READINGS FROM THE BIBLE

THE MACMILLAN COMPANY
NEW YORK • BOSTON • CHICAGO
DALLAS • ATLANTA • SAN FRANCISCO

MACMILLAN AND CO., LIMITED
LONDON • BOMBAY • CALCUTTA
MADRAS • MELBOURNE

THE MACMILLAN COMPANY
OF CANADA, LIMITED
TORONTO

READINGS FROM THE BIBLE

SELECTED AND EDITED BY
MARY ELLEN CHASE

THE MACMILLAN COMPANY
NEW YORK 1952

First printing

PRINTED IN THE UNITED STATES OF AMERICA

FOREWORD

This collection of biblical readings has been made in response not only to requests from students at Smith College who have taken my course, The Literature of the Bible, but also to many similar requests from persons who have found my book *The Bible and the Common Reader* both interesting and helpful. In choosing the selections I decided early to include only those which my students and I have read during our study of the Bible in any given year at Smith. So far as material is concerned, this book is, therefore, except for a few unimportant abridgments and the occasional necessary substitution of reference to certain passages in place of the passages themselves, an almost exact reproduction of the college course which I have given with ever increasing pleasure during the past fourteen years. The selections are placed in the order of our study: the Old Testament narratives first, with regard so far as possible to chronology; the poetry next, that of the great prophets, the Psalms, the Song of Songs, the poems on Wisdom, and the Book of Job; the passages from the New Testament last. This same order is used in the presentation and discussion of biblical literature in my book *The Bible and the Common Reader,* now being issued in a new and revised edition.

The brief introductions to the selections and the critical and explanatory notes have been written in order to clarify the reading. Those who desire fuller knowledge than such introductions and notes can give either of Hebrew history or of the background of the various passages will find both in the book named above.

I am quite aware that certain readers may miss many excerpts which they might wish included. In explanation of my choice, or even in justification of it, I would say that, on the basis of a relatively long experience in studying and teaching the Bible, I believe that the best of its literature will be found in these pages. I have taught my course at Smith on the idea and the principle that it is far better to know well the best of the Bible than to have a smattering of all of it (even if that were possible), especially in view of the recognized fact that a considerable portion of it is quite undistinguished as literature and even dull and meaningless to the modern reader. In short, I feel sure that a knowledge and appreciation of the selections given here will reveal the riches of biblical literature far more clearly than if more were included.

The form in which the material is compiled here is obviously a departure from that found in the usual Bible. The familiar division into verses was a quite arbitrary device used in the sixteenth century by English translators, but never employed in the Hebrew or Greek manuscripts. It has seemed best to arrange the prose in paragraphs. As to the poetry, it is placed in lines instead of in verses so that the original Hebrew "balance" or "parallelism" (that is, the form of Hebrew poetry) may be more clear.

No justification, at least in *my* mind, is necessary for using only the King James, or Authorized, Version. Not only does my course at Smith dictate such usage, but, in spite of various opinions as to the worth of more modern renderings, I myself am convinced that no other version, early or late, contains the dignity and the beauty of our incomparable translation of 1611. For more than three hundred years it has been the version best known to countless readers both in England and in America; and even today no other has become a serious rival simply because none has ever equaled, or even approached, its perfection of language. In the early seventeenth century it became our "noblest monument of English prose," and it remains that same monument today.

I can only hope that those who read these selections will derive at least a portion of the enjoyment and the satisfaction which have been mine in compiling them and in attempting, through the notes and suggestions, to make the reading of the Bible both a pleasurable and an exciting experience.

MARY ELLEN CHASE

Smith College
Northampton, Massachusetts
June, 1952

CONTENTS

THE POETRY OF THE OLD TESTAMENT

SELECTIONS FROM THE NEW TESTAMENT

OLD TESTAMENT NARRATIVES

THE reader who wisely begins his story of the Bible with the narratives of the Old Testament should at once become aware of certain characteristics of Hebrew prose which have been accurately preserved in the English translation; for a recognition of these will vastly increase his pleasure in reading. He will note its directness and simplicity, its economy, its lack of subordinate constructions; he will see at once that the diction is concrete rather than abstract and that it is rich in nouns and verbs, usually unaccompanied by many adjectives and adverbs. The Hebrew vocabulary was, in fact, very small in comparison with other languages; and the authors of the Bible were given to using the same words over and over again, partly because their words were relatively few, largely because they obviously believed that the practice of repetition added strength and emphasis to their writing. Indeed, this constant use of repetition, not only of words, but of phrases and even of ideas, is the most outstanding characteristic of the Hebrew writers. They employed also the use of understatement, often even of omission of what may seem to us necessary detail; yet they did this seemingly in order that the imaginations of their hearers, or readers, might supply those dramatic effects and meanings suggested if actually unexpressed. In other words, they relied upon the sound of the language itself, the pictorial value of its single concrete words, and upon its inner, and often symbolic, meaning and significance rather than upon elaboration of any sort. They were much given to the use of the direct question, a literary device which is common throughout the Bible and which does much to engage the reader's participation both in narrative and in poetry.

All of these distinctive traits of style and diction, if noted at the beginning, will contribute greatly both to the understanding and to the enjoyment of the passages which follow.

–I–

THE EARLIEST STORIES OF THE HEBREWS

In these five groups of readings, all of which come from the book of Genesis, we are first introduced to those myths and legends which were cherished by the Hebrew people. Nor are all of them exclusively Hebrew in origin. In the early records of other races there are similar tales of the creation of the world, of Edens lost because of the sin of man, and of a great flood which in some dim age covered the earth. But in no other literature have such stories been told with so much charm and power or with such insight into the changeless nature of man.

The tales of Abraham and of Isaac and the justly famous Jacob-Joseph saga may be called patriarchal, or epic. In these the Hebrew narrators have gathered together the traditions of their people in terms of their remote ancestors. Whether Abraham or Isaac, Jacob or Joseph, existed as individuals is questionable; but their names and experiences typify the life of the earliest Semitic wanderers from the east into the Land of Canaan.

Genesis is a book compiled by Hebrew scholars around the year 400 B.C., at which time the portion of the Old Testament known as the Pentateuch, or first five books, was gathered together. Its first chapter, one of the most beautiful in the Old Testament, is actually later in date than the remainder of Genesis. This chapter was written around 500 B.C. by an unknown author, whereas the stories of Adam and Eve, that of the flood, and those of the patriarchs were composed some centuries earlier. The Hebrew scholars wisely, however, disregarded the dates of actual composition in order to give a chronological account, as they believed, of their nation from its beginning.

1

THE CREATION OF THE WORLD

GENESIS I–2:3

In the beginning God created the heaven and the earth. And the earth was without form, and void; and darkness was upon the face of the deep. And the Spirit of God moved upon the face of the waters. And God said, Let there be light; and there was light. And God saw the light, that it was good; and God divided the light from the darkness. And God called the light Day, and the darkness he called Night. And the evening and the morning were the first day.

And God said, Let there be a firmament in the midst of the waters, and let it divide the waters from the waters. And God made the firmament, and divided the waters which were under the firmament from the waters which were above the firmament; and it was so. And God called the firmament Heaven. And the evening and the morning were the second day.

And God said, Let the waters under the heaven be gathered together unto one place, and let the dry land appear; and it was so. And God called the dry land Earth; and the gathering together of the waters called he Seas; and God saw that it was good. And God said, Let the earth bring forth grass, the herb yielding seed, and the fruit tree yielding fruit after his kind, whose seed is in itself, upon the earth; and it was so. And the earth brought forth grass, and herb yielding seed after his kind, and the tree yielding fruit, whose seed was in itself, after his kind; and God saw that it was good. And the evening and the morning were the third day.

And God said, Let there be lights in the firmament of the heaven, to divide the day from the night; and let them be for signs, and for seasons, and for days, and years; and let them be for lights in the firmament of the heaven, to give light upon the earth; and it was so. And God made two great lights: the greater light to rule the day, and the lesser light to rule the night; he made the stars also. And God set them in the firmament of the heaven, to give light upon the earth, and to rule over the day and over the night, and to divide the light from the darkness; and God saw that it was good. And the evening and the morning were the fourth day.

And God said, Let the waters bring forth abundantly the moving creature that hath life, and fowl that may fly above the earth in the open firmament of heaven. And God created great whales, and every living creature that moveth, which the waters brought forth abundantly, after their kind, and every winged fowl after his kind; and God saw that it was good. And God blessed them, saying, Be fruitful, and multiply, and fill the waters in the seas; and let fowl multiply in the earth. And the evening and the morning were the fifth day.

And God said, Let the earth bring forth the living creatures after his kind, cattle and creeping thing, and beast of the earth after his kind; and it was so. And God made the beast of the earth after his kind, and cattle after their kind, and everything that creepeth upon the earth after his kind; and God saw that it was good. And God said, Let us make man in our image, after our likeness; and let them have dominion over the fish of the sea, and over the fowl of the air, and over the cattle, and over all the earth, and over every creeping thing that creepeth upon the earth. So God created man in his own image, in the image of God created he him; male and female created he them. And God blessed them, and God said unto them, Be fruitful, and multiply, and replenish the earth, and subdue it, and have dominion over the fish of the sea, and over the fowl of the air, and over every living thing that moveth upon the earth. And God said, Behold, I have given you every herb bearing seed, which is upon the face of all the earth, and every tree, in the which is the fruit of a tree yielding seed; to you it shall be for meat. And to every beast of the earth, and to every fowl of the air, and to every thing that creepeth upon the earth, wherein there is life, I have given every green herb for meat; and it was so. And God saw every thing that he had made, and, behold, it was very good. And the evening and the morning were the sixth day.

Thus the heavens and the earth were finished, and all the host of them. And on the seventh day God ended his work which he had made; and he rested on the seventh day from all his work which he had made. And God blessed the seventh day, and sanctified it: because that in it he had rested from all his work which God created and made.

2

THE STORY OF ADAM AND EVE

GENESIS 2:4–4:15

These are the generations of the heavens and of the earth when they were created, in the day that the Lord God made the earth and the heavens, and every plant of the field before it was in the earth, and every herb of the field before it grew; for the Lord God had not caused it to rain upon the earth, and there was not a man to till the ground. But there went up a mist from the earth and watered the whole face of the ground. And the Lord God formed man of the dust of the ground, and breathed into his nostrils the breath of life; and man became a living soul.

And the Lord God planted a garden eastward in Eden; and there he put the man whom he had formed. And out of the ground made the Lord God to grow every tree that is pleasant to the sight and good for food; the tree of life also in the midst of the garden, and the tree of knowledge of good and evil.

And the Lord God took the man, and put him into the garden of Eden to dress it and to keep it. And the Lord God commanded the man, saying, Of every tree of the garden thou mayest freely eat; but of the tree of the knowledge of good and evil, thou shalt not eat of it; for in the day that thou eatest thereof thou shalt surely die.

And the Lord God said, It is not good that the man should be alone. I will make him an help-meet for him. And out of the ground the Lord God formed every beast of the field, and every fowl of the air; and brought them unto Adam[1] to see what he would call

[1] The name Adam comes from the Hebrew word *atham,* which means "man" in the sense of "mankind."

them; and whatsoever Adam called every living creature, that was the name thereof. And Adam gave names to all cattle, and to the fowl of the air, and to every beast of the field; but for Adam there was not found an help-meet for him. And the Lord God caused a deep sleep to fall upon Adam, and he slept; and he took one of his ribs, and closed up the flesh instead thereof; and the rib, which the Lord God had taken from man, made he a woman, and brought her unto the man. And Adam said, This is now bone of my bones, and flesh of my flesh; she shall be called Woman, because she was taken out of Man. Therefore shall a man leave his father and his mother, and shall cleave unto his wife; and they shall be one flesh. And they were both naked, the man and his wife, and were not ashamed.

Now the serpent was more subtile than any beast of the field which the Lord God had made. And he said unto the woman, Yea, hath God said, Ye shall not eat of every tree of the garden? And the woman said unto the serpent, We may eat of the fruit of the trees of the garden; but of the fruit of the tree which is in the midst of the garden, God hath said, Ye shall not eat of it, neither shall ye touch it, lest ye die. And the serpent said unto the woman, Ye shall not surely die; for God doth know that in the day ye eat thereof, then your eyes shall be opened, and ye shall be as gods, knowing good and evil. And when the woman saw that the tree was good for food, and that it was pleasant to the eyes, and a tree to be desired to make one wise, she took of the fruit thereof, and did eat, and gave also unto her husband with her; and he did eat. And the eyes of them both were opened, and they knew that they were naked; and they sewed fig leaves together and made themselves aprons.

And they heard the voice of the Lord God walking in the garden in the cool of the day; and Adam and his wife hid themselves from the presence of the Lord God amongst the trees of the garden. And the Lord God called unto Adam, and said unto him, Where art thou? And he said, I heard thy voice in the garden, and I was afraid, because I was naked; and I hid myself. And he said, Who told thee that thou wast naked? Hast thou eaten of the tree, whereof I commanded thee that thou shouldest not eat? And the man said, The woman whom thou gavest to be with me, she gave me of the tree, and I did eat. And the Lord God said unto the woman, What is this that thou hast done? And the woman said, The serpent beguiled me, and I did eat. And the Lord God said unto the serpent, Because thou hast done this, thou art cursed above all cattle, and above every beast of the field; upon thy belly shalt thou go, and dust shalt thou eat all the days of thy life. And I will put enmity between thee and the woman, and between thy seed and her seed; it shall bruise thy head, and thou shalt bruise his heel. Unto the woman he said, I will greatly multiply thy sorrow and thy conception. In sorrow thou shalt bring forth children; and thy desire shall be to thy husband, and he shall rule over thee. And unto Adam he said, Because thou hast hearkened unto the voice of thy wife, and hast eaten of the tree, of which I commanded thee, saying, Thou shalt not eat of it, cursed is the ground for thy sake. In sorrow shalt thou eat of it all the days of thy life. Thorns also and thistles shall it bring forth to thee; and thou shalt eat the herb of the field. In the sweat of thy face shalt thou eat bread, till thou return unto the ground; for out of it wast thou taken. For dust thou art, and unto dust shalt thou return.

And Adam called his wife's name Eve, because she was the mother of all living. Unto Adam also and to his wife did the Lord God make coats of skins, and clothed them. And the Lord God said, Behold, the man is become as one of us, to know good and evil. And now, lest he put forth his hand, and take also of the tree of life, and eat, and live forever, therefore the Lord God sent him forth from the garden of Eden, to till the ground from whence he was taken. So he drove out the man; and he placed at the east of the garden of Eden cherubim, and a flaming sword which turned every way, to keep the way of the tree of life.

And Adam knew Eve his wife; and she conceived and bare Cain, and she said, I have gotten a man from the Lord. And she again bare his brother Abel. And Abel was a keeper of sheep, but Cain was a tiller of the ground.

And in process of time it came to pass that Cain brought of the fruit of the ground an offering unto the Lord. And Abel, he also brought of the firstlings of his flock and of the fat thereof. And the Lord had respect unto Abel and to his offering; but unto Cain and to his offering he had not respect. And Cain was very wroth, and his countenance fell. And the Lord said unto Cain, Why art thou wroth? and why is thy countenance fallen? If thou doest well, shalt thou not be accepted? and if thou doest not well, sin lieth at the door.

And Cain talked with Abel his brother. And it came to pass, when they were in the field, that Cain rose up against Abel his brother and slew him. And the Lord said unto Cain, Where is Abel, thy brother? And he said, I know not. Am I my brother's keeper? And God said, What hast thou done? The voice of thy brother's blood crieth unto me from the ground. And now art thou cursed from the earth, which hath opened her mouth to receive thy brother's blood from thy hand. When thou tillest the ground, it shall not henceforth yield unto thee her strength. A fugitive and vagabond shalt thou be in the earth.

And Cain said unto the Lord, My punishment is greater than I can bear. Behold, thou hast driven me out this day from the face of the earth; and from thy face shall I be hid; and I shall be a fugitive and a vagabond in the earth; and it shall come to pass that every one that findeth me shall slay me.

And the Lord said unto him, Therefore whosoever slayeth Cain, vengeance shall be taken on him sevenfold. And the Lord set a mark upon Cain, lest any finding him should kill him.

3

THE GREAT FLOOD

FROM GENESIS 6–8

And it came to pass, when men began to multiply on the face of the earth and daughters were born unto them, that the sons of God saw the daughters of men that they were fair; and they took them wives of all which they chose.

And God saw that the wickedness of man was great in the earth, and that every imagination of the thoughts of his heart was only evil continually. And it repented the Lord that he had made man on the earth, and it grieved him at his heart. And the Lord said, I will destroy man whom I have created from the face of the earth, both man and beast, and the creeping thing, and the fowls of the air; for it repenteth me that I have made them. But Noah found grace in the eyes of the Lord. He was a just man and perfect in his generations, and Noah walked with God.

And God said unto Noah, The end of all flesh is come before me; for the earth is filled with violence through them; and, behold, I will destroy them with the earth. Make thee an ark of gopher wood; rooms shalt thou make in the ark, and shalt pitch it within and without with pitch. And this is the fashion which thou shalt make it of: The length of the ark shall be three hundred cubits,[1] the breadth of it fifty cubits, and the height of it thirty cubits. A window shalt thou make to the ark, and in a cubit shalt thou finish it above; and the door of the ark shalt thou set in the side thereof; with lower, second, and third stories shalt thou make it. And, behold, I, even I, do bring a flood of waters upon the earth, to destroy all flesh, wherein is the breath of life, from under heaven; and every thing that is in the earth shall die. But with thee will I establish my covenant; and thou shalt come into the ark, thou, and thy sons, and thy wife, and thy sons' wives with thee. And of every living thing of all flesh, two of every sort shalt thou bring into the ark, to keep them alive with thee; they shall be male and female. Of fowls after their kind, and of cattle after their kind, of every creeping thing of the earth after his kind, two of every sort shall come unto thee, to keep them alive. And take thou unto thee of all food that is eaten, and thou shalt gather it to thee; and it shall be for food for thee, and for them. Thus did Noah; according to all that God commanded him, so did he.

And the Lord said unto Noah, Come thou and all thy house into the ark; for thee have I seen righteous before me in this generation. Of every clean beast thou shalt take to thee by sevens, the male and his female; and of beasts that are not clean by two, the male and his female. Of fowls also of the air by sevens, the male and the

[1] A cubit was about 18 inches in length.

female, to keep seed alive upon the face of all the earth. For yet seven days, and I will cause it to rain upon the earth forty days and forty nights; and every living substance that I have made will I destroy from off the face of the earth. And Noah did according unto all that the Lord commanded him.

And Noah was six hundred years old when the flood of waters was upon the earth. And Noah went in, and his sons, and his wife, and his sons' wives with him, into the ark, because of the waters of the flood. Of clean beasts, and of beasts that are not clean, and of fowls, and of every thing that creepeth upon the earth, there went in two and two unto Noah into the ark, the male and the female, as God had commanded Noah. And it came to pass after seven days, that the waters of the flood were upon the earth. In the six hundredth year of Noah's life, in the second month, the seventeenth day of the month, the same day were all the fountains of the great deep broken up, and the windows of heaven were opened. And the rain was upon the earth forty days and forty nights. In the selfsame day entered Noah, and Shem, and Ham, and Japheth, the sons of Noah, and Noah's wife, and the three wives of his sons with them, into the ark; they, and every beast after his kind, and all the cattle after their kind, and every creeping thing that creepeth upon the earth after his kind, and every fowl after his kind, every bird of every sort. And they went in unto Noah into the ark, two and two of all flesh, wherein is the breath of life. And they that went in, went in male and female of all flesh, as God had commanded him; and the Lord shut him in.

And the flood was forty days upon the earth; and the waters increased, and bare up the ark, and it was lift up above the earth. And the waters prevailed, and were increased greatly upon the earth; and the ark went upon the face of the waters. And the waters prevailed exceedingly upon the earth; and all the high hills that were under the whole heaven were covered. Fifteen cubits upward did the water prevail; and the mountains were covered. And all flesh died that moved upon the earth, both of fowl, and of cattle, and of beast, and of every creeping thing that creepeth upon the earth, and every man; all in whose nostrils was the breath of life, of all that was in the dry land, died. And every living substance was destroyed which was upon the face of the ground, both man, and cattle, and the creeping things, and the fowl of the heaven; and they were destroyed from the earth; and Noah only remained alive, and they that were with him in the ark. And the waters prevailed upon the earth an hundred and fifty days.

And God remembered Noah, and every living thing and all the cattle that was with him in the ark. And God made a wind to pass over the earth, and the waters assuaged; the fountains also of the deep and the windows of heaven were stopped, and the rain from heaven was restrained; and the waters returned from off the earth continually. And after the end of the hundred and fifty days the waters were abated. And the ark rested in the seventh month, on the seventeenth day of the month, upon the mountains of Ararat. And the waters decreased continually until the tenth month; in the tenth month, on the first day of the month, were the tops of the mountains seen. And it came to pass at the end of forty days, that Noah opened the window of the ark which he had made, and he sent forth a raven, which went forth to and fro, until the waters were dried up from off the earth. Also he sent forth a dove from him, to see if the waters were abated from off the face of the ground; but the dove found no rest for the sole of her foot, and she returned unto him into the ark, for the waters were on the face of the whole earth. Then he put forth his hand, and took her, and pulled her in unto him into the ark. And he stayed yet other seven days; and again he sent forth the dove out of the ark; and the dove came in to him in the evening; and, lo, in her mouth was an olive leaf plucked off, so Noah knew that the waters were abated from off the earth. And he stayed yet other seven days; and sent forth the dove, which returned not again unto him any more.

And it came to pass in the six hundredth and first year, in the first month, the first day of the month, the waters were dried up from off the earth; and Noah removed the covering of the ark, and looked, and, behold, the face of the ground was dry. And in the second month, on the seven and twentieth day of the month, was the earth dried. And God spake unto Noah, saying, Go forth of the ark, thou, and thy wife, and thy sons, and thy sons' wives with thee. Bring forth with thee every living thing that is with thee, of all flesh, both of fowl, and of cattle, and of every creeping thing that creepeth upon the earth, that they may breed abundantly in the earth, and be fruitful, and multiply upon the earth. And Noah went forth, and his sons, and his wife, and his sons' wives with him; every beast, every creeping thing, and every fowl, and whatsoever creepeth upon the earth, after their kinds, went forth out of the ark. And Noah builded an altar unto the Lord; and took of every clean beast, and of every clean fowl, and offered burnt offerings on the altar. And the Lord smelled a sweet savor; and the Lord said in his heart, I will not again curse the ground any more for man's sake; for the imagination of man's heart is evil from his youth. Neither will I again smite any more every thing living, as I have done. While the earth remaineth, seedtime and harvest, and cold and heat, and summer and winter, and day and night shall not cease.

4

TALES OF ABRAHAM AND ISAAC

Abram, or Abraham, was, according to legend, the first patriarch recorded by Hebrew tradition, in other words, the father of the Hebrew nation. Genesis in an earlier chapter says that he was the son of Terah and that he came originally from Ur of the Chaldees, an ancient town in the valley of the Tigris and Euphrates rivers. Legend further implies that with his father he left Ur and journeyed northwestward upon command of God that these earliest Hebrews should leave a land given to the worship of strange deities; that he settled in Haran, some six hundred miles from Ur; and that at the age of seventy-five he went from Haran southward some two hundred miles to the Land of Canaan. To the religious motives ascribed for this pilgrimage should be added the fact that the earliest Semitic tribes, of which the Hebrews were but one, were inherently nomadic, wandering from place to place in search of pasturage for their flocks.

Any reliable date for this patriarchal age, typified by Abraham, is impossible to give; but perhaps we shall not be far wrong when we place it around 2000 B.C.

Abram and Lot

Now the Lord had said unto Abram, Get thee out of thy country, and from thy kindred, and from thy father's house, unto a land that I will show thee. And I will make of thee a great nation, and I will bless thee and make thy name great; and thou shalt be a blessing. And I will bless them that bless thee and curse him that curseth thee; and in thee shall all families of the earth be blessed.

So Abram departed, as the Lord had spoken unto him; and Lot went with him. And Abram was seventy and five years old when he departed out of Haran. And Abram took Sarai his wife, and Lot his brother's son, and all their substance that they had gathered and the souls that they had gotten in Haran; and they went forth to go into the land of Canaan, and into the land of Canaan they came. And Abram was very rich in cattle, in silver, and in gold. And Lot also, which went with Abram, had flocks, and herds, and tents. And the land was not able to bear them, that they might dwell together; for their substance was great, so that they could not dwell together.

And there was a strife between the herdmen of Abram's cattle and the herdmen of Lot's cattle. And Abram said unto Lot, Let there be no strife, I pray thee, between me and thee, and between my herdmen and thy herdmen; for we be brethren. Is not the whole land before thee? Separate thyself, I pray thee, from me. If thou wilt take the left hand, then I will go to the right; or if thou depart to the right hand, then I will go to the left.

And Lot lifted up his eyes, and beheld all the plain of Jordan, that it was well watered everywhere, even as the garden of the Lord. Then Lot chose him all the plain of Jordan; and Lot journeyed east. And they separated themselves the one from the other. Abram dwelt in the land of Canaan and Lot dwelt in the cities of the plain and pitched his tent toward Sodom. But the men of Sodom were wicked and sinners before the Lord exceedingly.

And the Lord said unto Abram after that Lot was separated from him, Lift up now thine eyes, and look from the place where thou art northward, and southward, and eastward, and westward; for all the land which thou seest, to thee will I give it and to thy seed forever. And I will make thy seed as the dust of the earth, so that if a man can number the dust of the earth, then shall thy seed also be numbered. Arise, walk through the land in the length of it and in the breadth of it, for I will give it unto thee.

Then Abram removed his tent, and came and dwelt in the plain of Mamre, which is in Hebron, and built there an altar unto the Lord.

Sarai and Hagar

Now Sarai, Abram's wife, bore him no children; and she had a handmaid, an Egyptian, whose name was Hagar. And Sarai said unto Abram, Behold now, the Lord hath restrained me from bearing; I pray thee, go in unto my maid; it may be that I may obtain children by her. And Abram hearkened to the voice of Sarai, and he went in unto Hagar and she conceived. And when she saw that she had conceived, her mistress was despised in her eyes.

And Sarai said unto Abram, My wrong be upon thee. I have given my maid into thy bosom; and when she saw that she had conceived, I was despised in her eyes. But Abram said unto Sarai, Behold, thy maid is in thy hand. Do to her as it pleaseth thee.

But when Sarai dealt hardly with her, Hagar fled from her face. And the angel of the Lord found her by a fountain of water in the wilderness. And he said, Hagar, whence camest thou? And she said, I flee from the face of my mistress Sarai. And the angel of the Lord said unto her, Return to thy mistress and submit thyself under her hands. I will multiply thy seed exceedingly, that it shall not be numbered for multitude. Behold thou art with child and shalt bear a son, and shalt call his name Ishmael, because the Lord hath heard thy affliction. And he will be a wild man; his hand will be against every man, and every man's hand against him.

And Abram was fourscore and six years old when Hagar bare Ishmael.

And when Abram was ninety years old and nine, the Lord appeared unto him and said, I am the Almighty God. Walk before me, and be thou perfect. And I will make my covenant between me and thee, and will multiply thee exceedingly.

And Abram fell on his face. And God talked with him, saying, Behold, my covenant is with thee, and thou shalt be a father of many nations. Neither shall thy name any more be called Abram, but thy name shall be Abraham.[1] As for Sarai thy wife, thou shalt not call her name Sarai, but Sarah shall her name be. And I will bless her, and give thee a son also of her; yea, I will bless her, and she shall be a mother of nations.

Then Abraham fell upon his face, and laughed, and said in his heart, Shall a child be born unto him that is a hundred years old? And shall Sarah, that is ninety years old, bear?

And God said, Sarah thy wife shall bear thee a son indeed; and thou shalt call his name Isaac; and I will establish my covenant with him for an everlasting covenant, and with his seed after him.

And the Lord appeared unto Abraham in the plains of Mamre; and he sat in the tent door in the heat of the day; and he lift up his eyes and looked, and, lo, three men stood by him; and, when he saw them, he ran to meet them from the tent door, and bowed himself toward the ground, and said, My Lord, if now I have found favor in thy sight, pass not away, I pray thee, from thy servant; let a little water, I pray you, be fetched, and wash your feet, and rest yourselves under the tree; and I will fetch a morsel of bread, and comfort ye your hearts. And they said, So do, as thou hast said. And Abraham hastened into the tent unto Sarah, and said, Make ready quickly three measures of fine meal, knead it, and make cakes upon the hearth. And Abraham ran unto the herd, and fetched a calf tender and good, and gave it unto a young man; and he hasted to dress it. And he took butter, and milk, and the calf which he had

[1] The name Abram in Hebrew means literally "a high father." Abraham means "the high father of a nation." Sarah means "a princess."

dressed, and set it before them; and he stood by them under the tree, and they did eat.

And they said unto him, Where is Sarah thy wife? And he said, Behold, in the tent, And one of them said, Lo, Sarah thy wife shall have a son. And Sarah heard it in the tent door, which was behind him.

Now Abraham and Sarah were old and well stricken in age; and it ceased to be with Sarah after the manner of women. Therefore Sarah laughed within herself, saying, After I am waxed old, shall I have pleasure, my lord being old also? And the Lord said unto Abraham, Wherefore did Sarah laugh, saying, Shall I of a surety bear a child, which am old? Is anything too hard for the Lord? At the time appointed I will return to thee, and Sarah shall have a son. Then Sarah denied, saying, I laughed not; for she was afraid. And he said, Nay; but thou didst laugh.

The Destruction of Sodom and Gomorrah

And the men rose up from thence, and looked toward Sodom; and Abraham went with them to bring them on the way. And the Lord said, Shall I hide from Abraham that thing which I do, seeing that Abraham shall surely become a great and mighty nation, and all the nations of the earth shall be blessed in him? For I know him, that he will command his children and his household after him, and they shall keep the way of the Lord to do justice and judgment, that the Lord may bring upon Abraham that which he hath spoken of him. And the Lord said, Because the cry of Sodom and Gomorrah is great, and because their sin is very grievous, I will go down now, and see whether they have done altogether according to the cry of it, which is come unto me; and if not, I will know.

And the men turned their faces from thence, and went toward Sodom; but Abraham stood yet before the Lord. And Abraham drew near, and said, Wilt thou also destroy the righteous with the wicked? Peradventure there be fifty righteous within the city, wilt thou also destroy and not spare the place for the fifty righteous that are therein? That be far from thee to do after this manner, to slay the righteous with the wicked. Shall not the Judge of all the earth do right? And the Lord said, If I find in Sodom fifty righteous within the city, then I will spare all the place for their sakes. And Abraham answered and said, Behold now, I have taken upon me to speak unto the Lord, which am but dust and ashes. Peradventure there shall lack five of the fifty righteous; wilt thou destroy all the city for lack of five? And he said, If I find there forty and five, I will not destroy it. And he spake unto him yet again, and said, Peradventure there shall be forty found there. And he said, I will not do it for forty's sake. And he said unto him, O let not the Lord be angry, and I will speak. Peradventure there shall thirty be found there. And he said, I will not do it if I find thirty there. And he said, Behold now, I have taken upon me to speak unto the Lord. Peradventure there shall be twenty found there. And he said, I will not destroy it for twenty's sake. And he said, O let not the Lord be angry, and I will speak yet but this once. Peradventure ten shall be found there. And he said, I will not destroy it for the ten's sake. And the Lord went his way, as soon as he had left communing with Abraham; and Abraham returned unto his place.

And angels came to Sodom at even; and Lot sat in the gate of Sodom. And they said unto Lot, Hast thou here any besides? Thy sons, and thy daughters, and whatsoever thou hast in the city, bring them out of this place; for we will destroy this place, because the cry of them is waxen great before the face of the Lord; and the Lord hath sent us to destroy it. And Lot went out, and spake unto his sons-in-law, which married his daughters, and said, Up, get you out of this place; for the Lord will destroy this city. But he seemed as one that mocked unto his sons-in-law.

And when the morning arose, then the angels hastened Lot, saying, Arise, take thy wife, and thy two daughters, which are here, lest thou be consumed in the iniquity of the city. And, while he lingered, the men laid hold upon his hand, and upon the hand of his wife, and upon the hand of his two daughters; and they brought him forth, and set him without the city. And it came to pass, when they had brought them forth abroad, that they said, Escape for thy life. Look not behind thee, neither stay thou in all the plain;

escape to the mountain, lest thou be consumed. And Lot said unto them, Oh, not so, my lord. Behold now, thy servant hath found grace in thy sight, and thou hast magnified thy mercy, which thou hast showed unto me in saving my life; and I cannot escape to the mountain, lest some evil take me, and I die. Behold now, this city is near to flee unto, and it is a little one. Oh, let me escape thither, and my soul shall live. And one of them said unto him, See, I have accepted thee concerning this thing also, that I will not overthrow this city, for the which thou hast spoken. Haste thee, escape thither; for I cannot do any thing till thou be come thither. Therefore the name of the city was called Zoar. Then the Lord rained upon Sodom and upon Gomorrah brimstone and fire from the Lord out of heaven; and he overthrew those cities, and all the plain, and all the inhabitants of the cities, and that which grew upon the ground. But his wife looked back from behind Lot, and she became a pillar of salt.

And Abraham gat up early in the morning to the place where he stood before the Lord; and he looked toward Sodom and Gomorrah, and toward all the land of the plain, and beheld, and, lo, the smoke of the country went up as the smoke of a furnace.

Hagar and Ishmael

And the Lord visited Sarah as he had said, and the Lord did unto Sarah as he had spoken. For Sarah conceived, and bare Abraham a son in his old age, at the set time of which God had spoken to him. And Abraham called the name of his son that was born unto him, Isaac. And Abraham circumcised his son Isaac being eight days old, as God had commanded him. And Abraham was an hundred years old when his son Isaac was born unto him. And Sarah said, God hath made me to laugh, so that all that hear will laugh with me. And she said, Who would have said unto Abraham that Sarah should have given children suck? For I have born him a son in his old age.

And the child grew and was weaned; and Abraham made a great feast the same day that Isaac was weaned. And Sarah saw the son of Hagar the Egyptian, which she had born unto Abraham, mocking. Wherefore she said unto Abraham, Cast out this bondwoman and her son; for the son of this bondwoman shall not be heir with my son, even with Isaac. And the thing was very grievous in Abraham's sight because of his son. And God said unto Abraham, Let it not be grievous in thy sight because of the lad and because of thy bondwoman. In all that Sarah hath said unto thee, hearken unto her voice; for in Isaac shall thy seed be called. And also of the son of the bondwoman will I make a nation, because he is thy seed.

And Abraham rose up early in the morning, and took bread and a bottle of water, and gave it unto Hagar, putting it on her shoulder, and the child, and sent her away. And she departed, and wandered in the wilderness of Beersheba. And the water was spent in the bottle, and she cast the child under one of the shrubs. And she went, and sat her down over against him a good way off, as it were a bowshot; for she said, Let me not see the death of the child. And she sat over against him, and lifted up her voice, and wept. And God heard the voice of the lad; and the angel of God called to Hagar out of heaven, and said unto her, What aileth thee, Hagar? Fear not; for God hath heard the voice of the lad where he is. Arise, lift up the lad, and hold him in thine hand; for I will make him a great nation. And God opened her eyes, and she saw a well of water; and she went and filled the bottle with water, and gave the lad drink. And God was with the lad; and he grew and dwelt in the wilderness, and became an archer.

The Sacrifice of Isaac

And it came to pass after these things that God did tempt Abraham, and said unto him, Abraham. And he said, Behold, here I am. And he said, Take now thy son, thine only son Isaac, whom thou lovest, and get thee into the land of Moriah; and offer him there for a burnt offering upon one of the mountains which I will tell thee of. And Abraham rose up early in the morning, and saddled his ass, and took two of his young men with him, and Isaac his son, and clave the wood for the burnt offering, and rose up, and went unto the place of which God had told him.

Then on the third day Abraham lifted up his eyes, and saw the place afar off. And Abraham said unto his young men, Abide ye here with the ass; and I and the lad will go yonder and worship, and come again to you. And Abraham took the wood of the burnt offering and laid it upon Isaac his son; and he took the fire in his hand, and a knife; and they went both of them together. And Isaac spake unto Abraham his father, and said, My father. And he said, Here am I, my son. And he said, Behold the fire and the wood; but where is the lamb for a burnt offering? And Abraham said, My son, God will provide himself a lamb for a burnt offering. So they went both of them together.

And they came to the place which God had told him of; and Abraham built an altar there, and laid the wood in order, and bound Isaac his son, and laid him on the altar upon the wood. And Abraham stretched forth his hand, and took the knife to slay his son. And the angel of the Lord called unto him out of heaven, and said, Abraham, Abraham. And he said, Here am I. And he said, Lay not thine hand upon the lad, neither do thou anything unto him; for now I know that thou fearest God, seeing thou hast not withheld thy son, thine only son, from me. And Abraham lifted up his eyes, and looked, and behold behind him a ram caught in a thicket by his horns; and Abraham went and took the ram, and offered him up for a burnt offering in the stead of his son.

And the angel of the Lord called unto Abraham out of heaven the second time, and said, By myself have I sworn, saith the Lord; for because thou hast done this thing, and hast not withheld thy son, thine only son, that in blessing I will bless thee, and in multiplying I will multiply thy seed as the stars of the heaven, and as the sand which is upon the seashore; and thy seed shall possess the gate of his enemies; and in thy seed shall all the nations of the earth be blessed.

And Abraham was old, and well stricken in age, and the Lord had blessed Abraham in all things. And Abraham said unto his eldest servant of his house, Put, I pray thee, thy hand under my thigh; and I will make thee swear by the Lord, the God of heaven, and the God of the earth, that thou shalt not take a wife unto my son of the daughters of the Canaanites, among whom I dwell; but thou shalt go unto my country and to my kindred, and take a wife unto my son Isaac. And the servant said unto him, Peradventure the woman will not be willing to follow me unto this land. Must I needs bring thy son again unto the land from whence thou camest? And Abraham said unto him, Beware thou that thou bring not my son thither again. The Lord God of heaven, which took me from my father's house, and from the land of my kindred, and which spake unto me, and that sware unto me, saying, Unto thy seed will I give this land; he shall send his angel before thee, and thou shalt take a wife unto my son from thence. And if the woman will not be willing to follow thee, then thou shalt be clear from this my oath. And the servant put his hand under the thigh of Abraham his master, and sware to him concerning that matter.

And the servant took ten camels of the camels of his master, and departed; and he went to Mesopotamia, unto the city of Nahor. And he made his camels to kneel down without the city by a well of water at the time of the evening, even the time that women go out to draw water. And he said, O Lord God of my master Abraham, I pray thee, send me good speed this day, and show kindness unto my master Abraham. Behold, I stand here by the well of water; and the daughters of the men of the city come out to draw water; and let it come to pass, that the damsel to whom I shall say, Let down thy pitcher, I pray thee, that I may drink; and she shall say, Drink, and I will give thy camels drink also; let the same be she that thou hast appointed for thy servant Isaac; and thereby shall I know that thou hast showed kindness unto my master.

And it came to pass, before he had done speaking, that, behold, Rebekah came out, who was born to Bethuel, son of Milcah, the wife of Nahor, Abraham's brother, with her pitcher upon her shoulder. And the damsel was very fair to look upon, a virgin, neither had any man known her; and she went down to the well, and filled her pitcher, and came up. And the servant ran to meet her, and said, Let me, I pray thee, drink a little water of thy pitcher. And she said, Drink, my lord; and she hasted, and let down her pitcher upon her hand, and gave him drink. And when she had done giving him drink, she said, I will draw water for thy camels also, until they have done drinking. And she hasted, and emptied her pitcher into the trough, and ran again unto the well to draw water, and drew for all his camels. And the man wondering at her held his peace. And it came to pass, as the camels had done drinking, that the man took a golden earring of half a shekel weight, and two bracelets for her hands of ten shekels weight of gold; and said, Whose daughter art thou? Tell me, I pray thee, is there room in thy father's house for us to lodge in? And she said unto him, I am the daughter of Bethuel, the son of Milcah, which she bare unto Nahor. She said moreover unto him, We have both straw and provender enough, and room to lodge in. And the man bowed down his head, and worshipped the Lord. And he said, Blessed be the Lord God of my master Abraham, who hath not left destitute my master of his mercy and his truth. And the damsel ran, and told them of her mother's house these things.

And Rebekah had a brother, and his name was Laban; and Laban ran out unto the man unto the well. And it came to pass, when he saw the earring, and bracelets upon his sister's hands, and when he heard the words of Rebekah his sister, that he came unto the man; and, behold, he stood by the camels at the well. And he said, Come in, thou blessed of the Lord; wherefore standest thou without? for I have prepared the house, and room for the camels. And the man came into the house; and Laban ungirded his camels, and gave straw and provender for the camels, and water to wash his feet, and the men's feet that were with him. And there was set meat before him to eat; but he said, I will not eat until I have told mine errand. And he said, Speak on.

And he said, I am Abraham's servant. And the Lord hath blessed my master greatly; and he is become great; and he hath given him flocks, and herds, and silver, and gold, and menservants, and maidservants, and camels, and asses. And Sarah my master's wife bare a son to my master when she was old; and unto him hath he given all that he hath. And my master made me swear, saying, Thou shalt not take a wife to my son of the daughters of the Canaanites, in whose land I dwell; but thou shalt go unto my father's house, and to my kindred, and take a wife unto my son. And I came this day unto the well, and behold, Rebekah came forth with her pitcher on her shoulder; and she went down unto the well, and drew water; and I said unto her, Let me drink, I pray thee. And she made haste, and let down her pitcher from her shoulder, and said, Drink, and I will give thy camels drink also. So I drank, and she made the camels drink also. And I put the earring upon her face, and the bracelets upon her hands. And I bowed down my head, and worshipped the Lord, and blessed the Lord God of my master Abraham, which had led me in the right way. And now if ye will deal kindly and truly with my master, tell me; and if not, tell me; that I may turn to the right hand, or to the left.

Then Laban and Bethuel answered and said, The thing proceedeth from the Lord; we cannot speak unto thee bad or good. Behold, Rebekah is before thee, take her, and go, and let her be thy master's son's wife, as the Lord hath spoken. And it came to pass, that, when Abraham's servant heard their words, he worshipped the Lord, bowing himself to the earth. And the servant brought forth jewels of silver, and jewels of gold, and raiment, and gave them to Rebekah; he gave also to her brother and to her mother precious things. And they did eat and drink, he and the men that were with him, and tarried all night; and they rose up in the morning, and he said, Send me away unto my master. And her brother and her mother said, Let the damsel abide with us a few days, at the least ten. After that she shall go. And he said unto them, Hinder me not, seeing the Lord hath prospered my way; send me away that I may go to my master. And they said, We will call the damsel, and enquire at her mouth. And they called Rebekah, and said unto her, Wilt thou go with this man? And she said, I will go.

And they sent away Rebekah their sister, and her nurse, and Abraham's servant, and his men. And they blessed Rebekah, and said unto her, Thou art our sister. Be thou the mother of thousands of millions, and let thy seed possess the gate of those which hate them.

And Rebekah arose, and her damsels, and they rode upon the camels and followed the man; and the servant took Rebekah, and went his way. And Isaac went out to meditate in the field at eventide; and he lifted up his eyes, and saw, and behold, the camels were coming. And Rebekah lifted up her eyes, and when she saw Isaac, she lighted off the camel. For she had said unto the servant, What man is this that walketh in the field to meet us? And the servant had said, It is my master. Therefore she took a veil, and covered herself. And the servant told Isaac all things that he had done. And Isaac brought her into his mother Sarah's tent, and took Rebekah, and she became his wife; and he loved her. And Isaac was comforted after his mother's death.

5

THE JACOB–JOSEPH SAGA

The saga which follows is one of the finest narratives of the Old Testament from various points of view: as a portrayal of the ancient Hebrew family and of that family coherence and pride always characteristic of the Jewish people; as a description of primitive pastoral life; as a document of religious and patriotic fervor; and as a literary achievement of the highest excellence. Written by two authors, unknown at least by name, somewhere between 850 and 750 B.C., it remains one of the masterpieces of all ancient literature and belongs among other great epics, such as the *Iliad* and the *Odyssey* or the sagas of northern lands.

The men who wrote it, in order to preserve for future generations those stories which had been told orally for centuries, were not only great dramatists, but wise psychologists as well. They understood that irony of situation which arises from the conflict of character, those ageless emotions which forever shape human life and destiny, jealousy and fear, love and revenge, pride, frustration, and bitterness. The vividness of their dialogue is unsurpassed; and the persons who portray themselves by it remain in our imaginations: Rebekah with her resourcefulness and cunning; Jacob with his craftiness and passion; the frustration and fury of Leah; the despair and pathos of Rachel; the final triumph of the embittered Esau.

They knew also how, in the fewest of words, to suggest the spirit of a place, the darkness at Bethel, the well in Padan-aram with its flocks; and, lastly, they could surround their saga with an atmosphere of time itself so that, as we read it, we become conscious not so much of the past as of an odd permanence in life, a changelessness which knows no beginning and, indeed, no end.[1]

Jacob

FROM GENESIS 27–35

And it came to pass, that when Isaac was old, and his eyes were dim so that he could not see, he called Esau his eldest son, and said unto him, My son. And he said unto him, Behold, here am I. And he said, Behold now, I am old, I know not the day of my death. Now therefore take, I pray thee, thy weapons, thy quiver and thy bow, and go out to the field, and take me some venison; and make me savory meat, such as I love, and bring it to me that I may eat, that my soul may bless thee before I die. And Rebekah heard when Isaac spake to Esau his son. And Esau went to the field to hunt for venison, and to bring it.

And Rebekah spake unto Jacob her son, saying, Behold, I heard thy father speak unto Esau thy brother, saying, Bring me venison, and make me savory meat, that I may eat, and bless thee before the Lord before my death. Now therefore, my son, obey my voice according to that which I command thee. Go now to the flock and fetch me from thence two good kids of the goats; and I will make them savory meat for thy father, such as he loveth; and thou shalt bring it to thy father, that he may eat, and that he may bless thee before his death. And Jacob said to Rebekah his mother, Behold, Esau my brother is a hairy man, and I am a smooth man; my father

[1] An extended treatment of the Jacob-Joseph saga may be found in *The Bible and the Common Reader,* Pt. II.

peradventure will feel me, and I shall seem to him as a deceiver; and I shall bring a curse upon me, and not a blessing. And his mother said unto him, Upon me be thy curse, my son; only obey my voice, and go fetch me them. And he went and fetched, and brought them to his mother; and his mother made savory meat, such as his father loved. And Rebekah took goodly raiment of her eldest son Esau, which were with her in the house, and put them upon Jacob her younger son; and she put the skins of the kids of the goats upon his hands, and upon the smooth of his neck; and she gave the savory meat and the bread, which she had prepared, unto the hand of her son Jacob.

And he came unto his father, and said, My father; and he said, Here am I. Who art thou, my son? And Jacob said unto his father, I am Esau thy firstborn; I have done according as thou badest me. Arise, I pray thee, sit and eat of my venison, that thy soul may bless me. And Isaac said unto his son, How is it that thou hast found it so quickly, my son? And he said, Because the Lord thy God brought it to me. And Isaac said unto Jacob, Come near, I pray thee, that I may feel thee, my son, whether thou be my very son Esau or not. And Jacob went near unto Isaac his father; and he felt him, and said, The voice is Jacob's voice, but the hands are the hands of Esau. And he discerned him not, because his hands were hairy, as his brother Esau's hands. So he blessed him. And he said, Art thou my very son Esau? And he said, I am. And he said, Bring it near to me, and I will eat of my son's venison, that my soul may bless thee. And he brought it near to him, and he did eat; and he brought him wine, and he drank. And his father Isaac said unto him, Come near now, and kiss me, my son. And he came near, and kissed him; and he smelled the smell of his raiment, and blessed him, and said, See, the smell of my son is as the smell of a field which the Lord hath blessed; therefore, God give thee of the dew of heaven, and the fatness of the earth, and plenty of corn and wine. Let people serve thee, and nations bow down to thee. Be lord over thy brethren, and let thy mother's sons bow down to thee. Cursed be every one that curseth thee, and blessed be he that blesseth thee.

And it came to pass, as soon as Isaac had made an end of blessing

Jacob and Jacob was yet scarce gone out from the presence of Isaac his father, that Esau his brother came in from his hunting. And he also had made savory meat, and brought it unto his father, and said unto his father, Let my father arise, and eat of his son's venison, that thy soul may bless me. And Isaac his father said unto him, Who art thou? And he said, I am thy son, thy firstborn Esau. And Isaac trembled very exceedingly, and said, Who? Where is he that hath taken venison, and brought it me, and I have eaten of all before thou camest, and have blessed him? Yea, and he shall be blessed. And when Esau heard the words of his father, he cried with a great and exceeding bitter cry, and said unto his father, Bless me, even me also, O my father! And he said, Thy brother came with subtilty, and hath taken away thy blessing. And Esau said, Is not he rightly named Jacob? For he hath supplanted me these two times. He took away my birthright; and, behold, now he hath taken away my blessing. And he said, Hast thou not reserved a blessing for me? And Isaac answered and said unto Esau, Behold, I have made him thy lord, and all his brethren have I given to him for servants; and with corn and wine have I sustained him; and what shall I do now unto thee, my son? And Esau said unto his father, Hast thou but one blessing, my father? Bless me, even me also, O my father! And Esau lifted up his voice, and wept. And Isaac his father answered and said unto him, Behold, thy dwelling shall be the fatness of the earth, and of the dew of heaven from above; and by thy sword shalt thou live, and shalt serve thy brother; and it shall come to pass when thou shalt have the dominion, that thou shalt break his yoke from off thy neck.

And Esau hated Jacob because of the blessing wherewith his father blessed him; and Esau said in his heart, The days of mourning for my father are at hand; then will I slay my brother Jacob.

And these words of Esau her elder son were told to Rebekah; and she sent and called Jacob her younger son and said unto him, Behold, thy brother Esau doth comfort himself, purposing to kill thee. Now, therefore, obey my voice and flee thou to Laban my brother to Haran, and tarry with him until thy brother's fury turn away and he forget that which thou hast done to him. Then will I send, and fetch you from thence.

And Rebekah said to Isaac, I am weary of my life because of the daughters of Heth.[2] If Jacob take a wife of the daughters of Heth, what good shall my life do to me? And Isaac called Jacob, and blessed him, and said, Thou shalt not take a wife of the daughters of Canaan. Arise, go to Padan-aram, to the house of thy mother's father, and take a wife of the daughters of Laban thy mother's brother.

And Jacob went out from Beersheba and went toward Haran. And he lighted upon a certain place, and tarried there all night, because the sun was set; and he took of the stones of that place, and put them for his pillows, and lay down in that place to sleep. And he dreamed, and behold a ladder set up on the earth, and the top of it reached to heaven; and behold the angels of God ascending and descending on it. And, behold! the Lord stood above it, and said, I am the Lord God of Abraham thy father, and the God of Isaac. The land whereon thou liest, to thee will I give it, and to thy seed; and thy seed shall be as the dust of the earth; and thou shalt spread abroad to the west, and to the east, and to the north, and to the south; and in thee and in thy seed shall all the families of the earth be blessed. And, behold, I am with thee, and will keep thee in all places whither thou goest, and will bring thee again into this land; for I will not leave thee, until I have done that which I have spoken to thee of.

And Jacob awaked out of his sleep, and he said, Surely the Lord is in this place; and I knew it not. And he was afraid, and said, How dreadful is this place! This is none other but the house of God, and this is the gate of heaven.

And Jacob rose up early in the morning, and took the stone that he had put for his pillows, and set it up for a pillar, and poured oil upon the top of it. And he called the name of that place Bethel;[3]

[2] Esau had married two Hittite girls, Judith and Bashemath, who were, in Rebekah's words, "a grief of mind" to her and to Isaac. Both objected to the marriage, not only because of the apparent unlikableness of the girls themselves, but because they were Hittites, a non-Semitic people.

[3] Bethel means in Hebrew "the house of God."

but the name of that city was called Luz at the first. And Jacob vowed a vow, saying, If God will be with me, and will keep me in this way that I go, and will give me bread to eat and raiment to put on, so that I come again to my father's house in peace, then shall the Lord be my God; and this stone, which I have set for a pillar, shall be God's house; and of all that thou shalt give me I will surely give the tenth unto thee.

Then Jacob went on his journey, and came into the land of the people of the east. And he looked, and behold a well in the field, and, lo, there were three flocks of sheep lying by it; for out of that well they watered the flocks; and a great stone was upon the well's mouth. And thither were all the flocks gathered; and they rolled the stone from the well's mouth, and watered the sheep, and put the stone again upon the well's mouth in his place. And Jacob said unto them, My brethren, whence be ye? And they said, Of Haran are we. And he said unto them, Know ye Laban the son of Nahor? And they said, We know him. And he said unto them, Is he well? And they said, He is well; and, behold, Rachel his daughter cometh with the sheep.

And Jacob said, Lo, it is yet high day, neither is it time that the cattle should be gathered together. Water ye the sheep, and go and feed them. And they said, We cannot, until all the flocks be gathered together, and till they roll the stone from the well's mouth. Then we water the sheep.

And while he yet spake with them, Rachel came with her father's sheep, for she kept them. And it came to pass, when Jacob saw Rachel the daughter of his mother's brother, and the sheep of Laban, that Jacob went near and rolled the stone from the well's mouth and watered the flock of Laban. And Jacob kissed Rachel, and lifted up his voice and wept. And Jacob told Rachel that he was Rebekah's son; and she ran and told her father, and it came to pass, when Laban heard the tidings of Jacob his sister's son, that he ran to meet him and embraced him and kissed him, and brought him to his house.

And Laban had two daughters. The name of the elder was Leah, and the name of the younger was Rachel. Leah was tendereyed;[4] but Rachel was beautiful and well favored. And Jacob loved Rachel and said to Laban, I will serve thee seven years for Rachel thy younger daughter. And Laban said, It is better that I give her to thee than that I should give her to another man. Abide with me. And Jacob served seven years for Rachel; and they seemed unto him but a few days, for the love he had to her.

And Jacob said unto Laban, Give me my wife, for my days are fulfilled, that I may go in unto her. And Laban gathered together all the men of the place and made a feast. And it came to pass in the evening that he took Leah his daughter and brought her to Jacob; and he went in unto her. And it came to pass that, in the morning, behold, it was Leah!

And Jacob said to Laban, What is this thou hast done unto me? Did I not serve with thee for Rachel? Wherefore then hast thou beguiled me? And Laban said, It must not be so done in our country to give the younger before the firstborn. Fulfil her week, and we will give thee this also for the service which thou shalt serve with me yet seven other years. And Jacob did so, and fulfilled her week; and he gave him Rachel to wife also. And he went in also unto Rachel; and he loved also Rachel more than Leah, and served with Laban yet seven other years.

And when the Lord saw that Leah was hated, he opened her womb; but Rachel was barren. And Leah conceived and bare a son; and she called his name Reuben, for she said, Surely the Lord hath looked upon my affliction. Now therefore my husband will love me. And she conceived again and bare a son, and said, Because the Lord hath heard that I was hated, he hath therefore given me this son also; and she called his name Simeon. And she conceived again and bare a son, and said, Now this time will my husband be joined unto me because I have borne him three sons. Therefore was his name called Levi. And she conceived again and bare a son, and she said, Now will I praise the Lord. Therefore she called his name Judah,

[4] This adjective is *not* complimentary. It means "sore-eyed."

and left bearing. And when Rachel saw that she bore Jacob no children, Rachel envied her sister, and said unto Jacob, Give me children, or else I die.

And Reuben went in the days of wheat harvest and found mandrakes[5] in the field and brought them unto his mother. Then Rachel said to Leah, Give me, I pray thee, of thy son's mandrakes. And Leah said unto her, Is it a small matter that thou hast taken my husband? And wouldest thou take away my son's mandrakes also? And Rachel said, Therefore he shall lie with thee tonight for thy son's mandrakes.

And Jacob came out of the field in the evening, and Leah went out to meet him and said, Thou must come in unto me; for surely I have hired thee with my son's mandrakes. And he lay with her that night. And God hearkened unto Leah, and she conceived and bare Jacob the fifth son. And she conceived again and bare Jacob the sixth son. And Leah said, God hath endued me with a good dowry. Now will my husband dwell with me because I have borne him six sons. And afterward she bore a daughter and called her name Dinah.[6]

And God remembered Rachel, and God hearkened to her and opened her womb. And she conceived and bare a son, and said, God hath taken away my reproach. And she called his name Joseph and said, The Lord shall add to me another son.

And it came to pass, when Rachel had borne Joseph, that Jacob said unto Laban, Send me away that I may go unto mine own place and to my country. Give me my wives and my children, for whom I have served thee, and let me go; for thou knowest my service which I have done thee. And Laban said unto him, I pray thee, if I have found favor in thine eyes, tarry; for I have learned by experience that the Lord hath blessed me for thy sake. Appoint me thy wages, and I will give it. And Jacob said unto him, Thou knowest how I have served thee and how thy cattle was with me. For it was

[5] Ancient superstition taught that to eat the root of the mandrake, or even to look upon it, would promote conception.

[6] The sad story of Dinah is told in Genesis 34.

little which thou hadst before I came, and it is now increased unto a multitude. And now, when shall I provide for mine own house also?

And Laban said, What shall I give thee? And Jacob said, Thou shalt not give me anything; but if thou wilt do this thing for me, I will again feed and keep thy flock: I will pass through all thy flock today, removing from thence all the speckled and spotted cattle, and all the brown among the sheep, and the spotted and speckled among the goats; and of such shall be my hire. And Laban said, Behold, I would it might be according to thy word. And he set three days' journey betwixt himself and Jacob; and Jacob fed the rest of Laban's flocks.

And Jacob took him rods of green poplar and of the hazel and chestnut tree and pilled white streaks in them. And he set the rods which he had pilled before the flocks in the gutters in the watering troughs when the flocks came to drink, that they should conceive when they came to drink. And the flocks conceived before the rods and brought forth cattle ring-streaked, speckled, and spotted. And Jacob increased exceedingly and had much cattle, and maidservants and menservants, and camels, and asses.

And he heard the words of Laban's sons, saying, Jacob hath taken away all that was our father's. And Jacob beheld the countenance of Laban, and, behold, it was not toward him as before. And the Lord said unto Jacob, Return unto the land of thy fathers and to thy kindred; and I will be with thee.

And Jacob sent and called Rachel and Leah to the field unto his flock, and said unto them, I see your father's countenance, that it is not toward me as before; but the God of my father hath been with me. And ye know that with all my power I have served your father. And your father hath deceived me and changed my wages ten times; but God suffered him not to hurt me. If he said thus, The speckled shall be thy wages, then all the cattle bare speckled; and if he said thus, The ring-streaked shall be thy hire, then bare all the cattle ring-streaked. Thus God hath taken away the cattle of your father and given them to me.

And Rachel and Leah answered and said unto him, Is there yet any portion or inheritance for us in our father's house? Are we not counted of him strangers? For he hath sold us and hath quite devoured also our money. Now, then, whatsoever God hath said unto thee, do.

Then Jacob rose up and set his sons and his wives upon camels. And he carried away all his cattle and all his goods which he had gotten in Padan-aram for to go to Isaac his father in the land of Canaan. And Laban went to shear his sheep; and Rachel had stolen the images[7] that were her father's. And Jacob stole away unawares to Laban, in that he told him not that he had fled. So he fled with all that he had; and he rose up and passed over the river, and set his face toward the mount Gilead.

And it was told Laban on the third day that Jacob was fled. And he took his brethren with him and pursued after him seven days' journey; and they overtook him in the mount Gilead. And Laban said to Jacob, What hast thou done that thou hast stolen away unawares to me and carried away my daughters as captives taken with the sword? Wherefore didst thou flee away secretly and didst not tell me, that I might have sent thee away with mirth and with songs, with tabret and with harp? And hast not suffered me to kiss my daughters? And now, though thou wouldest needs be gone because thou sore longedst after thy father's house, wherefore hast thou stolen my gods? And Jacob answered and said to Laban, Because I was afraid, for I said, Peradventure thou wouldest take by force thy daughters from me. With whomsoever thou findest thy gods, let him not live. For Jacob knew not that Rachel had stolen them.

And Laban went into Jacob's tent, and into Leah's tent, but he found them not. Then went he out of Leah's tent and entered into Rachel's tent. Now Rachel had taken the images and put them in the camel's furniture, and sat upon them. And Laban searched all the tent, but found them not. And Rachel said to her father, Let

[7] The actual nature and significance of these images, household gods, or *teraphim,* is unknown. They were small images made of clay, were obviously looked upon with superstitious reverence, and may have been used for purposes of divination.

it not displease my lord that I cannot rise up before thee, for the custom of women is upon me. And he searched, but found not the images.

And early in the morning Laban rose up and kissed his daughters and blessed them; and he departed and returned unto his place.

And Jacob went on his way. And he sent messengers before him to Esau his brother unto the country of Edom. And the messengers returned to Jacob saying, We came to thy brother Esau, and he cometh to meet thee and four hundred men with him. Then Jacob was greatly afraid and distressed; and he took of that which came to his hand a present for Esau his brother: two hundred she-goats and twenty he-goats, two hundred ewes and twenty rams, thirty milch camels with their colts, forty kine and ten bulls, twenty she-asses and ten foals. And he delivered them into the hand of his servants, and said, When Esau my brother meeteth thee and asketh thee saying, Whither goest thou? And who are these before thee? then shalt thou say, They be thy servant Jacob's; it is a present sent unto my lord Esau. So went the present before him.

And Jacob was left alone; and there wrestled a man with him until the breaking of the day. And when he saw that he prevailed not against Jacob, he touched the hollow of his thigh; and the hollow of Jacob's thigh was out of joint as he wrestled with him. And he said, Let me go, for the day breaketh. And Jacob said, I will not let thee go, except thou bless me. And he said unto him, What is thy name? And he said, Jacob. And he said, Thy name shall be called no more Jacob, but Israel; for as a prince hast thou power with God and with men, and hast prevailed. And Jacob said, Tell me, I pray thee, thy name. And he said, Wherefore is it that thou dost ask after my name? And he blessed him there. And Jacob called the name of the place Peniel; for, he said, I have seen God face to face, and my life is preserved.

And as he passed over Peniel, the sun rose upon him. And Jacob lifted up his eyes and, behold, Esau came and with him four hundred men. And Jacob divided the children unto Leah and unto Rachel, and unto the two handmaids. And he put the handmaids and their children foremost, and Leah and her children after, and Rachel and Joseph hindermost. And he passed over before them and bowed himself to the ground seven times until he came near to his brother.

And Esau ran to meet him and embraced him, and fell on his neck and kissed him; and they wept. And Esau lifted up his eyes and saw the women and the children, and said, Who are those with thee? And Joseph said, The children which God hath graciously given thy servant. Then the handmaidens came near, they and their children, and Leah also with her children, and they bowed themselves; and after came Joseph near and Rachel, and they bowed themselves.

And Esau said, What meanest thou by all this drove which I met? And Jacob said, These are to find grace in the sight of my lord. And Esau said, I have enough, my brother. Keep that thou hast unto thyself.

And God said unto Jacob, Arise, go up to Bethel, and make there an altar unto God that appeared unto thee when thou fleddest from the face of Esau thy brother. Then Jacob said unto his household, Put away the strange gods that are among you, and be clean and change your garments. And let us arise and go up to Bethel, and I will make there an altar unto God, who answered me in the day of my distress and was with me in the way which I went. And they journeyed and came to Bethel, and Jacob built there an altar.

And they journeyed from Bethel and there was but a little way to come to Ephrath;[8] and Rachel travailed, and she had hard labor. And it came to pass, when she was in hard labor, that the midwife said unto her, Fear not. Thou shalt have this son also. And it came to pass, as her soul was in departing (for she died), that she called his name Benoni;[9] but his father called him Benjamin.

[8] Ephrath is Bethlehem.
[9] Benoni means "son of my sorrow."

Joseph

FROM GENESIS 37–50

And Jacob dwelt in the land wherein his father was a stranger, in the land of Canaan. Joseph, being seventeen years old, was feeding the flock with his brethren; and Joseph brought unto his father their evil report. Now Israel loved Joseph more than all his children, because he was the son of his old age; and he made him a coat of many colors. And when his brethren saw that their father loved him more than all his brethren, they hated him, and could not speak peaceably unto him.

And Joseph dreamed a dream, and he told it his brethren; and they hated him yet the more. And he said unto them, Hear, I pray you, this dream which I have dreamed: Behold, we were binding sheaves in the field, and, lo, my sheaf arose, and also stood upright; and, behold, your sheaves stood round about, and made obeisance to my sheaf. And his brethren said to him, Shalt thou indeed reign over us? Or shalt thou indeed have dominion over us? And they hated him yet the more for his dreams and for his words.

And his brethren went to feed their father's flock in Shechem. And Israel said unto Joseph, Do not thy brethren feed the flock in Shechem? Come, and I will send thee unto them. And he said to him, Here am I. And he said to him, Go, I pray thee, see whether it be well with thy brethren, and well with the flocks; and bring me word again.

And when his brothers saw him afar off, even before he came near unto them, they conspired against him to slay him. And they said one to another, Behold, this dreamer cometh! Come now therefore, and let us slay him, and cast him into some pit; and we will say, Some evil beast hath devoured him; and we shall see what will become of his dreams. And Reuben heard it, and said unto them, Shed no blood, but cast him into this pit that is in the wilderness, and lay no hand upon him; that he might rid him out of their hands, to deliver him to his father again.

And it came to pass, when Joseph was come unto his brethren, that they stripped Joseph out of his coat, his coat of many colors that was on him; and they took him, and cast him into a pit; and the pit was empty, there was no water in it. And they sat down to eat bread; and they lifted up their eyes and looked, and, behold, a company of Ishmaelites came from Gilead, with their camels bearing spicery and balm and myrrh, going to carry it down to Egypt. And Judah said unto his brethren, What profit is it if we slay our brother and conceal his blood? Come, and let us sell him to the Ishmaelites, and let not our hand be upon him; for he is our brother and our flesh. And his brethren were content; and they drew and lifted up Joseph out of the pit, and sold Joseph to the Ishmaelites for twenty pieces of silver; and they brought Joseph into Egypt.

And Reuben returned unto the pit; and, behold, Joseph was not in the pit; and he rent his clothes. And he returned unto his brethren, and said, The child is not; and I, whither shall I go? And they took Joseph's coat, and killed a kid of the goats, and dipped the coat in the blood; and they sent the coat of many colors, and they brought it to their father, and said, This have we found; know now whether it be thy son's coat or no. And he knew it, and said, It is my son's coat; an evil beast hath devoured him. And Jacob rent his clothes, and put sackcloth upon his loins, and mourned for his son many days.

And Joseph was brought down to Egypt; and Potiphar, an officer of Pharaoh, captain of the guard, an Egyptian, bought him of the hands of the Ishmaelites, which had brought him down thither. And the Lord was with Joseph, and he was a prosperous man; and he was in the house of his master the Egyptian. And his master saw that the Lord was with him, and that the Lord made all that he did to prosper in his hand. And Joseph found grace in his sight; and he made him overseer over his house, and all that he had he put into his hand. And Joseph was a goodly person, and well favored.

And it came to pass after these things, that his master's wife cast her eyes upon Joseph; and she said, Lie with me. But he refused, and said unto his master's wife, Behold, my master hath committed all that he hath to my hand. There is none greater in this house than I; neither hath he kept back anything from me but thee, because thou art his wife. How then can I do this great wickedness, and sin against God? And it came to pass, as she spake to Joseph day by day, that he hearkened not unto her, to lie by her, or to be with her. And it came to pass about this time, that Joseph went into the house to do his business; and there was none of the men of the house there within. And she caught him by his garment, saying, Lie with me. And he left his garment in her hand, and fled, and got him out. And it came to pass, when she saw that he had left his garment in her hand and was fled forth, that she called unto the men of her house, and spake unto them, saying, See, he hath brought in an Hebrew unto us to mock us. He came in unto me to lie with me, and I cried with a loud voice; and it came to pass, when he heard that I cried, that he left his garment with me, and fled, and got him out. And she laid up his garment by her until his lord came home. And she spake unto him according to these words, saying, The Hebrew servant, which thou hast brought unto us, came in unto me to mock me; and it came to pass, as I lifted up my voice and cried, that he left his garment with me and fled out.

And it came to pass, when his master heard the words of his wife, that his wrath was kindled. And Joseph's master took him, and put him into the prison, a place where the king's prisoners were bound. But the Lord was with Joseph, and showed him mercy, and gave him favor in the sight of the keeper of the prison. And the keeper of the prison committed to Joseph's hand all the prisoners that were in the prison.

And it came to pass after these things, that the butler of the king of Egypt and his baker had offended their lord the king of Egypt. And Pharaoh was wroth, and he put them in ward in the house of the captain of the guard, into the prison, the place where Joseph was bound.

And they dreamed a dream both of them, each man his dream in one night, the butler and the baker of the king of Egypt, which were bound in the prison. And Joseph came in unto them in the morning, and looked upon them, and, behold, they were sad. And he asked them, saying, Wherefore look ye so sadly today? And they said unto him, We have dreamed a dream, and there is no interpreter of it. And Joseph said unto them, Do not interpretations belong to God? Tell me them, I pray you. And the chief butler told his dream to Joseph, and said to him: In my dream, behold, a vine was before me; and in the vine were three branches; and it was as though it budded, and her blossoms shot forth; and the clusters thereof brought forth ripe grapes; and Pharaoh's cup was in my hand; and I took the grapes, and pressed them into Pharaoh's cup, and I gave the cup into Pharaoh's hand. And Joseph said unto him, This is the interpretation of it: The three branches are three days; yet within three days shall Pharaoh lift up thine head, and restore thee unto thy place; and thou shalt deliver Pharaoh's cup into his hands, after the former manner when thou wast his butler. But think on me when it shall be well with thee, and show kindness, I pray thee, unto me, and make mention of me unto Pharaoh, and bring me out of this house. For indeed I was stolen away out of the land of the Hebrews; and here also have I done nothing that they should put me into the dungeon.

When the chief baker saw that the interpretation was good, he said unto Joseph, I also was in my dream, and, behold, I had three white baskets on my head; and in the uppermost basket there was of all manner of bakemeats for Pharaoh; and the birds did eat them out of the basket upon my head. And Joseph answered and said, This is the interpretation thereof: The three baskets are three days; yet within three days shall Pharaoh lift up thy head from off thee, and shall hang thee on a tree; and the birds shall eat thy flesh from off thee.

And it came to pass the third day, which was Pharaoh's birthday, that he made a feast unto all his servants. And he restored the chief butler unto his butlership again, and he gave the cup into Pharaoh's hand; but he hanged the chief baker, as Joseph had interpreted to them. Yet did not the chief butler remember Joseph, but forgat him.

And it came to pass at the end of two full years, that Pharaoh dreamed; and, behold, he stood by the river. And, behold, there came up out of the river seven well favored kine and fatfleshed; and they fed in a meadow. And, behold, seven other kine came up after them out of the river, ill favored and leanfleshed; and stood by the other kine upon the brink of the river. And the ill favored and leanfleshed kine did eat up the seven well favored and fat kine. So Pharaoh awoke. And he slept and dreamed the second time, and, behold, seven ears of corn came up upon one stalk, rank and good. And, behold, seven thin ears and blasted with the east wind sprung up after them. And the seven thin ears devoured the seven rank and full ears. And Pharaoh awoke, and, behold, it was a dream. And it came to pass in the morning that his spirit was troubled; and he sent and called for all the magicians of Egypt, and all the wise men thereof; and Pharaoh told them his dreams; but there was none that could interpret them unto Pharaoh.

Then spake the chief butler unto Pharaoh, saying, I do remember my faults this day. Pharaoh was wroth with his servants, and put me in ward in the captain of the guard's house, both me and the chief baker; and we dreamed a dream in one night, I and he. And there was there with us a young man, an Hebrew, servant to the captain of the guard; and we told him, and he interpreted to us our dreams. And it came to pass, as he interpreted to us, so it was; me he restored unto mine office, and him he hanged.

Then Pharaoh sent and called Joseph, and they brought him hastily out of the dungeon. And he shaved himself, and changed his raiment, and came in unto Pharaoh. And Pharaoh said unto Joseph, I have dreamed a dream, and there is none that can interpret it; and I have heard say of thee, that thou canst understand a dream to interpret it. And Joseph answered Pharaoh, saying, It is not in me. God shall give Pharaoh an answer of peace. And Pharaoh said unto Joseph, In my dream, behold, I stood upon the bank of the river; and, behold, there came up out of the river seven kine, fatfleshed and well favored; and they fed in a meadow; and, behold, seven other kine came up after them, poor and very ill favored and leanfleshed, such as I never saw in all the land of Egypt for badness. And the lean and the ill favored kine did eat up the first seven fat kine; and when they had eaten them up, it could not be known that they had eaten them; but they were still ill favored, as at the beginning. So I awoke. And I saw in my dream, and, behold, seven ears came up in one stalk, full and good; and, behold, seven ears, withered, thin, and blasted with the east wind, sprung up after them; and the thin ears devoured the seven good ears. And I told this unto the magicians; but there was none that could declare it to me.

And Joseph said unto Pharaoh, The dream of Pharaoh is one: God hath showed Pharaoh what he is about to do. The seven good kine are seven years; and the seven good ears are seven years; the dream is one. And the seven thin and ill favored kine that came up after them are seven years; and the seven empty ears, blasted with the east wind, shall be seven years of famine. This is the thing which I have spoken unto Pharaoh: What God is about to do he showeth unto Pharaoh. Behold, there come seven years of great plenty throughout all the land of Egypt; and there shall arise after them seven years of famine; and all the plenty shall be forgotten in the land of Egypt; and the famine shall consume the land; for it shall be very grievous. And for that the dream was doubled unto Pharaoh twice, it is because the thing is established by God, and God will shortly bring it to pass. Now therefore let Pharaoh look out a man discreet and wise, and set him over the land of Egypt. And let them gather all the food of those good years that come, and lay up corn under the hand of Pharaoh, and let them keep food in the cities. And that food shall be for store to the land against the seven years of famine, which shall be in the land of Egypt.

And the thing was good in the eyes of Pharaoh, and in the eyes of all his servants. And Pharaoh said unto his servants, Can we find such a one as this is, a man in whom the Spirit of God is? And Pharaoh said unto Joseph, Forasmuch as God hath showed thee all this, there is none so discreet and wise as thou art. Thou shalt be over my house, and according unto thy word shall all my people be ruled; only in the throne will I be greater than thou. And Pharaoh took off his ring from his hand, and put it upon Joseph's hand, and arrayed him in vestures of fine linen, and put a gold chain about his neck, and he made him to ride in the second chariot which he had; and he made him ruler over all the land of Egypt. And

Pharaoh gave him to wife Asenath the daughter of Potipherah priest of On.

And Joseph was thirty years old when he stood before Pharaoh king of Egypt. And Joseph went out from the presence of Pharaoh, and went throughout all the land of Egypt. And in the seven plenteous years the earth brought forth by handfuls. And he gathered up all the food of the seven years, which were in the land of Egypt, and laid up the food in the cities. And Joseph gathered corn as the sand of the sea, very much, until he left numbering; for it was without number. And unto Joseph were born two sons before the years of famine came, which Asenath bare unto him. And Joseph called the name of the first-born Manasseh; for God, said he, hath made me forget all my toil, and all my father's house. And the name of the second called he Ephraim; for God hath caused me to be fruitful in the land of my affliction.

And the seven years of plenteousness that was in the land of Egypt were ended. And the seven years of dearth began to come, according as Joseph had said; and the dearth was in all lands; but in all the land of Egypt there was bread. And Joseph opened all the storehouses, and sold unto the Egyptians; and the famine waxed sore in the land of Egypt. And all countries came into Egypt to Joseph for to buy corn, because that the famine was so sore in all lands.

Now when Jacob saw that there was corn in Egypt, Jacob said unto his sons, Why do ye look one upon another? And he said, Behold, I have heard that there is corn in Egypt. Get you down thither, and buy for us from thence, that we may live and not die.

And Joseph's ten brethren went down to buy corn in Egypt. But Benjamin, Joseph's brother, Jacob sent not with his brethren; for he said, Lest peradventure mischief befall him. And the sons of Israel came to buy corn, for the famine was in the land of Canaan. And Joseph's brethren came, and bowed down themselves before him with their faces to the earth. And Joseph saw his brethren, and he knew them, but made himself strange unto them, and spake roughly unto them; and he said unto them, Whence come ye? And they said, From the land of Canaan to buy food. And Joseph knew his brethren, but they knew not him. And Joseph remembered the dreams which he dreamed of them, and he said unto them, Ye are spies; to see the nakedness of the land ye are come. And they said unto him, Nay, my lord, but to buy food are thy servants come. We are all one man's sons; we are true men; thy servants are no spies. Thy servants are twelve brethren, the sons of one man in the land of Canaan; and, behold, the youngest is this day with our father, and one is not. And Joseph said unto them, Hereby ye shall be proved: By the life of Pharaoh ye shall not go forth hence, except your youngest brother come thither. Send one of you, and let him fetch your brother, and ye shall be kept in prison, that your words may be proved, whether there be any truth in you. And he put them all together into ward three days. And Joseph said unto them the third day, This do, and live, for I fear God: If ye be true men, let one of your brethren be bound in the house of your prison; go ye, carry corn for the famine of your houses; but bring your youngest brother unto me; so shall your words be verified, and ye shall not die.

And they said one to another, We are verily guilty concerning our brother Joseph in that we saw the anguish of his soul, when he besought us, and we would not hear; therefore is this distress come upon us. And Reuben answered them, saying, Spake I not unto you, saying, Do not sin against the child; and ye would not hear? Therefore, behold, also his blood is required. And they knew not that Joseph understood them; for he spake unto them by an interpreter. And he turned himself about from them, and wept, and returned to them again, and communed with them, and took from them Simeon, and bound him before their eyes.

Then Joseph commanded to fill their sacks with corn, and to restore every man's money into his sack, and to give them provision for the way; and thus did he unto them. And they laded their asses with the corn and departed thence. And as one of them opened his sack to give his ass provender in the inn, he espied his money; for, behold, it was in his sack's mouth. And he said unto his brethren, My money is restored; and, lo, it is even in my sack; and their heart failed them, and they were afraid, saying one to another, What is this that God hath done unto us?

And they came unto Jacob, their father, unto the land of Canaan and told him all that befell unto them, saying, The man who is the lord of the land spake roughly to us and took us for spies of the country. And we said unto him, We are true men; we are no spies; we be twelve brethren, sons of our father; one is not, and the youngest is this day with our father in the land of Canaan. And the man, the lord of the country, said unto us, Hereby shall I know that ye are true men: Leave one of your brethren here with me, and take food for the famine of your households, and be gone; and bring your youngest brother unto me; then shall I know that ye are no spies, but that ye are true men; so will I deliver you your brother, and ye shall traffic in the land.

And it came to pass as they emptied their sacks, that, behold, every man's bundle of money was in his sack; and when both they and their father saw the bundles of money, they were afraid. And Jacob their father said unto them, Me have ye bereaved of my children. Joseph is not, and Simeon is not, and ye will take Benjamin away; all these things are against me. And Reuben spake unto his father, saying, Slay my two sons, if I bring him not to thee; deliver him into my hand, and I will bring him to thee again. And he said, My son shall not go down with you; for his brother is dead, and he is left alone. If mischief befall him by the way in the which ye go, then shall ye bring down my gray hairs with sorrow to the grave.

And the famine was sore in the land. And it came to pass, when they had eaten up the corn which they had brought out of Egypt, their father said unto them, Go again, buy us a little food. And Judah spake unto him, saying, The man did solemnly protest unto us, saying, Ye shall not see my face except your brother be with you. If thou wilt send our brother with us, we will go down and buy thee food. But if thou wilt not send him, we will not go down. And Israel said, Wherefore dealt ye so ill with me, as to tell the man whether ye had yet a brother? And they said, The man asked us straitly of our state, and of our kindred, saying, Is your father yet alive? Have ye another brother? And we told him according to the tenor of these words. Could we certainly know that he would say, Bring your brother down? And Judah said unto Israel his father, Send the lad with me, and we will arise and go, that we may live, and not die, both we, and thou, and also our little ones. I will be surety for him; of my hand shalt thou require him. If I bring him not unto thee, and set him before thee, then let me bear the blame forever.

And their father Israel said unto them, If it must be so now, do this. Take of the best fruits of the land in your vessels, and carry down the man a present, a little balm, and a little honey, spices, and myrrh, nuts, and almonds. And take double money in your hand; and the money that was brought again in the mouth of your sacks, carry it again in your hand; peradventure it was an oversight. Take also your brother, and arise, go again unto the man, and God Almighty give you mercy before the man, that he may send away your other brother and Benjamin.

And the men took that present, and they took double money in their hand, and Benjamin, and rose up, and went down to Egypt, and stood before Joseph. And when Joseph saw Benjamin with them, he said to the ruler of his house, Bring these men home, and slay, and make ready; for these men shall dine with me at noon. And the man did as Joseph bade; and the man brought the men into Joseph's house.

And the men were afraid, because they were brought into Joseph's house. And they came near to the steward of Joseph's house, and they communed with him at the door of the house, and said, O sir, we came indeed down at the first time to buy food, and it came to pass, when we came to the inn, that we opened our sacks, and, behold, every man's money was in the mouth of his sack; we have brought it again in our hand. And other money have we brought down in our hands to buy food; we cannot tell who put our money in our sacks. And he said, Peace be to you, fear not; your God, and the God of your father, hath given you treasure in your sacks. And he brought Simeon out unto them.

And the man brought the men into Joseph's house, and gave them water, and they washed their feet; and he gave their asses provender. And they made ready the present against Joseph came at noon; for they heard that they should eat bread there. And when Joseph came home, they brought him the present which was in their hand into the house, and bowed themselves to him to the earth. And he asked them of their welfare, and said, Is your father well, the old man of whom ye spake? Is he yet alive? And they answered, Thy servant our father is in good health, he is yet alive. And he lifted up his eyes, and saw his brother Benjamin, his mother's son, and said, Is this your younger brother, of whom ye spake unto me? And he said, God be gracious unto thee, my son. And Joseph made haste; for his bowels did yearn upon his brother; and he sought where to weep; and he entered into his chamber, and wept there. And he washed his face, and went out, and refrained himself, and said, Set on bread. And they set on for him by himself, and for them by themselves, and for the Egyptians which did eat with him by themselves, because the Egyptians might not eat bread with the Hebrews. And they sat before him, the firstborn according to his birthright, and the youngest according to his youth; and the men marvelled one at another. And he took and sent messes unto them from before him; but Benjamin's mess was five times so much as any of theirs. And they drank, and were merry with him.

And Joseph commanded the steward of his house, saying, Fill the men's sacks with food, as much as they can carry, and put every man's money in his sack's mouth. And put my cup, the silver cup, in the sack's mouth of the youngest, and his corn money. And he did according to the word that Joseph had spoken.

As soon as the morning was light, the men were sent away, they and their asses. And when they were gone out of the city, and not yet far off, Joseph said unto his steward, Up, follow after the men; and when thou dost overtake them, say unto them, Wherefore have ye rewarded evil for good? Is not this it in which my lord drinketh, and whereby indeed he divineth? Ye have done evil in so doing. And he overtook them, and he spake unto them these same words.

And they said unto him, Wherefore saith my lord these words? God forbid that thy servants should do according to this thing. Behold, the money which we found in our sacks' mouths we brought again unto thee out of the land of Canaan; how then should we steal out of thy lord's house silver or gold? With whomsoever of thy servants it be found, both let him die, and we also will be my lord's bondmen. And he said, Now also let it be according unto your words. He with whom it is found shall be my servant; and ye shall be blameless. Then they speedily took down every man his sack to the ground, and opened every man his sack. And he searched, and began at the eldest, and left at the youngest; and the cup was found in Benjamin's sack.

Then they rent their clothes, and laded every man his ass, and returned to the city. And Judah and his brethren came to Joseph's house; for he was yet there; and they fell before him on the ground. And Joseph said unto them, What deed is this that ye have done? Wot ye not that such a man as I can certainly divine? And Judah said, What shall we say unto my lord? What shall we speak? or how shall we clear ourselves? God hath found out the iniquity of thy servants; behold, we are my lord's servants, both we, and he also with whom the cup is found. And he said, God forbid that I should do so; but the man in whose hand the cup is found, he shall be my servant; and as for you, get you up in peace unto your father.

Then Judah came near unto him, and said, Oh my lord, let thy servant, I pray thee, speak a word in my lord's ears, and let not thine anger burn against thy servant; for thou art even as Pharaoh. My lord asked his servants, saying, Have ye a father, or a brother? And we said unto my lord, We have a father, an old man, and a child of his old age, a little one; and his brother is dead, and he alone is left of his mother, and his father loveth him. And thou saidst unto thy servants, Bring him down unto me, that I may set mine eyes upon him. And we said unto my lord, The lad cannot leave his father; for if he should leave his father, his father would die. And thou saidst unto thy servants, Except your youngest brother come down with you, ye shall see my face no more. And it came to pass, when we came up unto thy servant my father, we told him the words of my lord. And our father said, Go again, and buy us a little food. And we said, We cannot go down; if our youngest brother be with us, then will we go down; for we may not see the man's face, except our youngest brother be with us. And thy servant my father said unto us, Ye know that my wife bare me two sons; and the one went out from me, and I said, Surely he is torn in pieces; and I saw him not since; and if ye take this also from me, and mischief befall him, ye shall bring down my gray hairs with sorrow to the grave. Now therefore, when I come to my father, and the lad be not with us, seeing that his life is bound up in the lad's life, it shall come to pass, when he seeth that the lad is not with us, that he will die; and thy servants shall bring down the gray hairs of our father with sorrow to the grave. Now therefore, I pray thee, let thy servant abide instead of the lad a bondman to my lord; and let the lad go up with his brethren. For how shall I go up to my father, and the lad be not with me?

Then Joseph could not refrain himself; and he cried, Cause every man to go out from me. And there stood no man with him while Joseph made himself known unto his brethren. And he wept aloud. And Joseph said unto his brethren, I am Joseph. Doth my father yet live? And his brethren could not answer him, for they were troubled at his presence. And Joseph said unto his brethren, Come near to me, I pray you. And they came near. And he said, I am Joseph your brother, whom ye sold into Egypt. Now therefore be not grieved nor angry with yourselves that ye sold me hither; for God did send me before you to preserve life. For these two years hath the famine been in the land; and yet there are five years, in the which there shall neither be earing nor harvest. And God sent me before you to preserve you a posterity in the earth and to save your lives by a great deliverance. So now, it was not you that sent me hither, but God; and he hath made me a father to Pharaoh, and lord of all his house, and a ruler throughout all the land of Egypt. Haste ye, and go up to my father, and say unto him, Thus saith thy son Joseph, God hath made me lord of all Egypt. Come down unto me, tarry not. And thou shalt dwell in the land of Goshen, and thou shalt be near unto me, thou, and thy children, and thy children's children, and thy flocks, and thy herds, and all that thou hast; and there will I nourish thee; for yet there are five years of famine. And ye shall tell my father of all my glory in Egypt, and of all that ye have seen; and ye shall haste and bring down my father hither. And he fell upon his brother Benjamin's neck, and wept; and Benjamin wept upon his neck. Moreover, he kissed all his brethren, and wept upon them; and after that his brethren talked with him.

And the fame thereof was heard in Pharaoh's house, saying, Joseph's brethren are come; and it pleased Pharaoh well and his servants. And Pharaoh said unto Joseph, Say unto thy brethren, This do ye; lade your beasts, and go, get you unto the land of Canaan; and take your father, and your households, and come unto me; and I will give you the good of the land of Egypt, and ye shall eat the fat of the land. And the children of Israel did so; and Joseph gave them wagons, according to the commandment of Pharaoh, and gave them provision for the way. To all of them he gave each man changes of raiment; but to Benjamin he gave three hundred pieces of silver and five changes of raiment. And to his father he sent after this manner: ten asses laden with the good things of Egypt, and ten she-asses laden with corn and bread and meat for his father by the way.

And they went up out of Egypt, and came into the land of Canaan, unto Jacob their father, and told him, saying, Joseph is yet alive, and he is governor over all the land of Egypt. And Jacob's heart fainted, for he believed them not. And they told him all the words of Joseph which he had said unto them; and when he saw the wagons which Joseph had sent to carry him, the spirit of Jacob their father revived. And he said, It is enough; Joseph my son is yet alive. I will go and see him before I die.

And Israel took his journey with all that he had and came to Beersheba, and offered sacrifices unto the God of his father Isaac. And God spake unto Israel in the visions of the night, and said, Jacob, Jacob. And he said, Here am I. And he said, I am God, the God of thy father. Fear not to go down into Egypt; for I will there make of thee a great nation. I will go down with thee into Egypt; and I will also surely bring thee up again. And Jacob rose up from Beersheba; and the sons of Israel carried Jacob their father, and their little ones, and their wives, in the wagons which Pharaoh had sent to carry them. And they took their cattle, and their goods which they had gotten in the land of Canaan, and came into Egypt, Jacob, and all his seed with him.

And Joseph made ready his chariot, and went up to meet Israel his father, to Goshen, and presented himself unto him; and he fell on his neck, and wept on his neck a good while. And Israel said unto Joseph, Now let me die, since I have seen thy face, because thou art yet alive.

And Israel dwelt in the land of Egypt, in the country of Goshen; and they had possessions therein, and grew, and multiplied exceedingly. And Jacob lived in the land of Egypt seventeen years; so the whole age of Jacob was an hundred and forty and seven years. And the time drew nigh that Israel must die; and he called his son Joseph, and said unto him, If now I have found grace in thy sight, put, I pray thee, thy hand under my thigh, and deal kindly and truly with me. Bury me not, I pray thee, in Egypt; but I will lie with my fathers, and thou shalt carry me out of Egypt, and bury me in their burying-place. And he said, I will do as thou hast said. And he said, Swear unto me, and he sware unto him. And Israel bowed himself upon the bed's head.

And Joseph fell upon his father's face, and wept upon him, and kissed him. And Joseph commanded his servants the physicians to embalm his father; and the physicians embalmed Israel. And forty days were fulfilled for him; for so are fulfilled the days of those which are embalmed; and the Egyptians mourned for him threescore and ten days. And when the days of his mourning were past, Joseph spake unto the house of Pharaoh, saying, My father made me swear, saying, Lo, I die; in my grave which I have digged for me in the land of Canaan, there shalt thou bury me. Now therefore let me go up, I pray thee, and bury my father, and I will come again. And Pharaoh said, Go up, and bury thy father, according as he made thee swear.

And Joseph went up to bury his father; and with him went up all the servants of Pharaoh, the elders of his house, and all the elders of the land of Egypt, and all the house of Joseph, and his brethren, and his father's house; only their little ones, and their flocks, and their herds, they left in the land of Goshen. And there went up with him both chariots and horsemen; and it was a very great company.

And his sons did unto Jacob according as he commanded them; for his sons carried him into the land of Canaan, and buried him in the cave of the field of Machpelah, which Abraham bought with the field for a possession of a burying-place. And Joseph returned into Egypt, he, and his brethren, and all that went up with him to bury his father. And Joseph dwelt in Egypt, he and his father's house; and Joseph lived an hundred and ten years.

And Joseph said unto his brethren, I die; and God will surely visit you and bring you out of this land unto the land which he sware to Abraham, to Isaac, and to Jacob. And Joseph took an oath of the children of Israel, saying, God will surely visit you, and ye shall carry up my bones from hence. So Joseph died, being an hundred and ten years old; and they embalmed him, and he was put in a coffin in Egypt.

-II-

THE GREAT LEADERS OF ANCIENT ISRAEL

C. 1250–1030 B.C.

These readings portray the life and fortunes of the Hebrew people during two centuries between the Exodus from Egypt, usually placed around 1250 B.C., and the accession of King Saul, about 1030 B.C. Although portions of the narratives are without doubt legendary in character, without solid basis in historical fact, we may be certain that the main outlines of the stories deal with actual history rather than with legend and tradition. We know that there was an exodus from Egypt; that Moses did exist as the greatest leader and teacher of his people; that Joshua was his successor; that the magnificent song of Deborah had its conception and creation in an actual battle; and that Samuel, although he is one of the most puzzling of characters, was responsible for the kingship of Saul. And if we are on less sure ground with the stories of Gideon, Jephthah, and Samson, they not only provide us with graphic and exciting narrative, but reveal interesting knowledge of the perils and problems of life in Canaan during these two centuries, often called the Period of the Judges of Israel.

When we begin these selections, certain Hebrew tribes are in Egypt (whence they had migrated some two or three centuries earlier) and under the bondage of the Pharaoh; when we conclude them, the tribes under Moses, Joshua, and others, after a sojourn in the wilderness south of the Dead Sea, have gradually conquered Canaan, or Palestine [1] as we know it, and have become a small, yet not unimportant, nation under a king, their chief enemies now being the Philistines on the western seacoast.

[1] The name Palestine is another form of the word Philistine. The early Hebrews did not use the term for Canaan.

1
MOSES

This material on Moses has been carefully selected from the books of Exodus and Deuteronomy. These books, together with Leviticus and Numbers, written by various authors over a period of four centuries and compiled about 400 B.C., comprise the so-called Torah, or Law, of the Hebrew people. Much of them means little to readers of today and is not in any way essential to a fair understanding either of Hebrew history or of Moses himself.

I have chosen only those chapters which reveal Moses as the deliverer of his people from Egypt, as the framer of their early laws and actually the founder of their nation, and as the great spiritual leader who, himself led by God, was the power behind the establishment of their national religion.

The careful reader will recognize that these readings on Moses are, so far as literary excellence is concerned, inferior to the Jacob-Joseph saga. But the story which they tell is indispensable to any knowledge of those events which, more than three thousand years ago, transformed a few thousand Hebrew tribesmen into a firmly united people.

And the children of Israel were fruitful, and increased abundantly, and multiplied, and waxed exceeding mighty; and the land was filled with them. Now there arose up a new king over Egypt, which knew not Joseph. And he said unto his people, Behold, the people of the children of Israel are more and mightier than we. Come on, let us deal wisely with them; lest they multiply, and it come to pass, that, when there falleth out any war, they join also unto our enemies, and fight against us, and so get them up out of the land. Therefore they did set over them taskmasters to afflict them with their burdens. But the more they afflicted them, the more they multiplied and grew. And the Egyptians were grieved because of the children of Israel. And they made the children of Israel to serve with rigor. And they made their lives bitter with hard bondage, in mortar, and in brick, and in all manner of service in the field.

And the king of Egypt spake to the Hebrew midwives and said,

When ye do the office of a midwife to the Hebrew women, if it be a son, then ye shall kill him. But the midwives feared God and did not as the king of Egypt commanded them, but saved the men children alive. Therefore God dealt well with the midwives; and the people multiplied and waxed very mighty.

And there went a man of the house of Levi, and took to wife a daughter of Levi. And the woman conceived, and bare a son; and when she saw him, that he was a goodly child, she hid him three months. And when she could not longer hide him, she took for him an ark of bulrushes, and daubed it with slime and with pitch, and put the child therein; and she laid it in the flags by the river's brink. And his sister stood afar off, to wit what would be done to him.

And the daughter of Pharaoh came down to wash herself at the river; and her maidens walked along by the river's side; and when she saw the ark among the flags, she sent her maid to fetch it. And when she had opened it, she saw the child; and, behold, the babe wept. And she had compassion on him, and said, This is one of the Hebrews' children. Then said his sister to Pharaoh's daughter, Shall I go and call to thee a nurse of the Hebrew women, that she may nurse the child for thee? And Pharaoh's daughter said to her, Go. And the maid went and called the child's mother. And Pharaoh's daughter said unto her, Take this child away, and nurse it for me, and I will give thee thy wages. And the woman took the child, and nursed it. And the child grew, and she brought him unto Pharaoh's daughter, and he became her son. And she called his name Moses.

And it came to pass in those days, when Moses was grown, that he went out unto his brethren, and looked on their burdens; and he spied an Egyptian smiting a Hebrew, one of his brethren. And he looked this way and that way, and when he saw that there was no man, he slew the Egyptian, and hid him in the sand. And when he went out the second day, behold, two men of the Hebrews strove together; and he said to him that did the wrong, Wherefore smitest thou thy fellow? And he said, Who made thee a prince and a judge over us? Intendest thou to kill me, as thou killedst the Egyptian? And Moses feared, and said, Surely this thing is known.

Now when Pharaoh heard this thing, he sought to slay Moses. But Moses fled from the face of Pharaoh and dwelt in the land of Midian; and he sat down by a well. Now the priest of Midian had seven daughters; and they came and drew water, and filled the troughs to water their father's flock. And the shepherds came and drove them away; but Moses stood up and helped them, and watered their flock. And when they came to their father, he said, How is it that ye are come so soon today? And they said, An Egyptian delivered us out of the hand of the shepherds, and also drew water enough for us, and watered the flock. And he said unto his daughters, And where is he? Why is it that ye have left the man? Call him, that he may eat bread. And Moses was content to dwell with the man; and he gave Moses Zipporah his daughter.

Now Moses kept the flock of Jethro his father-in-law, the priest of Midian; and he led the flock to the back side of the desert, and came to the mountain of God, even to Horeb. And the Angel of the Lord appeared unto him in a flame of fire out of the midst of a bush; and he looked, and, behold, the bush burned with fire, and the bush was not consumed. And Moses said, I will now turn aside, and see this great sight, why the bush is not burnt. And when the Lord saw that he turned aside to see, God called unto him out of the midst of the bush, and said, Moses, Moses. And he said, Here am I. And he said, Draw not nigh hither. Put off thy shoes from off thy feet; for the place whereon thou standest is holy ground. Moreover he said, I am the God of thy father, the God of Abraham, the God of Isaac, the God of Jacob. And Moses hid his face, for he was afraid to look upon God.

And the Lord said, I have surely seen the affliction of my people which are in Egypt, and have heard their cry by reason of their taskmaster; for I know their sorrows. And I am come down to deliver them out of the hand of the Egyptians, and to bring them up out of that land unto a good land and a large, unto a land flowing with milk and honey. Come now therefore, and I will send thee unto

Pharaoh, that thou mayest bring forth my people, the children of Israel, out of Egypt.

And Moses said unto God, Who am I that I should bring forth the children of Israel out of Egypt? And God said, Certainly I will be with thee; and this shall be a token unto thee that I have sent thee: When thou hast brought forth the people out of Egypt, ye shall serve God upon this mountain.

And Moses answered and said, But behold, they will not believe me, nor hearken unto my voice; for they will say, The Lord hath not appeared unto thee. And the Lord said, What is that in thy hand? And he said, A rod. And he said, Cast it on the ground. And he cast it on the ground, and it became a serpent; and Moses fled before it. And the Lord said unto Moses, Put forth thine hand, and take it by the tail. And he put forth his hand and caught it, and it became a rod in his hand.

And Moses said unto the Lord, O my Lord, I am not eloquent, but I am slow of speech, and of a slow tongue. And the Lord said unto him, Who hath made man's mouth? or who hath made the dumb, or the deaf, or the seeing, or the blind? Have not I, the Lord? Now therefore go, and I will be with thy mouth, and teach thee what thou shalt say. Is not Aaron the Levite thy brother? I know that he can speak well. And also, behold, he cometh forth to meet thee; and when he seeth thee, he will be glad in his heart. And thou shalt speak unto him, and put words in his mouth; and I will be with thy mouth, and with his mouth, and will teach you what ye shall do. And thou shalt take this rod in thine hand, wherewith thou shalt do signs.

The Bible gives here, Exodus 7–12, a legendary account of the ten plagues visited upon Pharaoh by God. The final tragedy, the death of the firstborn, follows.

Then Moses called for all the elders of Israel, and said unto them, Draw out and take you a lamb according to your families, and kill the Passover. And ye shall take a bunch of hyssop, and dip it in the blood that is in the basin, and strike the lintel and the two side posts with the blood that is in the basin; and none of you shall go out at the door of his house until the morning. For the Lord will pass through to smite the Egyptians; and when he seeth the blood upon the lintel, and on the two side posts, the Lord will pass over the door, and will not suffer the destroyer to come in unto your houses to smite you. And ye shall observe this thing for an ordinance to thee and to thy sons forever. And it shall come to pass, when ye be come to the land which the Lord will give you, according as he hath promised, that ye shall keep this service. And it shall come to pass, when your children shall say unto you, What mean ye by this service? that ye shall say, It is the sacrifice of the Lord's Passover, who passed over the houses of the children of Israel in Egypt, when he smote the Egyptians and delivered our houses. And the people bowed the head and worshipped. And the children of Israel went away, and did as the Lord had commanded Moses and Aaron.

And it came to pass, that at midnight the Lord smote all the firstborn in the land of Egypt, from the firstborn of Pharaoh that sat on his throne unto the firstborn of the captive that was in the dungeon; and all the firstborn of cattle. And Pharaoh rose up in the night, he, and all his servants and all the Egyptians; and there was a great cry in Egypt, for there was not a house where there was not one dead.

And God called for Moses and Aaron by night, and said, Rise up, and get you forth, both ye and the children of Israel. Also take your flocks and your herds, and be gone; and bless me also. And God led the people about through the way of the wilderness of the Red Sea. And the Lord went before them by day in a pillar of cloud to lead them the way, and by night in a pillar of fire to give them light.

And it was told the king of Egypt that the people fled; and the heart of Pharaoh and of his servants was turned against the people, and they said, Why have we done this, that we have let Israel go from serving us? And he made ready his chariot, and took his people with him; and he took six hundred chosen chariots, and captains over every one of them. And the Lord hardened the heart of

Pharaoh king of Egypt, and he pursued after the children of Israel, and overtook them encamping by the sea.

And when Pharaoh drew nigh, the children of Israel lifted up their eyes, and, behold, the Egyptians marched after them; and they were sore afraid. And the children of Israel cried out unto the Lord. And they said unto Moses, Because there were no graves in Egypt, hast thou taken us away to die in the wilderness? Wherefore hast thou dealt thus with us, to carry us forth out of Egypt? For it had been better for us to serve the Egyptians, than that we should die in the wilderness. And Moses said unto the people, Fear ye not, stand still, and see the salvation of the Lord, which he will show to you today; for the Egyptians whom ye have seen today, ye shall see them again no more forever. The Lord shall fight for you, and ye shall hold your peace.

And the Lord said unto Moses, Wherefore criest thou unto me? Speak unto the children of Israel that they go forward; but lift thou up thy rod, and stretch out thine hand over the sea, and divide it; and the children of Israel shall go on dry ground through the midst of the sea. And I, behold, I will harden the hearts of the Egyptians, and they shall follow them; and I will get me honor upon Pharaoh, and upon all his host, upon his chariots, and upon his horsemen. And the Egyptians shall know that I am the Lord.

And the angel of God, which went before the camp of Israel, removed and went behind them; and the pillar of the cloud went from before their face, and stood behind them; and it came between the camp of the Egyptians and the camp of Israel; and it was a cloud and darkness to them, but it gave light by night to these so that the one came not near the other all the night. And Moses stretched out his hand over the sea; and the Lord caused the sea to go back by a strong east wind all that night, and made the sea dry land, and the waters were divided. And the children of Israel went into the midst of the sea upon the dry ground; and the waters were a wall unto them on their right hand and on their left.

And the Egyptians pursued, and went in after them to the midst of the sea, even all Pharaoh's horses, his chariots, and his horsemen. And it came to pass, that in the morning watch the Lord looked unto the host of the Egyptians through the pillar of fire and of the cloud, and troubled the host of the Egyptians, and took off their chariot wheels, that they drave them heavily, so that the Egyptians said, Let us flee from the face of Israel; for the Lord fighteth for them against the Egyptians. And the Lord said unto Moses, Stretch out thine hand over the sea, that the waters may come again upon the Egyptians, upon their chariots, and upon their horsemen. And Moses stretched forth his hand over the sea, and the sea returned to his strength when the morning appeared; and the Egyptians fled against it; and the Lord overthrew the Egyptians in the midst of the sea. And the waters returned, and covered the chariots, and the horsemen, and all the host of Pharaoh that came into the sea after them. There remained not so much as one of them. But the children of Israel walked upon dry land in the midst of the sea; and the waters were a wall unto them on their right hand and on their left. Thus the Lord saved Israel that day out of the hand of the Egyptians; and Israel saw the Egyptians dead upon the seashore. And Israel saw that great work which the Lord did upon the Egyptians; and the people feared the Lord, and believed the Lord, and his servant Moses.

Then sang Moses and the children of Israel this song unto the Lord:

> I will sing unto the Lord, for he hath triumphed gloriously:
> The horse and his rider hath he thrown into the sea.

And the whole congregation of the children of Israel murmured against Moses and Aaron in the wilderness and said unto them, Would to God we had died by the hand of the Lord in the land of Egypt when we did eat bread to the full! For ye have brought us forth into this wilderness to kill this whole assembly with hunger.

Then said the Lord unto Moses, Behold, I will rain bread from heaven for you; and the people shall go out and gather a certain rate every day that I may prove them whether they will walk in my law, or no. And on the sixth day they shall prepare that which they bring in, and it shall be twice as much as they gather daily. And

Moses and Aaron said unto all the children of Israel, At even, then ye shall know that the Lord hath brought you out from the land of Egypt; and in the morning, then shall ye see the glory of the Lord.

And it came to pass that at even the quails came up and covered the camp, and in the morning the dew lay round about the host. And when the dew was gone up, behold, upon the face of the wilderness there lay a small round thing as small as the hoar frost on the ground. And when the children of Israel saw it, they said to one another, It is manna, for they wist not what it was. And it was like coriander seed, white; and the taste of it was like wafers made with honey. And Moses said unto them, This is the bread which the Lord hath given you to eat. Six days ye shall gather it, but on the seventh day, which is the sabbath, in it there shall be none. And it came to pass that there went out some of the people on the seventh day to gather, and they found none. And the Lord said, How long refuse ye to keep my commandments and my laws?

In the third month, when the children of Israel were gone forth out of the land of Egypt, the same day came they into the wilderness of Sinai; and there Israel camped before the mount. And Moses went up unto God, and the Lord called unto him out of the mountain, saying, Thus shalt thou say to the house of Jacob, and tell the children of Israel: Ye have seen what I did unto the Egyptians, and how I bare you on eagles' wings, and brought you unto myself. Now therefore, if ye will obey my voice indeed, and keep my covenant, then ye shall be a peculiar treasure unto me above all people. For all the earth is mine; and ye shall be unto me a kingdom of priests, and an holy nation. These are the words which thou shalt speak unto the children of Israel.

And Moses came and called for the elders of the people, and laid before their faces all these words which the Lord commanded him. And all the people answered together, and said, All that the Lord hath spoken we will do. And Moses returned the words of the people unto the Lord. And the Lord said unto Moses, Lo, I come unto thee in a thick cloud, that the people may hear when I speak with thee, and believe thee forever. And Moses told the words of the people unto the Lord.

And the Lord said unto Moses, Go unto the people, and sanctify them today and tomorrow, and let them wash their clothes, and be ready against the third day; for the third day the Lord will come down in the sight of all the people upon mount Sinai. And thou shalt set bounds unto the people round about, saying, Take heed to yourselves, that ye go not up into the mount, or touch the border of it. Whosoever toucheth the mount shall be surely put to death. And Moses went down from the mount unto the people, and sanctified the people; and they washed their clothes. And he said unto the people, Be ready against the third day.

And it came to pass on the third day in the morning, that there were thunders and lightnings, and a thick cloud upon the mount, and the voice of the trumpet exceeding loud, so that all the people that was in the camp trembled. And Moses brought forth the people out of the camp to meet with God; and they stood at the nether part of the mount. And mount Sinai was altogether on a smoke, because the Lord descended upon it in fire; and the smoke thereof ascended as the smoke of a furnace, and the whole mount quaked greatly. And when the voice of the trumpet sounded long, and waxed louder and louder, Moses spake, and God answered him by a voice. And the Lord came down upon mount Sinai, on the top of the mount; and the Lord called Moses up to the top of the mount; and Moses went up. And the Lord said unto Moses, Go down, charge the people, lest they break through unto the Lord to gaze, and many of them perish. And let the priests also, which come near to the Lord, sanctify themselves, lest the Lord break forth upon them. And Moses said unto the Lord, The people cannot come up to mount Sinai; for thou chargedst us, saying, Set bounds about the mount, and sanctify it. And the Lord said unto him, Away, get thee down, and thou shalt come up, thou, and Aaron with thee; but let not the priests and the people break through to come up unto the Lord, lest he break forth upon them. So Moses went down unto the people, and spake unto them.

And God spake all these words, saying, I am the Lord thy God, which have brought thee out of the land of Egypt, out of the house of bondage. Thou shalt have no other gods before me. Thou shalt not make unto thee any graven image, or any likeness of any thing that is in heaven above, or that is in the earth beneath, or that is in the water under the earth; thou shalt not bow down thyself to them, nor serve them; for I the Lord thy God am a jealous God, visiting the iniquity of the fathers upon the children unto the third and fourth generation of them that hate me; and showing mercy unto thousands of them that love me, and keep my commandments. Thou shalt not take the name of the Lord thy God in vain; for the Lord will not hold him guiltless that taketh his name in vain. Remember the sabbath day to keep it holy. Six days shalt thou labor, and do all thy work; but the seventh day is the sabbath of the Lord thy God. In it thou shalt not do any work, thou, nor thy son, nor thy daughter, thy manservant, nor thy maidservant, nor thy cattle, nor thy stranger that is within thy gates; for in six days the Lord made heaven and earth, the sea, and all that in them is, and rested the seventh day: wherefore the Lord blessed the sabbath day, and hallowed it. Honor thy father and thy mother, that thy days may be long upon the land which the Lord thy God giveth thee. Thou shalt not kill. Thou shalt not commit adultery. Thou shalt not steal. Thou shalt not bear false witness against thy neighbor. Thou shalt not covet thy neighbor's house, thou shalt not covet thy neighbor's wife, nor his manservant, nor his maidservant, nor his ox, nor his ass, nor any thing that is thy neighbor's.

And all the people saw the thunderings, and the lightnings, and the noise of the trumpet, and the mountain smoking; and when the people saw it, they removed, and stood afar off. And they said unto Moses, Speak thou with us, and we will hear; but let not God speak with us, lest we die. And Moses said unto the people, Fear not; for God is come to prove you, and that his fear may be before your faces, that ye sin not. And the people stood afar off, and Moses drew near unto the thick darkness where God was.

And when the people saw that Moses delayed to come down out of the mount, the people gathered themselves together unto Aaron, and said unto him, Up, make us gods, which shall go before us; for as for this Moses, the man that brought us up out of the land of Egypt, we wot not what is become of him. And Aaron said unto them, Break off the golden earrings which are in the ears of your wives, of your sons, and of your daughters, and bring them unto me. And all the people brake off the golden earrings which were in their ears, and brought them unto Aaron. And he received them at their hand, and fashioned it with a graving tool, after he had made a molten calf; and they said, These be thy gods, O Israel, which brought thee up out of the land of Egypt. And when Aaron saw it, he built an altar before it; and Aaron made proclamation, and said, Tomorrow is a feast to the Lord. And they rose up early on the morrow and offered burnt offerings, and brought peace offerings; and the people sat down to eat and to drink and rose up to play.

And the Lord said unto Moses, Go, get thee down; for thy people which thou broughtest out of the land of Egypt have corrupted themselves. And Moses turned, and went down from the mount, and the two tables of the testimony were in his hand. And the tables were the work of God, and the writing was the writing of God, graven upon the tables.

And it came to pass, as soon as he came nigh unto the camp, that he saw the calf, and the dancing; and Moses' anger waxed hot, and he cast the tables out of his hands, and brake them beneath the mount. And he took the calf which they had made and burnt it in the fire, and ground it to powder, and strewed it upon the water, and made the children of Israel drink of it.

And the Lord said unto Moses, Hew thee two tables of stone like unto the first; and I will write upon these tables the words that were in the first tables, which thou breakest. And be ready in the morning, and come up in the morning unto mount Sinai, and present thyself there to me in the top of the mount. And no man shall come up with thee, neither let any men be seen throughout all the mount; neither let the flocks nor herds feed before that mount.

And Moses hewed two tables of stone like unto the first; and he rose up early in the morning, and went up unto mount Sinai, as the Lord had commanded him, and took in his hand the two tables of stone. And the Lord descended in the cloud, and stood with him there, and proclaimed the name of the Lord. And the Lord passed by before him, and proclaimed: The Lord, The Lord God, merciful and gracious, long-suffering, and abundant in goodness and truth, keeping mercy for thousands, forgiving iniquity and transgression and sin; and that will by no means clear the guilty; visiting the iniquity of the fathers upon the children, and upon the children's children, unto the third and to the fourth generation. And Moses made haste, and bowed his head toward the earth and worshipped.

And Moses went up from the plains of Moab unto the mountains of Nebo, to the top of Pisgah, that is over against Jericho. And the Lord shewed him all the land of Gilead unto Dan, and all Naphtali, and the land of Ephraim, and Manasseh, and all the land of Judah, unto the utmost sea, and the south, and the plain of the valley of Jericho, the city of palm trees, unto Zoar. And the Lord said unto him, This is the land which I sware unto Abraham, unto Isaac, and unto Jacob, saying, I will give it unto thy seed. I have caused thee to see it with thine eyes, but thou shalt not go over thither.

So Moses the servant of the Lord died there in the land of Moab, according to the word of the Lord. And God buried him in a valley in the land of Moab, over against Bethpeor; but no man knoweth of his sepulchre unto this day. And Moses was an hundred and twenty years old when he died. His eye was not dim, nor his natural force abated.

And the children of Israel wept for Moses in the plains of Moab thirty days.[2]

[2] Other interesting accounts of Moses and the life of the Israelites in the wilderness may be found in Numbers 11, 12, 14, 20, 21, and in 22–24 (the story of Balaam and his talking ass).

2

JOSHUA

FROM JOSHUA 1–6

Now after the death of Moses the servant of the Lord, it came to pass that the Lord spake unto Joshua the son of Nun, saying, Moses my servant is dead. Now therefore arise, go over this Jordan, thou, and all this people, unto the land which I do give to them, even to the children of Israel. There shall not any man be able to stand before thee all the days of thy life. As I was with Moses, so I will be with thee. I will not fail thee, nor forsake thee. Have not I commanded thee? Be strong and of a good courage; be not afraid, neither be thou dismayed; for the Lord thy God is with thee whithersoever thou goest.

Then Joshua commanded the officers of the people, saying, Pass through the host, and command the people, saying, Prepare you victuals; for within three days ye shall pass over this Jordan, to go in to possess the land, which the Lord your God giveth you to possess it.

And Joshua the son of Nun sent out two men to spy secretly, saying, Go view the land, even Jericho. And they went, and came into an harlot's house, named Rahab, and lodged there. And it was told the king of Jericho, saying, Behold, there came men in hither tonight of the children of Israel to search out the country. And the king of Jericho sent unto Rahab, saying, Bring forth the men that are come to thee, which are entered into thine house; for they be come to search out all the country. And the woman took the two men, and hid them, and said thus, There came men unto me, but I wist not whence they were; and it came to pass, about the time of shutting of the gate, when it was dark, that the men went out. Whither the men went I wot not. Pursue after them quickly; for ye shall overtake them. But she had brought them up to the roof of the house, and hid them with the stalks of flax, which she had laid in order upon the roof. And the men pursued after them the way of Jordan unto the fords.

And, before they were laid down, she came up unto them upon the roof; and she said unto the men, I know that the Lord hath given you the land, and that your terror is fallen upon us, and that all the inhabitants of the land faint because of you. For we have heard how the Lord dried up the water of the Red Sea for you, when ye came out of Egypt. And as soon as we had heard these things, our hearts did melt, neither did there remain any more courage in any man, because of you; for the Lord your God, he is God in heaven above, and in earth beneath. Now therefore, I pray you, swear unto me by the Lord since I have showed you kindness, that ye will also show kindness unto my father's house, and give me a true token; and that ye will save alive my father, and my mother, and my brethren, and my sisters, and all that they have, and deliver our lives from death. And the men answered her, Our life for yours, if ye utter not this our business. And it shall be, when the Lord hath given us the land, that we will deal kindly and truly with thee.

Then she let them down by a cord through the window; for her house was upon the town wall, and she dwelt upon the wall. And she said unto them, Get you to the mountain, lest the pursuers meet you; and hide yourselves there three days, until the pursuers be returned; and afterward may ye go your way. And the men said unto her, Behold, when we come into the land, thou shalt bind this line of scarlet thread in the window which thou didst let us down by; and thou shalt bring thy father, and thy mother, and thy brethren, and all thy father's household home unto thee. And if thou utter this our business, then we will be quit of thine oath which thou hast made us to swear. And she said, According unto your words, so be it. And she sent them away, and they departed; and she bound the scarlet line in the window.

And they went and came unto the mountain and abode there three days until the pursuers were returned; and the pursuers sought them throughout all the way, but found them not. So the two men returned and came to Joshua and told him all things that befell them. And they said unto Joshua, Truly the Lord hath delivered into our hands all the land, for even all the inhabitants of the country do faint because of us.

And Joshua rose early in the morning and came to Jordan, he and all the children of Israel, and lodged there before they passed over. And it came to pass after three days, that the officers went through the host; and they commanded the people, saying, When ye see the ark of the covenant[1] of the Lord your God, and the priests bearing it, then ye shall remove from your place, and go after it.

And Joshua said unto the people, Sanctify yourselves, for tomorrow the Lord will do wonders among you. And Joshua spake unto the priests, saying, Take up the ark of the covenant, and pass over before the people. And they took up the ark of the covenant, and went before the people. And as they that bare the ark were come unto Jordan, and the feet of the priests that bare the ark were dipped in the brim of the water, it came to pass that the waters which came down from above stood and rose up, and the people passed over right against Jericho. And the priests that bare the ark of the covenant of the Lord stood firm on dry ground in the midst of Jordan, and all the Israelites passed over on dry ground, until all the people were passed clean over Jordan.

Now Jericho was straitly shut up because of the children of Israel; none went out and none came in. And the Lord said unto Joshua, See, I have given unto thine hand Jericho and the king thereof, and the mighty men of valor. And ye shall compass the city, and go round about the city once. Thus shalt thou do six days. And seven priests shall bear before the ark seven trumpets of rams' horns; and the seventh day ye shall compass the city seven times, and the

[1] In Exodus, 25–27, there is a long and detailed description of this Ark of the Covenant. It was evidently a box-like structure, made of the wood of the acacia tree, in size some 4 feet long by 2 feet wide and deep. It was always to the Israelites a sacred symbol of the presence of God, and contained, in the words of Exodus, a "testimony" which God gave to his people. What this testimony was is not actually known; but the most likely assumption is that it was a portion of manna. Throughout the Pentateuch it is clearly suggested that the Ark was kept in a Tabernacle, or tent, and that both constituted a Holy Place of worship.

priests shall blow with the trumpets. And it shall come to pass that when they make a long blast with the ram's horn, all the people shall shout with a great shout; and the wall of the city shall fall down flat, and the people shall ascend up, every man straight before him.

And it came to pass when Joshua had called the priests and spoken unto the people that the seven priests bearing the seven trumpets of rams' horns passed on before the Lord and blew with the trumpets; and the ark of the covenant of the Lord followed them. So the ark of the Lord compassed the city, going about it once. And the second day they compassed the city once. So they did six days.

And it came to pass on the seventh day that they rose early about the dawning of the day and compassed the city after the same manner seven times. And it came to pass at the seventh time, when the priests blew with the trumpets, Joshua said unto the people, Shout, for the Lord hath given you the city. And the city shall be accursed, and all that are therein. Only Rahab the harlot shall live, she and all that are with her in the house, because she hid the messengers that we sent.

And it came to pass, when the people shouted with a great shout, that the wall fell down flat so that the people went up into the city, every man straight before him, and they took the city. And they burnt the city with fire, and all that was therein. Only the silver and the gold, and the vessels of brass and iron they put into the treasury of the house of the Lord.

And Joshua saved Rahab the harlot alive and her father's household, and all that she had, because she hid the messengers which Joshua sent to spy out Jericho.

3

DEBORAH AND HER SONG

The story of Deborah and her famous Song have their source in a decisive victory won by the Israelites over the Canaanitish tribes, who, now thoroughly aroused to their danger, leagued together under their captain

Sisera in a last attempt to throw back the invaders. The date of this battle, upon which the fate of the Hebrew nation depended, was around 1150–1100 B.C. The Song of Deborah, written by an unknown poet, was doubtless composed soon after the victory and is, therefore, one of the earliest masterpieces of Hebrew literature.

We know little of Deborah herself. She was probably not a "judge" of Israel even though that position is assigned to her; but the story of her patriotism and faith, by which she incited Barak to victory, and the exciting tale of Jael and her hammer together form one of the most thrilling of narratives.

JUDGES 4–5

And the children of Israel again did evil[1] in the sight of the Lord. And the Lord sold them into the hand of Jabin, king of Canaan, that reigned in Hazor, the captain of whose hosts was Sisera. And the children of Israel cried unto the Lord, for he had nine hundred chariots of iron; and twenty years he mightily oppressed the children of Israel.

And Deborah, a prophetess, the wife of Lapidoth, she judged Israel at that time. And she dwelt under the palm tree of Deborah between Ramah and Bethel in mount Ephraim. And she sent and called Barak the son of Abinoam and said unto him, Hath not the Lord God of Israel commanded, saying, Go and draw toward mount Tabor, and take with thee ten thousand men of the children of Naphtali and of the children of Zebulun? And I will draw unto thee, to the river Kishon, Sisera, the captain of Jabin's army, with his chariots, and his multitude; and I will deliver him into thine hand. And Barak said unto her, If thou wilt go with me, then I will go; but if thou wilt not go with me, then I will not go. And she said, I will surely go with thee, notwithstanding the journey that thou takest shall not be for thine honor; for the Lord shall sell Sisera into the hand of a woman. And Deborah arose, and went with Barak to Kedesh. And Barak called Zebulun and Naphtali to Kedesh; and he went up with ten thousand men at his feet; and Deborah went up with him.

[1] This evil was the worship of Canaanitish gods, as related in Judges 2–3.

Now Heber the Kenite had severed himself from the Kenites, and pitched his tent unto the plain of Zaanaim, which is by Kedesh. And they showed Sisera that Barak the son of Abinoam was gone up to mount Tabor. And Sisera gathered together all his chariots, even nine hundred chariots of iron, and all the people that were with him unto the river of Kishon. And Deborah said unto Barak, Up; for this is the day in which the Lord hath delivered Sisera into thine hand. Is not the Lord gone out before thee? So Barak went down from mount Tabor, and ten thousand men after him. And the Lord discomfited Sisera, and all his chariots, and all his host, with the edge of the sword before Barak, so that Sisera lighted down off his chariot, and fled away on his feet. But Barak pursued after the chariots, and after the host; and all the host of Sisera fell upon the edge of the sword; and there was not a man left.

Howbeit Sisera fled away on his feet to the tent of Jael the wife of Heber the Kenite; for there was peace between Jabin the king of Hazor and the house of Heber the Kenite. And Jael went out to meet Sisera, and said unto him, Turn in, my lord, turn in to me; fear not. And when he had turned in unto her into the tent, she covered him with a mantle. And he said unto her, Give me, I pray thee, a little water to drink; for I am thirsty. And she opened a bottle of milk, and gave him drink, and covered him. And he said unto her, Stand in the door of the tent; and it shall be, when any man doth come and enquire of thee, and say, Is there any man here? that thou shalt say, No.

Then Jael Heber's wife took a nail of the tent, and took an hammer in her hand, and went softly unto him, and smote the nail into his temples, and fastened it into the ground; for he was fast asleep and weary. So he died. And, behold, as Barak pursued Sisera, Jael came out to meet him, and said unto him, Come, and I will show thee the man whom thou seekest. And when he came into her tent, behold, Sisera lay dead, and the nail was in his temple. So God subdued on that day Jabin the king of Canaan before the children of Israel. And the hand of the children of Israel prospered, and prevailed against Jabin the king of Canaan, until they had destroyed Jabin king of Canaan.

The song will be more clearly understood and appreciated if its four divisions are noted: The first is merely an introduction to the ode, or hymn, itself; the second describes the marching forth of God from Sinai to fight for His people and also the conditions prevailing in a fear-ridden country; the third recounts the rallying of the Hebrew tribes, with praise given to those who came and reproof to those who refused; the fourth, the finest part, relates the great battle, the death of Sisera, and the pathetic picture of his mother, waiting in vain for his return.

Then sang Deborah and Barak the son of Abinoam on that day, saying:

Praise ye the Lord for the avenging of Israel,
When the people willingly offered themselves.
Hear, O ye kings; give ear, O ye princes;
I, even I, will sing unto the Lord;
I will sing praise to the Lord God of Israel.

Lord, when thou wentest out of Seir,
When thou marchedst out of the field of Edom,
The earth trembled, and the heavens dropped,
The clouds also dropped water.
The mountains melted from before the Lord,
Even that Sinai from before the Lord God of Israel.
In the days of Shamgar the son of Anath,
In the days of Jael, the highways were unoccupied,
And the travellers walked through byways.
The inhabitants of the villages ceased, they ceased in Israel,
Until that I Deborah arose,
That I arose a mother in Israel.
They chose new gods;
Then was war in the gates:
Was there a shield or spear seen
Among forty thousand in Israel?
My heart is toward the governors of Israel,

That offered themselves willingly among the people.
Bless ye the Lord!
Speak, ye that ride on white asses,
Ye that sit in judgment,
And walk by the way.
They that are delivered from the noise of archers in the places of drawing water,
There shall they rehearse the righteous acts of the Lord,
Even the righteous acts toward the inhabitants of his villages in Israel:
Then shall the people of the Lord go down to the gates.

Awake, awake, Deborah!
Awake, awake! Utter a song!
Arise, Barak, and lead thy captivity captive, thou son of Abinoam!
Then he made him that remaineth have dominion over the nobles among the people:
The Lord made me have dominion over the mighty.
Out of Ephraim was there a root of them against Amalek:
After thee, Benjamin, among thy people:
Out of Machir came down governors,
And out of Zebulun they that handle the pen of the writer.
And the princes of Issachar were with Deborah;
Even Issachar, and also Barak,
He was sent on foot into the valley.
For the divisions of Reuben there were great thoughts of heart.
Why abodest thou among the sheepfolds,
To hear the bleatings of the flocks?
For the divisions of Reuben there were great searchings of heart.
Gilead abode beyond Jordan;
And why did Dan remain in ships?
Asher continued on the seashore,
And abode in his breaches.
Zebulun and Naphtali were a people that jeoparded their lives unto the death in the high places of the field.

The kings came and fought,
Then fought the kings of Canaan
In Taanach by the waters of Megiddo;
They took no gain of money.
They fought from heaven;
The stars in their courses fought against Sisera.
The river of Kishon swept them away,
That ancient river, the river Kishon.
O my soul, thou hast trodden down strength!
Then were the horse-hoofs broken by the means of the prancings,
The prancings of their mighty ones.
Curse ye Meroz, said the angel of the Lord,
Curse ye bitterly the inhabitants thereof!
Because they came not to the help of the Lord,
To the help of the Lord against the mighty.
Blessed above women shall Jael the wife of Heber the Kenite be!
Blessed shall she be above women in the tent!
He asked water, and she gave him milk;
She brought forth butter in a lordly dish.
She put her hand to the nail,
And her right hand to the workmen's hammer;
And with the hammer she smote Sisera,
She smote off his head,
When she had pierced and stricken through his temples.
At her feet he bowed, he fell, he lay down;
At her feet he bowed, he fell;
Where he bowed, there he fell down dead.
The mother of Sisera looked out at a window, and cried through the lattice,
Why is his chariot so long in coming?
Why tarry the wheels of his chariots?
Her wise ladies answered her,
Yea, she returned answer to herself,
Have they not sped? Have they not divided the prey?
To every man a damsel or two; to Sisera a prey of divers colors,

A prey of divers colors of needlework on both sides,
Meet for the necks of them that take the spoil?

So let all thine enemies perish, O Lord!
But let them that love him be as the sun when he goeth forth in
his might.

4

GIDEON

FROM JUDGES 6–7

And the children of Israel did evil in the sight of the Lord; and the Lord delivered them unto the hand of Midian seven years. And the hand of Midian prevailed against Israel. And because of the Midianites[1] the children of Israel made them the dens which are in the mountains, and caves, and strongholds. And so it was, when Israel had sown, that the Midianites came up, and the Amalekites, and the children of the east, even they came up against them. And they encamped against them, and destroyed the increase of the earth till thou come to Gaza, and left no sustenance for Israel, neither sheep, nor ox, nor ass. For they came up with their cattle and their tents, and they came as grasshoppers for multitude; for both they and their camels were without number. And they entered into the land to destroy it. And Israel was greatly impoverished because of the Midianites; and the children of Israel cried unto the Lord.

And there came an angel of the Lord, and sat under an oak which was in Ophrah, that pertained unto Joash the Abiezrite; and his son Gideon threshed wheat by the winepress to hide it from the Midianites. And the angel of the Lord appeared unto him and said unto him, The Lord is with thee, thou mighty man of valor. And Gideon said unto him, O my Lord, if the Lord be with us, why then is all this befallen us? And where be all his miracles which our fathers

[1] The Midianites were Bedouin tribes from the deserts east of the Jordan who, around 1100 B.C., made ravages against the Israelites in Canaan.

told us of, saying, Did not the Lord bring us up from Egypt? But now the Lord hath forsaken us, and delivered us into the hands of the Midianites. And the Lord said unto him, Surely I will be with thee, and thou shalt smite the Midianites as one man. And Gideon said unto God, If thou wilt save Israel by mine hand, as thou hast said, behold I will put a fleece of wool in the floor; and if the dew be on the fleece only, and it be dry upon all the earth besides, then shall I know that thou wilt save Israel by mine hand, as thou hast said. And it was so; for he rose up early on the morrow, and thrust the fleece together, and wringed the dew out of the fleece, a bowlful of water. And Gideon said unto God, Let not thine anger be hot against me; and I will speak but this once. Let me prove, I pray thee, but this once with the fleece; let it now be dry only upon the fleece, and upon all the ground let there be dew. And God did so that night; for it was dry upon the fleece only, and there was dew on all the ground.

Then Gideon and all the people that were with him rose up early, and pitched beside the well of Harod, so that the host of the Midianites were on the north side of them, by the hill of Moreh, in the valley. And the Lord said unto Gideon, The people that are with thee are too many for me to give the Midianites into their hands, lest Israel vaunt themselves against me, saying, Mine own hand hath saved me. Now therefore go to, proclaim in the ears of the people, saying, Whosoever is fearful and afraid, let him return and depart early from mount Gilead. And there returned of the people twenty and two thousand; and there remained ten thousand. And the Lord said unto Gideon, The people are yet too many. Bring them down unto the water, and I will try them for thee there; and it shall be, that of whom I say unto thee, This shall go with thee, the same shall go with thee; and of whomsoever I say unto thee, This shall not go with thee, the same shall not go.

So he brought down the people unto the water; and the Lord said unto Gideon, Every one that lappeth of the water with his tongue, as a dog lappeth, him shalt thou set by himself; likewise every one that boweth down upon his knees to drink. And the number of them that lapped, putting their hand to their mouth, were three hundred men; but all the rest of the people bowed down upon their knees to drink water. And the Lord said unto Gideon, By the three hundred men that lapped will I save you, and deliver the Midianites into thine hand; and let all the other people go every man unto his place. And Gideon sent all the rest of Israel every man unto his tent, and retained those three hundred men; and the host of Midian was beneath him in the valley.

And it came to pass the same night, that the Lord said unto him, Arise, get thee down unto the host; for I have delivered it into thine hand. But if thou fear to go down, go thou with Phurah thy servant down to the host; and thou shalt hear what they say; and afterward shall thine hands be strengthened to go down unto the host. Then went he down with Phurah his servant unto the outside of the armed men that were in the host. And the Midianites and the Amalekites and all the children of the east lay along in the valley like grasshoppers for multitude; and their camels were without number, as the sand by the seaside for multitude. And when Gideon was come, behold, there was a man that told a dream unto his fellow, and said, Behold, I dreamed a dream, and, lo, a cake of barley bread tumbled into the host of Midian, and came unto a tent, and smote it that it fell, and overturned it, that the tent lay along. And his fellow answered and said, This is nothing else save the sword of Gideon the son of Joash a man of Israel; for into his hand hath God delivered Midian and all the host.

And it was so, when Gideon heard the telling of the dream, and the interpretation thereof, that he worshipped, and returned into the host of Israel, and said, Arise; for the Lord hath delivered into your hand the host of Midian. And he divided the three hundred men into three companies, and he put a trumpet in every man's hand, with empty pitchers, and lamps within the pitchers. And he said unto them, Look on me, and do likewise; and, behold, when I come to the outside of the camp, it shall be that, as I do, so shall ye do. When I blow with a trumpet, I and all that are with me, then blow ye the trumpets also on every side of all the camp, and say, The sword of the Lord and of Gideon!

So Gideon and the hundred men that were with him came unto

the outside of the camp in the beginning of the middle watch; and they had but newly set the watch; and they blew the trumpets and brake the pitchers that were in their hands. And the three companies blew the trumpets, and brake the pitchers, and held the lamps in their left hands, and the trumpets in their right hands to blow withal; and they cried, The sword of the Lord, and of Gideon! And they stood every man in his place round about the camp; and all the host ran, and cried, and fled. And the three hundred blew the trumpets, and the Lord set every man's sword against his fellow, even throughout all the host; and the host fled. And the men of Israel gathered themselves together and pursued after the Midianites.[2]

5

JEPHTHAH

This brief and tragic story of Jephthah and of his ill fated daughter is one of the most beautifully written among Old Testament narratives. It illustrates admirably that genius for understatement and omission which has already been noted as characteristic of the Bible storytellers at their best. With its irony and its suggestion of the caprice of Fate, it seems almost more Greek than Hebrew and has often been compared, in its tone and treatment, to Greek tragedies.

FROM JUDGES 11

Now Jephthah the Gileadite was a mighty man of valor, and he was the son of a harlot; and Gilead begat Jephthah. And Gilead's wife bare him sons; and his wife's sons grew up, and they thrust out Jephthah, and said unto him, Thou shalt not inherit in our father's house; for thou art the son of a strange woman. Then Jephthah fled from his brethren, and dwelt in the land of Tob.

And it came to pass in process of time, that the children of Ammon made war against Israel. And it was so, that when the

[2] The reader is urged to read also Judges 9, the story of the revolt of Abimelech, the son of Gideon.

children of Ammon made war against Israel, the elders of Gilead went to fetch Jephthah out of the land of Tob. And they said unto Jephthah, Come, and be our captain, that we may fight with the children of Ammon. And Jephthah said unto the elders of Gilead, Did not ye hate me, and expel me out of my father's house? And why are ye come unto me now when ye are in distress? And the elders of Gilead said unto Jephthah, Therefore we turn again to thee now, that thou mayest go with us, and fight against the children of Ammon, and be our head over all the inhabitants of Gilead. And Jephthah said unto the elders of Gilead, If ye bring me home again to fight against the children of Ammon, and the Lord deliver them before me, shall I be your head? And the elders of Gilead said unto Jephthah, The Lord be witness between us, if we do not according to thy words.

And Jephthah vowed a vow unto the Lord and said, If thou shalt without fail deliver the children of Ammon into mine hands, then it shall be, that whatsoever cometh forth of the doors of my house to meet me when I return in peace from the children of Ammon, shall surely be the Lord's, and I will offer it up for a burnt offering.

So Jephthah passed over unto the children of Ammon, to fight against them; and the Lord delivered them into his hands. And he smote them from Aroer, even till thou come to Minnith, even twenty cities, and unto the plain of the vineyards, with a very great slaughter. Thus the children of Ammon were subdued before the children of Israel.

And Jephthah came to Mizpeh unto his house, and, behold, his daughter came out to meet him with timbrels and with dances. And she was his only child; beside her he had neither son nor daughter. And it came to pass, when he saw her, that he rent his clothes, and said, Alas, my daughter! thou hast brought me very low, and thou art one of them that trouble me; for I have opened my mouth unto the Lord, and I cannot go back. And she said unto him, My father, if thou hast opened thy mouth unto the Lord, do to me according to that which hath proceeded out of thy mouth; forasmuch as the Lord hath taken vengeance for thee of thine enemies, even of the children of Ammon. And she said unto her father, Let this thing be done for me: Let me alone two months, that I may go up and down upon the mountains and bewail my virginity, I and my fellows. And he said, Go.

And he sent her away for two months. And she went with her companions and bewailed her virginity upon the mountains. And it came to pass at the end of two months that she returned unto her father, who did with her according to his vow which he had vowed; and she knew no man. And it was a custom in Israel that the daughters of Israel went yearly to lament the daughter of Jephthah the Gileadite four days in a year.

6

SAMSON

The story of Samson, one of the most fascinating in the Old Testament, does not properly belong among these accounts of the leaders of ancient Israel. For they have their basis, at least, in history, whereas the Samson material is legendary and traditional. Samson was surely no "judge" of Israel, nor did he wage war against the Philistines. He is, instead, the hero of folklore, the subject of a cycle of folk tales which probably were known and loved by country people, even centuries before the written history of Israel began.

His brilliant author, without doubt the same man who wrote most of the Jacob-Joseph Saga, wisely wished to preserve at least some of these popular tales; and because he was himself an intensely religious and patriotic Israelite, he chose to introduce into his presentation of Samson certain elements which did not belong to the much earlier and purely oral stories. Thus the original folk hero, the Hebrew Hercules of popular fancy, became a youth consecrated to God, a "judge," and a warrior as well as a crude, boisterous, and somewhat mad "strong man."

But we can be grateful to his re-creator who gathered together these ancient tales of wandering storytellers, even though he chose to endow Samson with characteristics which in the beginning he never possessed. For the result is a powerful and appealing narrative in which both the comic and tragic are wonderfully blended together.[1]

[1] The chapter entitled "The Folk Tale of Samson" in *The Bible and the Common Reader,* Pt. II, will make the material which follows more clear to the reader.

And there was a certain man of Zorah whose name was Manoah; and his wife was barren. And the angel of the Lord appeared unto the woman and said unto her, Behold now, thou art barren; but thou shalt conceive and bear a son. And no razor shall come upon his head; for the child shall be a Nazarite[2] unto God from the womb; and he shall begin to deliver Israel out of the hand of the Philistines.

Then the woman came and told her husband, saying, A man of God came unto me, and his countenance was like the countenance of an angel of God, very terrible; but I asked not whence he was, neither told he me his name. But he said unto me, Behold, thou shalt conceive and bear a son; and the child shall be a Nazarite to God from the womb to the day of his death.

Then Manoah entreated the Lord, and said, O my Lord, let the man of God which thou didst send come again unto us, and teach us what we shall do unto the child that shall be born. And God hearkened to the voice of Manoah; and the angel of God came again unto the woman as she sat in the field; but Manoah her husband was not with her. And the woman made haste, and ran, and showed her husband, and said unto him, Behold, the man hath appeared unto me, that came unto me the other day. And Manoah arose, and went after his wife, and came to the man, and said unto him, Art thou the man that spakest unto the woman? And he said, I am. And Manoah said, Now let the words come to pass. How shall we order the child, and how shall we do unto him? And the angel of the Lord said unto Manoah, Of all that I said unto the woman let her beware. She may not eat of any thing that cometh of the vine, neither let her drink wine or strong drink, nor eat any unclean thing. All that I commanded her let her observe.

And Manoah said unto the angel of the Lord, I pray thee, let us detain thee, until we shall have made ready a kid for thee. And the angel of the Lord said unto Manoah, Though thou detain me,

[2] Nazarite, from the Hebrew word *nazar,* to separate, means one set apart, or consecrated to God.

I will not eat of thy bread; and if thou wilt offer a burnt offering, thou must offer it unto the Lord. For Manoah knew not that he was an angel of the Lord. And Manoah said unto the angel of the Lord, What is thy name, that when thy sayings come to pass we may do thee honor? And the angel of the Lord said unto him. Why askest thou thus after my name, seeing it is secret? So Manoah took a kid with a meat offering, and offered it upon a rock unto the Lord; and the angel did wondrously; and Manoah and his wife looked on. For it came to pass, when the flame went up toward heaven from off the altar, that the angel of the Lord ascended in the flame of the altar. And Manoah and his wife looked on it, and fell on their faces to the ground. But the angel of the Lord did no more appear to Manoah and to his wife. Then Manoah knew that he was an angel of the Lord. And Manoah said unto his wife, We shall surely die, because we have seen God. But his wife said unto him, If the Lord were pleased to kill us, he would not have received a burnt offering and a meat offering at our hands, neither would he have showed us all these things, nor would as at this time have told us such things as these. And the woman bare a son, and called his name Samson; and the child grew, and the Lord blessed him.

And Samson went down to Timnath, and saw a woman in Timnath of the daughters of the Philistines. And he came up and told his father and his mother, and said, I have seen a woman in Timnath of the daughters of the Philistines; now therefore get her for me to wife. Then his father and his mother said unto him, Is there never a woman among the daughters of thy brethren, or among all my people, that thou goest to take a wife of the uncircumcised Philistines? And Samson said unto his father, Get her for me; for she pleaseth me well.

Then went Samson down and his father and his mother to Timnath, and came to the vineyards of Timnath; and, behold, a young lion roared against him. And the Spirit of the Lord came mightily upon him, and he rent him as he would have rent a kid, and he had nothing in his hand; but he told not his father or his mother what he had done. And he went down and talked with the woman;

and she pleased Samson well. And after a time he returned to take her, and he turned aside to see the carcase of the lion; and, behold, there was a swarm of bees and honey in the carcase of the lion. And he took thereof in his hands and went on eating, and came to his father and mother, and he gave them and they did eat; but he told not them that he had taken the honey out of the carcase of the lion.

So his father went down unto the woman; and Samson made there a feast; for so used the young men to do. And it came to pass, when they saw him, that they brought thirty companions to be with him. And Samson said unto them, I will now put forth a riddle unto you: If ye can certainly declare it me within the seven days of the feast, and find it out, then I will give you thirty sheets and thirty change of garments; but if ye cannot declare it me, then shall ye give me thirty sheets and thirty change of garments. And they said unto him, Put forth thy riddle, that we may hear it. And he said unto them, Out of the eater came forth meat, and out of the strong came forth sweetness. And they could not in three days expound the riddle. And it came to pass on the seventh day, that they said unto Samson's wife, Entice thy husband, that he may declare unto us the riddle, lest we burn thee and thy father's house with fire. Have ye called us to take that we have?

And Samson's wife wept before him, and said, Thou dost but hate me, and lovest me not. Thou hast put forth a riddle unto the children of my people, and hast not told it me. And he said unto her, Behold, I have not told it my father nor my mother, and shall I tell it thee? And she wept before him the seven days, while their feast lasted; and it came to pass on the seventh day, that he told her, because she lay sore upon him; and she told the riddle to the children of her people. And the men of the city said unto him on the seventh day before the sun went down, What is sweeter than honey? and what is stronger than a lion? And he said unto them, If ye had not ploughed with my heifer, ye had not found out my riddle.

And the Spirit of the Lord came upon him, and he went down to Ashkelon, and slew thirty men of them, and took their spoil, and gave change of garments unto them which expounded the riddle. And his anger was kindled, and he went up to his father's house.

But Samson's wife was given to his companion, whom he had used as his friend.

But it came to pass in the time of wheat harvest that Samson visited his wife with a kid; and he said, I will go in to my wife into the chamber. But her father would not suffer him to go in. And her father said, I verily thought that thou hadst utterly hated her; therefore I gave her to thy companion. Is not her younger sister fairer than she? Take her, I pray thee, instead of her. And Samson said concerning them, Now shall I be more blameless than the Philistines, though I do them a displeasure.

And Samson went and caught three hundred foxes, and took firebrands, and turned tail to tail, and put a firebrand in the midst between two tails. And when he had set the brands on fire, he let them go into the corn of the Philistines and burnt up shocks, with the vineyards and the olives. Then the Philistines said, Who hath done this? And they answered, Samson the son-in-law of the Timnite, because he had taken his wife and given her to his companion. And the Philistines came up and burnt her and her father with fire.

And Samson said unto them, Though ye have done this, yet will I be avenged of you. And he smote them hip and thigh with a great slaughter. . . . And he found a new jawbone of an ass, and put forth his hand and took it, and slew a thousand men therewith. And Samson said:

> With the jawbone of an ass, heaps upon heaps;
> With the jaw of an ass have I slain a thousand men.

Then went Samson to Gaza and saw there a harlot, and went in unto her. And it was told the Philistines, saying, Samson is come hither. And they laid wait for him all night in the gate of the city and were quiet all the night, saying, In the morning when it is day, we shall kill him. And Samson lay till midnight, and arose at midnight and took the doors of the gate of the city, and the two posts, and went away with them, and put them upon his shoulders and carried them to the top of a hill that is before Hebron.

And it came to pass afterward, that he loved a woman in the valley of Sorek whose name was Delilah. And the lords of the Philistines came up unto her, and said, Entice him and see wherein his great strength lieth and by what means we may prevail against him; and we will give thee, everyone of us, eleven hundred pieces of silver. And Delilah said to Samson, Tell me, I pray thee, wherein thy great strength lieth, and wherewith thou mightest be bound to afflict thee. And Samson said unto her, If they bind me with seven green withes that were never dried, then shall I be weak, and be as another man. Then the lords of the Philistines brought up to her seven green withes which had not been dried, and she bound him with them. Now there were men lying in wait, abiding with her in the chamber. And she said unto him, The Philistines be upon thee, Samson! And he brake the withes as a thread of tow is broken when it toucheth the fire; so his strength was not known. And Delilah said unto Samson, Behold, thou hast mocked me, and told me lies. Now tell me, I pray thee, wherewith thou mightest be bound. And he said unto her, If they bind me fast with new ropes that never were occupied, then shall I be weak, and be as another man. Delilah therefore took new ropes and bound him therewith, and said unto him, The Philistines be upon thee, Samson! And there were liers in wait abiding in the chamber. And he brake them from off his arms like a thread. And Delilah said unto Samson, Hitherto thou hast mocked me, and told me lies. Tell me wherewith thou mightest be bound. And he said unto her, If thou weavest the seven locks of my head with the web. And she fastened it with a pin, and said unto him, The Philistines be upon thee, Samson! And he awaked out of his sleep, and went away with the pin of the beam, and with the web.

And she said unto him, How canst thou say, I love thee, when thine heart is not with me? Thou hast mocked me these three times, and hast not told me wherein thy great strength lieth. And it came to pass, when she pressed him daily with her words, and urged him, so that his soul was vexed unto death, that he told her all his heart, and said unto her, There hath not come a razor upon mine head; for I have been a Nazarite unto God from my mother's womb. If I be shaven, then my strength will go from me, and I shall become weak, and be like any other man.

And when Delilah saw that he had told her all his heart, she sent and called for the lords of the Philistines, saying, Come up this once, for he hath showed me all his heart. Then the lords of the Philistines came up unto her, and brought money in their hand. And she made him sleep upon her knees; and she called for a man, and she caused him to shave off the seven locks of his head; and his strength went from him. And she said, The Philistines be upon thee, Samson! And he awoke out of his sleep, and said, I will go out, as at other times before, and shake myself. And he wist not that the Lord was departed from him. But the Philistines took him and put out his eyes, and brought him down to Gaza, and bound him with fetters of brass; and he did grind in the prison house. Howbeit the hair of his head began to grow again after he was shaven.

Then the lords of the Philistines gathered them together for to offer a great sacrifice unto Dagon their god, and to rejoice; for they said, Our god hath delivered Samson our enemy into our hand. And when the people saw him, they praised their god; for they said, Our god hath delivered into our hands our enemy, and the destroyer of our country, which slew many of us. And it came to pass, when their hearts were merry that they said, Call for Samson, that he may make us sport. And they called for Samson out of the prison house; and he made them sport; and they set him between the pillars. And Samson said unto the lad that held him by the hand, Suffer me that I may feel the pillars whereupon the house standeth that I may lean upon them.

Now the house was full of men and women; and all the lords of the Philistines were there; and there were upon the roof about three thousand men and women that beheld while Samson made sport. And Samson called unto the Lord and said, O Lord God, remember me, I pray thee, and strengthen me, I pray thee, only this once, O God, that I may be at once avenged of the Philistines for my two eyes. And Samson took hold of the two middle pillars upon which the house stood, of one with his right hand and of the other with his left. And Samson said, Let me die with the Philistines. And he bowed himself with all his might; and the house fell upon all the lords and upon all the people that were therein. So the dead which he slew at his death were more than they which he slew in his life.

Then his brethren and all the house of his father came down and took him, and brought him up, and buried him in the burying-place of Manoah his father.

7
SAMUEL

Samuel, the last of the great leaders of ancient Israel, lived around 1050 B.C., between the days of the judges and the founding of the kingdom. His times were critical ones for his people, and the problems which concerned them are reflected in the narratives concerning him. By 1050 B.C., two centuries after the Exodus from Egypt, most of the Land of Canaan had been gradually conquered and the Canaanites as gradually absorbed into the Hebrew population. But a new danger now began to threaten from the Philistines on the southwestern coastal plain. These energetic people had come from the Aegean Islands and were, it is usually assumed, Cretan in origin. They possessed a culture and a military prowess far superior to those of their Hebrew neighbors; and for many years they proved the chief menace to the new nation of Israel.

The two long books (originally one) which bear the name of Samuel contain not only the most interesting and profound character studies of the Old Testament, but also many examples of superb literary composition. Actually, they deal more with the first kings of Israel, Saul and David, than they do with Samuel; and many of their chapters will be included in the stories of those kings. The books present a variety of material, written between 1000 and 500 B.C. by several authors of differing literary ability and compiled at a much later date. The very fact that the books are by several authors is no doubt responsible for the inconsistency in the character of Samuel. So many divergent activities are assigned to him by one or another author that it is difficult to determine what manner of man he was. Was he a gifted child and, later, a prophet? Did he really practice clairvoyance? Why is practically nothing told of his middle years? Did he become an unreasonable and resentful old man? With all these unanswered questions, it is certain that he was a judge and a leader of Israel, second only to Moses in the Hebrew mind. Perhaps, indeed, his very importance in Hebrew tradition and history resulted, as in the case of Moses, in much legendary material concerning him.

It has seemed best in the readings directly concerning Samuel to select the most interesting, whether they are historical or legendary in origin. More concerning him is contained in the story of Saul, with whom he was intimately and ironically connected.

FROM I SAMUEL 1–8

Now there was a certain man of Ramah, of mount Ephraim, and his name was Elkanah. And he had two wives; the name of the one was Hannah, and the name of the other Peninnah; and Peninnah had children, but Hannah had no children. And this man went up out of his city yearly to worship and to sacrifice unto the Lord of hosts in Shiloh. And the two sons of Eli, Hophni and Phinehas, the priests of the Lord, were there. And when the time was that Elkanah offered, he gave to Peninnah his wife and to all her sons and her daughters, portions; but unto Hannah he gave a worthy portion; for he loved Hannah, but the Lord had shut up her womb. And her adversary also provoked her sore, for to make her fret, because the Lord had shut up her womb. And as he did so year by year, when she went up to the house of the Lord, so Peninnah provoked her; therefore she wept, and did not eat. Then said Elkanah her husband to her, Hannah, why weepest thou? and why eatest thou not? and why is thy heart grieved? Am I not better to thee than ten sons?

So Hannah rose up after they had eaten in Shiloh, and after they had drunk. Now Eli the priest sat upon a seat by a post of the temple of the Lord. And she was in bitterness of soul, and prayed unto the Lord, and wept sore. And she vowed a vow, and said, O Lord of hosts, if thou wilt indeed look on the affliction of thine handmaid, and remember me, and not forget thine handmaid, but wilt give unto thine handmaid a man child, then I will give him unto the Lord all the days of his life, and there shall no razor come upon his head. And it came to pass, as she continued praying before the Lord, that Eli marked her mouth. Now Hannah, she spake in her heart; only her lips moved, but her voice was not heard; therefore Eli thought she had been drunken. And Eli said unto her, How long wilt thou be drunken? Put away thy wine from thee. And Hannah answered and said, No, my lord; I am a woman of a sorrowful spirit. I have drunk neither wine nor strong drink, but have poured out my soul before the Lord. Count not thine handmaid for a daughter of Belial; for out of the abundance of my complaint and grief have I spoken hitherto. Then Eli answered and said, Go in peace; and the God of Israel grant thee thy petition that thou hast asked of him. So the woman went her way, and did eat, and her countenance was no more sad.

And they rose up in the morning early, and worshipped before the Lord, and returned, and came to their house to Ramah; and Elkanah knew Hannah his wife; and the Lord remembered her. Wherefore it came to pass that she bare a son, and called his name Samuel, saying, Because I have asked him of the Lord. And the man Elkanah and all his house went up to offer unto the Lord the yearly sacrifice, and his vow. But Hannah went not up; for she said unto her husband, I will not go up until the child be weaned, and then I will bring him, that he may appear before the Lord, and there abide forever. And Elkanah her husband said unto her, Do what seemeth thee good. Tarry until thou have weaned him; only the Lord establish his word. So the woman abode, and gave her son suck until she weaned him.

And when she had weaned him, she took him up with her, with three bullocks, and one ephah of flour, and a bottle of wine, and brought him unto the house of the Lord in Shiloh; and the child was young. And they slew a bullock, and brought the child to Eli. And she said, Oh my lord, as thy soul liveth, my lord, I am the woman that stood by thee here, praying unto the Lord. For this child I prayed; and the Lord hath given me my petition which I asked of him. Therefore also I have lent him to the Lord. As long as he liveth he shall be lent to the Lord. And he worshipped the Lord there.

And Hannah prayed and said:

My heart rejoiceth in the Lord;
Mine horn is exalted in the Lord;
My mouth is enlarged over mine enemies;
Because I rejoice in thy salvation.
There is none holy as the Lord:
For there is none besides thee;
Neither is there any rock like our God.
The Lord killeth, and maketh alive;
He bringeth down to the grave, and bringeth up.
The Lord maketh poor, and maketh rich;
He bringeth low, and lifteth up.
He raiseth up the poor out of the dust,
And lifteth up the beggar from the dunghill,
To set them among princes,
And to make them inherit the throne of glory.
For the pillars of the earth are the Lord's,
And he hath set the world upon them.
He will keep the feet of his saints,
And the wicked shall be silent in darkness;
For by strength shall no man prevail.
The adversaries of the Lord shall be broken to pieces;
Out of heaven shall he thunder upon them.
The Lord shall judge the ends of the earth;
And he shall give strength unto his king,
And exalt the horn of his anointed.

Now the sons of Eli were sons of Belial; they knew not the Lord. And the priest's custom with the people was that, when any man offered sacrifice, the priest's servant came, while the flesh was in seething, with a fleshhook of three teeth in his hand; and he struck it into the pan, or kettle, or caldron, or pot; all that the fleshhook brought up the priest took for himself. So they did in Shiloh unto all the Israelites that came thither. Also before they burnt the fat, the priest's servant came, and said to the man that sacrificed, Give flesh to roast for the priest; for he will not have sodden flesh of thee, but raw.

And if any man said unto him, Let them not fail to burn the fat presently, and then take as much as thy soul desireth; then he would answer him, Nay; but thou shalt give it to me now; and if not, I will take it by force. Wherefore the sin of the young men was very great before the Lord.

But Samuel ministered before the Lord, being a child girded with a linen ephod. Moreover his mother made him a little coat, and brought it to him from year to year, when she came up with her husband to offer the yearly sacrifice.

And the child Samuel ministered unto the Lord before Eli. And it came to pass, when Eli was laid down in his place and his eyes began to wax dim that he could not see, and ere the lamp of God went out in the temple of the Lord, where the ark of God was, and Samuel was laid down to sleep, that the Lord called Samuel. And he answered, Here am I. And he ran unto Eli, and said, Here am I; for thou calledst me. And he said, I called not; lie down again. And he went and lay down. And the Lord called yet again, Samuel. And Samuel arose and went to Eli, and said, Here am I; for thou didst call me. And he answered, I called not, my son; lie down again. Now Samuel did not yet know the Lord, neither was the word of the Lord yet revealed unto him. And the Lord called Samuel again the third time. And he arose and went to Eli, and said, Here am I; for thou didst call me. And Eli perceived that the Lord had called the child. Therefore Eli said unto Samuel, Go, lie down; and it shall be, if he call thee, that thou shalt say, Speak, Lord; for thy servant heareth. So Samuel went and lay down in his place.

And the Lord came, and stood, and called as at other times, Samuel, Samuel. Then Samuel answered, Speak; for thy servant heareth. And the Lord said to Samuel, Behold, I will do a thing in Israel, at which both the ears of every one that heareth it shall tingle. In that day I will perform against Eli all the things which I have spoken concerning his house. When I begin, I will also make an end. For I have told him that I will judge his house forever for the iniquity which he knoweth, because his sons made themselves vile and he restrained them not.

And Samuel lay until the morning, and opened the doors of the house of the Lord. And Samuel feared to show Eli the vision. Then Eli called Samuel, and said, Samuel, my son. And he answered, Here am I. And he said, What is the thing that the Lord hath said unto thee? I pray thee hide it not from me. God do so to thee, and more also, if thou hide any thing from me of all things that he said unto thee. And Samuel told him every whit, and hid nothing from him. And he said, It is the Lord. Let him do what seemeth him good.

Now Israel went out against the Philistines to battle. And the Philistines put themselves in array against Israel; and when they joined battle, Israel was smitten before the Philistines; and they slew of the army in the field about four thousand men.

And when people were come into the camp, the elders of Israel said, Wherefore hath the Lord smitten us today before the Philistines? Let us fetch the ark of the covenant of the Lord out of Shiloh unto us, that when it cometh among us, it may save us out of the hand of our enemies. So the people sent to Shiloh, that they might bring from thence the ark of the covenant of the Lord of hosts, which dwelleth between the cherubim; and the two sons of Eli, Hophni and Phinehas, were there with the ark of the covenant of God. And when the ark of the covenant of the Lord came into the camp, all Israel shouted with a great shout, so that the earth rang again. And when the Philistines heard the noise of the shout, they said, What meaneth the noise of this great shout in the camp of the Hebrews? And they understood that the ark of the Lord was come into the camp. And the Philistines were afraid, for they said, God is come into the camp. And they said, Woe unto us! for there hath not been such a thing heretofore. Woe unto us! Who shall deliver us out of the hand of these mighty Gods? These are the Gods that smote the Egyptians with all the plagues in the wilderness. Be ye strong, and quit yourselves like men, O yc Philistines! that ye be not servants unto the Hebrews, as they have been to you. Quit yourselves like men, and fight.

And the Philistines fought, and Israel was smitten, and they fled every man into his tent; and there was a very great slaughter; for there fell of Israel thirty thousand footmen. And the ark of God was taken; and the two sons of Eli, Hophni and Phinehas, were slain.

And there ran a man out of the army, and came to Shiloh the same day, with his clothes rent, and with earth upon his head. And when he came, lo, Eli sat upon a seat by the wayside watching; for his heart trembled for the ark of God. And when the man came into the city, and told it, all the city cried out. And when Eli heard the noise of the crying, he said, What meaneth the noise of this tumult? And the man came in hastily, and told Eli. Now Eli was ninety and eight years old; and his eyes were dim, that he could not see. And the man said unto Eli, I am he that came out of the army, and I fled today out of the army. And he said, What is there done, my son? And the messenger answered, and said, Israel has fled before the Philistines, and there hath been also a great slaughter among the people, and thy two sons also, Hophni and Phinehas, are dead, and the ark of God is taken. And it came to pass, when he made mention of the ark of God, that he fell from off his seat backward by the side of the gate, and his neck brake, and he died; for he was an old man, and heavy.

And his daughter-in-law, Phinehas' wife, was with child, near to be delivered. And when she heard the tidings that the ark of God was taken, and that her father-in-law and her husband were dead, she bowed herself and travailed; for her pains came upon her. And about the time of her death the women that stood by her said unto her, Fear not; for thou hast borne a son. But she answered not, neither did she regard it. And she named the child Ichabod, saying, The glory is departed from Israel; because the ark of God was taken and because of her father-in-law and her husband. And she said, The glory is departed from Israel; for the ark of God is taken.[1]

And it came to pass when Samuel was old that he made his sons judges over Israel. And his sons walked not in his ways but turned

[1] Chapters 5, 6, and 7 of I Samuel may well be read here. They describe the misfortunes wrought upon the Philistines by the presence of the ark of God among them.

aside after lucre and took bribes and perverted judgment. Then all the elders of Israel came to Samuel and said unto him, Behold, thou art old, and thy sons walk not in thy ways. Now make us a king to judge us like all the nations.

But the thing displeased Samuel when they said, Give us a king to judge us. And Samuel prayed unto the Lord, and the Lord said unto him, Hearken unto the voice of the people in all that they say unto thee; for they have not rejected thee, but they have rejected me that I should not reign over them. Now therefore hearken unto their voice; yet protest solemnly unto them and show them the manner of the king that shall reign over them.

And Samuel told all the words of the Lord unto the people that asked of him a king. And he said: This will be the manner of the king that shall reign over you: He will take your sons and appoint them for himself, for his chariots, and to be his horsemen; and some shall run before his chariots. And he will appoint him captains over thousands, and captains over fifties; and will set them to ear his ground, and to reap his harvest, and to make his instruments of war, and instruments of his chariots. And he will take your daughters to be confectioners, and to be cooks, and to be bakers. And he will take your fields and your vineyards and your oliveyards, and give them to his servants. And he will take your menservants and your maidservants, and your goodliest young men, and your asses, and put them to his work. He will take the tenth of your sheep, and ye shall be his servants. And ye shall cry out in that day because of your king which ye shall have chosen.

Nevertheless the people refused to obey the voice of Samuel, and they said, Nay, but we will have a king over us that we also may be like all the nations and that our king may go out before us and fight our battles. And Samuel heard all the words of the people, and he rehearsed them in the ears of the Lord. And the Lord said to Samuel, Hearken unto their voice and make them a king.

-III-

THE FIRST TWO KINGS OF ISRAEL

SAUL

DAVID

THE two books of Samuel together with the first two chapters of I Kings form a body of material basically historical, though interspersed with legend. This is one of the most important portions of the Old Testament, not only because it affords valuable information on Hebrew history, but also because it contains literature of the highest order. Except for the first few chapters on Samuel, it is entirely devoted to the stories of Saul and David.

The material represents a compilation, gathered from the records and traditions of at least three hundred years. The earliest and best portion (II Samuel 9–20, I Kings 1–2) was composed around 1000 B.C. during the reign of David; the other parts were written later. The authors are unknown, by name.

SAUL

The following incidents which relate the disastrous life of Saul, the first king of Israel, have been assembled from I Samuel 9–31. Certain abridgments have been made, actually, I believe, to the improvement of the story, since the omission of unimportant and repetitious material enhances the unity and the power of one of the finest narratives of the Old Testament.

Although, according to the ancient Hebrew belief in retributive justice, Saul deserved punishment for his disobedience to God's commands, his punishment seems far greater than his sin deserved; and the modern reader will see in his story the great and moving tragedy which it unquestionably is. For Saul is the unwilling victim both of chance, which thrust upon him an undesired kingship, and of the fatal, yet common, human frailties of passionate affection and jealous pride, which eventually brought his natural melancholy to madness. From the capricious beginning of his story every incident of his ill starred life moves relentlessly toward its inevitable and bitter close.

Yet, whatever the original purpose of his skillful narrator, it is impossible to feel that Saul was not more sinned against than sinning. Quick to acknowledge his guilt and to ask forgiveness, devoted to God who departs from him, careful for his honor and that of his children after him, capable of admiring his hated rival, his nature throughout his story possesses both strength and nobility. And when in despair he goes to Endor to ask advice of the "wise woman" there (in itself an ironic return to the occult power which had set in progress his ruinous course), he is seen in these last hours of his life as one of the most appealing and convincing characters in the literature or in the history of any age.

1

Now there was a man of Benjamin, whose name was Kish, a mighty man of power. And he had a son, whose name was Saul, a choice young man and a goodly; and there was not among the children of Israel a goodlier person than he. From his shoulders and upward he was higher than any of the people.

And the asses of Kish Saul's father were lost. And Kish said to Saul his son, Take now one of the servants with thee, and arise, go seek the asses. And he passed through mount Ephraim, and passed through the land of Shalisha, but they found them not. Then they passed through the land of Shalim, and there they were not; and he passed through the land of the Benjamites, but they found them not. And when they were come to the land of Zuph, Saul said to his servant that was with him, Come, and let us return, lest my father leave caring for the asses and take thought for us. And he said unto him, Behold now, there is in this city a man of God. All that he saith cometh surely to pass. Now let us go thither; peradventure he can show us our way that we should go. Then said Saul to his servant, But, behold, if we go, what shall we bring the man? For the bread is spent in our vessels, and there is not a present to bring to the man of God. And the servant answered Saul again, and said, Behold I have here at hand the fourth part of a shekel of silver.

That will I give to the man of God to tell us our way. Then said Saul, Well said. Come, let us go.

And they went up into the city; and when they were come into the city, behold, Samuel came out against them. Now the Lord had told Samuel in his ear a day before Saul came, saying, Tomorrow about this time I will send thee a man out of the land of Benjamin, and thou shalt anoint him to be captain over my people Israel, that he may save my people out of the hand of the Philistines. And when Samuel saw Saul, the Lord said unto him, Behold the man whom I spoke to thee of. This same shall reign over my people.

Then Saul drew near to Samuel in the gate and said, Tell me, I pray thee, where the seer's house is. And Samuel answered Saul, and said, I am the seer. Ye shall eat with me today, and tomorrow I will let thee go, and will tell thee all that is in thine heart. And as for thine asses that were lost three days ago, set not thy mind on them; for they are found. And on whom is all the desire of Israel? Is it not on thee, and on all thy father's house? And Saul answered and said, Am not I a Benjamite of the smallest of the tribes of Israel? And my family the least of all the families of the tribe of Benjamin? Wherefore then speakest thou so to me?

And Samuel took Saul and his servant and brought them into the parlor and made them sit in the chiefest place among them that were bidden. And Samuel said unto the cook, Bring the portion which I gave thee, of which I said unto thee, Set it by thee. And the cook took up the shoulder and that which was upon it, and set it before Saul. And Samuel said, Behold that which is left. Set it before thee, and eat; for unto this time hath it been kept for thee.

And they arose early; and it came to pass, about the spring of the day, that Samuel called Saul to the top of the house, saying, Up, that I may send thee away. And Saul arose, and they went out both of them, he and Samuel, abroad. And as they were going down to the end of the city, Samuel said to Saul, Bid the servant pass on before us—and he passed on—but stand thou still a while that I may show thee the word of God.

Then Samuel took a vial of oil, and poured it upon his head, and kissed him, and said, Is it not because the Lord hath anointed thee to be captain over his inheritance? When thou art departed from me today, then thou shalt find two men by Rachel's sepulchre in the border of Benjamin; and they will say unto thee, The asses which thou wentest to seek are found; and, lo, thy father sorroweth for you, saying, What shall I do for my son?

2

And Samuel called the people together and said unto the children of Israel, Thus saith the Lord God of Israel, I brought up Israel out of Egypt, and delivered you out of the hand of the Egyptians, and out of the hand of all kingdoms, and of them that oppressed you; and ye have this day rejected your God, who himself saved you out of all your adversities and your tribulations; and ye have said unto him, Nay, but set a king over us. Now therefore present yourselves before the Lord by your tribes and by your thousands.

And when Samuel had caused all the tribes of Israel to come near, the tribe of Benjamin was taken. When he had caused the tribe of Benjamin to come near by their families, Saul the son of Kish was taken; and when they sought him, he could not be found. Therefore they enquired of the Lord further, if the man should come thither. And the Lord answered, Behold he hath hid himself among the stuff.[1]

And they ran and fetched him thence. And when he stood among the people, he was higher than any of the people from his shoulders and upward. And Samuel said to all the people, See ye him whom the Lord hath chosen, that there is none like him among all the people? And all the people shouted, and said, God save the king!

3

Now the sons of Saul were Jonathan, and Ishui, and Melchishua; and the names of his two daughters were Merab and Michal; and the name of Saul's wife was Ahinoam; and the name of the captain of his host was Abner, the son of Ner, Saul's uncle. And Kish was

[1] The baggage, or supply carts.

the father of Saul. And there was sore war against the Philistines all the days of Saul; and when Saul saw any strong man or any valiant man, he took him unto him.

And the Philistines gathered themselves together to fight with Israel, thirty thousand chariots and six thousand horsemen, and people as the sand which is on the seashore in multitude. When the men of Israel saw that they were in a strait (for the people were distressed), then the people did hide themselves in caves, and in thickets, and in rocks, and in high places, and in pits.

Now it came to pass upon a day that Jonathan the son of Saul said unto the young man that bore his armor, Come, and let us go over into the garrison of these uncircumcised. It may be that the Lord will work for us. But he told not his father. And his armor-bearer said unto him, Behold, I am with thee according to thy heart.

Then said Jonathan, Behold, we will pass over unto these men. If they say thus unto us, Tarry until we come to you, then we will not go up unto them. But if they say, Come up unto us, then we will go up; for the Lord hath delivered them into our hand; and this shall be a sign unto us.

And both of them discovered themselves unto the garrison of the Philistines; and the Philistines said, Behold, the Hebrews come forth out of the holes where they had hid themselves. Come up to us, and we will show you a thing. And Jonathan said to his armor-bearer, Come up after me, for the Lord hath delivered them into the hand of Israel.

And Jonathan climbed up upon his hands and upon his feet, and his armor-bearer after him; and the Philistines fell before Jonathan; and his armor-bearer slew after him. And that first slaughter which Jonathan and his armor-bearer made was about twenty men. And there was trembling in the host, in the field, and among all the people. And the watchmen of Saul looked, and behold, the multitude melted away, and they went beating down one another. Then said Saul, Number now, and see who is gone from us. And when they had numbered, behold, Jonathan and his armor-bearer were not there.

And Saul and all the people that were with him assembled themselves, and they came to the battle; and behold, every man's sword was against his fellow, and there was a very great discomfiture. Likewise all the men of Israel which had hid themselves, when they heard that the Philistines fled, even they also followed hard after them in the battle. So the Lord saved Israel that day.

And the men of Israel were distressed that day, for Saul had adjured the people, saying, Cursed be the man that eateth any food until evening, that I may be avenged on mine enemies. So none of the people tasted any food. And all they of the land came to a wood; and there was honey upon the ground. And when the people were come into the wood, behold, the honey dropped. But no man put his hand to his mouth, for the people feared the oath.

But Jonathan heard not when his father charged the people with the oath. Wherefore he put forth the end of the rod that was in his hand, and dipped it in an honeycomb, and put his hand to his mouth; and his eyes were enlightened.

Then answered one of the people, and said, Thy father straitly charged the people with an oath, saying, Cursed be the man that eateth any food this day. Then said Jonathan, My father hath troubled the land. See, I pray you, how mine eyes have been enlightened, because I tasted a little of this honey. How much more, if haply the people had eaten freely today of the spoil of their enemies which they found? for had there not been now a much greater slaughter among the Philistines? And they smote the Philistines that day from Michmash to Aijalon; and the people were very faint. And the people flew upon the spoil, and took sheep, and oxen, and calves, and slew them on the ground; and the people did eat them with the blood.

Then they told Saul, saying, Behold, the people sin against the Lord in that they eat with the blood. And Saul said, Draw ye near hither, all the chief of the people, and know and see wherein this sin hath been this day. For as the Lord liveth, which saveth Israel, though it be in Jonathan my son he shall surely die. Therefore Saul said unto the Lord God of Israel, Give a perfect lot. And Saul and Jonathan were taken. And Saul said, Cast lots between me and Jonathan my son. And Jonathan was taken.

Then Saul said to Jonathan, Tell me what thou hast done. And Jonathan told him and said, I did but taste a little honey with the end of the rod that was in mine hand, and, lo, I must die. And Saul answered, God do so and more also; for thou shalt surely die, Jonathan.

And the people said unto Saul, Shall Jonathan die, who hath wrought this great salvation in Israel? God forbid! As the Lord liveth, there shall not one hair of his head fall to the ground; for he hath wrought with God this day.

So the people rescued Jonathan, that he died not.

4

Samuel also said unto Saul, The Lord sent me to anoint thee to be king over his people, over Israel. Now therefore hearken thou unto the voice of the Lord. Thus saith the Lord of hosts: I remember that which Amalek did to Israel, how he laid wait for him in the way when he came up from Egypt. Now go and smite Amalek and utterly destroy all that they have and spare them not, but slay both man and woman, infant and suckling, ox and sheep, camel and ass.

And Saul gathered the people together and came to a city of Amalek and laid wait in the valley. And Saul smote the Amalekites; and he took Agag the king of the Amalekites alive, and utterly destroyed all the people with the edge of the sword. But Saul and the people spared Agag, and the best of the sheep, and of the oxen, and of the lambs, and would not utterly destroy them; but everything that was vile and refuse, that they destroyed utterly.

Then came the word of the Lord unto Samuel, saying: It repenteth me that I have set up Saul to be king, for he is turned back from following me and hath not performed my commandments. And it grieved Samuel, and he cried unto the Lord all night. And Samuel came to Saul, and Saul said unto him, Blessed be thou of the Lord. I have performed the commandment of the Lord. And Samuel said, What meaneth then this bleating of the sheep in mine ears and the lowing of the oxen which I hear? And Saul said, The people spared the best of the sheep and of the oxen to sacrifice unto the Lord thy God; but the rest we have utterly destroyed.

Then Samuel said unto Saul, Stay, and I will tell thee what the Lord hath said to me this night. And he said unto him, Say on. And Samuel said, When thou wast little in thine own sight, wast thou not made the head of the tribes of Israel, and the Lord anointed thee king over Israel? And the Lord said, Go and utterly destroy the Amalekites and fight against them until they be consumed. Wherefore then didst thou not obey the voice of the Lord?

And Saul said unto Samuel, Yea, I have obeyed the voice of the Lord and have brought Agag the king of Amalek and have utterly destroyed the Amalekites. But the people took of the sheep and oxen to sacrifice unto the Lord thy God. And Samuel said, Hath the Lord as great delight in burnt offerings and sacrifices as in obeying the voice of the Lord? Behold, to obey is better than sacrifice and to hearken than the fat of rams. Because thou hast rejected the word of the Lord, he hath also rejected thee from being king.

And Saul said, I have sinned, for I have transgressed the commandment of the Lord and thy words because I feared the people. Now therefore, I pray thee, pardon my sin and turn again with me that I may worship the Lord. And Samuel said, I will not return with thee, for thou hast rejected the word of the Lord, and the Lord hath rejected thee from being king over Israel.

And as Samuel turned about to go away, Saul laid hold upon the skirt of his mantle and it rent. And Samuel said, The Lord hath rent the kingdom of Israel from thee this day and hath given it to a neighbor of thine that is better than thou. Then Saul said, I have sinned. Yet honor me now, I pray thee, before the elders of my people and before Israel and turn again with me that I may worship the Lord thy God. So Samuel turned again; and Saul worshipped the Lord.

Then said Samuel, Bring ye hither to me Agag the king of the Amalekites. And Agag came unto him delicately. And Agag said, Surely the bitterness of death is past. And Samuel said, As thy sword hath made women childless, so shall thy mother be childless among women. And Samuel hewed Agag in pieces before the Lord.

Then Samuel went to Ramah; and Saul went up to his house, to Gibeah. And Samuel came no more to see Saul until the day of his death.

5

And the Lord said to Samuel: How long will ye mourn for Saul seeing I have rejected him? Fill thine horn with oil and go. I will send thee to Jesse the Bethlehemite, for I have provided me a king among his sons. Take a heifer with thee and say, I am come to sacrifice to the Lord. And call Jesse to the sacrifice, and I will show thee what thou shalt do, and thou shall anoint unto me him whom I name unto thee.

And Samuel came to Bethlehem and called Jesse and his sons to the sacrifice. And it came to pass when they were come, that he looked on Eliab and said, Surely the Lord's anointed is before him. But the Lord said unto Samuel, Look not on his countenance or on the height of his stature because I have refused him; for man looketh on the outward appearance, but the Lord looketh on the heart. Then Jesse called Abinadab and made him pass before Samuel. And he said, Neither hath the Lord chosen this. Then Jesse made Shammah to pass by. And he said, Neither hath the Lord chosen this. Again, Jesse made seven of his sons to pass before Samuel. And Samuel said unto Jesse, The Lord hath not chosen these. Are here all thy children? And he said, There remaineth yet the youngest, and, behold, he keepeth the sheep.

And Samuel said unto Jesse, Send and fetch him, for we will not sit down till he come hither. And he sent and brought him in. Now he was ruddy and withal of a beautiful countenance and goodly to look at. And the Lord said, Arise, anoint him, for this is he. Then Samuel took the horn of oil and anointed him in the midst of his brethren.

And the Spirit of the Lord came upon David from that day forward. But the Spirit of the Lord departed from Saul, and an evil spirit from the Lord troubled him.

And Saul's servants said unto him, Behold now, an evil spirit from God troubleth thee. Let our lord now command thy servants to seek out a man, who is a cunning player on a harp; and it shall come to pass, when the evil spirit from God is upon thee, that he shall play with his hand, and thou shalt be well. And Saul said unto his servants, Provide me now a man that can play well, and bring him to me. Then answered one of the servants, and said, Behold, I have seen a son of Jesse the Bethlehemite that is cunning in playing, and a mighty valiant man, and a man of war, and prudent in matters, and a comely person, and the Lord is with him. Wherefore Saul sent messengers unto Jesse, and said, Send me David thy son, which is with the sheep.

And Jesse took an ass laden with bread, and a bottle of wine, and a kid, and sent them by David his son unto Saul. And David came to Saul, and stood before him; and Saul loved him greatly; and he became his armor-bearer. And Saul sent to Jesse, saying, Let David, I pray thee, stand before me; for he hath found favor in my sight.

And it came to pass, when the evil spirit from God was upon Saul, that David took a harp, and played with his hand; so Saul was refreshed, and was well, and the evil spirit departed from him.[2]

6

And it came to pass that the soul of Jonathan was knit with the soul of David, and Jonathan loved him as his own soul. And Saul took him that day, and would let him go no more home to his father's house. Then Jonathan and David made a covenant. And Jonathan stripped himself of the robe that was upon him, and gave it to David, and his garments, even to his sword, and to his bow, and to his girdle.

And David went out whithersoever Saul sent him, and behaved himself wisely; and Saul set him over the men of war, and he was accepted in the sight of all the people, and also in the sight of Saul's

[2] In I Samuel 17 there is another version of David's entrance into the life of Saul: his slaying of the Philistine giant Goliath. Most readers are, of course, familiar with the famous story. It is, however, conceded by most scholars to be purely legendary, an example of those exploits which always arise around the figure of a popular hero.

servants. And it came to pass as they came, when David was returned from the slaughter of the Philistines, that the women came out of all cities of Israel, singing and dancing, to meet king Saul, with tabrets, with joy, and with instruments of music. And the women answered one another as they played and said,

Saul hath slain his thousands,
And David his ten thousands.

And Saul was very wroth, and the saying displeased him; and he said, They have ascribed unto David ten thousands, and to me they have ascribed but thousands. And what can he have more but the kingdom?

And Saul was afraid of David, because the Lord was with him and was departed from Saul. Therefore Saul removed him from him, and made him his captain over a thousand; and he went out and came in before the people. And David behaved himself wisely in all his ways; and the Lord was with him. Wherefore when Saul saw that he behaved himself very wisely, he was afraid of him. But all Israel and Judah loved David, because he went out and came in before them.

And Saul said to David, Behold my elder daughter Merab, her will I give thee to wife. Only be thou valiant for me and fight the Lord's battles. (For Saul said, Let not mine hand be upon him, but let the hand of the Philistines be upon him.) And David said unto Saul, Who am I, or my father's family in Israel, that I should be son-in-law to the king?

But it came to pass at the time when Merab should have been given to David, that she was given unto Adriel the Meholathite to wife. And Michal Saul's daughter loved David; and they told Saul, and the thing pleased him. And Saul said, I will give him her that she may be a snare to him and that the hand of the Philistines may be against him. And Saul commanded his servants, saying, Commune with David secretly and say, Behold, the king hath delight in thee, and all his servants love thee. Now therefore be the king's son-in-law. The king desireth not any dowry, but a hundred foreskins of the Philistines. And when his servants told David these words, it pleased David well to be the king's son-in-law. Wherefore David arose and went, he and his men, and slew of the Philistines two hundred men; and David brought their foreskins, and they gave them in full tale to the king. And Saul gave him Michal his daughter to wife. And Saul saw and knew that the Lord was with David and that Michal loved him. And Saul was yet the more afraid of David; and he became David's enemy continually.

And Saul spoke to Jonathan and to all his servants, that they should kill David. But Jonathan delighted much in David, and Jonathan told David, saying, Saul my father seeketh to kill thee. Now therefore, I pray thee, take heed to thyself until the morning, and abide in a secret place, and hide thyself; and I will go out and stand beside my father in the field where thou art, and I will commune with my father of thee; and what I see, that I will tell thee.

And Jonathan spoke good of David unto Saul his father, and said unto him, Let not the king sin against his servant, against David, because he hath not sinned against thee, and because his works have been to theeward very good. Wherefore then wilt thou sin against innocent blood, to slay David without a cause?

And Saul hearkened unto the voice of Jonathan; and Saul swore, As the Lord liveth, he shall not be slain. And Jonathan called David, and Jonathan showed him all those things. And Jonathan brought David to Saul, and he was in his presence, as in times past.

7

And there was war again; and David went out and fought with the Philistines and slew them with a great slaughter. And the evil spirit from the Lord was upon Saul as he sat in his house with his javelin in his hand. And David played his harp with his hand. And Saul sought to smite David even to the wall with the javelin, but he slipped away out of Saul's presence, and Saul smote the javelin into the wall.

Saul also sent messengers unto David's house to watch him and to slay him in the morning; and Michal David's wife told him, saying, If thou save not thy life tonight, tomorrow thou shalt be slain. So Michal let David down through a window; and he went and fled, and escaped. And Michal took an image and laid it in the bed, and put a pillow of goats' hair for his bolster, and covered it with a cloth. And when Saul sent messengers to take David, she said, He is sick. And Saul sent the messengers again to see David, saying, Bring him up to me in the bed that I may slay him. And when the messengers were come in, behold, there was an image in the bed with a pillow of goats' hair for his bolster.

So David fled and escaped and came to Samuel to Ramah and told him all that Saul had done to him. And he and Samuel went and dwelt in Naioth. . . . And Saul sent messengers to take David, and David fled from Naioth, and came and said before Jonathan, What have I done? And what is my sin before thy father that he seeketh my life? And Jonathan said, Thou shalt not die. Behold my father will do nothing either great or small but that he will show it me. Come, and let us go out into the field.

And they went out both of them into the field. And Jonathan said to David, Tomorrow is the new moon, and thou shalt be missed because thy seat will be empty. And when thou hast stayed three days, then thou shalt go down quickly and come to the place where thou didst hide thyself when the business was in hand and shalt remain by the stone Ezel. And I will shoot three arrows on the side thereof, as though I shot at a mark. And, behold, I will send a lad, saying, Go, find out the arrows. If I expressly say unto the lad, Behold, the arrows are on this side of thee, take them, then come thou, for there is peace to thee, and no hurt. But if I say thus unto the young man, Behold, the arrows are beyond thee, go thy way; for the Lord hath sent thee away. And as touching the matter which thou and I have spoken of, behold, the Lord be between thee and me forever.

So David hid himself in the field; and when the new moon was come, the king sat him down to eat meat. And the king sat upon his seat, as at other times, even upon a seat by the wall; and Jonathan arose, and Abner sat by Saul's side, and David's place was empty. Then Saul's anger was kindled against Jonathan, and he said unto him, As long as the son of Jesse liveth, thou shalt not be established, nor thy kingdom. Wherefore now send and fetch him unto me, for he shall surely die. And Jonathan answered and said, Wherefore shall he be slain? What hath he done? And Saul cast a javelin at him to smite him. So Jonathan arose from the table in fierce anger, for he was grieved for David because his father had done him shame.

And it came to pass in the morning that Jonathan went out into the field at the time appointed with David, and a little lad with him. And he said unto his lad, Run, find out now the arrows which I shoot. And as the lad ran, he shot an arrow beyond him. And when the lad was come to the place of the arrow which Jonathan had shot, Jonathan cried after the lad, and said, Is not the arrow beyond thee? And Jonathan cried after the lad, Make speed, haste, stay not. And Jonathan's lad gathered up the arrows, and came to his master. But the lad knew not anything; only Jonathan and David knew the matter. And Jonathan gave his artillery unto his lad, and said unto him, Go, carry them to the city.

And as soon as the lad was gone, David arose out of a place toward the south, and fell on his face to the ground, and bowed himself three times; and they kissed one another, and wept one with another. And Jonathan said to David, Go in peace, forasmuch as we have sworn both of us in the name of the Lord, saying, The Lord be between me and thee, and between my seed and thy seed forever. And David arose and departed; and Jonathan went into the city.

8

David therefore departed thence and escaped to the cave Adullam; and when his brethren and all his father's house heard it, they went down thither to him. And everyone that was in distress, and everyone that was in debt, and everyone that was discontented gathered themselves unto him; and he became a captain over them; and there were with him about four hundred men. And David abode in the wilderness in strongholds and remained in a mountain in the wilderness of Ziph. And Saul sought him every day, but God delivered him not into his hand. And David saw that Saul was come out to seek his life, and David was in the wilderness of Ziph in a wood. And Jonathan arose and went to David and strengthened his hand in God. And Jonathan said unto him, Fear not, for the hand of my father shall not find thee; and thou shalt be king over Israel and I shall be next unto thee; and that also my father knoweth. And they two made a covenant before the Lord; and David abode in the wood and Jonathan went to his house.

And it came to pass when Saul was returned from following the Philistines that it was told him, Behold, David is in the wilderness of Engedi. Then Saul took three thousand chosen men out of all Israel, and went to seek David and his men upon the rocks of the wild goats. And he came to the sheepcotes by the way, where was a cave; and Saul went in to cover his feet. And David and his men remained in the sides of the cave. And the men of David said unto him, Behold the day of which the Lord said unto thee, Behold, I will deliver thine enemy into thine hand, that thou mayest do to him as it shall seem good unto thee.

Then David arose, and cut off the skirt of Saul's robe privily. And it came to pass afterward, that David's heart smote him, because he had cut off Saul's skirt. And he said unto his men, The Lord forbid that I should do this thing unto my master, the Lord's anointed, to stretch forth mine hand against him, seeing he is the anointed of the Lord. So David stayed his servants with these words, and suffered them not to rise against Saul. But Saul rose up out of the cave, and went on his way. David also arose afterward, and went out of the cave, and cried after Saul, saying, My lord the king.

And when Saul looked behind him, David stooped with his face to the earth, and bowed himself. And David said to Saul, Wherefore hearest thou men's words saying, Behold, David seeketh thy hurt? Behold, this day thine eyes have seen how that the Lord had delivered thee today into mine hand in the cave; and some bade me kill thee; but mine eye spared thee; and I said, I will not put forth mine hand against my lord, for he is the Lord's anointed. Moreover, my father, see, yea, see the skirt of thy robe in my hand; for in that I cut off the skirt of thy robe, and killed thee not, know thou and see that there is neither evil nor transgression in mine hand, and I have not sinned against thee; yet thou huntest my soul to take it. After whom is the king of Israel come out? After whom dost thou pursue? After a dead dog, after a flea. The Lord therefore be judge, and judge between me and thee.

And it came to pass, when David had made an end of speaking, that Saul said, Is this thy voice, my son David? And Saul lifted up his voice and wept. And he said to David, Thou art more righteous than I; for thou hast rewarded me good whereas I have rewarded thee evil. And thou hast showed me this day how thou hast dealt well with me, forasmuch as when the Lord had delivered me into thine hand, thou killedst me not. And now, behold, I know well that thou shalt surely be king and that the kingdom of Israel shall be established in thine hand. Swear now therefore unto me by the Lord that thou wilt not cut off my seed after me and that thou wilt not destroy my name out of my father's house.

And David sware unto Saul. And Saul went home; but David and his men gat them up unto the stronghold.

9

Now Samuel was dead, and all Israel lamented him, and buried him in Ramah, even in his own city. And Saul had put away those that had familiar spirits and the wizards out of the land.

And the Philistines gathered themselves together, and came and pitched in Shunem; and Saul gathered all Israel together, and they pitched in Gilboa. And when Saul saw the host of the Philistines, he was afraid, and his heart greatly trembled. And when Saul inquired of the Lord, the Lord answered him not, neither by dreams, nor by lots, nor by prophets.

Then said Saul unto his servants, Seek me a woman that hath a familiar spirit that I may go to her and inquire of her. And his servants said to him, Behold, there is a woman that hath a familiar spirit at Endor. And Saul disguised himself, and put on other raiment, and he went and two men with him, and they came to the woman by night. And he said, I pray thee, divine unto me by the familiar spirit, and bring me him up, whom I shall name unto thee. And the woman said unto him, Behold, thou knowest what Saul hath done, how he hath cut off those that have familiar spirits and the wizards out of the land. Wherefore then layest thou a snare for my life, to cause me to die? And Saul sware to her by the Lord, saying, As the Lord liveth, there shall no punishment happen to thee for this thing.

Then said the woman, Whom shall I bring up unto thee? And he said, Bring me up Samuel. And when the woman saw Samuel, she cried with a loud voice; and the woman spake to Saul, saying, Why hast thou deceived me? For thou art Saul. And the king said unto her, Be not afraid; for what sawest thou? And the woman said unto Saul, I saw gods ascending out of the earth. And he said unto her, What form is he of? And she said, An old man cometh up, and he is covered with a mantle. And Saul perceived that it was Samuel; and he stooped with his face to the ground, and bowed himself.

And Samuel said to Saul, Why hast thou disquieted me, to bring me up? And Saul answered, I am sore distressed; for the Philistines make war against me, and God is departed from me, and answereth me no more, neither by prophets, nor by dreams; therefore I have called thee, that thou mayest make known unto me what I shall do. Then said Samuel, Wherefore then dost thou ask of me, seeing the Lord is departed from thee and is become thine enemy? And the Lord hath done as he spake by me; for the Lord hath rent the kingdom out of thine hand, and given it to thy neighbor, even to David. Because thou obeyedst not the voice of the Lord nor executedst his fierce wrath upon Amalek, therefore hath the Lord done this thing unto thee this day. Moreover the Lord will also deliver Israel with thee into the hand of the Philistines; and tomorrow shalt thou and thy sons be with me.

Then Saul fell straightway all along on the earth, and was sore afraid because of the words of Samuel; and there was no strength in him; for he had eaten no bread all the day, nor all the night. And the woman came unto Saul, and saw that he was sore troubled, and said unto him, Behold, thine handmaid hath obeyed thy voice, and I have put my life in my hand, and have hearkened unto thy words which thou spakest unto me. Now therefore, I pray thee, hearken thou also unto the voice of thine handmaid, and let me set a morsel of bread before thee; and eat, that thou mayest have strength, when thou goest on thy way. But he refused, and said, I will not eat. But his servants, together with the woman, compelled him; and he hearkened unto their voice. So he arose from the earth, and sat upon the bed. And the woman had a fat calf in the house; and she hasted and killed it, and took flour, and kneaded it, and did bake unleavened bread thereof. And she brought it before Saul, and before his servants; and they did eat. Then they rose up, and went away that night.

10

Now the Philistines fought against Israel; and the men of Israel fled from before the Philistines, and fell down slain in mount Gilboa. And the Philistines followed hard upon Saul and upon his sons; and the Philistines slew Jonathan, and Abinadab, and Melchishua, Saul's sons.

And the battle went sore against Saul, and the archers hit him; and he was sore wounded of the archers. Then said Saul unto his armor-bearer, Draw thy sword, and thrust me through therewith, lest these uncircumcised come and thrust me through and abuse me. But his armor-bearer would not, for he was sore afraid. Therefore Saul took a sword, and fell upon it. And when his armor-bearer saw that Saul was dead, he fell likewise upon his sword, and died with him. So Saul died, and his three sons, and his armor-bearer, and all his men, that same day together.

And when the men of Israel that were on the other side of the valley, and they that were on the other side of the Jordan, saw that the men of Israel fled and that Saul and his sons were dead, they forsook the cities and fled; and the Philistines came and dwelt in them. And it came to pass on the morrow, when the Philistines came to strip the slain, that they found Saul and his three sons fallen in mount Gilboa. And they cut off his head, and stripped off his armor, and sent into the land of the Philistines round about, to publish it in the house of their idols, and among the people. And they put his armor in the house of Ashtaroth; and they fastened his body to the wall of Bethshan.

And when the inhabitants of Jabesh-gilead heard of that which the Philistines had done to Saul, all the valiant men arose, and went all night, and took the body of Saul and the bodies of his sons from the wall of Bethshan, and came to Jabesh, and burnt them there. And they took their bones and buried them under a tree at Jabesh, and fasted seven days.

THE LAMENT OF DAVID OVER SAUL AND JONATHAN

II SAMUEL: I

This lament, one of the glories of ancient Hebrew literature and among the greatest elegies of any age, may well serve as an interlude between the stories of the two kings. It was written shortly before the year 1000 B.C., when David ascended the throne of Israel and doubtless immediately following the deaths of Saul and Jonathan. The poem is an expression of profound and genuine sorrow; and in its lack of sentimentalism and even of bitterness, in its simplicity, restraint, and extraordinary beauty, it will always remain, like the Song of Deborah, one of the earliest treasures of Hebrew poetry.

It is preceded here by the vivid picture of David's reception of the tragic news from Mount Gilboa and of the fate of the false messenger.

Now it came to pass after the death of Saul that on the third day, behold, a man came out of the camp from Saul with his clothes rent and earth upon his head; and when he came to David, he fell to the earth and did obeisance. And David said unto him, From whence comest thou? And he said unto him, Out of the camp of Israel am I escaped. And David said unto him, How went the matter? I pray thee, tell me. And he answered, The people are fled from the battle and many also are fallen and dead. And Saul and Jonathan his son are dead also.

And David said unto the young man that told him, How knowest thou that Saul and Jonathan be dead? And the young man said, As I happened by chance upon mount Gilboa, behold, Saul leaned upon his spear; and, lo, the chariots and horsemen followed hard after him. And when he looked behind him, he saw me and called unto me. And I answered, Here am I. And he said unto me, Who art thou? And I answered him, I am an Amalekite. He said unto me again, Stand, I pray thee, upon me and slay me; for anguish is come upon me because my life is yet whole in me. So I stood upon him, and slew him, because I was sure that he could not live after that he was fallen; and I took the crown that was upon his head and the bracelet that was on his arm, and have brought them hither unto my lord.

Then David took hold of his clothes and rent them, and likewise all the men that were with him. And they mourned, and wept, and fasted until even, for Saul and for Jonathan his son and for the people of the Lord, and for the house of Israel because they were fallen by the sword.

And David said unto the young man that told him, How wast thou not afraid to stretch forth thine hand to destroy the Lord's anointed? And David called one of the young men and said, Go near, and fall upon him. And he smote him that he died. And David said unto him, Thy blood be upon thy head; for thy mouth hath testified against thee, saying, I have slain the Lord's anointed.

And David lamented with this lamentation over Saul and over Jonathan his son:

The beauty of Israel is slain upon thy high places:
How are the mighty fallen!
Tell it not in Gath,
Publish it not in the streets of Askelon,
Lest the daughters of the Philistines rejoice,
Lest the daughters of the uncircumcised triumph.

Ye mountains of Gilboa,
Let there be no dew, neither let there be rain, upon you, nor fields of offerings:

For there the shield of the mighty is vilely cast away,
The shield of Saul, as though he had not been anointed with oil.
From the blood of the slain, from the fat of the mighty,
The bow of Jonathan turned not back,
And the sword of Saul returned not empty.

Saul and Jonathan were lovely and pleasant in their lives,
And in their death they were not divided:
They were swifter than eagles,
They were stronger than lions.
Ye daughters of Israel, weep over Saul,
Who clothed you in scarlet, with other delights,
Who put ornaments of gold upon your apparel.
How are the mighty fallen in the midst of the battle!
O Jonathan, thou wast slain in thine high places.
I am distressed for thee, my brother Jonathan:
Very pleasant hast thou been unto me;
Thy love to me was wonderful,
Passing the love of women.
How are the mighty fallen,
And the weapons of war perished!

DAVID

The entire book of II Samuel and the first two chapters of I Kings contain the account of the reign of David. The story of his fateful connection with Saul has already, in large part, been given in the preceding section: his young manhood, his marriage with Saul's daughter, his rise to popularity and power, his life as an outlaw. The following readings, devoted only to his kingship, continue to reveal him as one of the most many-sided and paradoxical of human beings.

That he was a great king in his generosity toward his enemies, in his devotion to the national religion, and in his successful efforts to increase the size and power of his country is surely true; that he was self-indulgent and crafty, unjust and even cruel, is equally true. Apparently the most unwise and weak of fathers, he brought upon himself the treachery and conspiracy of his sons; and the last years of his reign present a sad and tragic picture and anything but a noble portrait.

Few biographies have been written with greater objectiveness than this account of his life. The writer to whom we owe the most brilliant chapters, and who was almost certainly a member of David's court, has drawn him as he unquestionably was, a man of conflicting attributes, a romanticist from his boyhood and yet, upon occasion, the most sordid of realists. The confusion of his court and household with their crimes and intrigues; the ironic consequences visited upon behavior as ironic; the play of conflicting passions—these are all drawn with pitiless detail and matchless skill, the biographer standing quite outside his subject and exhibiting no personal bias or prejudice whatever.

The book of II Samuel, particularly chapters 9–20, clearly the work of one writer, has long been recognized as a work of superb literary composition. And as we admire the charm and the strength of that composition, we should remember that this unknown chronicler of the second king of Israel and of the finely drawn characters surrounding him was writing at a time when biography as an art did not exist. He had, therefore, no models before him; but it is quite clear that he needed none!

1

And it came to pass after this that David inquired of the Lord, saying, Shall I go up into any of the cities of Judah? And the Lord said unto him, Go up. And David said, Whither shall I go up? And he said, Unto Hebron. And David went up thither, and his two wives also, Ahinoam the Jezreelitess, and Abigail[1] Nabal's wife the Carmelite. And his men that were with him did David bring up; and they dwelt in the cities of Hebron. And the men of Judah came, and there they anointed David king over the house of Judah. But Abner, captain of Saul's host, took Ishbosheth the son of Saul and made him king over all Israel.

Now there was long war between the house of Saul and the house of David; but David waxed stronger and stronger, and the house of Saul waxed weaker and weaker. And unto David were born six sons in Hebron. And Abner sent messengers to David, saying, Make thy league with me, and my hand shall be with thee to bring all Israel unto thee. And David said, I will make a league

[1] An interesting account of Abigail is given in I Samuel 25.

with thee; but one thing I require of thee, Thou shalt not see my face except thou first bring Michal Saul's daughter when thou comest. And they sent and took her from her husband Phaltiel; and her husband went with her weeping behind her. Then said Abner unto him, Go, return. And he returned.

2

And when Abner was returned to Hebron, Joab[2] took him aside in the gate, to speak with him quietly, and smote him there under the fifth rib so that he died. So Joab slew Abner because he had slain Joab's brother Asahel at Gibeon in the battle. And when David heard it, he said, I and my kingdom are guiltless before the Lord forever from the death of Abner. Let it rest on the head of Joab and on all his father's house. And David said to Joab and to all the people that were with him, Rend your clothes and gird you with sackcloth, and mourn before Abner. And king David himself followed the bier. And they buried Abner in Hebron; and the king lifted up his voice and wept at the grave of Abner. And the king said: Know ye not that there is a prince and a great man fallen this day in Israel?

3

Then came all the tribes of Israel to David unto Hebron; and they anointed David king over Israel. (David was thirty years old when he began to reign, and he reigned forty years.) And the king and his men went to Jerusalem of the Jebusites, and David took the stronghold of Zion; the same is the city of David. And David went on and grew great, and the Lord God of hosts was with him. And David inquired of the Lord, saying, Shall I go up to the Philistines? And the Lord said unto David, Go up; for I will doubtless deliver the Philistines into thine hand. And David did so, as the Lord had commanded him, and smote the Philistines.

And David gathered together all the chosen men of Israel, and he arose and went with all the people that were with him to bring

[2] Joab was the captain of David's army.

up out of the house of Abinadab in Gibeah the ark of God, whose name is called by the name of the Lord of hosts that dwelleth between the cherubim. And they set the ark of God upon a new cart; and Uzzah and Ahio the sons of Abinadab drave the new cart. And David and all the house of Israel played before the Lord on all manner of instruments made of fir wood, even on harps, and on psalteries, and on timbrels, and on cornets, and on cymbals. And when they came to Nachon's threshing-floor, Uzzah put forth his hand to the ark of God and took hold of it, for the oxen shook it. And the anger of the Lord was kindled against Uzzah; and God smote him there for his error. And there he died by the ark of God.

And David was afraid of the Lord that day and said, How shall the ark of the Lord come to me? So David would not remove the ark of the Lord unto him into the city of David; and it continued in the house of Obededom the Gittite three months; and the Lord blessed Obededom and all his household.

And it was told king David, saying, The Lord hath blessed the house of Obededom. So David went and brought up the ark of God into the city of David with gladness. And when they that bare the ark of the Lord had gone six paces, he sacrificed oxen and fatlings. And David danced before the Lord with all his might; and he was girded with a linen ephod. So David and all the house of Israel brought up the ark of the Lord with shouting and with the sound of the trumpet.

And as the ark of the Lord came into the city of David, Michal Saul's daughter looked through a window and saw king David leaping and dancing before the Lord; and she despised him in her heart. And they brought in the ark of the Lord and set it in the midst of the tabernacle that David had pitched for it; and as soon as David had made an end of offering burnt offerings and peace offerings, he blessed the people and then returned to bless his household.

And Michal came out to meet David and said, How glorious was the king of Israel today, who uncovered himself in the eyes of the handmaids of his servants, as one of the vain fellows shamelessly uncovereth himself! And David said unto Michal, It was before the Lord which chose me before thy father and before all his house;

therefore *will* I play before the Lord. And I will yet be more vile and will be base in mine own sight; and of the maidservants which thou hast spoken of, of them shall I be had in honor.

Therefore Michal, the daughter of Saul, had no child unto the day of her death.

4

And after this it came to pass that David smote the Philistines and subdued them; and he smote Moab, and the king of Zobah. And when the Syrians of Damascus came to succor the king of Zobah, David slew of the Syrians two and twenty thousand men. And David did dedicate unto the Lord the silver and gold of all nations which he subdued. And David gat him a name when he returned from smiting the Syrians; and the Lord preserved David whithersoever he went. And David reigned over all Israel; and David executed judgment and justice unto all his people. And Joab was over the host; and David's sons were chief rulers.

And David said, Is there yet any that is left of the house of Saul that I may show him kindness for Jonathan's sake? And there was of the house of Saul a servant whose name was Ziba. And the king said unto him, Is there not yet any of the house of Saul that I may show the kindness of God unto him? And Ziba said unto the king, Jonathan hath yet a son which is lame on his feet. Then David sent and fetched Mephibosheth the son of Jonathan, and when he was come unto David, he fell on his face and did reverence. And David said unto him, Fear not; for I will surely show thee kindness for Jonathan thy father's sake, and I will restore thee all the land of Saul; and thou shalt eat bread at my table continually. So Mephibosheth dwelt in Jerusalem; for he did eat continually at the king's table; and he was lame on both his feet.

5

And it came to pass in an eveningtide that David arose from off his bed and walked upon the roof of the king's house. And from the roof he saw a woman washing herself; and the woman was very beautiful to look upon. And David sent and enquired after the woman. And one said, Is not this Bathsheba the wife of Uriah the Hittite?

And David sent messengers and took her; and she came in unto him and he lay with her; and she returned unto her house. And the woman conceived and sent and told David, and said, I am with child. And David sent to Joab, saying, Send me Uriah the Hittite. And Joab sent Uriah to David.

And when Uriah was come unto him, David demanded of him how Joab did, and how the people did, and how the war prospered. And David said to Uriah, Go down to thy house, and wash thy feet. And Uriah departed out of the king's house, and there followed him a mess of meat from the king. But Uriah slept at the door of the king's house with all the servants of his lord, and went not down to his house.

And when they had told David, saying, Uriah went not down unto his house, David said unto Uriah, Camest thou not from thy journey? Why then didst thou not go down unto thine house? And Uriah said unto David, The ark, and Israel, and Judah, abide in tents; and my lord Joab and the servants of my lord are encamped in the open fields. Shall I then go into mine house, to eat and to drink, and to lie with my wife? As thou livest, and as thy soul liveth, I will not do this thing. And David said to Uriah, Tarry here today also, and tomorrow I will let thee depart. So Uriah abode in Jerusalem that day and the morrow. And when David had called him, he did eat and drink before him; and he made him drunk; and at even he went out to lie on his bed with the servants of his lord, but went not down to his house.

And it came to pass in the morning that David wrote a letter to Joab, and sent it by the hand of Uriah. And he wrote in the letter, saying, Set ye Uriah in the forefront of the hottest battle, and retire ye from him, that he may be smitten, and die. And it came to pass, when Joab observed the city, that he assigned Uriah unto a place where he knew that valiant men were. And the men of the city went out, and fought with Joab; and there fell some of the people of the servants of David; and Uriah the Hittite died also.

Then Joab sent and told David all the things concerning the war, and charged the messenger, saying, When thou hast made an end of telling the matters of the war unto the king, and if so be that the king's wrath arise, and he say unto thee, Wherefore approached ye so nigh unto the city when ye did fight? Knew ye not that they would shoot from the wall? Why went ye nigh the wall? then say thou, Thy servant Uriah the Hittite is dead also.

So the messenger went, and came and showed David all that Joab had sent him for. And the messenger said unto David, Surely the men prevailed against us, and came out unto us into the field, and we were upon them even unto the entering of the gate. And the shooters shot from off the wall upon thy servants; and some of the king's servants be dead, and thy servant Uriah the Hittite is dead also.

Then David said unto the messenger, Thus shalt thou say unto Joab, Let not this thing displease thee, for the sword devoureth one as well as another. Make thy battle more strong against the city, and overthrow it.

And when the wife of Uriah heard that Uriah her husband was dead, she mourned for her husband. And when the mourning was past, David sent and fetched her to his house, and she became his wife, and bore him a son. But the thing that David had done displeased the Lord.

6

And the Lord sent Nathan the prophet unto David. And he came unto him, and said unto him, There were two men in one city; the one rich, and the other poor. The rich man had exceeding many flocks and herds; but the poor man had nothing, save one little ewe lamb, which he had bought and nourished up; and it grew up together with him, and with his children. It did eat of his own meat, and drank of his own cup, and lay in his bosom, and was unto him as a daughter. And there came a traveller unto the rich man; and he spared to take of his own flock, and of his own herd, to dress for the wayfaring man that was come unto him; but he took the poor man's lamb, and dressed it for the man that was come to him.

And David's anger was greatly kindled against the man; and he said to Nathan, As the Lord liveth, the man that hath done this thing shall surely die; and he shall restore the lamb fourfold, because he did this thing and because he had no pity.

And Nathan said to David, Thou art the man. Thus saith the Lord God of Israel, I anointed thee king over Israel, and I delivered thee out of the hand of Saul; and I gave thee the house of Israel and of Judah. Wherefore hast thou despised the commandment of the Lord, to do evil in his sight? Thou hast killed Uriah the Hittite with the sword, and hast taken his wife to be thy wife, and hast slain him with the sword of the children of Ammon. Now therefore the sword shall never depart from thine house, because thou hast despised me, and hast taken the wife of Uriah the Hittite to be thy wife. And David said unto Nathan, I have sinned against the Lord. And Nathan said unto David, The Lord also hath put away thy sin; thou shalt not die. Howbeit, because by this deed thou hast given great occasion to the enemies of the Lord to blaspheme, the child also that is born unto thee shall surely die.

And Nathan departed unto his house. And the Lord struck the child that Uriah's wife bare unto David, and it was very sick. David therefore besought God for the child; and David fasted, and went in, and lay all night upon the earth. And the elders of his house arose, and went to him, to raise him up from the earth; but he would not, neither did he eat bread with them. And it came to pass on the seventh day, that the child died. And the servants of David feared to tell him that the child was dead; for they said, Behold, while the child was yet alive, we spake unto him, and he would not hearken unto our voice. How will he then vex himself if we tell him that the child is dead?

But when David saw that his servants whispered, David perceived that the child was dead; therefore David said unto his servants, Is the child dead? And they said, He is dead. Then David arose from the earth, and washed, and anointed himself, and changed his apparel, and came into the house of the Lord, and worshipped. Then he came to his own house; and when he required, they set bread before him, and he did eat. Then said his servants unto him, What thing is this that thou hast done? Thou didst fast and weep for the child, while it was alive; but when the child was dead, thou didst rise and eat bread. And he said, While the child was yet alive, I fasted and wept; for I said, Who can tell whether God will be gracious to me, that the child may live? But now he is dead, wherefore should I fast? Can I bring him back again? I shall go to him, but he shall not return to me.

7

And it came to pass after this that Absalom the son of David had a fair sister, whose name was Tamar; and Amnon the son of David loved her. And Amnon was so vexed that he fell sick for his sister Tamar, for she was a virgin and Amnon thought it hard for him to do anything to her. But Amnon had a friend whose name was Jonadab; and Jonadab was a very subtile man. And he said unto Amnon, Why art thou, being the king's son, lean from day to day? Wilt thou not tell me? And Amnon said unto him, I love Tamar my brother Absalom's sister.

And Jonadab said unto him, Lay thee down on thy bed and make thyself sick; and when thy father cometh to see thee, say unto him, I pray thee, let my sister Tamar come and give me meat and dress the meat in my sight. So Amnon lay down and made himself sick; and when the king was come to see him, Amnon said, I pray thee, let Tamar my sister come and make me a couple of cakes in my sight that I may eat at her hand. Then David sent home to Tamar, saying, Go now to thy brother Amnon's house and dress him meat.

So Tamar went to her brother Amnon's house, and he was laid down. And she took flour and made cakes in his sight and did bake the cakes. And she took a pan and poured them out before him, but he refused to eat. And he said, Have out all men from me. And they went out every man from him. And Amnon said unto Tamar, Bring the meat into the chamber that I may eat of thine hand. And Tamar took the cakes which she had made and brought them into the chamber to Amnon her brother.

And when she had brought them unto him to eat, he took hold of her and said unto her, Come lie with me, my sister. And she answered him, Nay, my brother, do not force me; for no such thing ought to be done in Israel. Do not thou this folly. And I, whither shall I cause my shame to go? And as for thee, thou shalt be as one of the fools in Israel.

Howbeit Amnon would not hearken unto her voice; but being stronger than she, forced her and lay with her. Then he hated her exceedingly, so that the hatred wherewith he hated her was greater than the love wherewith he had loved her. And Amnon said unto her, Arise, be gone. And she said unto him, This evil in sending me away is greater than the other that thou didst unto me. But he would not hearken unto her.

And Tamar put ashes on her head and rent her garment of divers colors that was on her, and laid her hand on her head, and went on crying. But when king David heard of all these things, he was very wroth. So Tamar remained desolate in her brother Absalom's house. And Absalom hated Amnon because he had forced his sister Tamar.

And it came to pass after two full years that Absalom came to the king and said, Behold now, thy servant hath sheepshearers. Let the king, I beseech thee, and his servants go with thy servant. And the king said to Absalom, Nay, my son, let us not all now go, lest we be chargeable to thee. And Absalom pressed him; howbeit he would not go, but blessed him. Then said Absalom, Let my brother Amnon go with us. And the king said unto him, Why should he go with thee? But Absalom pressed him so that he let Amnon and all the king's sons go with him.

Now Absalom had commanded his servants, saying, Mark ye now when Amnon's heart is merry with wine, and when I say unto you, Smite Amnon, then kill him. Fear not, have I not commanded you? And the servants of Absalom did unto Amnon as Absalom had commanded. Then all the king's sons arose, and every man gat him up upon his mule, and fled.

And it came to pass that tidings came to David, saying, Absalom hath slain all the king's sons, and there is not one of them left. Then the king arose and tare his garments and lay on the earth. And Jonadab said, Let not my lord suppose that they have slain the king's sons, for Amnon only is dead. For this hath been determined by Absalom from the day Amnon forced his sister Tamar.

But Absalom fled and went to Geshur and was there three years. And the soul of king David longed to go forth unto Absalom; and he mourned for his son every day.

8

Now Joab perceived that the king's heart was toward Absalom. . . . And the king said unto Joab, Go, bring the young man Absalom again. So Joab arose and went to Geshur and brought Absalom to Jerusalem. And the king said, Let him turn to his own house, and let him not see my face. So Absalom returned to his own house and saw not the king's face. But in all Israel there was none to be so much praised as Absalom for his beauty; from the sole of his foot even to the crown of his head there was no blemish in him.

So Absalom dwelt two full years in Jerusalem and saw not the king's face. Therefore Absalom sent for Joab, but he would not come to him; and when he sent again the second time, he would not come. Therefore Absalom said unto his servants, See, Joab's field is near mine, and he hath barley there. Go and set it on fire. And Joab arose and came to Absalom and said, Wherefore have thy servants set my field on fire? And Absalom answered Joab, Wherefore am I come from Geshur? It had been good for me to have been there still. Now therefore let me see the king's face.

So Joab came to the king and told him; and when David had called for Absalom, he came to the king and bowed himself on his face to the ground before the king; and the king kissed Absalom.

. . . . But Absalom stole the hearts of the men of Israel; and he sent spies throughout all the tribes of Israel, saying, As soon as ye hear the sound of the trumpet, then ye shall say, Absalom reigneth in Hebron. And the conspiracy was strong, for the people increased continually with Absalom.

And there came a messenger to David saying, The hearts of the men of Israel are after Absalom. And David said unto all his servants that were with him at Jerusalem, Arise, and let us flee; for we shall not else escape from Absalom. And the king went forth and all his household after him and tarried in a place that was far off.

. . . And David numbered the people that were with him, and set captains of thousands and captains of hundreds over them. And David sent a third part of the people under the hand of Joab, and a third part under the hand of Abishai Joab's brother, and a third part under the hand of Ittai the Gittite. And the king said unto the people, I will surely go forth with you myself also. But the people answered, Thou shalt not go forth; for now thou art worth ten thousand of us. And the king said unto them, What seemeth you best, I will do. And the king stood by the gate side, and all the people came out by hundreds and by thousands. And the king commanded Joab and Abishai and Ittai, saying, Deal gently for my sake with the young man, even with Absalom. And all the people heard when the king gave all the captains charge concerning Absalom.

And Absalom met the servants of David. And Absalom rode upon a mule, and the mule went under the thick boughs of a great oak, and his head caught hold of the oak, and he was taken up between the heaven and the earth; and the mule that was under him went away. And a certain man saw it, and told Joab, and said, Behold, I saw Absalom hanged in an oak. And Joab said unto the man that told him, And, behold, thou sawest him, and why didst thou not smite him there to the ground? I would have given thee ten shekels of silver and a girdle. And the man said unto Joab, Though I should receive a thousand shekels of silver in mine hand, yet would I not put forth my hand against the king's son; for in our hearing the king charged thee and Abishai and Ittai, saying, Beware that none touch the young man Absalom. Then said Joab, I may not tarry thus with thee. And he took three darts in his hand and thrust them through the heart of Absalom while he was yet alive in the midst of the oak. And ten young men that bare Joab's armor compassed about and smote Absalom and slew him. And Joab blew the trumpet, and the people returned from pursuing after Israel. And they took Absalom and cast him into a great pit in the wood and laid a very great heap of stones upon him; and all Israel fled everyone to his tent.

And David sat between the two gates; and the watchman went up to the roof over the gate unto the wall, and lifted up his eyes, and looked, and behold a man running alone. And the watchman cried and told the king. And the king said, If he be alone, there is tidings in his mouth. And he came apace, and drew near. And the watchman saw another man running; and the watchman called unto the porter and said, Behold, another man running alone. And the king said, He also bringeth tidings. And the watchman said, Methinketh the running of the foremost is like the running of Ahimaaz the son of Zadok. And the king said, He is a good man and cometh with good tidings. And Ahimaaz called, and said unto the king, All is well. And he fell down to the earth upon his face before the king, and said, Blessed be the Lord thy God, which hath delivered up the men that lifted up their hand against my lord the king. And the king said, Is the young man Absalom safe? And Ahimaaz answered, When Joab sent the king's servant and me thy servant I saw a great tumult, but I knew not what it was.

And the king said unto him, Turn aside, and stand here. And he turned aside, and stood still. And behold Cushi came; and Cushi said, Tidings, my lord the king; for the Lord hath avenged thee this day of all them that rose up against thee. And the king said unto Cushi, Is the young man Absalom safe? And Cushi answered, The enemies of my lord the king, and all that rise against thee to do thee hurt, be as that young man is!

And the king was much moved, and went up to the chamber over the gate, and wept. And as he went, thus he said, O my son Absalom! my son, my son Absalom! Would God I had died for thee, O Absalom, my son, my son! [3]

[3] Chapters 15, 16, 17, and 18 of II Samuel may well be read for more details on the conspiracy of Absalom.

9

And it was told Joab, Behold, the king weepeth and mourneth for Absalom. And Joab came into the house of the king and said, Thou hast shamed this day the faces of all thy servants, which this day have saved thy life, and the lives of thy sons and of thy daughters, and the lives of thy wives, and the lives of thy concubines, in that thou lovest thine enemies and hatest thy friends. For this day I perceive that if Absalom had lived and all we had died this day, then it had pleased thee well. Now therefore arise, go forth, and speak comfortably unto thy servants; for I swear by the Lord if thou go not forth, there will not tarry one with thee this night, and that will be worse unto thee than all the evil that befell thee from thy youth until now.

Then the king arose and sat in the gate. And all the people came before the king, for Israel had fled every man to his tent. And all the people were at strife throughout all the tribes of Israel, saying, The king saved us out of the hand of our enemies and he delivered us out of the hand of the Philistines, and now he is fled out of the land because of Absalom. And Absalom, whom we anointed over us, is dead in battle. Now therefore why speak ye not a word of bringing the king back? And king David sent to the priests, saying, Speak unto the elders of Judah, saying, Why are ye the last to bring the king back to his house? Ye are my brethren, ye are my bones and my flesh. Wherefore then are ye the last to bring back the king?

And he bowed the heart of all the men of Judah even as the heart of one man, so that they sent this word unto the king, Return thou, and all thy servants. So the king returned and came to Jordan.

10

Now king David was old and stricken in years, and they covered him with clothes, but he gat no heat. Wherefore his servants said unto him, Let there be sought for my lord the king a young virgin; and let her lie in thy bosom that my lord the king may get heat. So they sought for a fair damsel throughout all the coasts of Israel and found Abishag a Shunammite and brought her to the king. And the damsel was very fair and cherished the king and ministered to him; but the king knew her not.

Then Adonijah the son of David exalted himself, saying, I will be king; and he prepared him chariots and horsemen. And his father had not displeased him at any time in saying, Why hast thou done so? And he conferred with Joab and with Abiathar the priest; and they, following Adonijah, helped him. But Zadok the priest and Benaiah, and Nathan the prophet, and the mighty men which belonged to David were not with Adonijah.

Wherefore Nathan spake unto Bathsheba the mother of Solomon saying, Hast thou not heard that Adonijah doth reign and David our lord knoweth it not? Now therefore let me, I pray thee, give thee counsel that thou mayest save thine own life and the life of thy son Solomon. Go and get thee unto king David and say unto him, Didst not thou, O king, swear unto thine handmaid, saying, Assuredly Solomon thy son shall reign after me, and he shall sit upon my throne? Why then doth Adonijah reign? Behold, while thou yet talkest there with the king, I also will come in after thee and confirm thy words.

And Bathsheba went in unto the king into the chamber; and Abishag the Shunammite ministered unto the king. And Bathsheba bowed, and did obeisance unto the king. And the king said, What wouldest thou? And she said unto him:

My lord, thou sworest by the Lord unto thine handmaid, saying, Assuredly Solomon thy son shall reign after me, and he shall sit upon my throne. And now, behold, Adonijah reigneth; and now, my lord the king, thou knowest it not. And he hath slain oxen and fat cattle and sheep in abundance, and hath called all the sons of the king, and Abiathar the priest and Joab the captain of the host; but Solomon thy servant hath he not called. And thou, my lord, O king, the eyes of all Israel are upon thee, that thou shouldest tell them who shall sit on the throne of my lord the king after him. Otherwise it shall come to pass, when my lord the king shall sleep with his fathers, that I and my son Solomon shall be counted offenders.

And, lo, while she yet talked with the king, Nathan the prophet also came in. And they told the king, saying, Behold, Nathan the prophet! And when he was come in before the king, he bowed himself before the king with his face to the ground. And Nathan said, My lord, O king, hast thou said, Adonijah shall reign after me, and he shall sit upon my throne? For he is gone down this day, and hath slain oxen and fat cattle and sheep in abundance, and hath called all the king's sons, and the captains of the host, and Abiathar the priest; and, behold, they eat and drink before him, and say, God save King Adonijah.

Then king David answered and said, Call me Bathsheba. And she stood before the king. And the king swore and said, Even as I swore unto thee by the Lord God of Israel, saying, Assuredly Solomon thy son shall reign after me, even so will I certainly do this day. Then Bathsheba bowed with her face to the earth and did reverence to the king. And king David said, Call me Zadok the priest, and Nathan, and Benaiah. And they came before the king. The king also said unto them, Take with you the servants of your lord and cause Solomon my son to ride upon mine own mule, and bring him down to Gihon; and let Zadok the priest and Nathan the prophet anoint him there king over Israel; and blow ye with the trumpet and say, God save King Solomon! For he shall be king in my stead, and I have appointed him to be ruler over Israel and over Judah.

And Adonijah and all the guests that were with him heard it as they had made an end of eating. And all that were with Adonijah were afraid and rose up and went every man his way. And Adonijah feared because of Solomon. And it was told Solomon, saying, Behold, Adonijah feareth king Solomon; for, lo, he hath caught hold on the horns of the altar, saying, Let King Solomon swear unto me today that he will not slay his servant with the sword. And Solomon said, If he will show himself a worthy man, there shall not a hair of him fall to the earth; but if wickedness shall be found in him, he shall die.

Now the days of David drew nigh that he should die; and he charged Solomon his son, saying, I go the way of all the earth. Be thou strong therefore, and show thyself a man, and keep the charge of the Lord thy God to walk in his ways, to keep his commandments and his judgments as it is written in the law of Moses. Moreover thou knowest also what Joab did to me and what he did unto Abner, whom he slew, and shed the blood of war in peace. Do therefore according to thy wisdom, and let not his hoar head go down to the grave in peace. But show kindness unto those who came to me when I fled because of Absalom thy brother.

So David slept with his fathers and was buried in the city of David.

-IV-

THE REIGN OF SOLOMON AND THE DIVISION OF THE KINGDOM

THESE readings on the reign of Solomon and on the subsequent division of the kingdom of Israel are included here not because of their literary merit, for they are clearly inferior in that respect to the readings from Samuel, but because without them one fails to get necessary information on the course of Hebrew history.

What manner of man Solomon really was is difficult to ascertain, since the account of him and of his reign is the work of several authors, one of whom at least depended largely on legend for his material. It is difficult to believe from what we actually know of this son of David that he possessed the "wisdom" popularly ascribed to him. Instead he seems anything but wise in his ambitious and costly building program, in his disastrous foreign marriages, and in the heavy debt with which he saddled his small country. He surely did not benefit his people by such projects and behavior. The poor among them became steadily poorer, discontented with their lot, and so fearful of Rehoboam's announcement of even heavier oppression that those in the north were won over to Jeroboam, who was thus able to lead a successful revolution upon the death of Solomon about 936 B.C. From that date Israel was divided into two kingdoms: the northern kingdom, Israel, centered in Samaria; the southern, Judah, with Jerusalem as its capital city.

FROM I KINGS 2:12–12

Then sat Solomon upon the throne of David his father; and his kingdom was established greatly.

And Adonijah came to Bathsheba the mother of Solomon. And she said, Comest thou peaceably? And he said, Peaceably. He said moreover, I have somewhat to say unto thee. And she said, Say on. And he said, Thou knowest that the kingdom was mine and that all Israel set their faces on me, that I should reign; howbeit the kingdom is turned about, and is become my brother's. And now I ask one petition of thee, deny me not. Speak, I pray thee, unto Solomon the king, that he give me Abishag the Shunammite to wife. And Bathsheba said, Well; I will speak for thee unto the king. Bathsheba therefore went unto King Solomon, to speak unto him for Adonijah. And the king rose up to meet her, and bowed himself unto her, and sat down on his throne, and caused a seat to be set for the king's mother; and she sat on his right hand. Then she said, I desire one small petition of thee. I pray thee, say me not nay. And the king said unto her, Ask on, my mother; for I will not say thee nay. And she said, Let Abishag the Shunammite be given to Adonijah thy brother to wife. And King Solomon answered and said unto his mother, And why dost thou ask Abishag the Shunammite for Adonijah? Ask for him the kingdom also; for he is mine elder brother; even for him, and for Abiathar the priest, and for Joab. Then King Solomon swore by the Lord, saying, God do so to me, and more also, if Adonijah have not spoken this word against his own life. Now therefore, as the Lord liveth, Adonijah shall be put to death this day. And King Solomon sent by the hand of Benaiah, and he fell upon Adonijah that he died.

And unto Abiathar the priest said the king, Get thee to Anathoth, unto thine own fields; for thou art worthy of death; but I will not at this time put thee to death, because thou barest the ark of the Lord God before David my father. So Solomon thrust out Abiathar from being priest unto the Lord.

Then tidings came to Joab; for Joab had turned after Adonijah, though he turned not after Absalom. And Joab fled unto the tabernacle of the Lord, and caught hold on the horns of the altar. And it was told King Solomon that Joab was fled unto the tabernacle of the Lord. Then Solomon sent Benaiah, saying, Go, fall upon him. And Benaiah came to the tabernacle of the Lord, and said unto him, Thus saith the king, Come forth. And he said, Nay; but I will die here. And Benaiah brought the king word again, saying, Thus said Joab, and thus he answered me. And the king said unto him, Do as he hath said, and fall upon him, and bury him. So Benaiah went up and fell upon Joab and slew him, and he was buried in his own house in the wilderness.

The Lord appeared to Solomon in a dream by night; and God said, Ask what I shall give thee. And Solomon said, Thou hast showed unto thy servant David my father great mercy, according as he walked before thee in truth, and in righteousness, and in uprightness of heart with thee. And now, O Lord my God, thou hast made thy servant king instead of David my father; and I am but a little child; I know not how to go out or come in. And thy servant is in the midst of thy people which thou hast chosen, a great people, that cannot be numbered nor counted for multitude. Give therefore thy servant an understanding heart to judge thy people, that I may discern between good and bad. And the speech pleased the Lord, that Solomon had asked this thing. And God said unto him, Because thou hast asked this thing, and hast not asked for thyself long life, neither hast asked riches for thyself, nor hast asked the life of thine enemies; but hast asked for thyself understanding to discern judgment; behold, I have done according to thy words. Lo, I have given thee a wise and an understanding heart, so that there was none like thee before thee, neither after thee shall any arise like unto thee. And I have also given thee that which thou hast not asked, both riches and honor; so that there shall not be any among the kings like unto thee all thy days. And if thou wilt walk in my ways, to keep my statutes and my commandments, as thy father David did walk, then I will lengthen thy days.

And Solomon awoke; and, behold, it was a dream. And he came to Jerusalem, and stood before the ark of the covenant of the Lord, and offered up burnt offerings, and offered peace offerings, and made a feast to all his servants.

Then came there two women that were harlots unto the king, and stood before him. And the one woman said, O my lord, I and this woman dwell in one house; and I was delivered of a child with her in the house. And it came to pass the third day after that I was delivered, that this woman was delivered also; and we were together; there was no stranger with us in the house, save we two in the house. And this woman's child died in the night, because she overlaid it. And she arose at midnight, and took my son from beside me, while thine handmaid slept, and laid it in her bosom, and laid her dead child in my bosom. And when I rose in the morning to give my child suck, behold, it was dead; but when I had considered it in the morning, behold, it was not my son, which I did bear. And the other woman said, Nay; but the living is my son, and the dead is thy son. And this said, No; but the dead is thy son, and the living is my son. Thus they spoke before the king.

And the king said, Bring me a sword. And they brought a sword before the king. And the king said, Divide the living child in two, and give half to the one and half to the other. Then spoke the woman whose the living child was unto the king, for her bowels yearned upon her son, and she said, O my lord, give her the living child, and in no wise slay it. But the other said, Let it be neither mine nor thine, but divide it. Then the king answered and said, Give her the living child, and in no wise slay it. She is the mother thereof. And all Israel heard of the judgment which the king had judged; and they feared the king; for they saw that the wisdom of God was in him to do judgment.

And Solomon made affinity with Pharaoh, king of Egypt, and took Pharaoh's daughter, and brought her into the city of David. And Solomon reigned over all kingdoms from the river unto the land of the Philistines and unto the border of Egypt. And Judah and Israel dwelt safely, every man under his vine and under his fig tree from Dan to Beersheba, all the days of Solomon. And Solomon had forty thousand stalls of horses for his chariots and twelve thousand horsemen. And all king Solomon's drinking vessels were of gold, none were of silver; it was nothing accounted of in the days of Solomon. For the king had at sea a navy with the navy of Hiram. Once in three years came the navy from Tarshish,[1] bringing gold, and silver, ivory and apes and peacocks. So king Solomon exceeded all the kings of the earth for riches and for wisdom.

And Hiram king of Tyre sent his servants unto Solomon. And Solomon sent to Hiram, saying, Thou knowest how that David my father could not build a house unto the name of the Lord his God, for the wars which were about him on every side. But now the Lord

[1] Tarshish is generally thought to have been a port in what is now Spain.

my God hath given me rest on every side; and, behold, I purpose to build a house unto the name of the Lord my God. Now therefore command thou that they hew me cedar trees out of Lebanon; and my servants shall be with thy servants; for thou knowest that there is not among us any that can skill to hew timber like unto the Sidonians. And Hiram sent to Solomon, saying, I will do all thy desire concerning timber of cedar and concerning timber of fir. My servants shall bring them down from Lebanon unto the sea; and I will convey them in floats unto the place that thou shalt appoint me.

And it came to pass in the fourth year of Solomon's reign over Israel, in the second month, that he began to build the house of the Lord. In the fourth year was the foundation of the house laid, and in the eleventh year was the house finished throughout all the parts thereof. So was he seven years in building it.[2]

And when the queen of Sheba heard of the fame of Solomon concerning the name of the Lord, she came to prove him with hard questions. And she came to Jerusalem with a very great train, with camels that bare spices, and very much gold, and precious stones; and when she was come to Solomon, she communed with him of all that was in her heart. And Solomon told her all her questions. There was not anything hid from the king, which he told her not. And when the queen of Sheba had seen all Solomon's wisdom, and the house that he had built, and the meat of his table, and the sitting of his servants, and the attendance of his ministers, and their apparel, and his cupbearers, and his ascent by which he went up unto the house of the Lord, there was no more spirit in her. And she said to the king, It was a true report that I heard in mine own land of thy acts and of thy wisdom. Howbeit I believed not the words until I came, and mine eyes had seen it; and, behold, the half was not told me. Thy wisdom and prosperity exceedeth the fame which I heard. Happy are thy men, happy are these thy servants, which stand continually before thee, and that hear thy wisdom. Blessed be the Lord thy God, which delighted in thee, to set thee on the throne of

[2] A detailed description of the temple which Solomon built is given in I Kings 6–7.

Israel. And she gave the king an hundred and twenty talents of gold, and of spices very great store, and precious stones. There came no more such abundance of spices as these which the queen of Sheba gave to king Solomon. And king Solomon gave unto the queen of Sheba all her desire, whatsoever she asked, beside that which Solomon gave her of his royal bounty. So she turned and went to her own country, she and her servants.

But king Solomon loved many strange women, together with the daughter of Pharaoh, women of the nations concerning which the Lord said unto the children of Israel, Ye shall not go in unto them; for surely they will turn your heart after their gods. Solomon clave unto these in love. And it came to pass, when Solomon was old, that his wives turned away his heart after other gods; and his heart was not perfect with the Lord his God. For Solomon went after Ashtoreth the goddess of the Sidonians and after Milcom the abomination of the Ammonites. And Solomon did evil in the sight of the Lord, and went not fully after the Lord, as did David his father. Then did Solomon build a high place for Chemosh the abomination of Moab in the hill that is before Jerusalem, and for Molech the abomination of the children of Ammon. And likewise did he for all his strange wives, which burnt incense and sacrificed unto their gods.

And the Lord was angry with Solomon, because his heart was turned from the Lord God of Israel, which had appeared unto him twice, and had commanded him concerning this thing, that he should not go after other gods; but he kept not that which the Lord commanded. Wherefore the Lord said unto Solomon, Forasmuch as this is done of thee, and thou hast not kept my covenant and my statutes, which I have commanded thee, I will surely rend the kingdom from thee, and will give it to thy servant. Notwithstanding in thy days I will not do it for David thy father's sake: but I will rend it out of the hand of thy son.

And Jeroboam the son of Nebat even he lifted up his hand against the king. And the man Jeroboam was a mighty man of valor. Solomon sought therefore to kill Jeroboam; and Jeroboam arose and fled into Egypt and was in Egypt until the death of Solomon.

And the time that Solomon reigned in Jerusalem over all Israel was forty years. And Solomon slept with his fathers, and was buried in the city of David. And Rehoboam his son reigned in his stead.

And Rehoboam went to Shechem; for all Israel were come to Shechem to make him king. And it came to pass, when Jeroboam the son of Nebat, who was yet in Egypt, heard of it, that they sent and called him. And Jeroboam and all the congregation of Israel came, and spoke unto Rehoboam, saying, Thy father made our yoke grievous. Now therefore make thou the grievous service of thy father and his heavy yoke which he put upon us, lighter, and we will serve thee. And he said unto them, Depart yet for three days, then come again to me. And the people departed.

And King Rehoboam consulted with the old men, that stood before Solomon his father while he yet lived, and said, How do ye advise that I may answer this people? And they spoke unto him, saying, If thou wilt be a servant unto this people this day, and wilt serve them, and answer them, and speak good words to them, then they will be thy servants forever. But he forsook the counsel of the old men, which they had given him, and consulted with the young men that were grown up with him, and which stood before him. And he said unto them, What counsel give ye that we may answer this people, who have spoken to me, saying, Make the yoke which thy father did put upon us lighter?

And the young men that were grown up with him spoke unto him, saying, Thus shalt thou speak unto this people: My little finger shall be thicker than my father's loins. And now whereas my father did lade you with a heavy yoke, I will add to your yoke. My father hath chastised you with whips, but I will chastise you with scorpions.

So Jeroboam and all the people came to Rehoboam the third day, as the king had appointed. And the king answered the people roughly, and forsook the old men's counsel that they gave him, and spoke to them after the counsel of the young men, saying, My father made your yoke heavy, and I will add to your yoke. My father also chastised you with whips, but I will chastise you with scorpions.

So when all Israel saw that the king hearkened not unto them, the people answered the king, saying, What portion have we in David? Neither have we inheritance in the son of Jesse. To your tents, O Israel! Now see to thine own house, David. So Israel rebelled against the house of David unto this day. And it came to pass, when all Israel heard that Jeroboam was come again, that they sent and called him unto the congregation, and made him king over all Israel. There was none that followed the house of David, but the tribe of Judah only.

-V-

ELIJAH AND ELISHA

In the book of Kings (originally one book), among many rather dull and obscure chapters dealing with the rulers of both northern and southern kingdoms, there are found certain narratives neither obscure nor dull. These well told, lively, and important stories center about two of the most extraordinary figures in the Old Testament, Elijah and his disciple Elisha. That they were actual historical characters there is little, if any, doubt; and yet it is not surprising that legends also clustered about them, for they were supermen, in truth. They lived about 850 B.C., nearly a century after the division of the kingdom; and their fiery purpose in life was to bring home to the northern kingdom of Israel the sins of its kings and of its people. They are often called "the speaking prophets," for, although they apparently wrote nothing, they were surely forerunners of the greater prophets to come a century later.

The northern kingdom afforded them rich ground for their missionary zeal. Insecurely established under Jeroboam, and from the nature of its situation infiltrated by foreigners, it had early become drawn toward idolatrous worship of strange gods. It lacked the more stable foundation of the house of David, which continued to rule the southern kingdom; and its kings, with few exceptions, were weak men. Syria to the north and the rising power of the Assyrian Empire to the east were dangerous and threatening neighbors. Most of the incidents which have to do with Elijah and Elisha center about King Ahab of Israel (875–853 B.C.) and his wicked wife Jezebel. The famine which forms a background for the narratives was an actual condition prevailing for some years at this time.

The stories, unfortunately few, which have survived concerning these fanatical but devoted men are obviously but part of a popular cycle of tales concerning them.

ELIJAH

FROM I KINGS 17, 18, 19, 21

And Elijah the Tishbite, who was of the inhabitants of Gilead, said unto Ahab, As the Lord God of Israel liveth, before whom I stand, there shall not be dew nor rain these years, but according to my word. And the word of the Lord came unto him, saying, Get thee hence, and turn thee eastward, and hide thyself by the brook Cherith that is before Jordan. And it shall be, that thou shalt drink of the brook; and I have commanded the ravens to feed thee there. So he went and did according unto the word of the Lord; for he went and dwelt by the brook Cherith that is before Jordan. And the ravens brought him bread and flesh in the morning, and bread and flesh in the evening; and he drank of the brook. And it came to pass, after a while, that the brook dried up because there had been no rain in the land.

And the word of the Lord came unto him, saying, Arise, get thee to Zarephath, which belongeth to Zidon, and dwell there. Behold, I have commanded a widow woman there to sustain thee. So he arose, and went to Zarephath. And when he came to the gate of the city, behold, the widow woman was there gathering of sticks; and he called to her, and said, Fetch me, I pray thee, a little water in a vessel, that I may drink. And as she was going to fetch it, he called to her, and said, Bring me, I pray thee, a morsel of bread in thine hand. And she said, As the Lord thy God liveth, I have not a cake, but an handful of meal in a barrel, and a little oil in a cruse; and, behold, I am gathering two sticks, that I may go in and dress it for me and my son, that we may eat it, and die. And Elijah said unto her, Fear not; go and do as thou hast said; but make me thereof a little cake first, and bring it unto me, and after make for thee and for thy son. For thus saith the Lord God of Israel, The barrel of meal shall not waste, neither shall the cruse of oil fail, until the day that the Lord sendeth rain upon the earth. And she went and did according to the saying of Elijah; and she and he and her house did eat many days. And the barrel of meal wasted not, neither did the cruse of oil fail, according to the word of the Lord, which he spake by Elijah.

And it came to pass, after these things, that the son of the woman, the mistress of the house, fell sick; and his sickness was so sore that there was no breath left in him. And she said unto Elijah, What have I to do with thee, O thou man of God? Art thou come unto me to call my sin to remembrance and to slay my son? And he said unto her, Give me thy son. And he took him out of her bosom, and carried him up into a loft, where he abode, and laid him upon his own bed. And he cried unto the Lord, and said, O Lord my God, hast thou also brought evil upon the widow with whom I sojourn, by slaying her son? And he stretched himself upon the child three times, and cried unto the Lord, and said, O Lord my God, I pray thee, let this child's soul come into him again. And the Lord heard the voice of Elijah; and the soul of the child came into him again, and he revived. And Elijah took the child, and brought him down out of the chamber into the house, and delivered him unto his mother. And Elijah said, See, thy son liveth. And the woman said to Elijah, Now by this I know that thou art a man of God, and that the word of the Lord in thy mouth is truth.

And it came to pass after many days, that the word of the Lord came to Elijah in the third year, saying, Go, show thyself unto Ahab; and I will send rain upon the earth. And Elijah went to show himself unto Ahab. And there was a sore famine in Samaria. And Ahab called Obadiah, which was the governor of his house. (Now Obadiah feared the Lord greatly; for it was so, when Jezebel cut off the prophets of the Lord, that Obadiah took an hundred prophets, and hid them by fifty in a cave, and fed them with bread and water.) And Ahab said unto Obadiah, Go into the land, unto all fountains of water, and unto all brooks. Peradventure we may find grass to save the horses and mules alive, that we lose not all the beasts. So they divided the land between them, to pass throughout it: Ahab went one way by himself, and Obadiah went another way by himself.

And as Obadiah was in the way, behold, Elijah met him; and he knew him, and fell on his face, and said, Art thou that my lord Elijah? And he answered him, I am. Go, tell thy lord, Behold, Elijah is here. And he said, What have I sinned, that thou wouldest deliver thy servant into the hand of Ahab to slay me? As the Lord thy God liveth, there is no nation or kingdom whither my lord hath not sent to seek thee; and when they said, He is not there; he took an oath of the kingdom and nation, that they found thee not. And now thou sayest, Go, tell thy lord, Behold, Elijah is here. And it shall come to pass, as soon as I am gone from thee, that the Spirit of the Lord shall carry thee whither I know not; and so when I come and tell Ahab, and he cannot find thee, he shall slay me; but I thy servant fear the Lord from my youth. Was it not told my lord what I did when Jezebel slew the prophets of the Lord, how I hid an hundred men of the Lord's prophets by fifty in a cave, and fed them with bread and water? And now thou sayest, Go, tell thy lord, Behold, Elijah is here; and he shall slay me. And Elijah said, As the Lord of hosts liveth, before whom I stand, I will surely show myself unto him today. So Obadiah went to meet Ahab, and told him; and Ahab went to meet Elijah.

And it came to pass, when Ahab saw Elijah, that Ahab said unto him, Art thou he that troubleth Israel? And he answered, I have not troubled Israel; but thou, and thy father's house, in that ye have forsaken the commandments of the Lord, and thou hast followed Baalim. Now therefore send, and gather to me all Israel unto mount Carmel, and the prophets of Baal four hundred and fifty, and the prophets of the groves four hundred, which eat at Jezebel's table. So Ahab sent unto all the children of Israel, and gathered the prophets together unto mount Carmel.

And Elijah came unto all the people, and said, How long halt ye between two opinions? If the Lord be God, follow him; but if Baal, then follow him. And the people answered him not a word. Then said Elijah unto the people, I, even I only, remain a prophet of the Lord; but Baal's prophets are four hundred and fifty men. Let them therefore give us two bullocks; and let them choose one bullock for themselves, and cut it in pieces, and lay it on wood, and put no fire under; and I will dress the other bullock, and lay it on wood, and put no fire under. And call ye on the name of your gods, and I will call on the name of the Lord; and the God that answereth by fire, let him be God. And all the people answered and said, It is well spoken. And Elijah said unto the prophets of Baal, Choose you one bullock for yourselves, and dress it first, for ye are many; and call on the name of your gods, but put no fire under. And they took the bullock which was given them, and they dressed it, and called on the name of Baal from morning even until noon, saying, O Baal, hear us! But there was no voice, nor any that answered. And they leaped upon the altar which was made. And it came to pass at noon that Elijah mocked them, and said, Cry aloud; for he *is* a God! Either he is talking, or he is pursuing, or he is in a journey, or peradventure he sleepeth, and must be awaked. And they cried aloud, and cut themselves after their manner with knives and lancets, till the blood gushed out upon them. And it came to pass, when midday was past, and they prophesied until the time of the offering of the evening sacrifice, that there was neither voice, nor any to answer, nor any that regarded.

And Elijah said unto all the people, Come near unto me. And all the people came near unto him. And he repaired the altar of the Lord that was broken down. And Elijah took twelve stones, according to the number of the tribes of the sons of Jacob; and with the stones he built an altar in the name of the Lord; and he made a trench about the altar, as great as would contain two measures of seed. And he put the wood in order, and cut the bullock in pieces, and laid him on the wood, and said, Fill four barrels with water, and pour it on the burnt sacrifice, and on the wood. And he said, Do it the second time; and they did it the second time. And he said, Do it the third time; and they did it the third time. And the water ran round about the altar, and he filled the trench also with water. And it came to pass, at the time of the offering of the evening sacrifice, that Elijah the prophet came near, and said, Lord God of Abraham, Isaac, and of Israel, let it be known this day that thou art God in Israel, and that I am thy servant, and that I have done all these things at thy word. Hear me, O Lord, hear me, that this people may know that thou art the Lord God, and that thou hast turned their heart back again. Then the fire of the Lord fell, and consumed the burnt sacrifice, and the wood, and the stones, and the dust, and licked up the water that was in the trench. And when all the people saw it, they fell on their faces; and they said, The Lord, he is the God! The Lord, he is the God! And Elijah said unto them, Take the prophets of Baal; let not one of them escape. And they took them; and Elijah brought them down to the brook Kishon, and slew them there.

And Elijah said unto Ahab, Get thee up, eat and drink; for there is a sound of abundance of rain. So Ahab went up to eat and to drink. And Elijah went up to the top of Carmel; and he cast himself down upon the earth, and put his face between his knees, and said to his servant, Go up now, look toward the sea. And he went up, and looked, and said, There is nothing. And he said, Go again seven times. And it came to pass at the seventh time, that he said, Behold, there ariseth a little cloud out of the sea, like a man's hand. And he said, Go up, say unto Ahab, prepare thy chariot, and get thee down, that the rain stop thee not. And it came to pass in the meanwhile, that the heaven was black with clouds and wind, and there was a great rain. And Ahab rode, and went to Jezreel. And the hand of the Lord was on Elijah; and he girded up his loins, and ran before Ahab to the entrance of Jezreel.

And Ahab told Jezebel all that Elijah had done, and withal how he had slain all the prophets with the sword. Then Jezebel sent a messenger unto Elijah, saying, So let the gods do to me, and more also, if I make not thy life as the life of one of them by tomorrow about this time. And when he saw that, he arose, and went for his life, and came to Beersheba, which belongeth to Judah, and left his servant there.

But he himself went a day's journey into the wilderness and came and sat down under a juniper tree; and he requested for himself that he might die, and said, It is enough; now, O Lord, take away my life; for I am not better than my fathers. And as he lay and slept under a juniper tree, behold, then an angel touched him, and said unto him, Arise and eat. And he looked, and, behold, there was a cake baken on the coals, and a cruse of water at his head. And he did eat and drink, and laid him down again. And the angel of the Lord came again the second time, and touched him, and said, Arise and eat; because the journey is too great for thee. And he arose, and did eat and drink, and went in the strength of that meat forty days and forty nights unto Horeb the mount of God.

And he came thither unto a cave, and lodged there; and, behold, the word of the Lord came to him, and he said unto him, What doest thou here, Elijah? And he said, I have been very jealous for the Lord God of hosts; for the children of Israel have forsaken thy covenant, thrown down thine altars, and slain thy prophets with the sword; and I, even I only, am left; and they seek my life, to take it away. And he said, Go forth, and stand upon the mount before the Lord. And, behold, the Lord passed by, and a great and strong wind rent the mountains, and brake in pieces the rocks before the Lord; but the Lord was not in the wind; and after the wind an earthquake; but the Lord was not in the earthquake; and after the earthquake a fire; but the Lord was not in the fire; and after the fire a still small voice. And it was so, when Elijah heard it that he wrapped his face in his mantle, and went out, and stood in the entering in of the cave. And, behold, there came a voice unto him, and said, What doest thou here, Elijah? And he said, I have been very jealous for the Lord God of hosts, because the children of Israel have forsaken thy covenant, thrown down thine altars, and slain thy prophets with the sword; and I, even I only, am left; and they seek my life, to take it away. And the Lord said unto him, Go, return on thy way to the wilderness of Damascus; and when thou comest, anoint Hazael to be king over Syria; and Jehu the son of Nimshi shalt thou anoint to be king over Israel; and Elisha the son of Shaphat, shalt thou anoint to be prophet in thy room. And it shall come to pass, that him that escapeth the sword of Hazael shall Jehu slay; and him that escapeth from the sword of Jehu shall Elisha slay. Yet I have left me seven thousand in Israel, all the knees which have not bowed unto Baal, and every mouth which hath not kissed him.

So he departed thence, and found Elisha the son of Shaphat, who was ploughing with twelve yoke of oxen before him, and he with the twelfth; and Elijah passed by him, and cast his mantle upon him. And he left the oxen, and ran after Elijah, and said, Let me, I pray thee, kiss my father and my mother, and then I will follow thee. And he said unto him, Go back again; for what have I done to thee? And he returned back from him, and took a yoke of oxen, and slew them, and boiled their flesh with the instruments of the oxen, and gave unto the people, and they did eat. Then he arose, and went after Elijah, and ministered unto him.

And it came to pass after these things, that Naboth the Jezreelite had a vineyard, which was in Jezreel, hard by the palace of Ahab king of Samaria. And Ahab spoke unto Naboth, saying, Give me thy vineyard, that I may have it for a garden of herbs, because it is near unto my house; and I will give thee for it a better vineyard than it; or, if it seem good to thee, I will give thee the worth of it in money. And Naboth said to Ahab, The Lord forbid it me, that I should give the inheritance of my fathers unto thee. And Ahab came into his house heavy and displeased because of the word which Naboth the Jezreelite had spoken to him. And he laid him down upon his bed, and turned away his face, and would eat no bread.

But Jezebel his wife came to him, and said unto him, Why is thy spirit so sad, that thou eatest no bread? And he said unto her, Because I spoke unto Naboth the Jezreelite, and said unto him, Give me thy vineyard for money; or else, if it please thee, I will give thee another vineyard for it; and he answered, I will not give thee my vineyard.

And Jezebel his wife said unto him, Dost thou now govern the kingdom of Israel? Arise, and eat bread, and let thine heart be merry. I will give thee the vineyard of Naboth the Jezreelite.

So she wrote letters in Ahab's name, and sealed them with his seal, and sent the letters unto the elders and to the nobles that were in his city, dwelling with Naboth. And she wrote in the letters, saying, Proclaim a fast, and set Naboth on high among the people; and set two men, sons of Belial, before him, to bear witness against him, saying, Thou didst blaspheme God and the king. And then carry him out, and stone him, that he may die.

And the men of his city, even the elders and the nobles who were the inhabitants in his city, did as Jezebel had sent unto them, and as it was written in the letters which she had sent unto them. They proclaimed a fast, and set Naboth on high among the people. And there came in two men, children of Belial, and sat before him; and the men of Belial witnessed against him, even against Naboth in the presence of the people, saying, Naboth did blaspheme God and the king. Then they carried him forth out of the city, and stoned him with stones, that he died.

Then they sent to Jezebel, saying, Naboth is stoned, and is dead. And it came to pass, when Jezebel heard that Naboth was stoned, and was dead, that Jezebel said to Ahab, Arise, take possession of the vineyard of Naboth the Jezreelite which he refused to give thee for money; for Naboth is not alive, but dead.

And it came to pass, when Ahab heard that Naboth was dead, that Ahab rose up to go down to the vineyard of Naboth the Jezreelite to take possession of it. And the word of the Lord came to Elijah the Tishbite saying, Arise, go down to meet Ahab king of Israel, which is in Samaria. Behold, he is in the vineyard of Naboth, whither he is gone down to possess it. And thou shalt speak unto him, saying, Thus saith the Lord, Hast thou killed, and also taken possession? And thou shalt speak unto him, saying, Thus saith the Lord, In the place where dogs licked the blood of Naboth shall dogs lick thy blood, even thine.

And Ahab said to Elijah, Hast thou found me, O mine enemy? And he answered, I have found thee, because thou hast sold thyself to work evil in the sight of the Lord. Behold, I will bring evil upon thee and will take away thy posterity for the provocation wherewith thou hast provoked me to anger and made Israel to sin. And of Jezebel also spoke the Lord, saying, The dogs shall eat Jezebel by the wall of Jezreel.

And it came to pass when Ahab heard these words that he rent his clothes and put sackcloth on his flesh, and fasted, and went softly. And the word of the Lord came to Elijah the Tishbite saying:

Seest thou how Ahab humbleth himself before me? Because he humbleth himself before me, I will not bring the evil in his days; but in his son's days will I bring the evil upon his house.

ELISHA

FROM II KINGS 4, 5, 9

And it fell on a day that Elisha passed to Shunem, where was a great woman; and she constrained him to eat bread. And so it was, that as oft as he passed by, he turned in thither to eat bread. And she said unto her husband, Behold now, I perceive that this is an holy man of God, which passeth by us continually. Let us make a little chamber, I pray thee, on the wall; and let us set for him there a bed, and a table, and a stool, and a candlestick; and it shall be, when he cometh to us, that he shall turn in thither.

And it fell on a day, that he came thither, and he turned into the chamber, and lay there. And he said to Gehazi his servant, Call this Shunammite. And when he had called her, she stood before him. And he said unto him, Say now unto her, Behold, thou hast been careful for us with all this care. What is to be done for thee? Wouldest thou be spoken for to the king, or to the captain of the host? And she answered, I dwell among my own people. And he said, What then is to be done for her? And Gehazi answered, Verily she hath no child, and her husband is old. And he said, Call her. And when he had called her, she stood in the door. And he said, About this season, according to the time of life, thou shalt embrace a son. And she said, Nay, my lord, thou man of God, do not lie unto thine handmaid. And the woman conceived, and bare a son at that season that Elisha had said unto her.

And when the child was grown, it fell on a day, that he went out to his father to the reapers. And he said unto his father, My head, my head. And he said to a lad, Carry him to his mother. And when he had taken him, and brought him to his mother, he sat on her knees till noon, and then died. And she went up, and laid him on the bed of the man of God, and shut the door upon him, and went out. And she called unto her husband, and said, Send me, I pray thee, one of the young men and one of the asses that I may run to the man of God, and come again. And he said, Wherefore wilt thou go to him today? It is neither new moon nor sabbath. And she said, It shall be well. Then she saddled an ass, and said to her servant, Drive, and go forward. Slack not thy riding for me, except I bid thee.

So she went and came unto the man of God to mount Carmel. And it came to pass, when the man of God saw her afar off, that he said to Gehazi his servant, Behold, yonder is that Shunammite! Run now, I pray thee, to meet her, and say unto her, Is it well with thee? Is it well with thy husband? Is it well with the child? And she answered, It is well. And when she came to the man of God to the hill, she caught him by the feet; but Gehazi came near to thrust her away. And the man of God said, Let her alone; for her soul is vexed within her; and the Lord hath hid it from me and hath not told me. Then she said, Did I desire a son of my lord? Did I not say, Do not deceive me? Then he said to Gehazi, Gird up thy loins, and take my staff in thine hand, and go thy way. If thou meet any man, salute him not; and if any salute thee, answer him not again; and lay my staff upon the face of the child. And the mother of the child said, As the Lord liveth, and as thy soul liveth, I will not leave thee. And he arose, and followed her.

And Gehazi passed on before them, and laid the staff upon the face of the child; but there was neither voice, nor hearing. Wherefore he went again to meet him, and told him, saying, The child is not awaked. And when Elisha was come into the house, behold, the child was dead, and laid upon his bed. He went in therefore, and shut the door upon them twain, and prayed unto the Lord. And he went up, and lay upon the child, and put his mouth upon his mouth, and his eyes upon his eyes, and his hands upon his hands; and he stretched himself upon the child; and the flesh of the child waxed warm. Then he returned, and walked in the house to and fro and went up, and stretched himself upon him; and the child sneezed seven times, and the child opened his eyes. And he called Gehazi, and said, Call this Shunammite. So he called her. And when she was come in unto him, he said, Take up thy son. Then she went in, and fell at his feet, and bowed herself to the ground, and took up her son, and went out.

Now Naaman, captain of the host of the king of Syria, was a great man with his master and honorable because by him the Lord had given deliverance to Syria. He was also a mighty man of valor, but he was a leper. And the Syrians had brought away captive out of the land of Israel a little maid; and she waited on Naaman's wife. And she said to her mistress, Would God my lord were with the prophet that is in Samaria! For he would recover him of his leprosy.

And one went in and told his lord, saying, Thus and thus said the maid that is of the land of Israel. And the king of Syria said, Go to, go, and I will send a letter unto the king of Israel.

And Naaman departed and took with him ten talents of silver, and six thousand pieces of gold, and ten changes of raiment. And he brought the letter to the king of Israel, saying: Now when this letter is come unto thee, behold, I have therewith sent Naaman my servant to thee that thou mayest recover him of his leprosy. And it came to pass, when the king of Israel had read the letter, that he rent his clothes, and said, Am I God, to kill and to make alive, that this man doth send unto me to recover a man of his leprosy? Wherefore consider, I pray you, and see how he seeketh a quarrel against me.

And it was so, when Elisha the man of God had heard that the king of Israel had rent his clothes, that he sent to the king, saying, Wherefore hast thou rent thy clothes? Let him come now to me, and he shall know that there is a prophet in Israel.

So Naaman came with his horses and with his chariot, and stood at the door of the house of Elisha. And Elisha sent a messenger unto him, saying, Go and wash in Jordan seven times, and thy flesh shall come again to thee, and thou shalt be clean.

But Naaman was wroth, and went away, and said, Behold, I thought, he will surely come out to me, and stand, and call on the name of the Lord his God, and strike his hand over the place, and recover the leper. Are not Abana and Pharpar, rivers of Damascus, better than all the waters of Israel? May I not wash in them, and be clean? So he turned and went away in a rage. And his servants came near, and spoke unto him, and said, My father, if the prophet had bid thee do some great thing, wouldest thou not have done it? How much rather then, when he saith to thee, Wash, and be clean?

Then went he down, and dipped himself seven times in Jordan, according to the saying of the man of God; and his flesh came again like unto the flesh of a little child, and he was clean. And he returned to the man of God, he and all his company, and came and stood before him; and he said, Behold, now I know that there is no God in all the earth, but in Israel. Now therefore, I pray thee, take a blessing of thy servant.

But Elisha said, As the Lord liveth, before whom I stand, I will receive none. And he urged him to take it; but he refused. And Naaman said, Shall there not then, I pray thee, be given to thy servant two mules' burden of earth? For thy servant will henceforth offer neither burnt offering nor sacrifice unto other gods, but unto the Lord. In this thing the Lord pardon thy servant, that when my master goeth into the house of Rimmon to worship there, and he leaneth on my hand, and I bow myself in the house of Rimmon; when I bow down myself in the house of Rimmon, the Lord pardon thy servant in this thing. And Elisha said unto him, Go in peace. So he departed from him a little way.

But Gehazi the servant of Elisha said, Behold, my master hath spared this Syrian in not receiving at his hands that which he brought, but, as the Lord liveth, I will run after him and take somewhat of him. So Gehazi followed after Naaman. And when Naaman saw him running after him, he lighted down from the chariot to meet him and said, Is all well? And Gehazi said, All is well. My master hath sent me, saying, Behold there be come to me from mount Ephraim two young men of the sons of the prophets. Give them, I pray thee, a talent of silver and two changes of garments.

And Naaman said, Be content, take two talents. And he urged him and bound two talents of silver in two bags, with two changes of garments, and laid them upon two of his servants; and they bore them before him. And when Gehazi came to the tower, he took them from their hand, and bestowed them in the house; and he let the men go, and they departed.

But he went in, and stood before his master. And Elisha said, Whence comest thou, Gehazi? And he said, Thy servant went no whither. And Elisha said unto him, Went not mine heart with thee when the man turned again from his chariot to meet thee? Is it a time to receive money, and to receive garments, and oliveyards and vineyards, and sheep and oxen, and menservants and maidservants? The leprosy therefore of Naaman shall cleave unto thee and unto thy seed forever.

And Gehazi went out from his presence a leper as white as snow.

And Elisha the prophet called one of the children of the prophets, and said unto him, Gird up thy loins and take this box of oil in thine hand and go to Ramoth-gilead. And when thou comest hither, look out there Jehu the son of Nimshi, and go in and make him arise from among his brethren and carry him to an inner chamber. Then take the box of oil and say, Thus saith the Lord, I have anointed thee king over Israel.

So the young man went to Ramoth-gilead. And when he came, behold, the captains of the host were sitting; and he said, I have an errand to thee, O captain. And Jehu said, Unto which of all us? And he said, To thee, O captain. And Jehu arose and went into the house. And he poured the oil on his head and said unto him, Thus saith the Lord God of Israel, I have anointed thee king over the people of the Lord, even over Israel. And thou shalt smite the house of Ahab thy master that I may avenge the blood of my servants the prophets and the blood of all the servants of the Lord at the hand of Jezebel. And the dogs shall eat Jezebel in the portion of Jezreel, and there shall be none to bury her.

So Jehu rode in a chariot and went to Jezreel, for king Joram the son of Ahab lay there. And there stood a watchman on the tower in Jezreel, and he spied the company of Jehu as he came and said, I see a company. And Joram said, Take a horseman and send to meet them, and let him say, Is it peace? So there went one on horseback to meet Jehu and said, Thus saith the king, Is it peace? And Jehu said, What hast thou to do with peace? Turn thee behind me.

And the watchman told, saying, The messenger came to them, but he cometh not again. Then Joram sent out a second on horseback, which came to them, and said, Thus saith the king, Is it peace? And Jehu answered, What hast thou to do with peace? Turn thee behind me. And the watchman told, saying, He came even unto them and cometh not again. And the driving is like the driving of Jehu the son of Nimshi; for he driveth furiously.

And Joram said, Make ready. And his chariot was made ready. And Joram king of Israel went out against Jehu and met him in the portion of Naboth. And it came to pass when Joram saw Jehu, that he said, Is it peace, Jehu? And he answered, What peace, so long as the whoredoms of thy mother Jezebel and her witchcrafts are so many?

And Joram turned his hands and fled. And Jehu drew a bow with his full strength and smote Joram between his arms, and the arrow went out at his heart, and he sunk down in his chariot. Then said Jehu to his captain, Take up and cast him in the portion of the field of Naboth; for remember how that, when I and thou rode together after Ahab his father, the Lord laid this burden upon him. Surely I have seen yesterday the blood of Naboth, saith the Lord, and I will requite thee in this plot, saith the Lord. Now therefore take and cast him into the plot of ground, according to the word of the Lord.

And when Jehu was come to Jezreel, Jezebel heard of it; and she painted her face, and tired her head, and looked out at a window. And as Jehu entered in at the gate, he lifted up his face to the window, and said, Who is on my side? Who? And there looked out to him two or three eunuchs.

And he said, Throw her down. So they threw her down; and some of her blood was sprinkled on the wall, and on the horses; and he trod her under foot. And when he was come in, he did eat and drink, and said, Go, see now this cursed woman, and bury her; for she *is* a king's daughter. And they went to bury her; but they found no more of her than the skull, and the feet, and the palms of her hands.

Wherefore they came again, and told him. And he said, This is the word of the Lord, which he spoke by his servant Elijah the Tishbite, saying, In the portion of Jezreel shall dogs eat the flesh of Jezebel; and the carcase of Jezebel shall be as dung upon the face of the field in the portion of Jezreel; so that they shall not say, This is Jezebel.

-VI-

TWO SHORT STORIES
RUTH
JONAH

In closing these readings in Old Testament prose, we cannot do better than to include two well known and admirably written short stories, Ruth and Jonah.[1] These stories, among the most delightful of any literature, have one thing in common: each is written to emphasize the idea that God is no respecter of persons, but is the Father of all men everywhere. But there the resemblance ceases.

Ruth is a pastoral tale, often called an idyl. It is set "in the days when the judges ruled"; but its message is that of its own day, when "foreign" marriages were causing much anxiety among the Jewish people. The unknown author is clearly saying in his charming and courteous story that the problem is not necessarily such a grave one, and he uses the happy marriage of a Moabitess to an Israelite to prove his point. Jonah, on the other hand, is a piece of ironic comedy, and relates an amusing contest of wits between Jonah and God, who teaches Jonah a good lesson by a kind of practical joking, distinctly human. In its sharp and ironic treatment it is one of the most original and imaginative of all Old Testament narratives.

Both stories were written far later than the material we have been reading; Ruth around 450 B.C., and Jonah perhaps a hundred years afterward.

[1] The book of Esther is also a short story, or perhaps better, a short novel. It is not included here, partly because of space, largely because as narrative it is inferior to Ruth and Jonah both in treatment and in tone. It is a nationalistic story which exalts the Jews above their enemies. It may, however, well be read both for pleasure and for information. It is discussed in *The Bible and the Common Reader*, Pt. II.

RUTH

RUTH 1–4

Now it came to pass in the days when the judges ruled, that there was a famine in the land. And a certain man of Bethlehem-judah went to sojourn in the country of Moab, he, and his wife, and his two sons. And the name of the man was Elimelech, and the name of his wife Naomi, and the name of his two sons Mahlon and Chilion. And they came into the country of Moab and continued there. And Elimelech Naomi's husband died; and she was left and her two sons. And they took them wives of the women of Moab; the name of the one was Orpah, and the name of the other Ruth; and they dwelled there about ten years. And Mahlon and Chilion died also, both of them; and the woman was left of her two sons and her husband.

Then she rose with her daughters-in-law, that she might return from the country of Moab; for she had heard in the country of Moab how that the Lord had visited his people in giving them bread. Wherefore she went forth out of the place where she was, and her two daughters-in-law with her; and they went on their way to return unto the land of Judah. And Naomi said unto her two daughters-in-law, Go, return each to her mother's house. The Lord deal kindly with you, as ye have dealt with the dead and with me. The Lord grant you that ye may find rest, each of you in the house of her husband. Then she kissed them; and they lifted up their voice and wept. And they said unto her, Surely we will return with thee unto thy people. And Naomi said, Turn again, my daughters. Why will ye go with me? Are there yet any more sons in my womb, that they may be your husbands? Turn again, my daughters, go your way; for I am too old to have an husband. If I should say I have hope, if I should have an husband also tonight, and should also bear sons, would ye tarry for them till they were grown? Would ye stay for them from having husbands? Nay, my daughters; for it grieveth me much for your sakes that the hand of the Lord is gone out against me. And they lifted up their voice and wept again; and Orpah kissed her mother-in-law, but Ruth clave unto her. And she said, Behold, thy sister-in-law is gone back unto her people, and unto her gods. Return thou after thy sister-in-law. And Ruth said, Entreat me not to leave thee, or to return from following after thee; for whither thou goest, I will go; and where thou lodgest, I will lodge. Thy people shall be my people, and thy God my God. Where thou diest, will I die, and there will I be buried. The Lord do so to me, and more also, if aught but death part thee and me. When she saw that she was steadfastly minded to go with her, then she left speaking unto her.

So they two went until they came to Bethlehem. And it came to pass, when they were come to Bethlehem, that all the city was moved about them, and they said, Is this Naomi? And she said unto them, Call me not Naomi, call me Mara; for the Almighty hath dealt very bitterly with me. I went out full, and the Lord hath brought me home again empty. Why then call ye me Naomi, seeing the Lord hath testified against me, and the Almighty hath afflicted me? So Naomi returned, and Ruth the Moabitess, her daughter-in-law, with her, and they came to Bethlehem in the beginning of barley harvest.

And Naomi had a kinsman of her husband's, a mighty man of wealth, of the family of Elimelech; and his name was Boaz. And Ruth the Moabitess said unto Naomi, Let me now go to the field, and glean ears of corn after him in whose sight I shall find grace. And she said unto her, Go, my daughter. And she went, and came, and gleaned in the field after the reapers; and her hap was to light on a part of the field belonging to Boaz.

And, behold, Boaz came from Bethlehem, and said unto the reapers, The Lord be with you. And they answered him, The Lord bless thee. Then said Boaz unto his servant that was set over the reapers, Whose damsel is this? And the servant that was set over the reapers answered and said, It is the Moabitish damsel that came back with Naomi out of the country of Moab; and she said, I pray you, let me glean and gather after the reapers among the sheaves. So she came, and hath continued even from the morning until now, that she tarried a little in the house. Then said Boaz unto Ruth,

Hearest thou not, my daughter? Go not to glean in another field, neither go from hence, but abide here fast by my maidens. Let thine eyes be on the field that they do reap, and go thou after them. Have I not charged the young men that they shall not touch thee? And when thou art athirst, go unto the vessels, and drink of that which the young men have drawn.

Then she fell on her face, and bowed herself to the ground, and said unto him, Why have I found grace in thine eyes, that thou shouldst take knowledge of me, seeing I am a stranger? And Boaz answered and said unto her, It hath fully been showed me all that thou hast done unto thy mother-in-law since the death of thine husband; and how thou hast left thy father and thy mother and the land of thy nativity, and art come unto a people which thou knewest not heretofore. The Lord recompense thy work, and a full reward be given thee of the Lord God of Israel, under whose wings thou art come to trust. Then she said, Let me find favor in thy sight, my lord; for that thou hast comforted me, and for that thou hast spoken friendly unto thine handmaid, though I be not like unto one of thine handmaidens. And Boaz said unto her, At mealtime come thou hither, and eat of the bread, and dip thy morsel in the vinegar. And she sat beside the reapers; and he reached her parched corn, and she did eat, and was sufficed, and left. And when she was risen up to glean, Boaz commanded his young men, saying, Let her glean even among the sheaves, and reproach her not; and let fall also some of the handfuls of purpose for her, and leave them that she may glean them, and rebuke her not. So she gleaned in the field until even, and beat out that she had gleaned; and it was about an ephah of barley.

And she took it up and went into the city; and her mother-in-law saw what she had gleaned; and she brought forth, and gave to her that she had reserved after she was sufficed. And her mother-in-law said unto her, Where hast thou gleaned today? And where wroughtest thou? Blessed be he that did take knowledge of thee. And she showed her mother-in-law with whom she had wrought, and said, The man's name with whom I wrought today is Boaz. And Naomi said unto her, Blessed be he of the Lord, who hath not left off his kindness to the living and to the dead. And Naomi said unto her, The man is near of kin unto us, one of our next kinsmen. And Ruth said, He said unto me also, Thou shalt keep fast by my young men, until they have ended all my harvest. And Naomi said unto Ruth, It is good, my daughter, that thou go out with his maidens, that they meet thee not in any other field. So she kept fast by the maidens of Boaz to glean unto the end of barley harvest and of wheat harvest; and she dwelt with her mother-in-law.

Then Naomi said unto her, My daughter, shall I not seek rest for thee, that it may be well with thee? And now is not Boaz of our kindred, with whose maidens thou wast? Behold, he winnoweth barley tonight in the threshingfloor. Wash thyself therefore, and anoint thee, and put thy raiment upon thee, and get thee down to the floor; but make not thyself known unto the man until he shall have done eating and drinking. And it shall be, when he lieth down, that thou shalt mark the place where he shall lie, and thou shalt go in, and uncover his feet, and lay thee down; and he will tell thee what thou shalt do. And she said unto her, All that thou sayest unto me I will do.

And she went down unto the floor, and did according to all that her mother-in-law bade her. And when Boaz had eaten and drunk, and his heart was merry, he went to lie down at the end of the heap of corn; and she came softly and uncovered his feet, and laid her down. And it came to pass at midnight, that the man was afraid, and turned himself; and, behold, a woman lay at his feet. And he said, Who art thou? And she answered, I am Ruth thine handmaid. Spread therefore thy skirt over thine handmaid; for thou art a near kinsman. And he said, Blessed be thou of the Lord, my daughter; for thou hast showed more kindness in the latter end than at the beginning, inasmuch as thou followedst not young men, whether poor or rich. And now, my daughter, fear not; I will do to thee all that thou requirest; for all the city of my people doth know that thou art a virtuous woman. And now it is true that I am thy near kinsman; howbeit there is a kinsman nearer than I. Tarry this night, and it shall be in the morning, that if he will perform unto thee the part of a kinsman, well; let him do the kinsman's part; but if he will not do the part of a kinsman to thee, then will I do the part of a kinsman to thee, as the Lord liveth. Lie down until the morning. And she lay at his feet until the morning; and she rose up before one could know another. And he said, Let it not be known that a woman came into the floor. Also he said, Bring the veil that thou hast upon thee, and hold it. And when she held it, he measured six measures of barley, and laid it on her; and she went into the city.

And when she came to her mother-in-law, she said, Who art thou, my daughter? And she told her all that the man had done to her. And she said, These six measures of barley gave he me; for he said to me, Go not empty unto thy mother-in-law. Then she said, Sit still, my daughter, until thou know how the matter will fall; for the man will not be in rest until he have finished the thing this day.

Then went Boaz up to the gate, and sat him down there. And, behold, the kinsman of whom Boaz spake came by; unto whom he said, Ho, such a one! Turn aside, sit down here. And he turned aside, and sat down. And he took ten men of the elders of the city, and said, Sit ye down here. And they sat down. And he said unto the kinsman, Naomi, that is come again out of the country of Moab, selleth a parcel of land, which was our brother Elimelech's; and I thought to advertise thee, saying, Buy it before the inhabitants, and before the elders of my people. If thou wilt redeem it, redeem it; but if thou wilt not redeem it, then tell me, that I may know; for there is none to redeem it besides thee; and I am after thee. And he said, I will redeem it. Then said Boaz, What day thou buyest the field of the hand of Naomi, thou must buy it also of Ruth the Moabitess, the wife of the dead, to raise up the name of the dead upon his inheritance. And the kinsman said, I cannot redeem it for myself, lest I mar mine own inheritance. Redeem thou my right to thyself; for I cannot redeem it. Now this was the manner in former time in Israel concerning redeeming, and concerning changing, for to confirm all things: a man plucked off his shoe and gave it to his neighbor; and this was a testimony in Israel.

Therefore the kinsman said unto Boaz, Buy it for thee. So he drew off his shoe. And Boaz said unto the elders and unto all the people, Ye are witnesses this day that I have bought all that was Elimelech's and all that was Chilion's and Mahlon's of the hand of Naomi. Moreover, Ruth the Moabitess have I purchased to be my wife, to raise up the name of the dead upon his inheritance. Ye are witnesses this day. And all the people that were in the gate, and the elders said, We are witnesses. The Lord make the woman that is come into thine house like Rachel and like Leah, which two did build the house of Israel.

So Boaz took Ruth, and she was his wife; and when he went in unto her, the Lord gave her conception and she bare a son. And the woman said unto Naomi, Blessed be the Lord which hath not left thee this day without a kinsman, that his name may be famous in Israel. And he shall be unto thee a restorer of thy life and a nourisher of thine old age; for thy daughter-in-law, which loveth thee, which is better to thee than seven sons, hath borne him.

And Naomi took the child and laid it in her bosom and became nurse unto it. And the women her neighbors gave it a name, saying, There is a son born to Naomi! And they called his name Obed. He is the father of Jesse, the father of David.

JONAH

JONAH 1–3

Now the word of the Lord came unto Jonah the son of Amittai, saying, Arise, go to Nineveh; that great city, and cry against it; for their wickedness is come up before me. But Jonah rose up to flee unto Tarshish from the presence of the Lord, and went down to Joppa. And he found a ship going to Tarshish; so he paid the fare thereof, and went down into it, to go with them unto Tarshish from the presence of the Lord.

But the Lord sent out a great wind into the sea, and there was a mighty tempest in the sea, so that the ship was like to be broken. Then the mariners were afraid, and cried every man unto his god, and cast forth the wares that were in the ship into the sea, to lighten it of them. But Jonah was gone down into the sides of the ship; and he lay, and was fast asleep. So the shipmaster came to him, and said unto him, What meanest thou, O sleeper? Arise, call upon thy God, if so be that God will think upon us, that we perish not. And they said every one to his fellow, Come, and let us cast lots, that we may know for whose cause this evil is upon us. So they cast lots, and the lot fell upon Jonah. Then said they unto him, Tell us, we pray thee, for whose cause this evil is upon us? What is thine occupation? and whence comest thou? What is thy country? and of what people art thou? And he said unto them, I am a Hebrew; and I fear the Lord, the God of heaven, which hath made the sea and the dry land. Then were the men exceedingly afraid, and said unto him, Why hast thou done this? For the men knew that he fled from the presence of the Lord, because he had told them. Then said they unto him, What shall we do unto thee, that the sea may be calm unto us? And he said unto them, Take me up, and cast me forth into the sea; so shall the sea be calm unto you; for I know that for my sake this great tempest is upon you.

Nevertheless the men rowed hard to bring it to the land, but they could not; for the sea wrought, and was tempestuous against them. Wherefore they cried unto the Lord, and said, We beseech thee, O Lord, we beseech thee, let us not perish for this man's life, and lay not upon us innocent blood; for thou, O Lord, hast done as it pleased thee. So they took up Jonah and cast him forth into the sea; and the sea ceased from her raging. Then the men feared the Lord exceedingly, and offered a sacrifice unto the Lord, and made vows.

Now the Lord had prepared a great fish to swallow up Jonah. And Jonah was in the belly of the fish three days and three nights. Then Jonah prayed unto the Lord his God out of the fish's belly, and said:

I cried by reason of mine affliction unto the Lord,
And he heard me;
Out of the belly of hell cried I,
And thou heardest my voice.
For thou hadst cast me into the deep, in the midst of the seas;

And the floods compassed me about:
All thy billows and thy waves passed over me.
Then I said, I am cast out of thy sight;
Yet I will look again toward thy holy temple.
The waters compassed me about, even to the soul:
The depth closed me round about,
The weeds were wrapped about my head.
I went down to the bottoms of the mountains;
The earth with her bars was about me for ever:
Yet hast thou brought up my life from corruption, O Lord my God.
When my soul fainted within me I remembered the Lord:
And my prayer came in unto thee, into thine holy temple.
They that observe lying vanities forsake their own mercy.
But I will sacrifice unto thee with the voice of thanksgiving;
I will pay that that I have vowed.
Salvation is of the Lord.[1]

And the Lord spake unto the fish, and it vomited out Jonah upon the dry land.

And the word of the Lord came unto Jonah the second time, saying, Arise, go unto Nineveh, that great city, and preach unto it the preaching that I bid thee. So Jonah arose and went unto Nineveh, according to the word of the Lord. Now Nineveh was an exceeding great city of three days' journey. And Jonah began to enter into the city a day's journey, and he cried, and said, Yet forty days, and Nineveh shall be overthrown!

So the people of Nineveh believed God, and proclaimed a fast, and put on sackcloth, from the greatest of them even to the least of them. For word came unto the king of Nineveh, and he arose from his throne, and he laid his robe from him, and covered him with sackcloth, and sat in ashes. And he caused it to be proclaimed and published through Nineveh by the decree of the king and his nobles, saying, Let neither man nor beast, herd nor flock, taste any

[1] This song of Jonah was probably not in the original story, but is a later addition.

thing. Let them not feed, nor drink water. But let man and beast be covered with sackcloth, and cry mightily unto God; yea, let them turn every one from his evil way, and from the violence that is in their hands. Who can tell if God will turn and repent, and turn away from his fierce anger, that we perish not? And God saw their works, that they turned from their evil way; and God repented of the evil that he had said that he would do unto them; and he did it not.

But it displeased Jonah exceedingly, and he was very angry. And he prayed unto the Lord, and said, I pray thee, O Lord, was not this my saying when I was yet in my country? Therefore I fled before unto Tarshish; for I knew that thou art a gracious God, and merciful, slow to anger, and of great kindness, and repentest thee of the evil. Therefore now, O Lord, take, I beseech thee, my life from me; for it is better for me to die than to live.

Then said the Lord, Doest thou well to be angry? So Jonah went out of the city, and sat on the east side of the city, and there made him a booth, and sat under it in the shadow, till he might see what would become of the city. And the Lord God prepared a gourd, and made it to come up over Jonah that it might be a shadow over his head, to deliver him from his grief. So Jonah was exceeding glad of the gourd. But God prepared a worm when the morning rose the next day, and it smote the gourd that it withered. And it came to pass, when the sun did arise, that God prepared a vehement east wind; and the sun beat upon the head of Jonah, that he fainted, and wished in himself to die, and said, It is better for me to die than to live. And God said to Jonah, Doest thou well to be angry for the gourd? And he said, I do well to be angry, even unto death. Then said the Lord, Thou hast had pity on the gourd, for the which thou hast not labored, neither madest it grow, which came up in a night, and perished in a night. And should not I spare Nineveh, that great city, wherein are more than sixscore thousand persons that cannot discern between their right hand and their left hand; [2] and also much cattle?

[2] God is referring here, in this much exaggerated number, to the babies of Nineveh.

THE POETRY OF THE OLD TESTAMENT

In [illegible] emotional [illegible] the poetry of the Old Testament, the reader must understand something of its [illegible] form. The [illegible] used is the most striking feature [illegible] [illegible] [illegible] [illegible] of one [illegible] [illegible] [illegible]; the [illegible] is [illegible] of [illegible] parallelism of the lines [illegible] [illegible] that the two lines together [illegible]. This results in effect in a repetition of thought [illegible] of the thought.

There are several forms of this parallelism, three of which will be explained and illustrated here. The first, and most frequently used, is [illegible] synonymous parallelism. In this form the same thought is expressed in two or sometimes three [illegible] [illegible] [illegible] Examples:

The heavens declare the glory of God;
And the firmament sheweth his handywork.

or

Blessed above women shall Jael the wife of Heber the Kenite be,
Blessed shall she be [illegible]

Another [illegible] [illegible] [illegible] [illegible] second line [illegible] [illegible] [illegible] [illegible] [illegible] [illegible] [illegible] [illegible]

I [illegible]
And [illegible]

When I consider thy heavens, the work of thy fingers,
The moon and the stars, which thou hast ordained;
What is man, that thou art mindful of him?
And the son of man, [illegible]

A third kind [illegible] [illegible] [illegible] [illegible] [illegible] the line [illegible] [illegible] [illegible] thought. Example:

In order to enjoy and appreciate the poetry of the Old Testament, the reader must understand something of its characteristic form. The Hebrew poet used as the most striking feature of his verse, not rhyme, or even meter in our sense of that word, but rather a method of balance, or *parallelism*, of his lines, or sometimes of the two halves of one line. This results, in effect, in a repetition of thought accompanied often by similar words.

There are several forms of this parallelism, three of which will be explained and illustrated here. The most commonly used is known as *synonymous parallelism*. In this form the same thought is expressed in two, or sometimes in three or more, succeeding lines. Examples are:

The heavens declare the glory of God;
And the firmament showeth his handiwork.

or

Blessed above women shall Jael the wife of Heber the Kenite be;
Blessed shall she be above women in the tent.

Another common form is called *synthetic parallelism*. Here the second line, and sometimes the third as well, completes the first by giving the result of the first, or by exemplifying the first, and thus *synthesizing*, or joining, the thoughts of each. Examples are:

I cried unto the Lord with my voice,
And he heard me out of his holy hill.

or

When I consider thy heavens, the work of thy fingers,
The moon and the stars which thou hast ordained,
What is man that thou art mindful of him?
And the son of man that thou visitest him?

A third form, often used, is termed *antithetical parallelism*, since the final line, or lines, contrasts with the preceding by a directly opposite thought. Examples are:

Weeping may endure for a night;
But joy cometh in the morning.

or

A thousand shall fall at thy side,
And ten thousand at thy right hand;
But it shall not come nigh thee.

There are various other forms identified by scholars; but the three described here and most commonly used are sufficient to make the reading of the poetry relatively clear and intelligible. If the reader is interested in a more detailed account, he will find a full and excellent article in Hastings' *Dictionary of the Bible* and a shorter explanation in *The Bible and the Common Reader,* Pt. I.

– I –

THE HEBREW PROPHETS AND THEIR POETRY

Among ancient peoples the Hebrews were unique in the possession of prophets. Just as Greece revered her philosophers and as Rome honored her statesmen, so Israel extolled her prophets, always great teachers and often major poets as well.

In order more fully to appreciate the prophetic readings selected here, it is well to understand both the meaning of prophecy and the historical background which was responsible for its appearance in Israel and Judah. Our word "prophet" comes from a Greek word meaning "to speak in place of" or "to speak for." The Hebrew prophet devoutly believed that he was speaking for God, in other words, that he was delivering *in place of God* a divine message to God's people. Around 750–700 B.C., the time of the first prophets, Amos, Hosea, Micah, and Isaiah, the religious, social, and political situation in both Israel and Judah was causing alarm to the more thoughtful of their people. In the northern kingdom at this time matters were even more desperate than in the southern. The religious apostasy which Elijah and Elisha had deplored a century earlier had increased; a brief period of freedom from war had resulted in an era of prosperity, which in its turn had encouraged luxurious living and injustice toward the poor; a succession of weak rulers had not recognized the dangers threatening from the rising power of the Assyrian Empire, which in 722 B.C. was to conquer and annihilate the northern kingdom. Judah, more secure among its hills, more strong in its house of David, was for two more centuries to be spared such conquest and annihilation; but its tragedy was coming, as Isaiah too well knew.

Such, most briefly, was the background which called forth the Hebrew prophets. Further explanation will be given in the introductions to each. Since the arrangement of prophetic material in the Bible is often puzzling and even sometimes chronologically out of place, it has seemed best, for purposes of clearness, to rearrange it and, so far as possible, to supply titles for the individual poems and occasional prose passages.

The reader should also note references to material not included in the selections, but well worth careful attention.[1]

1

THE PROPHET AMOS

Amos, the first of the prophets, was, as he declares in his description of his call by God, a herdsman, tending his flocks in the wilderness of Tekoa above the Dead Sea, a lonely region which by its very isolation must have offered him encouragement for his thoughts. Although he was himself a Judean, his prophetic warnings were delivered at Bethel in Israel, where he probably journeyed to sell the wool from his sheep. Convinced that he was called to be a spokesman for God, he spares in his bitter and direful addresses none of those who gathered about the wells, shrines, and market places. He pronounces the certain doom of the rich who, living in luxury in their winter and their summer houses, delight in food and drink and oppress the poor; of the frivolous women of Israel, whom he terms "kine of Bashan"; and of all who, turning away from the righteousness demanded by God, either perform meaningless rituals in their own places of worship or follow after strange gods.

Because of his vigorous, ironic style, his terse and tense sentences, now in questions, now in commands, and his lack of forbearance and even of mercy, Amos is often called "the prophet of doom." But he should be remembered also for a conception of God revolutionary for his day: a God who cares not only for His "chosen people" but for the Ethiopians, the hated Philistines of the past, and the neighboring Syrians, the enemies of Israel.

FROM AMOS 1–9

The Prophet's Call

Then answered Amos, and said to Amaziah, priest of Bethel:

I was no prophet, neither was I a prophet's son;
But I was a herdsman, and a gatherer of sycamore fruit;

[1] An extended treatment on the meaning and significance of Hebrew prophecy is given in *The Bible and the Common Reader,* Pt. II.

And the Lord took me as I followed the flock,
And the Lord said unto me,
Go, prophesy unto my people Israel.
Now therefore hear thou the word of the Lord:
Thou sayest, Prophesy not against Israel,
And drop not thy word against the house of Isaac.
Therefore thus saith the Lord:
Thy wife shall be a harlot in the city,
And thy sons and thy daughters shall fall by the sword,
And thy land shall be divided by line;
And thou shalt die in a polluted land;
And Israel shall surely go into captivity forth of his land.

The Sins of Israel [2]

Thus saith the Lord:
For three transgressions of Israel,
And for four,
I will not turn away the punishment thereof;
Because they sold the righteous for silver,
And the poor for a pair of shoes;
That pant after the dust of the earth on the head of the poor,
And turn aside the way of the meek:
And a man and his father will go in unto the same maid,
To profane my holy name;
And they lay themselves down upon clothes laid to pledge by every altar,
And they drink the wine of the condemned in the house of their god.

Yet destroyed I the Amorite before them,
Whose height was like the height of the cedars,
And he was strong as the oaks;
Yet I destroyed his fruit from above,
And his roots from beneath.

[2] These stanzas on the transgressions of Israel are a climax to the recital of similar transgressions on the part of neighboring peoples. See Amos 1–2.

Also I brought you up from the land of Egypt,
And led you forty years through the wilderness,
To possess the land of the Amorite.
And I raised up of your sons for prophets,
And of your young men for Nazarites.
Is it not even thus, O ye children of Israel?
Saith the Lord.
But ye gave the Nazarites wine to drink,
And commanded the prophets,
Saying, Prophesy not.

Behold, I am pressed under you,
As a cart is pressed that is full of sheaves.
Therefore the flight shall perish from the swift,
And the strong shall not strengthen his force,
Neither shall the mighty deliver himself;
Neither shall he stand that handleth the bow;
And he that is swift of foot shall not deliver himself;
Neither shall he that rideth the horse deliver himself.
And he that is courageous among the mighty
Shall flee away naked in that day,
Saith the Lord.

The Lovers of Ease and Luxury

Woe to them that are at ease in Zion,
And trust in the mountain of Samaria.
Ye that put far away the evil day,
And cause the seat of violence to come near;
That lie upon beds of ivory,
And stretch themselves upon their couches,
And eat the lambs out of the flock,
And the calves out of the midst of the stall;
That chant to the sound of the viol,
And invent to themselves instruments of music;
That drink wine in bowls,

And anoint themselves with the chief ointments:
Therefore now shall they go captive with the first that go captive,
And the banquet of them that stretched themselves shall be removed.

For, behold, the Lord commandeth,
And he will smite the great house with breaches,
And the little house with clefts.
And I will smite the winter house with the summer house;
And the houses of ivory shall perish,
And the great houses shall have an end,
Saith the Lord.

The Women of Israel

Hear this word, ye kine of Bashan,
That are in the mountain of Samaria,
Which oppress the poor, which crush the needy,
Which say to their masters, Bring, and let us drink.
The Lord God hath sworn by his holiness,
That, lo, the days shall come upon you,
That he will take you away with hooks,
And your posterity with fishhooks.
And ye shall go out at the breaches,
Every cow at that which is before her;
And ye shall cast them into the palace,
Saith the Lord.

True Religion

God speaks:

I hate, I despise your feast days,
And I will not smell in your solemn assemblies.
Though ye offer me burnt offerings and your meat offerings,
I will not accept them;
Neither will I regard the peace offerings of your fat beasts.

Take thou away from me the noise of thy songs;
For I will not hear the melody of thy viols.
But let judgment run down as waters,
And righteousness as a mighty stream.

God as Father of All

Are ye not as children of the Ethiopians unto me,
O children of Israel? saith the Lord.
Have not I brought up Israel out of the land of Egypt?
And the Philistines from Caphtor,
And the Syrians from Kir?
Behold, the eyes of the Lord God are upon the sinful kingdom,
And I will destroy it from off the face of the earth;
Saving that I will not utterly destroy the house of Jacob,
Saith the Lord.

2
THE PROPHET HOSEA

Hosea, who probably wrote his book or uttered his prophecies a few years later than Amos, was a northern Israelite and, unlike Amos, a townsman rather than a dweller in the wilderness. Also unlike Amos, he was a man of tenderness and mercy, who was chiefly concerned not with any new and more liberal idea of God, but rather with Him as the bereaved Father of His backsliding children of Israel. Hosea's subjects are the same: the luxury of the rich, the injustice to the poor, the following after false goods, the apathy of Israel.

The first three chapters of his book,[1] which are written in prose, suggest that his sympathy and sadness arose from a tragic personal experience in his own life: the faithlessness of his wife Gomer whom, in spite of her adultery, Hosea at God's command forgives and reclaims as his wife. Perhaps this tragedy accounts for the theme of harlotry which runs throughout Hosea's poetry. Like his own wife, Israel has played the harlot with God, who is the symbol of a devoted husband to His people and who has never ceased to love them.

[1] These opening chapters, not given here, may well be read.

Hosea's poetry lacks the vigor and strength of that of Amos. His broken and plaintive lines suggest grief instead of anger. Yet to many he is the most lovable of the prophets because of the sympathy and underlying tenderness which mark his poetry. The many beautiful similes which he constantly uses prove a sensitive imagination and add immeasurably to the charm of his verse. And he never wholly despairs as to the fate of his people. Always he sounds the hope that they will awake and return unto God.

FROM HOSEA 1–14

The Grief of God over His Children

When Israel was a child, then I loved him,
And called my son out of Egypt.
As I called them, so they went from me;
They sacrificed unto Baalim,
And burned incense to graven images.
I taught Ephraim [2] also to go, taking them by their arms;
But they knew not that I healed them.
I drew them with cords of a man, with bands of love;
And I was to them as they that take off the yoke on their jaws,
And I laid meat unto them.

He shall not return into the land of Egypt,
But the Assyrian shall be his king,
Because they refused to return.
And the sword shall abide on his cities,
And shall consume his branches, and devour them,
Because of their own counsels,
And my people are bent to backsliding from me;
Though they called them to the most High,
None at all would exalt him.
And now they sin more and more,
And have made them molten images of their silver;

[2] Ephraim is another name for Israel, the northern kingdom.

Therefore they shall be as the morning cloud,
And as the early dew that passeth away,
As the chaff that is driven with the whirlwind,
And as the smoke out of the chimney.
O Israel, thou hast destroyed thyself;
But in me is thine help.
I will be thy king:
Where is any other that may save thee in all thy cities?

How shall I give thee up, Ephraim?
How shall I deliver thee, Israel?
Mine heart is turned within me,
My repentings are kindled together.
I will not execute the fierceness of mine anger,
I will not return to destroy Ephraim:
For I am God, and not man;
The Holy One in the midst of thee.

The Final Redemption of Israel

God speaks:

O Ephraim, what shall I do unto thee?
O Judah, what shall I do unto thee?
For your goodness is as a morning cloud,
And as the early dew it goeth away.
I know Ephraim, and Israel is not hid from me.
For now, O Ephraim, thou committest whoredom,
And Israel is defiled.
For I desired mercy, and not sacrifice,
And the knowledge of God more than burnt offerings.
I have seen a horrible thing in the house of Israel:
There is the whoredom of Ephraim, Israel is defiled.
O Israel, return unto the Lord thy God;
For thou hast fallen by thine iniquity.
Take with you words, and turn to the Lord:

Israel speaks:

Come and let us return unto the Lord:
For he hath torn, and he will heal us;
He hath smitten and he will bind us up.
After two days will he revive us;
In the third day he will raise us up,
And we shall live in his sight.
Then shall we know, if we follow on to know the Lord:
His going forth is prepared as the morning,
And he shall come unto us as the rain,
As the latter and former rain unto the earth.

God speaks:

I will heal their backsliding, I will love them freely,
For mine anger is turned away from them.
I will be as the dew unto Israel:
He shall grow as the lily, and cast forth his roots as Lebanon;
His branches shall spread, and his beauty shall be as the olive tree.
They that dwell under his shadow shall return;
They shall revive as the corn and grow as the vine.
Ephraim shall say, What have I to do any more with idols?
I have heard God and observed him:
I am like a green fir tree;
From me is thy fruit found.
Who is wise, and he shall understand these things?
Prudent, and he shall know them?
For the ways of the Lord are right,
And the just shall walk in them.

3

THE PROPHET ISAIAH

Isaiah is, without doubt, the chief of all the Hebrew prophets. He was a statesman, an adviser to kings, as well as a prophetic teacher; a man of truly exalted religious conceptions; and a poet unsurpassed in the beauty and nobility of his language. He was born in Jerusalem around 770–760 B.C., and for forty years prophesied and taught in that city. Tradition says that he was of aristocratic birth, and it is very probable that he did come from a well known family, for he seems to have had early access to the kings of Judah.

His life was filled with concern and anxiety over the fate of his country. In 722 B.C. he saw the northern kingdom of Israel conquered by Assyria and its people driven into exile. He saw Judah become a vassal state of the same empire, and recognized that its complete conquest also might well be only a matter of time. He labored with kings, inferior to him in intelligence, to avert this disaster; and, above all else, he strove to reform the social evils of his day and to bring back his people to a sense of their dependence upon God.

The long book of sixty-six chapters called by his name has been the subject of much study on the part of scholars. Quite obviously most of it was not written by him, but by authors of a far later date. His own writings are scattered throughout chapters 1–39, most of those unquestionably his being contained in chapters 1–12. Since the arrangement of even these twelve chapters is not chronological, it has seemed wise to rearrange the selections given here. Isaiah's work should begin with chapter 6, which records in magnificent poetic prose his vision as a young man in the Temple at Jerusalem in the year 740 B.C.

The poetry of Isaiah is distinguished not only for its exalted expression, but also for its breadth and variety of subject matter and of style, as the readings will bear witness. He was the first among the prophets to express certain religious ideas: the vision of final peace in the world; the coming of a Messiah who will ensure that peace; the idea of Jerusalem as the symbol of the City of God; and, above all else, the conception of worship as the highest spiritual expression of man. These ideas run throughout his poetry.

FROM ISAIAH 1–12

The Prophet's Call

In the year that King Uzziah died I saw also the Lord sitting upon a throne, high and lifted up, and his train filled the temple. Above it stood the seraphim; each one had six wings; with twain he covered his face, and with twain he covered his feet, and with twain he did fly. And one cried unto another, and said, Holy, holy, holy, is the Lord of Hosts! The whole earth is full of his glory. And the posts of the door moved at the voice of him that cried, and the house was filled with smoke.

Then said I, Woe is me! for I am undone, because I am a man of unclean lips, and I dwell in the midst of a people of unclean lips. For mine eyes have seen the King, the Lord of Hosts.

Then flew one of the seraphim unto me, having a live coal in his hand, which he had taken with the tongs from off the altar; and he laid it upon my mouth, and said, Lo, this hath touched thy lips; and thine iniquity is taken away, and thy sin purged.

Also I heard the voice of the Lord, saying, Whom shall I send, and who will go for us? Then said I, Here am I. Send me.

The Song of the Vineyard

Now will I sing to my well beloved
A song of my beloved touching his vineyard.

My well beloved hath a vineyard
In a very fruitful hill.
And he fenced it and gathered out the stones thereof,
And planted it with the choicest vine,
And built a tower in the midst of it,
And also made a winepress therein.
And he looked that it should bring forth grapes,
And it brought forth wild grapes.

And now, O inhabitants of Jerusalem and men of Judah,
Judge, I pray you, betwixt me and my vineyard.
What could have been done more to my vineyard
That I have not done in it?
Wherefore, when I looked that it should bring forth grapes,
Brought it forth wild grapes?

And now go to! I will tell you
What I will do to my vineyard:
I will take away the hedge thereof, and it shall be eaten up;
And break down the wall thereof, and it shall be trodden down;
And I will lay it waste: It shall not be pruned nor digged;
But there shall come up briers and thorns.
I will also command the clouds
That they rain no rain upon it.

For the vineyard of the Lord of Hosts is the house of Israel,
And the men of Judah his pleasant plant;
And he looked for judgment, but behold oppression;
For righteousness, but behold a cry.

Two Prophetic Poems on the Desolation of Judah

1

Hear, O heavens, and give ear, O earth,
For the Lord hath spoken:

I have nourished and brought up children,
And they have rebelled against me.
The ox knoweth his owner,
And the ass his master's crib,
But Israel doth not know,
My people doth not consider.

Ah, sinful nation, a people laden with iniquity!
A seed of evildoers, children that are corrupters!
They have forsaken the Lord,
They have provoked the Holy One of Israel unto anger,
They are gone away backward.

Why should ye be stricken any more?
Ye will revolt more and more.
The whole head is sick and the whole heart faint.

From the sole of the foot even unto the head
There is no soundness in it;
But wounds, and bruises, and putrifying sores;
They have not been closed, neither bound up,
Neither mollified with ointment.

Your country is desolate, your cities are burned with fire,
Your land, strangers devour it in your presence,
And it is desolate, as overthrown by strangers.
And the daughter of Zion is left as a cottage in a vineyard,
As a lodge in a garden of cucumbers,
As a besieged city.
Except the Lord of Hosts had left unto us a very small remnant,
We should have been as Sodom,
We should have been like unto Gomorrah.

2

Enter into the rock, and hide thee in the dust,
For fear of the Lord, and for the glory of his majesty.
The lofty looks of man shall be humbled,
And the haughtiness of men shall be bowed down,
And the Lord alone shall be exalted in that day.
For the day of the Lord of Hosts
Shall be upon every one that is proud and lofty,
And upon every one that is lifted up;
And he shall be brought low;
And upon all the cedars of Lebanon, that are high and lifted up,
And upon all the oaks of Bashan,
And upon all the high mountains,
And upon all the hills that are lifted up,
And upon every high tower,
And upon every fenced wall,
And upon all the ships of Tarshish,
And upon all pleasant pictures.
And the loftiness of man shall be bowed down,

And the haughtiness of men shall be made low;
And the Lord alone shall be exalted in that day.
And the idols he shall utterly abolish.
And they shall go into the holes of the rocks,
And into the caves of the earth,
For fear of the Lord, and for the glory of his majesty,
When he ariseth to shake terribly the earth.

In that day a man shall cast his idols of silver, and his idols of gold,
Which they made each one for himself to worship,
To the moles and to the bats;
To go into the clefts of the rocks,
And into the tops of the ragged rocks,
For fear of the Lord, and for the glory of his majesty,
When he ariseth to shake terribly the earth.
Cease ye from man, whose breath is in his nostrils;
For wherein is he to be accounted of?

The Daughters of Zion

Because the daughters of Zion are haughty,
And walk with stretched forth necks and wanton eyes,
Walking and mincing as they go,
And making a tinkling with their feet:
Therefore the Lord will smite with a scab
The crown of the head of the daughters of Zion,
And the Lord will discover their secret parts.
In that day the Lord will take away
The bravery of their tinkling ornaments about their feet,
And their cauls, and their round tires like the moon,
The chains, and the bracelets, and the mufflers,
The bonnets, and the ornaments of the legs,
And the headbands, and the tablets, and the earrings,
The rings, and nose jewels,
The changeable suits of apparel,
And the mantles, and the wimples, and the crisping pins,
The glasses, and the fine linen, and the hoods, and the veils.

And it shall come to pass,
That instead of sweet smell there shall be stink;
And instead of a girdle a rent;
And instead of well set hair baldness;
And instead of a stomacher a girding of sackcloth;
And burning instead of beauty.
Thy men shall fall by the sword,
And thy mighty in the war.
And her gates shall lament and mourn,
And she being desolate shall sit upon the ground.

The Sins of Jerusalem and Judah

Hear the word of the Lord,
Ye rulers of Sodom!
Give ear unto the law of our God,
Ye people of Gomorrah!
To what purpose is the multitude of your sacrifices unto me?
Saith the Lord.
I am full of the burnt offerings of rams,
And the fat of fed beasts;
And I delight not in the blood of bullocks,
Or of lambs, or of he-goats.
When ye come to appear before me,
Who hath required this at your hand,
To tread my courts?
Bring no more vain oblations;
Incense is an abomination unto me;
The new moons and sabbaths, the calling of assemblies,
I cannot away with;
It is iniquity, even the solemn meeting.
Your new moons and your appointed feasts my soul hateth;
They are a trouble unto me; I am weary to bear them.
And when ye spread forth your hands,
I will hide mine eyes from you;
Yea, when ye make many prayers,

I will not hear;
Your hands are full of blood.
How is the faithful city become a harlot!
It was full of judgment; righteousness lodged in it;
But now murderers.
Thy silver is become dross,
Thy wine is mixed with water.
Thy princes are rebellious and companions of thieves;
Every one loveth gifts and followeth after rewards.
They judge not the fatherless,
Neither doth the cause of the widow come unto them.

Wash you, make you clean;
Put away the evil of your doings from before mine eyes.
Cease to do evil;
Learn to do well;
Seek judgment, relieve the oppressed,
Judge the fatherless, plead for the widow.
Come now, and let us reason together,
Saith the Lord:
Though your sins be as scarlet,
They shall be white as snow;
Though they be red like crimson,
They shall be as wool.
If ye be willing and obedient,
Ye shall eat the good of the land.
But if ye refuse and rebel,
Ye shall be devoured with the sword;
For the mouth of the Lord hath spoken it.

The Coming of Assyria

And he will lift up an ensign to the nations from far,
And will hiss unto them from the end of the earth;
And behold they shall come with speed swiftly.
None shall be weary nor stumble among them;
None shall slumber nor sleep.

Neither shall the girdle of their loins be loosed,
Nor the latchet of their shoes be broken.
Whose arrows are sharp and all their bows bent;
Their horses' hoofs shall be counted like flint,
And their wheels like a whirlwind.
Their roaring shall be like a lion;
They shall roar like young lions;
Yea, they shall roar and lay hold of the prey,
And shall carry it away safe, and none shall deliver it.
And in that day they shall roar against them
Like the roaring of the sea;
And if one look unto the land, behold darkness and sorrow;
And the light is darkened in the heavens thereof.

The Messianic Poems

1

And it shall come to pass in the last days
That the mountain of the Lord's house
Shall be established in the top of the mountains,
And shall be exalted above the hills;
And all nations shall flow unto it.
And many people shall go and say:
Come ye, and let us go up to the mountain of the Lord,
To the house of the God of Jacob.
And he will teach us of his ways,
And we will walk in his paths;
For out of Zion shall go forth the law,
And the word of the Lord from Jerusalem.
And he shall judge among the nations,
And shall rebuke many people;
And they shall beat their swords into plowshares
And their spears into pruning-hooks.
Nation shall not lift up sword against nation,
Neither shall they learn war any more.

2

The people that walked in darkness
Have seen a great light;
They that dwell in the land of the shadow of death,
Upon them hath the light shined.
Thou hast multiplied the nation, increased the joy;
They joy before thee according to the joy in harvest,
And as men rejoice when they divide the spoil.
For thou hast broken the yoke of his burden,
And the staff of his shoulder,
The rod of his oppressor,
As in the day of Midian.
For unto us a child is born, unto us a son is given;
And the government shall be upon his shoulder;
And his name shall be called
Wonderful, Counsellor, The mighty God,
The everlasting Father, The Prince of Peace.
Of the increase of his government and peace
There shall be no end,
Upon the throne of David, and upon his kingdom,
To order it, and to establish it
With judgment and with justice
From henceforth even forever.
The zeal of the Lord of Hosts will perform this.

3

And there shall come forth a rod out of the stem of Jesse,
And a Branch shall grow out of his roots.
And the spirit of the Lord shall rest upon him,
The spirit of wisdom and understanding,
The spirit of counsel and might,
The spirit of knowledge and of the fear of the Lord;
And shall make him of quick understanding in the fear of the Lord.

And he shall not judge after the sight of his eyes,
Neither reprove after the hearing of his ears;
But with righteousness shall he judge the poor,
And reprove with equity for the meek of the earth.
And he shall smite the earth with the rod of his mouth,
And with the breath of his lips shall he slay the wicked.
And righteousness shall be the girdle of his loins,
And faithfulness the girdle of his reins.
The wolf also shall dwell with the lamb,
And the leopard shall lie down with the kid;
And the calf and the young lion and the fatling together;
And a little child shall lead them.
And the cow and the bear shall feed;
Their young ones shall lie down together,
And the lion shall eat straw like the ox.
And the sucking child shall play on the hole of the asp,
And the weaned child shall put his hand on the cockatrice's den.
They shall not hurt nor destroy
In all my holy mountain:
For the earth shall be full of the knowledge of the Lord,
As the waters cover the sea.

The New Jerusalem

In that day shall the branch of the Lord be beautiful and glorious,
And the fruit of the earth shall be excellent and comely
For them that are escaped of Israel.
And it shall come to pass that he that is left in Zion
And he that remaineth in Jerusalem
Shall be called holy,
Even every one that is written among the living in Jerusalem.
And the Lord will create upon every dwelling place of mount Zion
And upon her assemblies
A cloud and smoke by day,
And the shining of a flaming fire by night,
And upon all, the glory shall be a defense.

And in that day thou shalt say, O Lord, I will praise thee!
Though thou wast angry with me,
Thine anger is turned away and thou comfortedst me.
Behold, God is my salvation.
I will trust and not be afraid;
For the Lord Jehovah is my strength and my song;
He also is become my salvation.
Sing unto the Lord,
For he hath done excellent things:
This is known in all the earth.
Cry out and shout, thou inhabitant of Zion!
For great is the Holy One of Israel
In the midst of thee.

4

THE PROPHET MICAH

Micah was a contemporary of Isaiah. He came from the small village of Moresheth near the once-famous Philistine city of Gath. His brief book of seven chapters is characterized for the most part by intense and even angry upbraidings of both Israel and Judah for the same sins which burdened the minds of Amos and Isaiah: idolatry, luxury, the oppression of the poor. Yet in chapter 4, obviously influenced by Isaiah, he echoes the beautiful hopes of his fellow prophet about the cessation of war; and in chapter 6 he defines in noble words what he believes to be the quality and the essence of true religion. He is, indeed, distinguished among the prophets and perhaps best remembered by countless readers for this poem, given here as his chief contribution to prophetic poetry.

True Religion

Wherewith shall I come before the Lord,
And bow myself before the high God?
Shall I come before him with burnt offerings,
With calves of a year old?
Will the Lord be pleased with thousands of rams,

Or with ten thousands of rivers of oil?
Shall I give my firstborn for my transgression,
The fruit of my body for the sin of my soul?
He hath showed thee, O man, what is good.
And what doth the Lord require of thee,
But to do justly, and to love mercy,
And to walk humbly with thy God?

5

THE PROPHET JEREMIAH

None among the great Hebrew prophets is so difficult to introduce and even partially to explain as is Jeremiah. His long book of fifty-two chapters, many of which are written in undistinguished prose, contains a vast variety of material: the prophet's laments and confessions, denunciations and warnings; his biography, supposedly dictated to Baruch, his companion and secretary; and various oracles against foreign nations. Moreover, Jeremiah because of his sadness and despair has through the centuries come to be regarded only as "the weeping prophet" and unfortunately avoided because of his "pessimism." Perhaps also the early but false assumption that he was the author of Lamentations, an anonymous and elaborate dirge on the Fall of Jerusalem, has contributed to the general misconception of him and hence to a lack of understanding of his actual character and stature and of a real appreciation of his poetry.

For Jeremiah in many ways is the most appealing of the prophets. More tender and sensitive by nature than any of them, except Hosea, whom he resembles in personality, ideas, and literary expression, he spent his life in a hopeless endeavor to save his country from the siege and conquest of Babylon, finally accomplished in 586 B.C. Reviled and persecuted by weak and vacillating kings of Judah, hated and misunderstood by his people, he nevertheless kept secure and invulnerable his personal integrity and his absolute reliance upon God. Of all the prophets, his sense of personal communion with God as the one necessity of man's life on earth is the deepest; and much of the sadness and grief rightly attributed to him arose from the bitter fact that he could not persuade others of this inner truth. He was thus one of the most solitary of men, moved always by a spiritual vision and idealism unattainable and even undesired by those whom he tried to teach. Unlike Amos, Hosea, and

Isaiah, he does not deal so much with the social sins of his people as with their religious apostasy, their hardness of heart, and their spiritual apathy and blindness.

Jeremiah came of a priestly family living in the hill village of Anathoth near Jerusalem. His many references to birds, to the fields, and to farm animals in his poetry show his love of the country and his homesickness for it. For he was destined to spend in Jerusalem the stormy years between 626 and 586 B.C., and to wage a losing battle against the certain destruction of that city, which to him, as to Isaiah one hundred years earlier, was the City of God.

The passages chosen from his writings (some of them taken out of their places and reassembled for the sake of greater clearness and unity) illustrate certain characteristics of him as man and poet: his overwhelming sorrow over the fate of his country which results in poetry filled with minor tones and cadences; his moments of despair over himself and his failure; his sense of communion with God; his never vanquished and even exultant hope of the final restoration of all Israel and of that New Covenant which God would at last make with His repentant children.[1]

The Prophet's Call

FROM JEREMIAH I

Then the word of the Lord came unto me saying:

Before I formed thee in the belly, I knew thee;
And before thou camest out of the womb, I sanctified thee;
And I ordained thee a prophet unto the nations.

Then said I: Ah, Lord God! behold, I cannot speak; for I am a child. But the Lord said unto me: Say not, I am a child; for thou shalt go to all that I shall send thee and whatsoever I command thee, thou shalt speak. Be not afraid of their faces; for I am with thee to deliver thee, saith the Lord.

[1] Readers are urged to learn more of Jeremiah's labors as a statesman and prophet from his biographical chapters, 26–45, and also from II Kings 18–25, which gives an account of the rulers of his day and of the siege of Jerusalem by Nebuchadnezzar of Babylon. They are referred also to *The Bible and the Common Reader*, Pt. II, for a fuller treatment of Jeremiah's background.

Then the Lord put forth his hand and touched my mouth. And the Lord said unto me: Behold, I have put my words in thy mouth. See, I have this day set thee over the nations and over the kingdoms, to root out and to pull down and to destroy, and to throw down, to build, and to plant.

Moreover, the word of the Lord came unto me, saying: Jeremiah, what seest thou? And I said, I see a rod of an almond tree. Then said the Lord unto me: Thou hast well seen; for I will hasten my word to perform it. And the word of the Lord came unto me the second time, saying: What seest thou? And I said, I see a seething pot, and the face thereof is toward the north.

Then the Lord said unto me: Out of the north an evil shall break forth upon all the inhabitants of the land. For, lo, I will call all the families of the kingdoms of the north; and they shall come, and they shall set every one his throne at the entering of the gates of Jerusalem, and against all the walls thereof round about, and against all the cities of Judah. And I will utter my judgments against them touching all their wickedness, who have forsaken me, and have burned incense unto other gods, and worshipped the works of their own hands. Thou therefore gird up thy loins, and arise, and speak unto them all that I command thee. Be not dismayed at their faces, lest I confound thee before them. For, behold, I have made thee this day a defenced city, and an iron pillar, and brazen walls against the whole land, against the kings of Judah, against the princes thereof, against the priests thereof, and against the people of the land. And they shall fight against thee; but they shall not prevail against thee; for I am with thee, saith the Lord, to deliver thee.

The Sins of Judah

FROM JEREMIAH 7–8

God speaks:

Seest thou not what they do in the cities of Judah
And in the streets of Jerusalem?
The children gather wood, and the fathers kindle the fire,

And the women knead their dough to make cakes to the Queen of Heaven,
And to pour out drink offerings unto other gods
That they may provoke me to anger.
Do they provoke me to anger? saith the Lord.
Do they not provoke themselves to the confusion of their own faces?
Behold, mine anger and my fury shall be poured out upon this place,
Upon man, and upon beast, and upon the trees of the field,
And upon the fruit of the ground;
And it shall burn, and shall not be quenched.

At that time, saith the Lord, they shall bring out the bones of the kings of Judah,
And the bones of the princes, and the bones of the priests,
And the bones of the prophets, and the bones of the inhabitants of Jerusalem
Out of their graves,
And they shall spread them before the sun and the moon,
And all the host of heaven whom they have loved,
And whom they have served, and after whom they have walked,
And whom they have sought and whom they have worshipped.
They shall not be gathered nor be buried;
They shall be for dung upon the face of the earth.

Why then is this people of Jerusalem slidden back?
They hold fast deceit, they refuse to return.
Yea, the stork in the heaven knoweth her appointed times,
And the turtle and the crane and the swallow observe the time of their coming;
But my people know not the judgment of the Lord.
I will surely consume them, saith the Lord.
There shall be no grapes on the vine,
Nor figs on the fig tree,
And the leaf shall fade;
And the things that I have given them shall pass away from them.

Then will I cause to cease from the cities of Judah
And from the streets of Jerusalem
The voice of mirth and the voice of gladness,
The voice of the bridegroom and the voice of the bride;
For the land shall be desolate.

The Dark Days to Come

FROM JEREMIAH 4–6

Thus saith the Lord:

I will bring evil from the north,
And a great destruction.
The lion is come up from his thicket,
And the destroyer of the Gentiles is on his way.
He is gone forth from his place to make thy land desolate,
And thy cities shall be laid waste, without an inhabitant.
And it shall come to pass at that day
That the heart of the king shall perish,
And the heart of the princes;
And the priests shall be astonished,
And the prophets shall wonder.

Lo, I will bring a nation upon you from far, O house of Israel.
It is a mighty nation, it is an ancient nation,
A nation whose language thou knowest not,
Neither understandest what they say.
Their quiver is as an open sepulchre;
They are all mighty men.
They shall lay hold on bow and spear;
They are cruel and have no mercy;
Their voice roareth like the sea,
And they ride upon horses.
They shall eat up thine harvest and thy bread
Which thy sons and thy daughters should eat.
They shall eat up thy flocks and thine herds;
They shall eat up thy vines and thy fig trees.

They shall impoverish thy fenced cities.
The whole land shall be desolate,
The whole city shall flee
For the noise of the horsemen and bowmen.
They shall go into thickets and climb up upon the rocks.
Every city shall be forsaken, and not a man dwell therein.

And when thou art spoiled, what wilt thou do?
Though thou clothest thyself with crimson,
Though thou deckest thee with ornaments of gold,
Though thou rentest thy face with painting,
In vain shalt thou make thyself fair;
Thy lovers will despise thee, they will seek thy life.
For I have heard a voice as of a woman in travail,
And the anguish as of her that bringeth forth her first child:
The voice of the daughter of Zion,
That bewaileth herself, that spreadeth her hands,
Saying, Woe is me now!

Jeremiah Curses His Birth

FROM JEREMIAH 15 AND 20

Woe is me, my mother,
That thou hast borne me a man of strife
And a man of contention to the whole earth!
Cursed be the day wherein I was born!
Let not the day wherein my mother bare me be blessed!
Cursed be the man who brought tidings to my father, saying,
A man child is born unto thee, making him very glad!
Let that man be as the cities which the Lord overthrew;
Let him hear the cry in the morning
And the shouting at noontide,
Because he slew me not from the womb!
O that my mother might have been my grave
And her womb always great with me!
Wherefore came I forth from the womb

To see labor and sorrow
That my days should be consumed with shame?

A Prayer of Jeremiah

FROM JEREMIAH 14

O Lord, though our iniquities testify against us,
Do thou forgive for thy name's sake.
For our backslidings are many;
We have sinned against thee.
O the hope of Israel, the Savior thereof in time of trouble,
Why shouldest thou be as a stranger in the land?
And as a wayfaring man that turneth aside to tarry for a night?
Why shouldest thou be as a man astonished?
As a mighty man that cannot save?
Yet thou, O Lord, art in the midst of us,
And we are called by thy name;
Leave us not.

Hast thou utterly rejected Judah?
Hath thy soul loathed Zion?
Why hast thou smitten us, and there is no healing for us?
We looked for peace, and there is no good,
For the time of healing, and behold trouble!
We acknowledge, O Lord, our wickedness,
And the iniquity of our fathers,
For we have sinned against thee.
Do not abhor us, for thy name's sake,
Do not disgrace the throne of thy glory.
Remember, break not thy covenant with us!
Are there any among the vanities of the Gentiles
That can cause rain?
Or make the heavens give showers?
Art not thou he, O Lord our God?
Therefore we will wait upon thee,
For thou hast made all these things.

Jeremiah's Lament for Israel

FROM JEREMIAH 8

When I would comfort myself against sorrow,
My heart is faint within me.
Behold the voice of the cry of the daughter of my people
Because of them that dwell in a far country:
Is not the Lord in Zion? Is not her king in her?
The harvest is past, the summer is ended,
And we are not saved.

For the hurt of the daughter of my people am I hurt;
Astonishment hath taken hold on me.
Is there no balm in Gilead?
Is there no physician there?

A Dirge for Israel

FROM JEREMIAH 9

God speaks in sorrow:

For the mountains will I take up a weeping and wailing,
And for the habitations of the wilderness a lamentation,
Because they are burned up so that none can pass through them.
Both the fowl of the heavens and the beast are fled;
They are gone.

Consider ye, and call for the mourning women,
That they may come;
And send for cunning women,
That they may come.
And let them make haste and take up a wailing for us
That our eyes may run down with tears,
And our eyelids gush out with waters.
For a voice of wailing is heard out of Zion:
How are we spoiled! We are greatly confounded
Because we have forsaken the land,
Because our dwellings have cast us out.

Yet hear the word of the Lord, O ye women,
And let your ear receive the word of his mouth,
And teach your daughters wailing,
And every one her neighbor lamentation.
For death is come up into our windows
And is entered into our palaces
To cut off the children from without
And the young men from the streets.

The Restoration of the People of God

FROM JEREMIAH 31

At the same time, saith the Lord,
Will I be the God of all the families of Israel,
And they shall be my people.
Thus saith the Lord:
The people which were left of the sword found grace in the wilderness;
Even Israel, when I went to cause him to rest.
The Lord hath appeared of old unto me, saying:
Yea, I have loved thee with an everlasting love;
Therefore with lovingkindness have I drawn thee.
Again I will build thee,
And thou shalt be built, O virgin of Israel:
Thou shalt again be adorned with thy tabrets,
And shalt go forth in the dances of them that make merry.
Thou shalt yet plant vines upon the mountains of Samaria;
The planters shall plant and shall eat them as common things.

For there shall be a day that the watchmen upon mount Ephraim shall cry,
Arise ye, and let us go up to Zion unto the Lord our God!
For thus saith the Lord:
Sing with gladness for Jacob,
And shout among the chief of the nations:
Publish ye, praise ye, and say,

O Lord, save thy people, the remnant of Israel.
Behold, I will bring them from the north country,
And gather them from the coasts of the earth,
And with them the blind and the lame,
The woman with child and her that travaileth with child together;
A great company shall return thither.
They shall come with weeping,
And with supplications will I lead them.
I will cause them to walk by the rivers of water
In a straight way, wherein they shall not stumble.
For I am a father to Israel,
And Ephraim is my firstborn.

Hear the word of the Lord, O ye nations,
And declare it in the isles thereof:
He that scattered Israel will gather him
And keep him, as a shepherd doth his flock.
For the Lord hath redeemed Jacob,
And ransomed him from the hand that was stronger than he.
Therefore they shall come and sing in the height of Zion,
And shall flow together to the goodness of the Lord,
For wheat, and for wine, and for oil,
And for the young of the flock and of the herd;
And their soul shall be as a watered garden,
And they shall not sorrow any more at all.
Then shall the virgin rejoice in the dance,
Both young men and old together;
For I will turn their mourning into joy,
I will comfort them and make them rejoice from their sorrow.

Thus saith the Lord:
A voice was heard in Ramah,
Lamentation and bitter weeping;
Rachel, weeping for her children,
Refused to be comforted for her children,
Because they were not.

Thus saith the Lord:
Refrain thy voice from weeping,
And thine eyes from tears,
For thy work shall be rewarded, saith the Lord;
And they shall come again from the land of the enemy.
And there is hope in thine end, saith the Lord,
That thy children shall come again to their own border.

Behold, the days come, saith the Lord,
That I will make a new covenant with the house of Israel,
And with the house of Judah:
Not according to the covenant that I made with their fathers
In the day that I took them by the hand
To bring them out of the land of Egypt.
But this shall be the covenant that I will make with the house of
 Israel:
I will put my law in their inward parts,
And I will write it in their hearts,
And I will be their God,
And they shall be my people.
And they shall teach no more every man his neighbor,
And every man his brother, saying, Know the Lord;
For they shall all know me,
From the least unto the greatest of them, saith the Lord.
I will forgive their iniquity,
And I will remember their sin no more.

6

NAHUM

FROM NAHUM 2–3[1]

Although Nahum is numbered among the Hebrew prophets, he was instead a great patriot and poet, as is evident from the one poem of his which has been preserved. This poem, which we may call *A Vision of*

[1] The first of the three chapters which comprise the book of Nahum does not belong to the original poem. It is a psalm added by some editor at a much later date.

the Destruction of Nineveh, was written sometime between 625 and 612 B.C., at which later date Nineveh was destroyed by the combined forces of the Medes and the Babylonians.

There is every reason for the fierce and bitter hatred which fills Nahum's description of the "bloody city," her frenzied attempts at defense against her enemies, her final overthrow. For one hundred years the great Assyrian Empire had instilled terror into both Israel and Judah. Despoiling and annexing the northern kingdom in 722, she had exacted tribute from Judah, dominated its policies, and threatened its destruction also; and when her rapid decline began about the year 625 and her own downfall became inevitable, Nahum's exultant, awful words may be read as the revengeful thoughts and hopes of thousands of his people.

His poem ranks with the Song of Deborah, written five centuries earlier, as an unsurpassed example of the ancient poetry of war. The sense of confusion and terror within the stricken city, the hurried orders for its defense, the brilliant, ironic images of its former grandeur and evil power, the details of the siege—all these show the power of Nahum as a poet. And the final quiet epilogue, or epitaph, which describes the city as a place where even shepherds slumber while freed nations clap their hands, makes clear the range of his genius.

A Vision of the Destruction of Nineveh

He that dasheth in pieces is come up before thy face.
Keep the munition,
Watch the way, make thy loins strong,
Fortify thy power mightily.

The shield of his mighty men is made red,
The valiant men are in scarlet;
The chariots shall be with flaming torches
In the day of his preparation,
And the fir trees shall be terribly shaken.
The chariots shall rage in the streets,
They shall jostle one against another in the broad ways;
They shall seem like torches,
They shall run like the lightnings.

They shall stumble in their walk;
They shall make haste to the wall thereof,
And the defence shall be prepared.

The gates of the rivers shall be opened,
And the palace shall be dissolved.
And Huzzab [2] shall be led away captive,
She shall be brought up,
And her maids shall lead her as with the voice of doves,
Taboring upon their breasts.
But Nineveh is of old like a pool of water;
Yet they shall flee away.
Stand, stand, shall they cry,
But none shall look back.

She is empty, and void, and waste;
And the heart melteth, and the knees smite together,
And much pain is in all loins,
And the faces of them all gather blackness.
Where is the dwelling of the lions?
And the feeding place of the young lions
Where the lion and the lion's whelp walked
And none made them afraid?

Woe to the bloody city!
It is all full of lies and robbery!
The horseman lifteth up the bright sword and the glittering spear,
And there is a multitude of slain,
And a great number of carcases.
There is no end of their corpses;
They stumble upon their corpses:
Because of the multitude of the whoredoms of the well favored harlot,
The mistress of witchcrafts,
That selleth nations through her whoredoms,
And families through her witchcrafts.

[2] Huzzab means the Queen of Assyria.

Behold, I am against thee, saith the Lord of Hosts,
And I will show the nations thy nakedness,
And the kingdoms thy shame.
And I will cast abominable filth upon thee,
And make thee vile, and will set thee as a gazingstock.
And it shall come to pass that all they that look upon thee shall flee from thee,
And say, Nineveh is laid waste!
Who will bemoan her?
Whence shall I seek comforters for thee?

Art thou better than populous No,[3]
That was situate among the rivers,
That had the waters round about it,
Whose rampart was the sea.
And whose wall was from the sea?
Ethiopia and Egypt were her strength
And it was infinite.
Yet was she carried away;
She went into captivity.
Her young children were dashed in pieces at the top of all the streets,
And they cast lots for her honorable men,
And all her great men were bound in chains.

Thou also shalt be drunken; thou shalt be hid;
Thou also shalt seek strength because of the enemy.
All thy strongholds shall be like fig trees with the first ripe figs;
If they be shaken, they shall even fall into the mouth of the eater.
Behold, thy people in the midst of thee are women;
The gates of thy land shall be set wide open unto thine enemies;
The fire shall devour thy bars.

Draw thee waters for the siege, fortify thy strongholds;
Go into clay, and tread the mortar,

[3] No was the ancient city of Thebes.

Make strong the brickkiln.
There shall the fire devour thee;
The sword shall cut thee off,
It shall eat thee up like the cankerworm;
Make thyself many as the cankerworm,
Make thyself many as the locusts.

Thou hast multiplied thy merchants above the stars of heaven:
The cankerworm spoileth, and fleeth away.
Thy crowned are as the locusts,
And thy captains as the great grasshoppers,
Which camp in the hedges in the cold day,
But when the sun ariseth they flee away,
And their place is not known where they are.

* * *

Thy shepherds slumber, O king of Assyria!
Thy nobles shall dwell in the dust!
Thy people is scattered upon the mountains,
And no man gathereth them.
There is no healing of thy bruise;
Thy wound is grievous.
All that hear the bruit of thee shall clap the hands over thee:
For upon whom hath not thy wickedness passed continually?

7

THE UNKNOWN POET, OR SECOND-ISAIAH

During the fifty years which the exiled Hebrews spent in Babylon, following the destruction of Jerusalem by Nebuchadnezzar in 586 B.C., two personalities stand out against the dark background of subjection and defeat: one, that of Ezekiel, and the other, that of a young man whose actual name has been lost but who is known to us as Second-Isaiah, simply because his poems were preserved in the manuscript of the book of Isaiah.

Ezekiel, although he is numbered among the major prophets because of the scope of his work, was not a great writer. His long book, written mostly in prose, is repetitious, often obscure and, in comparison with the work of the earlier prophets, unquestionably dull. Perhaps among all its forty-eight chapters only one may be read with interest and profit (chapter 37), that which portrays the vision of Ezekiel in the valley of bones and through which he symbolically expresses his hope and confidence that these dead and dry bones may again rise to life and strength. Yet Ezekiel, though not a literary genius, was a most important figure in Hebrew history, and should for that reason receive his just due.

Taken with the first of the exiles to Babylon in 597 B.C., after Nebuchadnezzar's first attack upon Jerusalem, he spent his many years there, apparently as a pastor to the Jewish community. It was he who, fired by the determination that the faith of his people must be preserved even though that people were temporarily lost in exile, actually preserved that faith and with consuming care insisted upon the preservation also of its outward forms. Through this insistence upon rites and ceremonies, priesthoods, the observance of holy days, the keeping of the Jewish Law, he kept alive in an alien empire the religious institutions of a nation. He has rightly been called the Father of Jewish Ritualism.

In contrast to his prose passages filled with visions and symbols is the lyrical and rhapsodic poetry of Second-Isaiah, often called "the Unknown Poet." He was, like Ezekiel, an unwilling sojourner in Babylon; but he brought a very different message to his homesick people. Instead of the observance of the Law in synagogue and temple, he sang of the love of God, not only for those of his race, but for all mankind. No poet among the prophets (and he was more poet than prophet) wrote with such unrestrained hope and joy. His poetry is filled with imagery and fancy, rapture and ecstasy. He writes of the blind who shall see, the lame who shall walk, the crooked places which shall be made straight. His poems possess one underlying theme, suggested or expressed: the ultimate return to Jerusalem through the mercy of God, who still loves his people, who is God of all, and without whose stiength all men are incomplete and helpless.

His best poems, mostly contained in Isaiah 40 to 55 and rearranged here for the sake of sequence and clearness, have certain qualities which the reader will do well to note: the quality of song, which is heightened in its effect by the great number of musical images; the many figures of speech, similes, metaphors, personifications; the use of ecstatic commands and of rhetorical questions, which give the effect of climax; and the ever recurring theme of the new in place of the old, new light and life, new and good tidings.

Both the poetry and the teaching of this unknown poet comprise a kind of spiritual epic, which not only aroused the hope and the faith of his own people, but, above all other Old Testament writings, had a direct influence upon Christian thought. Five hundred years before the Christian Era he is writing of redemption, of the meaning of suffering in the sense of atonement, of the worth of the individual in the eyes of God. In his tender solicitude for human pain, in his understanding of the minds of men, and in his infectious joy through faith in God, he could move the hearts of people as no other Old Testament poet could do. Nor has this power ever been limited to his own people or to his own time.

The Prophet's Call

Comfort ye, comfort ye my people,
Saith your God.
Speak ye comfortably to Jerusalem,
And cry unto her,
That her warfare is accomplished,
That her iniquity is pardoned:
For she hath received of the Lord's hand
Double for all her sins.

The voice of him that crieth in the wilderness,
Prepare ye the way of the Lord,
Make straight in the desert a highway for our God.
Every valley shall be exalted,
And every mountain and hill shall be made low;
And the crooked shall be made straight,
And the rough places plain;
And the glory of the Lord shall be revealed,
And all flesh shall see it together:
For the mouth of the Lord hath spoken it.

The voice said, Cry.
And he said, What shall I cry?
All flesh is grass,
And all the goodliness thereof is as the flower of the field.
The grass withereth, the flower fadeth
Because the spirit of the Lord bloweth upon it;
Surely the people is grass.
The grass withereth, the flower fadeth;
But the word of our God shall stand forever.

O Zion, that bringest good tidings,
Get thee up into the high mountain!
O Jerusalem, that bringest good tidings,
Lift up thy voice with strength!
Lift it up,
Be not afraid;
Say unto the cities of Judah,
Behold your God!

Behold, the Lord God will come with strong hand,
And his arm shall rule for him;
Behold, his reward is with him,
And his work before him.
He shall feed his flock like a shepherd:
He shall gather the lambs with his arm,
And carry them in his bosom,
And shall gently lead those that are with young.

Poems on the Nature of God

1

Who hath measured the waters in the hollow of his hand,
And meted out heaven with the span,
And comprehended the dust of the earth in a measure,

And weighed the mountains in scales,
And the hills in a balance?

Who hath directed the Spirit of the Lord,
Or being his counsellor hath taught him?
With whom took he counsel,
And who instructed him,
And taught him in the path of judgment,
And taught him knowledge,
And showed to him the way of understanding?

Behold, the nations are as a drop of a bucket,
And are counted as the small dust of the balance.
Behold, he taketh up the isles as a very little thing.
And Lebanon is not sufficient to burn,
Nor the beasts thereof sufficient for a burnt offering.
All nations before him are as nothing;
And they are counted to him less than nothing, and vanity.

2

To whom then will ye liken God?
Or with what likeness will ye compare unto him?
The workman melteth a graven image,
And the goldsmith spreadeth it over with gold,
And casteth silver chains.
He that is so impoverished that he hath no oblation
Chooseth a tree that will not rot;
He seeketh a cunning workman to prepare a graven image
That shall not be moved.
Have ye not known? Have ye not heard?
Hath it not been told you from the beginning?
Have ye not understood from the foundations of the earth?
It is he that sitteth upon the circle of the earth,
And the inhabitants thereof are as grasshoppers;
It is he that stretcheth out the heavens as a curtain,

And spreadeth them out as a tent to dwell in;
That bringeth the princes to nothing;
He maketh the judges of the earth as vanity.
Yea, they shall not be planted;
Yea, they shall not be sown;
Yea, their stock shall not take root in the earth.
And he shall also blow upon them, and they shall wither,
And the whirlwind shall take them away as stubble.

3

To whom then will ye liken me,
Or shall I be equal?
Saith the Holy One.
Lift up your eyes on high,
And behold who hath created these things,
That bringeth out their host by number;
He calleth them all by names by the greatness of his might,
For that he is strong in power, not one faileth.
Why sayest thou, O Jacob, and speakest, O Israel,
My way is hid from the Lord,
And my judgment is passed over from my God?
Hast thou not known? Hast thou not heard
That the everlasting God,
The Lord, the Creator of the ends of the earth,
Fainteth not, neither is weary?
There is no searching of his understanding.

He giveth power to the faint;
And to them that have no might he increaseth strength.
Even the youths shall faint and be weary,
And the young men shall utterly fall.
But they that wait upon the Lord shall renew their strength;
They shall mount up with wings as eagles;
They shall run, and not be weary;
And they shall walk, and not faint.

Poems on the Love of God and on His Promises of a Return Home

1

When the poor and needy seek water, and there is none,
And their tongue faileth for thirst,
I the Lord will hear them,
I the God of Israel will not forsake them.
I will open rivers in high places,
And fountains in the midst of the valleys;
I will make the wilderness a pool of water,
And the dry land springs of water.
I will plant in the wilderness the cedar,
The shittah tree,[1] and the myrtle, and the oil tree;
I will set in the desert the fir tree,
And the pine, and the box tree together,
That they may see, and know,
And consider, and understand together
That the hand of the Lord hath done this,
And the Holy One of Israel hath created it.

2

When thou passest through the waters,
I will be with thee;
And through the rivers,
They shall not overflow thee.
When thou walkest through the fire,
Thou shalt not be burned,
Neither shall the flame kindle upon thee.
For I am the Lord thy God,
The Holy One of Israel, thy Savior.
Fear not, for I am with thee;
I will bring thy seed from the east,
And gather thee from the west;

[1] The shittah tree was the acacia, or locust.

I will say to the north, Give up,
And to the south, Keep not back.
Bring my sons from far,
And my daughters from the ends of the earth.
Bring forth the blind people that have eyes,
And the deaf that have ears.

I, even I, am the Lord,
And beside me there is no savior.
Yea, before the day was, I am He,
And there is none that can deliver out of my hand.
I will work, and who shall let it?
I am the Lord, your Holy One,
The Creator of Israel, your King.
Thus saith the Lord, which maketh a way in the sea,
And a path in the mighty waters.

Remember ye not the former things,
Neither consider the things of old.
Behold, I will do a new thing!
Now it shall spring forth. Shall ye not know it?
I will even make a way in the wilderness,
And rivers in the desert.
The beast of the field shall honor me,
The dragons and the owls,
Because I give waters in the wilderness
And rivers in the desert
To give drink to my people, my chosen.
This people have I formed for myself,
And they shall show forth my praise.

3

Thus saith God, the Lord,
He that created the heavens and stretched them out;
He that spread forth the earth

And that which cometh out of it;
He that giveth breath unto the people upon it,
And spirit to them that walk therein:
I the Lord have called thee in righteousness,
I will hold thine hand, and will keep thee;
And give thee for a covenant of the people,
For a light of the Gentiles,
To open the blind eyes,
To bring out the prisoners from the prison,
And them that sit in darkness out of the prison house.
I am the Lord, that is my name,
And my glory will I not give to another,
Neither my praise to graven images.
Behold, the former things are come to pass,
And new things do I declare;
Before they spring forth I tell you of them.
Sing unto the Lord a new song,
And his praise from the end of the earth!
Ye that go down to the sea, and all that is therein,
The isles, and the inhabitants thereof;
Let the wilderness and the cities thereof lift up their voice,
Let the inhabitants of the rock sing,
Let them shout from the tops of the mountains,
Let them give glory unto the Lord,
And declare his praise in the islands.

I will make waste mountains and hills,
And dry up all their herbs;
And I will make the rivers islands,
And I will dry up the pools.
And I will bring the blind by a way that they knew not;
I will lead them in paths that they have not known;
I will make darkness light before them,
And crooked things straight.
These things will I do unto them,
And not forsake them.

4

(The poem which follows, chapter 35 of the book of Isaiah, is not included in those chapters usually accorded to the unknown poet, or Second-Isaiah. Its subject, imagery, and style, however, would seem to mark him as its author.)

The wilderness and the solitary place shall be glad for them;
And the desert shall rejoice and blossom as the rose.
It shall blossom abundantly,
And rejoice even with joy and singing;
The glory of Lebanon shall be given unto it,
The excellency of Carmel and Sharon;
They shall see the glory of the Lord
And the excellency of our God.
Strengthen ye the weak hands,
And confirm the feeble knees.
Say to them that are of a fearful heart, Be strong, fear not,
Behold your God will come with vengeance,
Even God with a recompense,
He will come and save you.
Then the eyes of the blind shall be opened,
And the ears of the deaf shall be unstopped;
Then shall the lame man leap as a hart,
And the tongue of the dumb sing:
For in the wilderness shall waters break out,
And streams in the desert;
And the parched ground shall become a pool,
And the thirsty land springs of water.
In the habitation of dragons where each lay
Shall be grass with reeds and rushes.
And a highway shall be there, and a way,
And it shall be called, The Way of Holiness.
The unclean shall not pass over it,
But it shall be for the wayfaring men,
Who, though fools, shall not err therein.
No lion shall be there,

Nor any ravenous beast shall go up thereon,
It shall not be found there.
But the redeemed shall walk there,
And the ransomed of the Lord shall return
And come to Zion with songs and everlasting joy upon their heads;
They shall obtain joy and gladness,
And sorrow and sighing shall flee away.

A Call to Awake

Awake, awake!
Put on thy strength, O Zion!
Put on thy beautiful garments, O Jerusalem, the holy city!
For henceforth there shall no more come into thee
The uncircumcised and the unclean.
Shake thyself from the dust;
Arise, and sit down, O Jerusalem;
Loose thyself from the bands of thy neck,
O captive daughter of Zion.
For thus saith the Lord,
Ye have sold yourselves for nought;
And ye shall be redeemed without money.

How beautiful upon the mountains
Are the feet of him that bringeth good tidings,
That publisheth peace;
That bringeth good tidings of good,
That publisheth salvation;
That saith unto Zion, Thy God reigneth!
Thy watchmen shall lift up the voice;
With the voice together shall they sing:
For they shall see eye to eye,
When the Lord shall bring again Zion.

Break forth into joy,
Sing together, ye waste places of Jerusalem:

For the Lord hath comforted his people,
He hath redeemed Jerusalem.
The Lord hath made bare his holy arm
In the eyes of all the nations;
And all the ends of the earth
Shall see the salvation of our God.

In Praise of Cyrus, King of Media

(Cyrus, who conquered Babylon in 538 B.C. and who shortly afterward gave permission to the exiled Jews to return home, is here extolled as the deliverer, and as the "anointed" of God.)

Thus saith the Lord to his anointed,
To Cyrus, whose right hand I have held
To subdue nations before him;
And I will loose the loins of kings,
To open before him the two-leaved gates;
And the gates shall not be shut.
I will go before thee,
And make the crooked places straight;
I will break in pieces the gates of brass,
And cut in sunder the bars of iron;
And I will give thee the treasures of darkness,
And hidden riches of secret places,
That thou mayest know that I, the Lord,
Which call thee by thy name, am the God of Israel.
For Jacob my servant's sake,
And Israel mine elect,
I have even called thee by thy name;
I have surnamed thee, though thou hast not known me.
I am the Lord, and there is none else,
There is no God beside me;
I girded thee, though thou hast not known me:
That they may know from the rising of the sun,
And from the west, that there is none beside me.
I am the Lord,

And there is none else.
I form the light, and create darkness;
I make peace, and create evil:
I the Lord do all these things.

The Suffering Servant

(This poem, chapter 53 of the book of Isaiah, is familiar to many readers, who look upon it as a Messianic poem which foretells the future sufferings of Christ; and, indeed, the material of the poem would seem to justify that assumption. Nevertheless, according to the best biblical scholars, the assumption is a false one. Our unknown poet is instead writing of the Israelitish people as the suffering servant of God. They have, through their years of punishment and exile, sacrificed themselves for the salvation of other nations, for whose transgressions also they have been wounded. As one reads the poem, among the most beautiful in Old Testament poetry, one will realize that these other nations are speaking in praise of Israel.)

Who hath believed our report?
And to whom is the arm of the Lord revealed?
For he shall grow up before him as a tender plant,
And as a root out of a dry ground;
He hath no form nor comeliness;
And when we shall see him, there is no beauty that we should desire him.
He is despised and rejected of men;
A man of sorrows, and acquainted with grief;
And we hid as it were our faces from him;
He was despised, and we esteemed him not.

Surely he hath borne our griefs,
And carried our sorrows;
Yet we did esteem him stricken,
Smitten of God, and afflicted.
But he was wounded for our transgressions,
He was bruised for our iniquities;
The chastisement of our peace was upon him;

And with his stripes we are healed.
All we like sheep have gone astray;
We have turned every one to his own way;
And the Lord hath laid on him
The iniquity of us all.

He was oppressed, and he was afflicted,
Yet he opened not his mouth;
He is brought as a lamb to the slaughter,
And as a sheep before her shearers is dumb,
So he openeth not his mouth.
He was taken from prison and from judgment;
And who shall declare his generation?
For he was cut off out of the land of the living,
For the transgression of my people was he stricken.
And he made his grave with the wicked,
And with the rich in his death,
Because he had done no violence,
Neither was any deceit in his mouth.

Yet it pleased the Lord to bruise him;
He hath put him to grief;
When thou shalt make his soul an offering for sin,
He shall see his seed, he shall prolong his days,
And the pleasure of the Lord shall prosper in his hand.
He shall see of the travail of his soul and be satisfied;
By his knowledge shall my righteous servant justify many,
For he shall bear their iniquities.

Therefore will I divide him a portion with the great,
And he shall divide the spoil with the strong,
Because he hath poured out his soul unto death.
And he was numbered with the transgressors,
And he bare the sin of many,
And made intercession for the transgressors.[2]

[2] A longer explanation of this poem will be found in *The Bible and the Common Reader*, Pt. II.

Two Poems on the Days to Come

1

Sing, O barren, thou that didst not bear!
Break forth into singing and cry aloud,
Thou that didst not travail with child.
Enlarge the place of thy tent,
And let them stretch forth the curtains of thine habitations.
For thou shalt break forth on the right hand and on the left,
And thy seed shall inherit the Gentiles
And make the desolate cities to be inhabited.
Fear not; for thou shalt not be ashamed;
Neither be thou confounded; for thou shalt not be put to shame;
For thou shalt forget the shame of thy youth,
And shalt not remember the reproach of thy widowhood any more.
For thy Maker is thine husband;
The Lord of Hosts is his name;
And thy Redeemer the Holy One of Israel;
The God of the whole earth shall he be called.

For a small moment have I forsaken thee;
But with great mercies will I gather thee.
In a little wrath I hid my face from thee for a moment;
But with everlasting kindness will I have mercy on thee,
Saith the Lord thy Redeemer.
For this is as the waters of Noah unto me;
For as I have sworn that the waters of Noah should no more go over the earth;
So have I sworn that I would not be wroth with thee, nor rebuke thee.
For the mountains shall depart,
And the hills be removed;
But my kindness shall not depart from thee,
Neither shall the covenant of my peace be removed,
Saith the Lord that hath mercy on thee.

O thou afflicted,
Tossed with tempest, and not comforted,
Behold, I will lay thy stones with fair colors,
And lay thy foundations with sapphires.
And I will make thy windows of agates,
And thy gates of carbuncles,
And all thy borders of pleasant stones.
And all thy children shall be taught of the Lord;
And great shall be the peace of thy children.

2

Ho, every one that thirsteth, come ye to the waters!
And he that hath no money, come ye, buy, and eat,
Yea, buy wine and milk without money and without price!
Wherefore do ye spend money for that which is not bread?
And your labor for that which satisfieth not?
Hearken diligently unto me, and eat ye that which is good,
And let your soul delight itself in fatness.
Incline your ear and come unto me,
Hear and your soul shall live;
And I will make an everlasting covenant with you,
Even the sure mercies of David.

For my thoughts are not your thoughts,
Neither are your ways my ways, saith the Lord.
For as the heavens are higher than the earth,
So are my ways higher than your ways,
And my thoughts than your thoughts.
For as the rain cometh down and the snow from heaven,
And returneth not hither, but watereth the earth,
And maketh it bring forth and bud
That it may give seed to the sower and bread to the eater;
So shall my word be that goeth forth out of my mouth:
It shall not return unto me void,
But it shall accomplish that which I please,
And it shall prosper in the thing whereto I sent it.

For ye shall go out with joy and be led forth with peace.
The mountains and the hills shall break forth before you into
  singing,
And all the trees of the field shall clap their hands.
Instead of the thorn shall come up the fir tree,
And instead of the brier shall come up the myrtle tree;
And it shall be to the Lord for a name,
For an everlasting sign that shall not be cut off.

8

THIRD-ISAIAH

Another unknown poet and prophet, whose work is also placed in the book of Isaiah, is called Third-Isaiah. His poems are contained within chapters 56–66, although scholars are by no means certain, or even agreed, as to how much of the material in these chapters was actually written by him. We are quite safe, however, in assigning the two poems given here to his authorship. The best of his poetry, these poems are rich and beautiful in both style and imagery and clearly show the influence of Second-Isaiah, even though their writer never attained the literary stature of his forerunner.

Third-Isaiah wrote at least one hundred years later than Second-Isaiah and during the difficult and disappointing years following the Return to Jerusalem in 536 B.C. His message to his discouraged people of Judea is one of hope for the future; his pictures are those of prosperity and peace, when foreign kings shall come to see the ultimate greatness of Jerusalem, when trade once more shall flourish, and when her rebuilt walls and gates shall be called Salvation and Praise.[1]

The Prophet's Call

The spirit of the Lord God is upon me;
Because the Lord hath anointed me
To preach good tidings unto the meek;
He hath sent me to bind up the brokenhearted,

[1] A description of the troublous conditions following the Return is given in *The Bible and the Common Reader,* Pt. I.

To proclaim liberty to the captives,
And the opening of the prison to them that are bound;
To proclaim the acceptable year of the Lord,
And the day of vengeance of our God;
To comfort all that mourn;
To appoint unto them that mourn in Zion,
To give unto them beauty for ashes,
The oil of joy for mourning,
The garment of praise for the spirit of heaviness,
That they might be called trees of righteousness,
The planting of the Lord, that he might be glorified.

And they shall build the old wastes,
They shall raise up the former desolations,
And they shall repair the waste cities,
The desolations of many generations.
And strangers shall stand and feed your flocks,
And the sons of the alien shall be your plowmen and your vine-dressers.
But ye shall be named the Priests of the Lord;
Men shall call you the Ministers of our God;
Ye shall eat the riches of the Gentiles,
And in their glory shall ye boast yourselves.

For your shame ye shall have double;
And for confusion they shall rejoice in their portion;
Therefore in their land they shall possess the double:
Everlasting joy shall be unto them.
For I the Lord love judgment,
I hate robbery for burnt offering;
And I will direct their work in truth,
And I will make an everlasting covenant with them.
And their seeds shall be known among the Gentiles,
And their offspring among the people;
All that see them shall acknowledge them,
That they are the seed which the Lord hath blessed.

I will greatly rejoice in the Lord,
My soul shall be joyful in my God;
For he hath clothed me with the garments of salvation,
He hath covered me with the robe of righteousness,
As a bridegroom decketh himself with ornaments,
And as a bride adorneth herself with her jewels.
For as the earth bringeth forth her bud,
And as the garden causeth the things that are sown in it to spring forth;
So the Lord God will cause righteousness and praise
To spring forth before all the nations.

The Glories of the Future

Arise, shine! for thy light is come,
And the glory of the Lord is risen upon thee.
For, behold, the darkness shall cover the earth,
And gross darkness the people;
But the Lord shall arise upon thee,
And his glory shall be seen upon thee.
And the Gentiles shall come to thy light,
And kings to the brightness of thy rising.

Lift up thine eyes round about, and see!
All they gather themselves together, they come to thee!
Thy sons shall come from far,
And thy daughters shall be nursed at thy side.
Then thou shalt see, and flow together,
And thine heart shall fear, and be enlarged;
Because the abundance of the sea shall be converted unto thee,
The forces of the Gentiles shall come unto thee.

The multitude of camels shall cover thee,
The dromedaries of Midian and Ephah;
All they from Sheba shall come;
They shall bring gold and incense,

And they shall show forth the praises of the Lord.
All the flocks of Kedar shall be gathered together unto thee,
The rams of Nabaioth shall minister unto thee;
They shall come up with acceptance on mine altar,
And I will glorify the house of my glory.

Who are these that fly as a cloud,
And as the doves to their windows?
Surely the isles shall wait for me,
And the ships of Tarshish first,
To bring thy sons from far,
Their silver and their gold with them,
Unto the name of the Lord thy God,
And to the Holy One of Israel, because he hath glorified thee.

And the sons of strangers shall build up thy walls,
And their kings shall minister unto thee.
For in my wrath I smote thee,
But in my favor have I had mercy on thee.
Therefore thy gates shall be open continually,
They shall not be shut day or night
That men may bring unto thee the forces of the Gentiles,
And that their kings may be brought.
For the nation and kingdom that will not serve thee shall perish.
Yea, those nations shall be utterly wasted.

The glory of Lebanon shall come unto thee,
The fir tree, the pine tree, and the box together,
To beautify the place of my sanctuary;
And I will make the place of my feet glorious.
The sons also of them that afflicted thee shall come bending unto thee,
And all they that despised thee shall bow themselves down at the soles of thy feet;
And they shall call thee: The City of the Lord,
The Zion of the Holy One of Israel.

Violence shall no more be heard in thy land,
Wasting nor destruction within thy borders;
But thou shalt call thy walls Salvation,
And thy gates Praise.
The sun shall be no more thy light by day,
Neither for brightness shall the moon give light unto thee;
But the Lord shall be unto thee an everlasting light,
And thy God thy glory.

-II-

THE PSALMS

If we say that the Psalms are the best known portion of the Old Testament, or perhaps even of the entire Bible, there will be few to quarrel with us. Yet there are countless readers of the Bible who know little about their origin, their place in Hebrew literature as a whole, and their divisions into distinctive types, a knowledge which, once attained, will make the reading of them far more intelligent and intelligible, not to say enjoyable.

The Psalms have often been called *The Hymn Book of the Jewish People*; and although this definition is far from conclusive, or even exact, it will perhaps serve our purpose better than any other. A great number of psalms, as is clear from the notations placed above them in most editions of the Bible, were used in the liturgical worship of the Second Temple, completed in Jerusalem in 516 B.C.; and yet perhaps even a greater number were written and collected for the purpose of private devotion and enjoyment. We should, therefore, think of them not alone as a hymnbook, but also as an anthology of religious poetry.[1]

The old tradition that David wrote the Psalms has long been known by scholars to be quite untrue. Few of them were written before 500 B.C.; and most of them date between 400–100 B.C., around which later date the Psalter was compiled. The careful reader will note at once that these poems which make up the Psalter are very different in material and in style from ancient Hebrew poems like the Song of Deborah or David's Lament, or even from the poetry of the earlier prophets. Whereas this earlier poetry is simple, concise, and restrained in style, the Psalms in contrast are far more elaborate in language and in imagery, far less restrained in expression. The ancient poetry belongs to what is often called the Classical Age of Hebrew Literature, which can be approximately dated from the Exodus (*c.* 1250 B.C.) to the Exile (586 B.C.); the Psalms, like the poetry of the Second and the Third

[1] A more extended treatment of the Psalms is given in *The Bible and the Common Reader,* Pt. II. An excellent presentation may be found in Robert H. Pfeiffer's *Introduction to the Old Testament,* Pt. V (New York, Harper and Brothers, 1941). Another is included in Theodore H. Robinson's *Poetry of the Old Testament* (London, Gerald Duckworth & Co., Ltd., 1948).

Isaiahs, that of Job, the Song of Songs, and the writers of the Poems on Wisdom, belong to the Romantic Age, from 586 B.C. onward.

The reader who takes the trouble to examine the book of Psalms in his Bible will note that it is made up of five clearly defined collections of songs and hymns, which may well have been separate anthologies, compiled at different times and joined together when the final edition of the book was made. He will see that each collection is separated from the one following by a kind of doxology; that the first collection ends with Psalm 41, the second with 72, the third with 89, the fourth with 106, and the fifth with 150.

In a collection of Readings such as this it is obviously necessary to select those psalms which are generally conceded to be the most beautiful. And it has seemed wise also to arrange those selected in groups which characterize them as to their material. I have, therefore, divided them into two main divisions: those which praise the greatness and the glory of God in His manifold creations; and those which present the manifold emotions of the human heart. Again, I have subdivided the second group, which is much larger and more varied than the first, into different types of psalms: (1) songs of personal gratitude and praise to God; (2) songs known as *pilgrim songs* because they were clearly composed to be sung by people journeying from their distant homes to Jerusalem for religious festivals; (3) songs called *occasional songs,* since they record certain incidents in the past of the Hebrew people; and (4) songs of meditation and reflection by the individual on his own interpretation and understanding of God.

It is my conviction that the careful reading of the psalms given here, with an intelligent understanding of their meaning and of their place in the Psalter as a whole, will make this beautiful portion of the Old Testament much more valuable to the reader than any attempt to read the entire collection.

1

PSALMS ON THE GLORY OF GOD IN HIS CREATIONS

PSALM 8

O Lord our Lord,
How excellent is thy name in all the earth!
Who hast set thy glory above the heavens.
Out of the mouth of babes and sucklings hast thou ordained strength
Because of thine enemies,
That thou mightest still the enemy and the avenger.
When I consider thy heavens, the work of thy fingers,
The moon and the stars, which thou hast ordained,
What is man, that thou art mindful of him?
And the son of man, that thou visitest him?
For thou hast made him a little lower than the angels,
And hast crowned him with glory and honor.
Thou madest him to have dominion over the works of thy hands;
Thou hast put all things under his feet;
All sheep and oxen,
Yea, and the beasts of the field;
The fowl of the air, and the fish of the sea,
And whatsoever passeth through the paths of the seas.
O Lord our Lord,
How excellent is thy name in all the earth!

PSALM 19

The heavens declare the glory of God;
And the firmament showeth his handiwork.
Day unto day uttereth speech,
And night unto night showeth knowledge.
There is no speech nor language,
Where their voice is not heard.

Their line is gone out through all the earth,
And their words to the end of the world.
In them hath he set a tabernacle for the sun,
Which is as a bridegroom coming out of his chamber,
And rejoiceth as a strong man to run a race.
His going forth is from the end of the heaven,
And his circuit unto the ends of it:
And there is nothing hid from the heat thereof.
The law of the Lord is perfect, converting the soul;
The testimony of the Lord is sure, making wise the simple;
The statutes of the Lord are right, rejoicing the heart;
The commandment of the Lord is pure, enlightening the eyes;
The fear of the Lord is clean, enduring forever;
The judgments of the Lord are true and righteous altogether.
More to be desired are they than gold, yea, than much fine gold;
Sweeter also than honey and the honeycomb.
Moreover by them is thy servant warned;
And in keeping of them there is great reward.
Who can understand his errors?
Cleanse thou me from secret faults.
Keep back thy servant also from presumptuous sins;
Let them not have dominion over me: then shall I be upright,
And I shall be innocent from the great transgression.
Let the words of my mouth, and the meditation of my heart, be acceptable in thy sight,
O Lord, my strength, and my redeemer.

PSALM 95 (IN PART)

O come, let us sing unto the Lord;
Let us make a joyful noise to the rock of our salvation.
Let us come before his presence with thanksgiving,
And make a joyful noise unto him with psalms.
For the Lord is a great God,
And a great King above all gods.
In his hand are the deep places of the earth;

The strength of the hills is his also.
The sea is his, and he made it,
And his hands formed the dry land.
O come, let us worship and bow down;
Let us kneel before the Lord our maker.
For he is our God;
And we are the people of his pasture, and the sheep of his hand.

PSALM 104

Bless the Lord, O my soul.
O Lord my God, thou art very great!
Thou art clothed with honor and majesty.
Who coverest thyself with light as with a garment;
Who stretchest out the heavens like a curtain;
Who layeth the beams of his chambers in the waters;
Who maketh the clouds his chariot;
Who walketh upon the wings of the wind;
Who maketh his angels spirits;
His ministers a flaming fire;
Who laid the foundations of the earth,
That it should not be removed forever.
Thou coveredst it with the deep as with a garment;
The waters stood above the mountains.
At thy rebuke they fled;
At the voice of thy thunder they hasted away.
They go up by the mountains; they go down by the valleys
Unto the place which thou hast founded for them.
Thou hast set a bound that they may not pass over,
That they turn not again to cover the earth.
He sendeth the springs into the valleys,
Which run among the hills.
They give drink to every beast of the field;
The wild asses quench their thirst.
By them shall the fowls of the heaven have their habitation,
Which sing among the branches.

He watereth the hills from his chambers;
The earth is satisfied with the fruit of thy works.
He causeth the grass to grow for the cattle,
And herb for the service of man,
That he may bring forth food out of the earth,
And wine that maketh glad the heart of man,
And oil to make his face to shine,
And bread which strengtheneth man's heart.
The trees of the Lord are full of sap,
The cedars of Lebanon, which he hath planted,
Where the birds make their nests.
As for the stork, the fir trees are her house;
The high hills are a refuge for the wild goats,
And the rocks for the conies.
He appointed the moon for seasons;
The sun knoweth his going down.
Thou makest darkness, and it is night,
Wherein all the beasts of the forest do creep forth.
The young lions roar after their prey,
And seek their meat from God.
The sun ariseth, they gather themselves together,
And lay them down in their dens.
Man goeth forth unto his work
And to his labor until the evening.
O Lord, how manifold are thy works!
In wisdom hast thou made them all.
The earth is full of thy riches.
So is this great and wide sea,
Wherein are things creeping innumerable,
Both small and great beasts.
There go the ships;
There is that leviathan, whom thou hast made to play therein.
These wait all upon thee,
That thou mayest give them their meat in due season.
That thou givest them they gather;
Thou openest thine hand, they are filled with good;

Thou hidest thy face, they are troubled;
Thou takest away their breath, they die,
And return to their dust.
Thou sendest forth thy spirit, they are created,
And thou renewest the face of the earth.
The glory of the Lord shall endure forever;
The Lord shall rejoice in his works.
He looketh on the earth, and it trembleth;
He toucheth the hills, and they smoke.
I will sing unto the Lord as long as I live;
I will sing praise to my God while I have my being.
My meditation of him shall be sweet;
I will be glad in the Lord.
Let the sinners be consumed out of the earth,
And let the wicked be no more.
Bless thou the Lord, O my soul!
Praise ye the Lord!

PSALM 147

Praise ye the Lord!
For it is good to sing praises unto our God;
For it is pleasant, and praise is comely.
The Lord doth build up Jerusalem;
He gathereth together the outcasts of Israel.
He healeth the broken in heart,
And bindeth up their wounds.
He telleth the number of the stars;
He calleth them all by their names.
Great is our Lord, and of great power;
His understanding is infinite.
The Lord lifteth up the meek;
He casteth the wicked down to the ground.
Sing unto the Lord with thanksgiving;
Sing praise upon the harp unto our God,
Who covereth the heaven with clouds,
Who prepareth rain for the earth,

Who maketh grass to grow upon the mountains.
He giveth to the beast his food,
And to the young ravens which cry.
He delighteth not in the strength of the horse;
He taketh not pleasure in the legs of a man.
The Lord taketh pleasure in them that fear him,
In those that hope in his mercy.
Praise the Lord, O Jerusalem!
Praise thy God, O Zion!
For he hath strengthened the bars of thy gates;
He hath blessed thy children within thee.
He maketh peace in thy borders,
And filleth thee with the finest of the wheat.
He sendeth forth his commandment upon earth;
His word runneth very swiftly.
He giveth snow like wool;
He scattereth the hoarfrost like ashes.
He casteth forth his ice like morsels:
Who can stand before his cold?
He sendeth out his word, and melteth them;
He causeth his wind to blow, and the waters flow.
He showeth his word unto Jacob,
His statutes and his judgments unto Israel.
He hath not dealt so with any nation,
And as for his judgments, they have not known them.
Praise ye the Lord!

PSALM 148

Praise ye the Lord!
Praise ye the Lord from the heavens;
Praise him in the heights.
Praise ye him, all his angels;
Praise ye him, all his hosts.
Praise ye him, sun and moon;
Praise him, all ye stars of light.
Praise him, ye heavens of heavens,

And ye waters that be above the heavens!
Let them praise the name of the Lord:
For he commanded, and they were created.
He hath also established them forever and ever;
He hath made a decree which shall not pass.
Praise the Lord from the earth,
Ye dragons, and all deeps,
Fire and hail, snow and vapors,
Stormy wind fulfilling his word,
Mountains and all hills,
Fruitful trees and all cedars,
Beasts and all cattle,
Creeping things and flying fowl,
Kings of the earth and all people,
Princes and all judges of the earth;
Both young men and maidens,
Old men and children,
Let them praise the name of the Lord.
For his name alone is excellent;
His glory is above the earth and heaven.
He also exalteth the horn of his people,
The praise of all his saints;
Even of the children of Israel, a people near unto him.
Praise ye the Lord!

II

PSALMS REFLECTING PERSONAL EMOTIONS

1

Songs of Gratitude and Praise

PSALM 23

The Lord is my shepherd; I shall not want.
He maketh me to lie down in green pastures;
He leadeth me beside the still waters;
He restoreth my soul.

He leadeth me in the paths of righteousness for his name's sake.
Yea, though I walk through the valley of the shadow of death,
I will fear no evil: for thou art with me;
Thy rod and thy staff they comfort me.
Thou preparest a table before me in the presence of mine enemies;
Thou anointest my head with oil; my cup runneth over.
Surely goodness and mercy shall follow me all the days of my life,
And I will dwell in the house of the Lord forever.

PSALM 27

The Lord is my light and my salvation; whom shall I fear?
The Lord is the strength of my life; of whom shall I be afraid?
When the wicked, even mine enemies and my foes,
Came upon me to eat up my flesh, they stumbled and fell.
Though a host should encamp against me,
My heart shall not fear;
Though war should rise against me,
In this will I be confident.
One thing have I desired of the Lord, that will I seek after:
That I may dwell in the house of the Lord all the days of my life,
To behold the beauty of the Lord, and to enquire in his temple.
For in the time of trouble he shall hide me in his pavilion;
In the secret of his tabernacle shall he hide me;
He shall set me up upon a rock.
And now shall mine head be lifted up above mine enemies round about me;
Therefore will I offer in his tabernacle sacrifices of joy;
I will sing, yea, I will sing praises unto the Lord.
Hear, O Lord, when I cry with my voice;
Have mercy also upon me, and answer me.
When thou saidst, Seek ye my face, my heart said unto thee,
Thy face, Lord, will I seek.
Hide not thy face far from me;
Put not thy servant away in anger;
Thou hast been my help;

Leave me not, neither forsake me, O God of my salvation.
When my father and my mother forsake me,
Then the Lord will take me up.
Teach me thy way, O Lord,
And lead me in a plain path,
Because of mine enemies.
Deliver me not over unto the will of mine enemies;
For false witnesses are risen up against me,
And such as breathe out cruelty.
I had fainted, unless I had believed to see the goodness of the Lord
in the land of the living.
Wait on the Lord!
Be of good courage, and he shall strengthen thine heart,
Wait, I say, on the Lord.

PSALM 91

He that dwelleth in the secret place of the Most High
Shall abide under the shadow of the Almighty.
I will say of the Lord, He is my refuge and my fortress;
My God; in him will I trust.
Surely he shall deliver thee from the snare of the fowler,
And from the noisome pestilence.
He shall cover thee with his feathers,
And under his wings shalt thou trust.
His truth shall be thy shield and buckler.
Thou shalt not be afraid for the terror by night;
Nor for the arrow that flieth by day;
Nor for the pestilence that walketh in darkness;
Nor for the destruction that wasteth at noonday.
A thousand shall fall at thy side,
And ten thousand at thy right hand;
But it shall not come nigh thee.
Only with thine eyes shalt thou behold
And see the reward of the wicked.
Because thou hast made the Lord, which is my refuge,

Even the most High, thy habitation;
There shall no evil befall thee,
Neither shall any plague come nigh thy dwelling.
For he shall give his angels charge over thee,
To keep thee in all thy ways.
They shall bear thee up in their hands,
Lest thou dash thy foot against a stone.
Thou shalt tread upon the lion and adder;
The young lion and the dragon shalt thou trample under feet.
Because he hath set his love upon me, therefore will I deliver him:
I will set him on high, because he hath known my name.
He shall call upon me, and I will answer him;
I will be with him in trouble;
I will deliver him, and honor him.
With long life will I satisfy him,
And show him my salvation.

PSALM 103

Bless the Lord, O my soul,
And all that is within me, bless his holy name!
Bless the Lord, O my soul,
And forget not all his benefits:
Who forgiveth all thine iniquities;
Who healeth all thy diseases;
Who redeemeth thy life from destruction;
Who crowneth thee with lovingkindness and tender mercies;
Who satisfieth thy mouth with good things,
So that thy youth is renewed like the eagle's.
The Lord executeth righteousness,
And judgment for all that are oppressed.
He made known his ways unto Moses,
His acts unto the children of Israel.
The Lord is merciful and gracious,
Slow to anger, and plenteous in mercy.
He will not always chide,

Neither will he keep his anger forever.
He hath not dealt with us after our sins,
Nor rewarded us according to our iniquities.
For as the heaven is high above the earth,
So great is his mercy toward them that fear him.
As far as the east is from the west,
So far hath he removed our transgressions from us.
Like as a father pitieth his children,
So the Lord pitieth them that fear him.
For he knoweth our frame;
He remembereth that we are dust.
As for man, his days are as grass;
As a flower of the field, so he flourisheth.
For the wind passeth over it, and it is gone;
And the place thereof shall know it no more.
But the mercy of the Lord is from everlasting to everlasting upon them that fear him,
And his righteousness unto children's children;
To such as keep his covenant,
And to those that remember his commandments to do them.
The Lord hath prepared his throne in the heavens;
And his kingdom ruleth over all.
Bless the Lord, ye his angels,
That excel in strength, that do his commandments,
Hearkening unto the voice of his word.
Bless ye the Lord, all ye his hosts;
Ye ministers of his, that do his pleasure.
Bless the Lord, all his works
In all places of his dominion,
Bless the Lord, O my soul!

PSALM 107 (in part)

O give thanks unto the Lord, for he is good;
For his mercy endureth forever!
Let the redeemed of the Lord say so,

Whom he hath redeemed from the hand of the enemy;
And gathered them out of the lands,
From the east, and from the west,
From the north, and from the south.
They wandered in the wilderness in a solitary way;
They found no city to dwell in.
Hungry and thirsty,
Their soul fainted in them.
Then they cried unto the Lord in their trouble,
And he delivered them out of their distresses;
And he led them forth by the right way,
That they might go to a city of habitation.
Oh that men would praise the Lord for his goodness,
And for his wonderful works to the children of men!
For he satisfieth the longing soul,
And filleth the hungry soul with goodness.
Such as sit in darkness and in the shadow of death,
Being bound in affliction and iron,
Because they rebelled against the words of God,
And condemned the counsel of the Most High.
Therefore he brought down their heart with labor;
They fell down, and there was none to help.
Then they cried unto the Lord in their trouble,
And he saved them out of their distresses.
He brought them out of darkness and the shadow of death,
And brake their bands in sunder.
Oh that men would praise the Lord for his goodness,
And for his wonderful works to the children of men!
For he hath broken the gates of brass,
And cut the bars of iron in sunder.
Fools, because of their transgression
And because of their iniquities, are afflicted;
Their soul abhorreth all manner of meat;
And they draw near unto the gates of death.
Then they cry unto the Lord in their trouble,
And he saveth them out of their distresses.

He sent his word, and healed them,
And delivered them from their destructions.
Oh that men would praise the Lord for his goodness,
And for his wonderful works to the children of men!
And let them sacrifice the sacrifices of thanksgiving,
And declare his works with rejoicing.
They that go down to the sea in ships,
That do business in great waters;
These see the works of the Lord,
And his wonders in the deep.
For he commandeth, and raiseth the stormy wind,
Which lifteth up the waves thereof.
They mount up to the heaven, they go down again to the depths:
Their soul is melted because of trouble.
They reel to and fro, and stagger like a drunken man,
And are at their wit's end.
Then they cry unto the Lord in their trouble,
And he bringeth them out of their distresses.
He maketh the storm a calm,
So that the waves thereof are still.
Then are they glad because they be quiet;
So he bringeth them unto their desired haven.
Oh that men would praise the Lord for his goodness,
And for his wonderful works to the children of men!

2

Pilgrim Songs

PSALM 84

How amiable are thy tabernacles,
O Lord of Hosts!
My soul longeth, yea, even fainteth for the courts of the Lord;
My heart and my flesh crieth out for the living God.
Yea, the sparrow hath found a house,
And the swallow a nest for herself, where she may lay her young,

Even thine altars, O Lord of hosts,
My King, and my God!
Blessed are they that dwell in thy house!
They will be still praising thee.
Blessed is the man whose strength is in thee;
In whose heart are the ways of them,
Who, passing through the valley of Baca, make it a well;
The rain also filleth the pools.
They go from strength to strength,
Every one of them in Zion appeareth before God.
O Lord God of Hosts, hear my prayer!
Give ear, O God of Jacob!
Behold, O God our shield,
And look upon the face of thine anointed.
For a day in thy courts is better than a thousand.
I had rather be a doorkeeper in the house of my God,
Than to dwell in the tents of wickedness.
For the Lord God is a sun and shield;
The Lord will give grace and glory;
No good thing will he withhold from them that walk uprightly.
O Lord of Hosts,
Blessed is the man that trusteth in thee!

PSALM 121

I will lift up mine eyes unto the hills,
From whence cometh my help.
My help cometh from the Lord,
Which made heaven and earth.
He will not suffer thy foot to be moved;
He that keepeth thee will not slumber.
Behold, he that keepeth Israel
Shall neither slumber nor sleep.
The Lord is thy keeper;
The Lord is thy shade upon thy right hand.
The sun shall not smite thee by day,

Nor the moon by night.
The Lord shall preserve thee from all evil;
He shall preserve thy soul.
The Lord shall preserve thy going out and thy coming in
From this time forth, and even forevermore.

PSALM 122

I was glad when they said unto me,
Let us go into the house of the Lord.
Our feet shall stand within thy gates, O Jerusalem.
Jerusalem is builded as a city that is compact together;
Whither the tribes go up, the tribes of the Lord,
Unto the testimony of Israel,
To give thanks unto the name of the Lord.
For there are set thrones of judgment,
The thrones of the house of David.
Pray for the peace of Jerusalem;
They shall prosper that love thee.
Peace be within thy walls,
And prosperity within thy palaces.
For my brethren and companions' sakes,
I will now say, Peace be within thee.
Because of the house of the Lord our God
I will seek thy good.

PSALM 125

They that trust in the Lord shall be as mount Zion,
Which cannot be removed, but abideth forever.
As the mountains are round about Jerusalem,
So the Lord is round about his people
From henceforth, even forever.
For the rod of the wicked shall not rest upon the lot of the righteous,
Lest the righteous put forth their hands unto iniquity.
Do good, O Lord, unto those that be good,
And to them that are upright in their hearts.

As for such as turn aside unto their crooked ways,
The Lord shall lead them forth with the workers of iniquity;
But peace shall be upon Israel.

PSALM 48

Great is the Lord, and greatly to be praised
In the city of our God, in the mountain of his holiness.
Beautiful for situation, the joy of the whole earth,
Is mount Zion, on the sides of the north,
The city of the great King.
God is known in her palaces for a refuge.
For, lo, the kings were assembled,
They passed by together.
They saw it, and so they marvelled;
They were troubled, and hastened away.
Fear took hold upon them there,
And pain, as of a woman in travail.
Thou breakest the ships of Tarshish with an east wind.
As we have heard, so have we seen
In the city of the Lord of Hosts, in the city of our God.
God will establish it forever.
We have thought of thy loving kindness, O God,
In the midst of thy temple.
According to thy name, O God,
So is thy praise unto the ends of the earth.
Thy right hand is full of righteousness.
Let mount Zion rejoice,
Let the daughters of Judah be glad,
Because of thy judgments.
Walk about Zion, and go round about her;
Tell the towers thereof.
Mark ye well her bulwarks, consider her palaces,
That ye may tell it to the generation following.
For this God is our God forever and ever;
He will be our guide even unto death.

3
Occasional Songs

PSALM 126

When the Lord turned again the captivity of Zion,
We were like them that dream.
Then was our mouth filled with laughter,
And our tongue with singing.
Then said they among the heathen,
The Lord hath done great things for them.
The Lord hath done great things for us,
Whereof we are glad.
Turn again our captivity, O Lord,
As the streams in the south.
They that sow in tears shall reap in joy.
He that goeth forth and weepeth, bearing precious seed,
Shall doubtless come again with rejoicing, bringing his sheaves with him.

PSALM 137

By the rivers of Babylon,
There we sat down; yea, we wept,
When we remembered Zion.
We hanged our harps
Upon the willows in the midst thereof.
For there they that carried us away captive required of us a song;
And they that wasted us required of us mirth, saying,
Sing us one of the songs of Zion!
How shall we sing the Lord's song in a strange land?
If I forget thee, O Jerusalem,
Let my right hand forget her cunning!
If I do not remember thee,
Let my tongue cleave to the roof of my mouth;
If I prefer not Jerusalem

Above my chief joy.
Remember, O Lord, the children of Edom
In the day of Jerusalem,
Who said, Rase it, rase it,
Even to the foundation thereof.
O daughter of Babylon, who art to be destroyed,
Happy shall he be that rewardeth thee as thou hast served us!
Happy shall he be that taketh and dasheth thy little ones against the stones! [2]

4

Songs of Meditation and Reflection

PSALM 90

Lord, thou hast been our dwelling place
In all generations.
Before the mountains were brought forth,
Or ever thou hadst formed the earth and the world,
Even from everlasting to everlasting, thou art God.
Thou turnest man to destruction;
And sayest, Return, ye children of men.
For a thousand years in thy sight
Are but as yesterday when it is past,
And as a watch in the night.
Thou carriest them away as with a flood; they are as a sleep:
In the morning they are like grass which groweth up.
In the morning it flourisheth, and groweth up;
In the evening it is cut down, and withereth.
For we are consumed by thine anger,
And by thy wrath are we troubled.
Thou hast set our iniquities before thee,
Our secret sins in the light of thy countenance.
For all our days are passed away in thy wrath;
We spend our years as a tale that is told.
The days of our years are threescore years and ten;

[2] Other occasional psalms are 78, 135, and 136.

And if by reason of strength they be fourscore years,
Yet is their strength labor and sorrow;
For it is soon cut off, and we fly away.
Who knoweth the power of thine anger?
Even according to thy fear, so is thy wrath.
So teach us to number our days
That we may apply our hearts unto wisdom.
Return, O Lord, how long?
And let it repent thee concerning thy servants.
O satisfy us early with thy mercy,
That we may rejoice and be glad all our days.
Make us glad according to the days wherein thou hast afflicted us,
And the years wherein we have seen evil.
Let thy work appear unto thy servants,
And thy glory unto their children.
And let the beauty of the Lord our God be upon us;
And establish thou the work of our hands upon us;
Yea, the work of our hands establish thou it.

PSALM 139

O Lord, thou hast searched me, and known me.
Thou knowest my downsitting and mine uprising,
Thou understandest my thought afar off.
Thou compassest my path and my lying down,
And art acquainted with all my ways.
For there is not a word in my tongue,
But lo, O Lord, thou knowest it altogether.
Thou hast beset me behind and before,
And laid thine hand upon me.
Such knowledge is too wonderful for me;
It is high, I cannot attain unto it.
Whither shall I go from thy spirit?
Or whither shall I flee from thy presence?
If I ascend up into heaven, thou art there;
If I make my bed in hell, behold, thou art there;

If I take the wings of the morning,
And dwell in the uttermost parts of the sea,
Even there shall thy hand lead me,
And thy right hand shall hold me.
If I say, Surely the darkness shall cover me,
Even the night shall be light about me;
Yea, the darkness hideth not from thee,
But the night shineth as the day;
The darkness and the light are both alike to thee.
For thou hast possessed my reins;
Thou hast covered me in my mother's womb.
I will praise thee; for I am fearfully and wonderfully made;
Marvellous are thy works;
And that my soul knoweth right well.
My substance was not hid from thee when I was made in secret,
And curiously wrought in the lowest parts of the earth.
Thine eyes did see my substance, yet being unperfect;
And in thy book all my members were written,
Which in continuance were fashioned
When as yet there was none of them.
How precious also are thy thoughts unto me, O God!
How great is the sum of them!
If I should count them, they are more in number than the sand.
When I awake, I am still with thee.
Surely thou wilt slay the wicked, O God;
Depart from me therefore, ye bloody men.
For they speak against thee wickedly,
And thine enemies take thy name in vain.
Do not I hate them, O Lord, that hate thee?
And am not I grieved with those that rise up against thee?
I hate them with perfect hatred:
I count them mine enemies.
Search me, O God, and know my heart!
Try me, and know my thoughts!
And see if there be any wicked way in me,
And lead me in the way everlasting.

- III -

THE SONG OF SONGS

Of all biblical poetry, perhaps the most difficult to read with the understanding and pleasure which it deserves is contained in that short book of eight chapters entitled in most Bibles *The Song of Solomon.* This book, since it has little, if any, connection with King Solomon, should be called instead, *The Song of Songs.* There are several reasons for this difficulty in reading: The poems which make up the book are mostly fragments placed together in no clear or even orderly sequence; the speakers or singers of most of them, apparently a young man and his sweetheart, are not easily identified; and the songs themselves have been, through many centuries, subjected to odd interpretations.

In order to justify or to explain the presence in the Bible of poetry clearly dealing with the passion of human love, early Jewish and Christian scholars saw the book as a parable, or an allegory, symbolizing the love of God for His people or the love of Christ for His Church. This explanation, which still is given in many Bibles, is, of course, completely untenable. The Song of Songs is a mutilated yet very beautiful anthology of quite secular poetry, written probably around 250 B.C. The songs extol the natural love of one human being for another; they are filled with the atmosphere and the imagery of spring in Palestine; their sensuous, elaborate, and even grotesque figures of speech, so unlike those of earlier Hebrew verse, suggest foreign influences, Egyptian, Persian, or perhaps even Greek; and although they differ radically from any other biblical poetry, they add immeasurably to the richness, variety, and, indeed, humanity of our Bible.

The selections given here have been rearranged so that the love lyrics sung by a lover and his mistress stand out as clearly as possible as units; the familiar and charming poem which describes the spring has been placed by itself, as have the beautiful and well known lines descriptive of the strength of human love; and the verses usually ascribed to wedding guests who sing of a bride's beauty and grace are, in their turn, placed alone.

A Girl Longs for Her Lover

Let him kiss me with the kisses of his mouth,
For thy love is better than wine.
Because of the savor of thy good ointments,
Thy name is as ointment poured forth.
I am black,[1] but comely, O ye daughters of Jerusalem;
As the tents of Kedar, as the curtains of Solomon.
Look not upon me because I am black,
Because the sun hath looked upon me.
My mother's children were angry with me;
They made me the keeper of the vineyards;
But mine own vineyard have I not kept.
Tell me, O thou whom my soul loveth, where thou feedest,
Where thou makest thy flock to rest at noon?
For why should I be as one that turneth aside
By the flocks of thy companions?

A Duet Between a Lover and His Sweetheart

He sings:

> I have compared thee, O my love,
> To a company of horses in Pharaoh's chariots.
> Thy cheeks are comely with rows of jewels,
> Thy neck with chains of gold.
> We will make thee borders of gold
> With studs of silver.

She sings:

> A bundle of myrrh is my well beloved unto me;
> He shall lie all night betwixt my breasts.
> My beloved is unto me as a cluster of camphire
> In the vineyards of Engedi.

[1] She means that she is tanned by the sun.

He sings:

Behold, thou art fair, my love!
Behold, thou art fair!
Thou hast dove's eyes.

She sings:

Behold, thou art fair, my beloved, yea, pleasant!
Also our bed is green.
The beams of our house are cedar,
And our rafters of fir.
I am the rose of Sharon,
And the lily of the valleys.

He sings:

As the lily among thorns,
So is my love among the daughters.

She sings:

As the apple tree among the trees of the wood,
So is my beloved among the sons.
I sat down under his shadow with great delight,
And his fruit was sweet to my taste.
He brought me to the banqueting house,
And his banner over me was love.
Stay me with flagons,
Comfort me with apples,
For I am sick from love!
His left hand is under my head,
And his right hand doth embrace me.
I charge you, O ye daughters of Jerusalem,
By the roes and by the hinds of the field,
That ye stir not up, nor awake my love
Till he please.

A Lover Describes His Sweetheart

Behold, thou art fair, my love!
Behold, thou art fair!
Thou hast dove's eyes within thy locks.
Thy hair is as a flock of goats
That appear from mount Gilead.
Thy teeth are like a flock of sheep
That are even shorn,
That came up from the washing.
Thy lips are like a thread of scarlet,
And thy speech is comely.
Thy temples are like a piece of pomegranate within thy locks.
Thy neck is like the tower of David builded for an armory,
Whereon there hang a thousand bucklers,
All shields of mighty men.
Thy two breasts are like two young roes that are twins,
Which feed among the lilies.
Thou art all fair, my love,
There is no spot in thee!
Thy lips, O my spouse, drop as the honeycomb;
Honey and milk are under thy tongue;
And the smell of thy garments is like the smell of Lebanon.
A garden inclosed is my sister,[1] my spouse,
A spring shut up, a fountain sealed,
A fountain of gardens,
A well of living waters,
And streams from Lebanon.

A Girl Describes Her Lover

What is thy beloved more than another beloved,
O thou fairest among women?
What is thy beloved more than another beloved,
That thou dost so charge us?

[2] This is an Egyptian term signifying "sweetheart."

My beloved is white and ruddy,
The chiefest among ten thousand.
His head is as the most fine gold;
His locks are bushy and black as a raven.
His eyes are as the eyes of doves by the rivers of waters,
Washed with milk and fitly set.
His cheeks are as a bed of spices,
As sweet flowers.
His lips like lilies, dropping sweet-smelling myrrh.
His hands are as gold rings set with the beryl.
His belly is as bright ivory, overlaid with sapphires.
His legs are as pillars of marble, set upon sockets of fine gold.
His countenance is as Lebanon,
Excellent as the cedars.
His mouth is most sweet; yea, he is altogether lovely.
This is my beloved, and this is my friend,
O daughters of Jerusalem!

Wedding Guests Sing to a Bride Who Dances Before Them

How beautiful are thy feet with shoes,
O prince's daughter!
The joints of thy thighs are like jewels,
The work of the hands of a cunning workman.
Thy navel is like a round goblet,
Which wanteth not liquor;
Thy belly is like an heap of wheat
Set about with lilies.
Thy two breasts are like two young roes that are twins.
Thy neck is as a tower of ivory.
Thine eyes like the fishpools in Heshbon, by the gate of Bathrabbim.
Thy nose is as the tower of Lebanon
Which looketh toward Damascus.
Thine head upon thee is like Carmel,
And the hair of thine head like purple.
The king is held in the galleries!

How fair and how pleasant art thou,
O love, for delights!

A Lover Sings of Spring in Palestine

My beloved spake, and said unto me:
Rise up, my love, my fair one, and come away!
For, lo, the winter is past,
The rain is over and gone;
The flowers appear on the earth;
The time of the singing of birds is come,
And the voice of the turtle is heard in our land.
The fig tree putteth forth her green figs,
And the vines with the tender grape give a good smell.
Arise, my love, my fair one, and come away!

A Poem in Praise of Love

Set me as a seal upon thine heart, as a seal upon thine arm:
For love is strong as death;
Jealousy is cruel as the grave;
The coals thereof are coals of fire,
Which hath a most vehement flame.
Many waters cannot quench love,
Neither can the floods drown it!
If a man would give all the substance of his house for love,
It would utterly be contemned.

-IV-

THE BOOK OF JOB

THE Book of Job holds rightful place both as the greatest literary masterpiece of the Bible and as one of the greatest masterpieces of all literature. It is ranked with Dante's *Divine Comedy* and Milton's *Paradise Lost,* both of which show its influence upon their authors, with the *Iliad* and the *Odyssey,* with the *Aeneid* and with Shakespeare. To read it with intelligence and understanding is surely to enjoy the deepest reading pleasure which the Bible can afford. But because the right reading of it assumes a recognition of the eternal problem with which it deals, as well as an awareness of its form, its various and distinctive parts, and the literary qualities which make it great, certain information and suggestions for that reading will, I hope, prove valuable.

This superb work of Hebrew poetry is unique among all the material of the Bible, whether in prose or poetry, because of the subject with which it deals and because of the attitude of its unknown author toward that subject. The theme of the book is the ancient and unsolvable problem of pain and suffering in the life of man. In itself this theme is unusual in biblical literature, for it presupposes a speculative or even philosophical bent of mind on the part of an author. Now the Hebrews were not, by nature, a speculative people. Unlike the Greeks, for example, they did not often question or try to solve the *whys* of human life; indeed, among all the many biblical writers only the authors of Ecclesiastes and Job can be termed reflective or philosophical. This lack of philosophical speculation on the part of the Hebrews can be explained partly by themselves, as a people given to seeing, hearing, loving, and describing the world about them rather than to pondering upon its mysteries, and partly by their religious training, which from the beginning had taught them that to obey the Law of God would result in happiness and prosperity, whereas to disobey that divinely established Law would result in punishment and, therefore, in misery. This traditional and orthodox teaching was held tenaciously by them in spite of the evidences about them which would seem to deny, or at least to question, its validity.

But the author of Job clearly rebelled against the easy acceptance of this doctrine. Writing his great poem probably around 450–400 B.C., he refutes the weak and reiterative arguments of Job's three orthodox friends, Eliphaz, Bildad, and Zophar, who would explain Job's sufferings by the inherited tenets of their ancestral faith. Nor is he content to deal only with Job's anguish and with its obvious injustice. He is even more concerned with the whole mystery of human sorrow. For if God, the creator of all things, is by the very fact of His creation responsible for all that is, then He must be responsible for evil as well as for good. How, then, can He be considered just in His dealing with men?

This, in brief, is the theme, or argument, of the Book of Job, an argument which occupies twenty-five of its forty-two chapters and is, therefore, by far its major portion. But since its relation to the other parts of Job should be understood, let us look carefully at the form of the book in order to become aware of its distinct parts; for it should be read with these parts clearly in mind. Indeed, if the reader is wise, he will read and study each part before he attempts to see the book as a whole.

There are five divisions of the book: (1) the prologue, which is contained in chapters 1 and 2, and the epilogue, which completes the prologue and is given in the last ten verses of the book, from chapter 42:7 to the close; (2) the argument, which runs from chapters 3 to 27, inclusive, and which is divided into three cycles, 3–14, 15–21, and 22–27; (3) the monologues of Job, chapters 29, 30, and 31; (4) the speeches of a young man named Elihu, chapters 32–37, inclusive; and (5) the words spoken by God to Job out of the whirlwind and Job's reply, chapters 38 to 42:7. Each of these parts will be explained at greater length in the notes preceding each in the readings which follow.

The literary qualities of the Book of Job are at once superior to, and different from, those of other great Hebrew poetry; and these qualities are seen at their best in chapters 3, 29, 30, 31, 38, 39, 40, and 41. Its author was obviously not only a learned man, but also one of extreme sensitiveness. No other among the Hebrew poets sees as does he "the wonderful works of God" in all their manifold aspects. No other uses figures of speech, similes, metaphors, personifications, with his wealth and beauty. And no other is equally gifted with the ability to effect quick and various changes of style, so evident, for example, in the superb third chapter where the slow, solemn, and measured accents of the first verses change to the plaintive and melodious tones of those of the second half of the poem.

And now a necessary explanation of the book as it appears in the following pages: Any abridgment or cutting of Job by the omission of verses from its most significant and beautiful chapters seems to me unfortunate. These should surely be allowed to stand as they are in all their glory and majesty. The argument, however, is another matter. This can, it seems to me, be abridged with really great profit to the reader and with little, if any, loss. There are good reasons, I think, for this conviction: the three cycles, in which each of Job's three friends speaks and is answered by Job, are repetitive both in material and in thought. The second cycle repeats the points of the first and contains less good poetry. The third cycle is, as is generally acknowledged by the best scholars, obscure in many places because of defects in the original manuscripts; and this obscurity results often in confusion as to who is actually speaking. Because of these features I have decided to include in the argument only the first cycle (with the addition, in brackets, of two significant passages from the second), but to give this cycle in full, exactly as it stands in the King James Version. The careful reader who becomes familiar with this one cycle will understand the points of all three and will be spared much unnecessary repetition and no little confusion.

Abridgment, perhaps drastic, has also been employed in the speeches of Elihu. These speeches are not only held by the best scholars to be a later insertion in the original text and hence not written by the author of Job, but they are as well of distinctly inferior literary quality to the rest of the poem. Only enough of them is given here to preserve the continuity of the whole.

This abridgment of the book has, so far as I know, not heretofore been attempted; but I believe that it affords the best and wisest way to become thoroughly familiar with this greatest work of Old Testament literature.[1]

1

THE PROLOGUE AND THE EPILOGUE

The prologue and the epilogue form the framework within which the great poem is set. Written in vivid and picturesque prose, they tell, or perhaps retell, the story of an upright man named Job, who lived in a land called Uz, and of the wager made by God and Satan concerning

[1] This introduction, even with the notes to each division, is necessarily brief. A far more extended description of the book is given in *The Bible and the Common Reader*, Pt. II. Although there are, of course, countless more learned articles and books on Job, perhaps the relative brevity of this chapter will be of greater value than more exhaustive treatments.

him. This story has all the characteristics of some ancient folk tale which may well have been current when the author of Job wrote his book and which he decided to utilize in order to give that book both form and a deeper meaning. For it should be carefully noted that, whereas in the old tale Job neither curses his fate nor asks why just men suffer, in the poem itself the author, apparently dissatisfied with Job's acceptance, develops his own conception of Job as a man who both rebels and questions.

The Prologue

There was a man in the land of Uz, whose name was Job; and that man was perfect and upright, and one that feared God, and eschewed evil. And there were born unto him seven sons and three daughters. His substance also was seven thousand sheep, and three thousand camels, and five hundred yoke of oxen, and five hundred she-asses, and a very great household; so that this man was the greatest of all the men of the east. And his sons went and feasted in their houses, every one his day; and sent and called for their three sisters to eat and to drink with them. And it was so, when the days of their feasting were gone about, that Job sent and sanctified them, and rose up early in the morning, and offered burnt offerings according to the number of them all; for Job said, It may be that my sons have sinned, and cursed God in their hearts. Thus did Job continually.

Now there was a day when the sons of God came to present themselves before the Lord, and Satan came also among them. And the Lord said unto Satan, Whence comest thou? Then Satan answered the Lord, and said, From going to and fro in the earth, and from walking up and down in it. And the Lord said unto Satan, Hast thou considered my servant Job, that there is none like him in the earth, a perfect and an upright man, one that feareth God, and escheweth evil? Then Satan answered the Lord, and said, Doth Job fear God for nought? Hast not thou made an hedge about him, and about his house, and about all that he hath on every side? Thou hast blessed the work of his hands, and his substance is increased in the land. But put forth thine hand now, and touch all that he hath, and he will curse thee to thy face. And the Lord said unto Satan,

Behold, all that he hath is in thy power; only upon himself put not forth thine hand. So Satan went forth from the presence of the Lord.

And there was a day when his sons and his daughters were eating and drinking wine in their eldest brother's house: and there came a messenger unto Job, and said, The oxen were plowing, and the asses feeding beside them; and the Sabeans fell upon them, and took them away. Yea, they have slain the servants with the edge of the sword; and I only am escaped alone to tell thee. While he was yet speaking, there came also another, and said, The fire of God is fallen from heaven, and hath burned up the sheep, and the servants, and consumed them; and I only am escaped alone to tell thee. While he was yet speaking, there came also another, and said, The Chaldeans made out three bands, and fell upon the camels, and have carried them away, yea, and slain the servants with the edge of the sword; and I only am escaped alone to tell thee. While he was yet speaking, there came also another, and said, Thy sons and thy daughters were eating and drinking wine in their eldest brother's house; and, behold, there came a great wind from the wilderness, and smote the four corners of the house, and it fell upon the young men, and they are dead; and I only am escaped alone to tell thee.

Then Job arose, and rent his mantle, and shaved his head, and fell down upon the ground, and worshipped, and said, Naked came I out of my mother's womb, and naked shall I return thither. The Lord gave, and the Lord hath taken away. Blessed be the name of the Lord!

In all this Job sinned not, nor charged God foolishly.

Again there was a day when the sons of God came to present themselves before the Lord, and Satan came also among them to present himself before the Lord. And the Lord said unto Satan, From whence comest thou? And Satan answered the Lord, and said, From going to and fro in the earth, and from walking up and down in it. And the Lord said unto Satan, Hast thou considered my servant Job, that there is none like him in the earth, a perfect and an upright man, one that feareth God, and escheweth evil? And still he holdeth fast his integrity, although thou movedst me against him to destroy him without cause. And Satan answered the Lord, and said, Skin for skin! Yea, all that a man hath will he give for his life. But put forth thine hand now, and touch his bone and his flesh, and he will curse thee to thy face. And the Lord said unto Satan, Behold, he is in thine hand; but save his life.

So went Satan forth from the presence of the Lord, and smote Job with sore boils from the sole of his foot unto his crown. And he took him a potsherd to scrape himself withal; and he sat down among the ashes. Then said his wife unto him, Dost thou still retain thine integrity? Curse God, and die! But he said unto her, Thou speakest as one of the foolish women speaketh. What, shall we receive good at the hand of God, and shall we not receive evil? In all this Job did not sin with his lips.

Now when Job's three friends heard of all this evil that was come upon him, they came every one from his own place: Eliphaz the Temanite, and Bildad the Shuhite, and Zophar the Naamathite. For they had made an appointment together to come to mourn with him and to comfort him. And when they lifted up their eyes afar off, and knew him not, they lifted up their voice and wept; and they rent every one his mantle and sprinkled dust upon their heads toward heaven.

So they sat down with him upon the ground seven days and seven nights, and none spake a word unto him. For they saw that his grief was very great.

The Epilogue

The epilogue is given here instead of at the close of the Book of Job, where it appears in the Bible. The reader will, of course, be aware upon reading it that it suggests the omission of much material. What this material was we have no means of knowing, what words God spoke to Job, what his friends said to him, or what he replied. These matters were obviously at one time given in the old folk tale. We can only assume from the nature and style of the prologue and epilogue that these were far different in character and in treatment from those of the great poem which follows.

And it was so that, after the Lord had spoken these words unto

Job, the Lord said to Eliphaz the Temanite: My wrath is kindled against thee and against thy two friends; for ye have not spoken of me the thing that is right, as my servant Job hath. Therefore take unto you now seven bullocks and seven rams and go to my servant Job, and offer up for yourselves a burnt offering. And my servant Job shall pray for you (for him I will accept), lest I deal with you after your folly in that ye have not spoken of me the thing which is right, like my servant Job.

So Eliphaz the Temanite and Bildad the Shuhite and Zophar the Naamathite went and did according as the Lord commanded them. The Lord also accepted Job. And the Lord turned the captivity of Job when he prayed for his friends; also, the Lord gave Job twice as much as he had before.

Then came there unto him all his brethren, and all his sisters, and all they that had been of his acquaintance before, and did eat bread with him in his house. And they bemoaned him and comforted him over all the evil that the Lord had brought upon him. Every man also gave him a piece of money, and every one an earring of gold.

So the Lord blessed the latter end of Job more than his beginning; for he had fourteen thousand sheep, and six thousand camels, and a thousand yoke of oxen, and a thousand she-asses. He had also seven sons and three daughters. And he called the name of the first, Jemima; and the name of the second, Kezia; and the name of the third, Keren-happuch. And in all the land there were no women found so fair as the daughters of Job; and their father gave them inheritance among their brethren.

After this Job lived an hundred and forty years, and saw his sons and his sons' sons, even four generations. So Job died, being old and full of days.

2

THE ARGUMENT

In the argument which follows, the reader will note that the words of Job's three friends are always dictated by their religious teaching. Their thoughts do not progress, but rather are constantly repeated. They maintain again and again that God is just, that Job *must* have sinned, and that but one way lies open to him; namely, to acknowledge his sin and to repent. When Job refuses to believe them, they deride and mock him for his irreverent daring to contend with God.

Job's arguments, on the contrary, do progress. After his cursing of his fate in the unsurpassed third chapter, he dares to accuse God of injustice, not alone toward Job, but toward all men; he proclaims his own innocence, saying that God Himself knows this; he swears that he will maintain his honesty and independence of mind. And throughout all that he says, two facts are evident: (1) the fate of all mankind concerns him as much as does his own suffering; (2) his faith in God does not waver, even although he is "full of confusion" and although God hides in darkness his mysterious ways with men.

The glory of this argument, old but ever new, lies, of course, in the intellectual honesty of Job. Although he is faced with a venerable religious teaching, reiterated by his three voluble friends, he is nevertheless faced also with the plain facts of human experience; and he has the independence and dignity to insist that these facts take precedence over the tenets of the faith handed down to him. That God honors him for this independence of thought is shown at the close of the poem.

After this opened Job his mouth, and cursed his day. And Job spake, and said:

Let the day perish wherein I was born,
And the night in which it was said,
There is a man child conceived.
Let that day be darkness.
Let God not regard it from above,
Neither let the light shine upon it.
Let darkness and the shadow of death stain it;
Let a cloud dwell upon it;
Let the blackness of the day terrify it.
As for that night, let darkness seize upon it.
Let it not be joined unto the days of the year,
Let it not come into the number of the months.
Lo, let that night be solitary,
Let no joyful voice come therein.
Let them curse it that curse the day

Who are ready to raise up their mourning.
Let the stars of the twilight thereof be dark;
Let it look for light, but have none,
Neither let it see the dawning of the day:
Because it shut not up the doors of my mother's womb,
Nor hid sorrow from mine eyes.
Why died I not from the womb?
Why did I not give up the ghost when I came out of the belly?
Why did the knees prevent me?
Or why the breasts that I should suck?

For now should I have lain still and been quiet,
I should have slept; then had I been at rest,
With kings and counsellors of the earth,
Which built desolate places for themselves;
Or with princes that had gold,
Who filled their houses with silver;
Or as an hidden untimely birth I had not been,
As infants which never saw light.
There the wicked cease from troubling;
And there the weary be at rest.
There the prisoners rest together;
They hear not the voice of the oppressor.
The small and great are there;
And the servant is free from his master.

Wherefore is light given to him that is in misery,
And life unto the bitter in soul;
Which long for death, but it cometh not;
And dig for it more than for hid treasures;
Which rejoice exceedingly,
And are glad, when they can find the grave?
Why is light given to a man whose way is hid,
And whom God hath hedged in?
For my sighing cometh before I eat,
And my roarings are poured out like the waters.

For the thing which I greatly feared is come upon me,
And that which I was afraid of is come unto me.
I was not in safety, neither had I rest, neither was I quiet;
Yet trouble came.

Then Eliphaz the Temanite answered, and said:

If we assay to commune with thee, wilt thou be grieved?
But who can withhold himself from speaking?
Behold, thou hast instructed many,
And thou hast strengthened the weak hands.
Thy words have upholden him that was falling,
And thou hast strengthened the feeble knees.
But now it is come upon thee, and thou faintest;
It toucheth thee, and thou art troubled.
Is not this thy fear, thy confidence, thy hope,
And the uprightness of thy ways?
Remember, I pray thee, whoever perished, being innocent?
Or where were the righteous cut off?
Even as I have seen:
They that plow iniquity and sow wickedness, reap the same.
By the blast of God they perish,
And by the breath of his nostrils are they consumed.
The roaring of the lion, and the voice of the fierce lion,
And the teeth of the young lions, are broken.
The old lion perisheth for lack of prey,
And the stout lion's whelps are scattered abroad.

Now a thing was secretly brought to me,
And mine ear received a little thereof.
In thoughts from the visions of the night
When deep sleep falleth on men,
Fear came upon me, and trembling
Which made all my bones to shake.
Then a spirit passed before my face;
The hair of my flesh stood up.
It stood still, but I could not discern the form thereof;

An image was before mine eyes.
There was silence, and I heard a voice, saying:
Shall mortal man be more just than God?
Shall a man be more pure than his Maker?
Behold, he put no trust in his servants,
And his angels he charged with folly.
How much less in them that dwell in houses of clay,
Whose foundation is in the dust,
Which are crushed before the moth?
They are destroyed from morning to evening,
They perish forever without any regarding it.
Doth not their excellency which is in them go away?
They die, even without wisdom.

Call now, if there be any that will answer thee.
And to which of the saints wilt thou turn?
For wrath killeth the foolish man,
And envy slayeth the silly one.
I have seen the foolish taking root,
But suddenly I cursed his habitation.
His children are far from safety,
And they are crushed in the gate,
Neither is there any to deliver them;
Whose harvest the hungry eateth up,
And taketh it even out of the thorns,
And the robber swalloweth up their substance.
Although affliction cometh not forth of the dust,
Neither doth trouble spring out of the ground,
Yet man is born unto trouble,
As the sparks fly upward.

I would seek unto God,
And unto God would I commit my cause,
Which doeth great things and unsearchable,
Marvellous things without number:
Who giveth rain upon the earth,

And sendeth waters upon the fields,
To set up on high those that be low,
That those which mourn may be exalted to safety.
He disappointeth the devices of the crafty,
So that their hands cannot perform their enterprise.
He taketh the wise in their own craftiness;
And the counsel of the froward is carried headlong.
They meet with darkness in the daytime,
And grope in the noonday as in the night.
But he saveth the poor from the sword, from their mouth,
And from the hand of the mighty.
So the poor hath hope,
And iniquity stoppeth her mouth.
Behold, happy is the man whom God correcteth;
Therefore despise not thou the chastening of the Almighty.
For he maketh sore, and bindeth up;
He woundeth, and his hands make whole.
He shall deliver thee in six troubles;
Yea, in seven shall there no evil touch thee.
In famine he shall redeem thee from death,
And in war from the power of the sword.
Thou shalt be hid from the scourge of the tongue,
Neither shalt thou be afraid of destruction when it cometh.
At destruction and famine thou shalt laugh,
Neither shalt thou be afraid of the beasts of the earth,
For thou shalt be in league with the stones of the field,
And the beasts of the field shall be at peace with thee.
And thou shalt know that thy tabernacle shall be in peace,
And thou shalt visit thy habitation, and shalt not sin.
Thou shalt know also that thy seed shall be great,
And thine offspring as the grass of the earth.
Thou shalt come to thy grave in a full age,
Like as a shock of corn cometh in in his season.

Lo this, we have searched it, so it is.
Hear it, and know thou it for thy good.

But Job answered, and said:

Oh that my grief were thoroughly weighed
And my calamity laid in the balances together!
For now it would be heavier than the sand of the sea;
Therefore my words are swallowed up.
For the arrows of the Almighty are within me,
The poison whereof drinketh up my spirit.
The terrors of God do set themselves in array against me.
Doth the wild ass bray when he hath grass?
Or loweth the ox over his fodder?
Can that which is unsavory be eaten without salt?
Or is there any taste in the white of an egg?
The things that my soul refused to touch are as my sorrowful meat.
Oh that I might have my request,
And that God would grant me the thing I long for!
Even that it would please God to destroy me,
That he would let loose his hand and cut me off!
Then should I yet have comfort,
Yea, I would harden myself in sorrow.
Let him not spare,
For I have not concealed the words of the Holy One.
What is my strength that I should hope?
And what is mine end that I should prolong my life?
Is my strength the strength of stones?
Or is my flesh of brass?
Is not my help in me?
And is wisdom driven quite from me?

To him that is afflicted pity should be showed from his friend,
But he forsaketh the fear of the Almighty.
My brethren have dealt deceitfully as a brook,
And as the stream of brooks they pass away;
Which are blackish by reason of the ice,
And wherein the snow is hid.
What time they wax warm, they vanish;

When it is hot, they are consumed out of their place.
The paths of their way are turned aside,
They go to nothing, and perish.
The troops of Tema looked,
The companies of Sheba waited for them;
They were confounded because they had hoped,
They came thither and were ashamed.
For now ye are nothing;
Ye see my casting down and are afraid.
Did I say, Bring unto me?
Or, Give a reward for me of your substance?
Or, Deliver me from the enemy's hand?
Or, Redeem me from the hand of the mighty?
Teach me, and I will hold my tongue,
And cause me to understand wherein I have erred.
How forcible are right words!
But what doth your arguing reprove?
Do ye imagine to reprove words,
And the speeches of one that is desperate, which are as wind?
Yea, ye overwhelm the fatherless,
And ye dig a pit for your friend.
Now therefore be content, look upon me;
For it is evident to you if I lie.
Return, I pray you, let it not be iniquity,
Yea, return again, my righteousness is in it.
Is there iniquity in my tongue?
Cannot my taste discern perverse things?

Is there not an appointed time to man upon earth?
Are not his days also like the days of a hireling?
As a servant earnestly desireth the shadow,
And as an hireling looketh for the reward of his work,
So am I made to possess months of vanity,
And wearisome nights are appointed to me.
When I lie down, I say, When shall I arise and the night be gone?
And I am full of tossings to and fro unto the dawning of the day.

My flesh is clothed with worms and clods of dust;
My skin is broken, and become loathsome.
My days are swifter than a weaver's shuttle,
And are spent without hope.
O remember that my life is wind!
Mine eye shall no more see good.
The eye of him that hath seen me shall see me no more;
Thine eyes are upon me, and I am not.
As the cloud is consumed and vanisheth away,
So he that goeth down to the grave shall come up no more.
He shall return no more to his house,
Neither shall his place know him any more.

Job speaks to God:

Therefore I will not refrain my mouth;
I will speak in the anguish of my spirit;
I will complain in the bitterness of my soul.
Am I a sea, or a whale,
That thou settest a watch over me?
When I say, My bed shall comfort me,
My couch shall ease my complaint;
Then thou scarest me with dreams,
And terrifiest me through visions;
So that my soul chooseth strangling,
And death rather than my life.
I loathe it; I would not live alway:
Let me alone; for my days are vanity.
What is man, that thou shouldest magnify him?
And that thou shouldest set thine heart upon him?
And that thou shouldest visit him every morning,
And try him every moment?
How long wilt thou not depart from me,
Nor let me alone till I swallow down my spittle?
I have sinned. What shall I do unto thee, O thou preserver of men?
Why hast thou set me as a mark against thee,

So that I am a burden to myself?
And why dost thou not pardon my transgression,
And take away mine iniquity?
For now shall I sleep in the dust,
And thou shalt seek me in the morning,
But I shall not be.

Then answered Bildad the Shuhite, and said:

How long wilt thou speak these things?
And how long shall the words of thy mouth be like a strong wind?
Doth God pervert judgment?
Or doth the Almighty pervert justice?
If thy children have sinned against him,
And he have cast them away for their transgression;
If thou wouldest seek unto God betimes,
And make thy supplication to the Almighty;
If thou wert pure and upright,
Surely now he would awake for thee,
And make the habitation of thy righteousness prosperous.
Though thy beginning was small,
Yet thy latter end should greatly increase.

For enquire, I pray thee, of the former age,
And prepare thyself to the search of their fathers
(For we are but of yesterday and know nothing,
Because our days upon earth are a shadow).
Shall not they teach thee and tell thee
And utter words out of their heart?
Can the rush grow up without mire?
Can the flag grow without water?
Whilst it is yet in his greenness and not cut down,
It withereth before any other herb.
So are the paths of all that forget God;
And the hypocrite's hope shall perish,
Whose hope shall be cut off,

And whose trust shall be a spider's web.
He shall lean upon his house, but it shall not stand;
He shall hold it fast, but it shall not endure.
He is green before the sun,
And his branch shooteth forth in his garden.
His roots are wrapped about the heap,
And seeth the place of stones.
If he destroy him from his place,
Then it shall deny him, saying, I have not seen thee.
Behold, this is the joy of his way,
And out of the earth shall others grow.
Behold, God will not cast away a perfect man,
Neither will he help the evil-doers;
Till he fill thy mouth with laughing
And thy lips with rejoicing.
They that hate thee shall be clothed with shame,
And the dwelling place of the wicked shall come to nought.

Then Job answered, and said:

I know it is so of a truth:
But how should man be just with God?
If he will contend with him,
He cannot answer him one of a thousand.
He is wise in heart, and mighty in strength.
Who hath hardened himself against him, and hath prospered?
Which removeth the mountains, and they know not;
Which overturneth them in his anger.
Which shaketh the earth out of her place,
And the pillars thereof tremble.
Which commandeth the sun, and it riseth not;
And sealeth up the stars.
Which alone spreadeth out the heavens,
And treadeth upon the waves of the sea.
Which maketh Arcturus, Orion, and Pleiades,
And the chambers of the south.
Which doeth great things past finding out,

Yea, and wonders without number.
Lo, he goeth by me, and I see him not;
He passeth on also, but I perceive him not.
Behold, he taketh away, who can hinder him?
Who will say unto him, What doest thou?
If God will not withdraw his anger,
The proud helpers do stoop under him.
How much less shall I answer him,
And choose out my words to reason with him?
Whom, though I were righteous, yet would I not answer,
But I would make supplication to my judge.
If I had called, and he had answered me;
Yet would I not believe that he had hearkened unto my voice;
For he breaketh me with a tempest,
And multiplieth my wounds without cause.
He will not suffer me to take my breath,
But filleth me with bitterness.
If I speak of strength, lo, he is strong;
And if of judgment, who shall set me a time to plead?
If I justify myself, mine own mouth shall condemn me;
If I say, I am perfect, it shall also prove me perverse.
Though I were perfect, yet would I not know my soul;
I would despise my life.
This is one thing, therefore I said it,
He destroyeth the perfect and the wicked.
If the scourge slay suddenly,
He will laugh at the trial of the innocent.
The earth is given into the hand of the wicked;
He covereth the faces of the judges thereof.
If not, where, and who is he?
Now my days are swifter than a post;
They flee away, they see no good.
They are passed away as the swift ships,
As the eagle that hasteth to the prey.
If I say, I will forget my complaint,
I will leave off my heaviness, and comfort myself,

I am afraid of all my sorrows,
I know that thou wilt not hold me innocent.
If I be wicked, why then labor I in vain?
If I wash myself with snow water,
And make my hands never so clean,
Yet shalt thou plunge me in the ditch,
And mine own clothes shall abhor me.
For he is not a man, as I am, that I should answer him,
And we should come together in judgment.
Neither is there any daysman betwixt us,
That might lay his hand upon us both.
Let him take his rod away from me,
And let not his fear terrify me.
Then would I speak, and not fear him; but it is not so with me.
My soul is weary of my life;
I will leave my complaint upon myself;
I will speak in the bitterness of my soul.

Job speaks to God:

I will say unto God, Do not condemn me;
Show me wherefore thou contendest with me.
Is it good unto thee that thou shouldest oppress,
That thou shouldest despise the work of thine hands,
And shine upon the counsel of the wicked?
Hast thou eyes of flesh?
Or seest thou as man seeth?
Are thy days as the days of man?
Are thy years as man's days,
That thou enquirest after mine iniquity,
And searchest after my sin?
Thou knowest that I am not wicked;
And there is none that can deliver out of thine hand.
Thine hands have made me
And fashioned me together round about;
Yet thou dost destroy me.

Remember, I beseech thee, that thou hast made me as the clay;
And wilt thou bring me into dust again?
Hast thou not poured me out as milk,
And curdled me like cheese?
Thou hast clothed me with skin and flesh,
And hast fenced me with bones and sinews.
Thou hast granted me life and favor,
And thy visitation hath preserved my spirit.
And these things hast thou hid in thine heart;
I know that this is with thee.
If I sin, then thou markest me,
And thou wilt not acquit me from mine iniquity.
If I be wicked, woe unto me;
And if I be righteous, yet will I not lift up my head.
I am full of confusion; therefore see thou mine affliction,
For it increaseth. Thou huntest me as a fierce lion;
And again thou showest thyself marvellous upon me.
Thou renewest thy witnesses against me,
And increasest thine indignation upon me;
Changes and war are against me.
Wherefore then hast thou brought me forth out of the womb?
Oh that I had given up the ghost, and no eye had seen me!
I should have been as though I had not been;
I should have been carried from the womb to the grave.
Are not my days few? Cease then,
And let me alone, that I may take comfort a little,
Before I go whence I shall not return,
Even to the land of darkness and the shadow of death;
A land of darkness, as darkness itself;
And of the shadow of death, without any order,
And where the light is as darkness.

Then answered Zophar the Naamathite, and said:

Should not the multitude of words be answered?
And should a man full of talk be justified?

Should thy lies make men hold their peace?
And when thou mockest,
Shall no man make thee ashamed?
For thou hast said, My doctrine is pure,
And I am clean in thine eyes.
But oh that God would speak, and open his lips against thee,
And that he would show thee the secrets of wisdom,
That they are double to that which is!
Know therefore that God exacteth of thee
Less than thine iniquity deserveth.
Canst thou by searching find out God?
Canst thou find out the Almighty unto perfection?
It is as high as heaven. What canst thou do?
Deeper than hell. What canst thou know?
The measure thereof is longer than the earth,
And broader than the sea.
If he cut off, and shut up,
Or gather together, then who can hinder him?
For he knoweth vain men;
He seeth wickedness also. Will he not then consider it
For vain man would be wise,
Though man be born like a wild ass's colt.
If thou prepare thine heart,
And stretch out thine hands toward him,
If iniquity be in thine hand, put it far away,
And let not wickedness dwell in thy tabernacles.
For then shalt thou lift up thy face without spot;
Yea, thou shalt be steadfast, and shalt not fear,
Because thou shalt forget thy misery,
And remember it as waters that pass away.
And thine age shall be clearer than the noonday;
Thou shalt shine forth, thou shalt be as the morning.
And thou shalt be secure, because there is hope;
Yea, thou shalt dig about thee,
And thou shalt take thy rest in safety.
Also thou shalt lie down, and none shall make thee afraid.

Yea, many shall make suit unto thee.
But the eyes of the wicked shall fail,
And they shall not escape,
And their hope shall be as the giving up of the ghost.

And Job answered, and said:

No doubt but ye are the people,
And wisdom shall die with you.
But I have understanding as well as you;
I am not inferior to you;
Yea, who knoweth not such things as these?
I am as one mocked of his neighbor,
Who calleth upon God, and he answereth him.
The just upright man is laughed to scorn.
He that is ready to slip with his feet
Is as a lamp despised in the thought of him that is at ease.
The tabernacles of robbers prosper,
And they that provoke God are secure,
Into whose hand God bringeth abundantly.
But ask now the beasts, and they shall teach thee;
And the fowls of the air, and they shall tell thee;
Or speak to the earth, and it shall teach thee;
And the fishes of the sea shall declare unto thee.
Who knoweth not in all these
That the hand of the Lord hath wrought this?
In whose hand is the soul of every living thing,
And the breath of all mankind.
Doth not the ear try words?
And the mouth taste his meat?
With the ancient is wisdom;
And in length of days understanding.
With him is wisdom and strength,
He hath counsel and understanding.
Behold, he breaketh down, and it cannot be built again;
He shutteth up a man, and there can be no opening.

Behold, he withholdeth the waters, and they dry up;
Also he sendeth them out, and they overturn the earth.
With him is strength and wisdom;
The deceived and the deceiver are his.
He leadeth counsellors away spoiled,
And maketh the judges fools.
He looseth the bond of kings,
And girdeth their loins with a girdle.
He leadeth princes away spoiled,
And overthroweth the mighty.
He removeth away the speech of the trusty,
And taketh away the understanding of the aged.
He poureth contempt upon princes,
And weakeneth the strength of the mighty.
He discovereth deep things out of darkness,
And bringeth out to light the shadow of death.
He increaseth the nations, and destroyeth them;
He enlargeth the nations, and straiteneth them again.
He taketh away the heart
Of the chief of the people of the earth,
And causeth them to wander
In a wilderness where there is no way.
They grope in the dark without light,
And he maketh them to stagger like a drunken man.

Lo, mine eye hath seen all this,
Mine ear hath heard and understood it.
What ye know, the same do I know also;
I am not inferior unto you.
Surely I would speak to the Almighty,
And I desire to reason with God.
But ye are forgers of lies,
Ye are all physicians of no value.
O that ye would altogether hold your peace,
And it should be your wisdom.
Hear now my reasoning,

And hearken to the pleadings of my lips.
Will ye speak wickedly for God?
And talk deceitfully for him?
Will ye accept his person?
Will ye contend for God?
Is it good that he should search you out?
Or as one man mocketh another, do ye so mock him?
He will surely reprove you,
If ye do secretly accept persons.
Shall not his excellency make you afraid?
And his dread fall upon you?
Your remembrances are like unto ashes,
Your bodies to bodies of clay.
Hold your peace, let me alone, that I may speak,
And let come on me what will.
Wherefore do I take my flesh in my teeth,
And put my life in mine hand?
Though he slay me, yet will I trust in him;
But I will maintain mine own ways before him.
He also shall be my salvation;
For an hypocrite shall not come before him.
[For I know that my Redeemer liveth,
And that he shall stand at the latter day upon the earth;
And though after my skin worms destroy this body,
Yet in my flesh I shall see God;
Whom I shall see for myself and mine eyes shall behold, and not another,
Though my reins be consumed within me.]

Hear diligently my speech,
And my declaration with your ears.

Job speaks to God:

Behold now, I have ordered my cause;
I know that I shall be justified.
Who is he that will plead with me?

For now, if I hold my tongue, I shall give up the ghost.
Only do not two things unto me,
Then will I not hide myself from thee:
Withdraw thine hand far from me;
And let not thy dread make me afraid.
Then call thou, and I will answer;
Or let me speak, and answer thou me.
How many are mine iniquities and sins?
Make me to know my transgression and my sin.
Wherefore hidest thou thy face,
And holdest me for thine enemy?
Wilt thou break a leaf driven to and fro?
And wilt thou pursue the dry stubble?
For thou writest bitter things against me,
And makest me to possess the iniquities of my youth.
Thou puttest my feet also in the stocks,
And lookest narrowly unto all my paths.
Thou settest a print upon the heels of my feet.

Man that is born of a woman
Is of few days, and full of trouble.
He cometh forth like a flower, and is cut down;
He fleeth also as a shadow, and continueth not.
And dost thou open thine eyes upon such an one,
And bringest me into judgment with thee?
Who can bring a clean thing out of an unclean? Not one.
Seeing his days are determined, the number of his months are with thee,
Thou hast appointed his bounds that he cannot pass;
Turn from him, that he may rest,
Till he shall accomplish, as an hireling, his day.
For there is hope of a tree, if it be cut down, that it will sprout again,
And that the tender branch thereof will not cease.
Though the root thereof wax old in the earth,
And the stock thereof die in the ground;
Yet through the scent of water it will bud,

And bring forth boughs like a plant.
But man dieth, and wasteth away;
Yea, man giveth up the ghost, and where is he?
As the waters fail from the sea,
And the flood decayeth and drieth up,
So man lieth down, and riseth not.
Till the heavens be no more, they shall not awake,
Nor be raised out of their sleep.
O that thou wouldest hide me in the grave,
That thou wouldest keep me secret, until thy wrath be past,
That thou wouldest appoint me a set time, and remember me!
If a man die, shall he live again?
All the days of my appointed time will I wait,
Till my change come.
Thou shalt call, and I will answer thee;
Thou wilt have a desire to the work of thine hands.
For now thou numberest my steps;
Dost thou not watch over my sin?
My transgression is sealed up in a bag,
And thou sewest up mine iniquity.
And surely the mountain falling cometh to nought,
And the rock is removed out of his place.
The waters wear the stones;
Thou washest away the things
Which grow out of the dust of the earth;
And thou destroyest the hope of man.
Thou prevailest forever against him, and he passeth;
Thou changest his countenance, and sendest him away.
His sons come to honor, and he knoweth it not;
And they are brought low, but he perceiveth it not of them.
But his flesh upon him shall have pain,
And his soul within him shall mourn.

Job questions his three friends concerning the life of man:

[What is the Almighty that we should serve him?
And what profit should we have, if we pray unto him?

One dieth in his full strength, being wholly at ease and quiet;
And another dieth in the bitterness of his soul, and never eateth
with pleasure.
They shall lie down alike in the dust,
And the worms shall cover them.
Behold, I know your thoughts,
And the devices which ye wrongfully imagine against me.
For ye say, Where is the house of the prince?
And where are the dwelling places of the wicked?
Have ye not asked them that go by the way?
And do ye not know their tokens:
That the wicked is reserved to the day of destruction?
They shall be brought forth to the day of wrath,
Who shall repay him for what he hath done?
Yet shall he be brought to the grave,
And he shall remain in the tomb.
The clods of the valley shall be sweet unto him;
And every man shall draw after him
As there are innumerable before him.

How then comfort ye me in vain,
Seeing in your answers there remaineth falsehood?]

3

THE MONOLOGUES OF JOB

After Job's three friends, horrified by his boldness and blasphemy, have become silent, Job, as though talking to himself, utters three soliloquies, or monologues. In these noble poems is found some of the most beautiful language of the book.

The Remembrance of Things Past

Oh that I were as in months past,
As in the days when God preserved me;
When his candle shined upon my head,

And when by his light I walked through darkness;
As I was in the days of my youth,
When the secret of God was upon my tabernacle;
When the Almighty was yet with me,
When my children were about me;
When I washed my steps with butter,
And the rock poured me out rivers of oil;
When I went out to the gate through the city,
When I prepared my seat in the street!
The young men saw me, and hid themselves;
And the aged arose and stood up.
The princes refrained talking,
And laid their hand on their mouth.
The nobles held their peace,
And their tongue cleaved to the roof of their mouth.
When the ear heard me, then it blessed me;
And when the eye saw me, it gave witness to me,
Because I delivered the poor that cried,
And the fatherless, and him that had none to help him.
The blessing of him that was ready to perish came upon me;
And I caused the widow's heart to sing for joy.
I put on righteousness, and it clothed me;
My judgment was as a robe and a diadem.
I was eyes to the blind,
And feet was I to the lame.
I was a father to the poor;
And the cause which I knew not I searched out.
And I brake the jaws of the wicked,
And plucked the spoil out of his teeth.
Then I said, I shall die in my nest,
And I shall multiply my days as the sand.
My root was spread out by the waters,
And the dew lay all night upon my branch.
My glory was fresh in me,
And my bow was renewed in my hand.
Unto me men gave ear, and waited,

And kept silence at my counsel.
After my words they spake not again;
And my speech dropped upon them.
And they waited for me as for the rain;
And they opened their mouth wide as for the latter rain.
If I laughed on them, they believed it not;
And the light of my countenance they cast not down.
I chose out their way, and sat chief,
And dwelt as a king in the army,
As one that comforteth the mourners.

The Sorrows of the Present

But now they that are younger than I have me in derision,
Whose fathers I would have disdained
To have set with the dogs of my flock.
Yea, whereto might the strength of their hands profit me,
In whom old age was perished?
For want and famine they were solitary,
Fleeing into the wilderness in former time desolate and waste.
Who cut up mallows by the bushes,
And juniper roots for their meat.
They were driven forth from among men
(They cried after them as after a thief)
To dwell in the cliffs of the valleys,
In caves of the earth, and in the rocks.
Among the bushes they brayed;
Under the nettles they were gathered together.
They were children of fools, yea, children of base men;
They were viler than the earth.
And now am I their song,
Yea, I am their byword.
They abhor me, they flee far from me,
And spare not to spit in my face.
Because he hath loosed my cord, and afflicted me,
They have also let loose the bridle before me.

Upon my right hand rise the youth; they push away my feet,
And they raise up against me the ways of their destruction.
They mar my path, they set forward my calamity,
They have no helper.
They came upon me as a wide breaking in of waters;
In the desolation they rolled themselves upon me.
Terrors are turned upon me;
They pursue my soul as the wind;
And my welfare passeth away as a cloud.
And now my soul is poured out upon me;
The days of affliction have taken hold upon me.
My bones are pierced in me in the night season,
And my sinews take no rest.
By the great force of my disease is my garment changed;
It bindeth me about as the collar of my coat.
He hath cast me into the mire,
And I am become like dust and ashes.

I cry unto thee, and thou dost not hear me;
I stand up, and thou regardest me not.
Thou art become cruel to me;
With thy strong hand thou opposest thyself against me.
Thou liftest me up to the wind; thou causest me to ride upon it,
And dissolvest my substance.
For I know that thou wilt bring me to death,
And to the house appointed for all living.
Howbeit he will not stretch out his hand to the grave,
Though they cry in his destruction.

Did not I weep for him that was in trouble?
Was not my soul grieved for the poor?
When I looked for good, then evil came unto me;
And when I waited for light, there came darkness.
My bowels boiled, and rested not;
The days of affliction prevented me.
I went mourning without the sun;

I stood up, and I cried in the congregation.
I am a brother to dragons,
And a companion to owls.
My skin is black upon me,
And my bones are burned with heat.
My harp also is turned to mourning,
And my organ into the voice of them that weep.

The Ethical Code of Job

I made a covenant with mine eyes;
Why then should I think upon a maid?
For what portion of God is there from above?
And what inheritance of the Almighty from on high?
Is not destruction to the wicked?
And a strange punishment to the workers of iniquity?
Doth not he see my ways,
And count all my steps?
If I have walked with vanity,
Or if my foot hath hasted to deceit;
Let me be weighed in an even balance,
That God may know mine integrity.
If my step hath turned out of the way,
And mine heart walked after mine eyes,
And if any blot hath cleaved to mine hands,
Then let me sow, and let another eat;
Yea, let my offspring be rooted out.
If mine heart have been deceived by a woman,
Or if I have laid wait at my neighbor's door;
Then let my wife grind unto another,
And let others bow down upon her.
For this is an heinous crime;
Yea, it is an iniquity to be punished by the judges.
For it is a fire that consumeth to destruction,
And would root out all mine increase.
If I did despise the cause of my manservant

Or of my maidservant, when they contended with me,
What then shall I do when God riseth up?
And when he visiteth, what shall I answer him?
Did not he that made me in the womb make him?
And did not one fashion us in the womb?
If I have withheld the poor from their desire,
Or have caused the eyes of the widow to fail,
Or have eaten my morsel myself alone,
And the fatherless hath not eaten thereof
(For from my youth he was brought up with me,
As with a father,
And I have guided her from my mother's womb).
If I have seen any perish for want of clothing,
Or any poor without covering;
If his loins have not blessed me,
And if he were not warmed with the fleece of my sheep;
If I have lifted up my hand against the fatherless,
When I saw my help in the gate;
Then let mine arm fall from my shoulder blade,
And mine arm be broken from the bone.
For destruction from God was a terror to me,
And by reason of his highness I could not endure.
If I have made gold my hope,
Or have said to the fine gold, Thou art my confidence;
If I rejoiced because my wealth was great,
And because mine hand had gotten much;
If I beheld the sun when it shined,
Or the moon walking in brightness;
And my heart hath been secretly enticed,
Or my mouth hath kissed my hand;
This also were an iniquity to be punished by the judge,
For I should have denied the God that is above.
If I rejoiced at the destruction of him that hated me,
Or lifted up myself when evil found him
(Neither have I suffered my mouth to sin
By wishing a curse to his soul).

If the men of my tabernacle said not,
Oh that we had of his flesh! we cannot be satisfied.
The stranger did not lodge in the street,
But I opened my doors to the traveler.
If I covered my transgressions as Adam,
By hiding mine iniquity in my bosom;
Did I fear a great multitude,
Or did the contempt of families terrify me,
That I kept silence, and went not out of the door?
Oh that one would hear me!
Behold, my desire is, that the Almighty would answer me,
And that mine adversary had written a book.
Surely I would take it upon my shoulder,
And bind it as a crown to me.
I would declare unto him the number of my steps;
As a prince would I go near unto him.
If my land cry against me,
Or that the furrows likewise thereof complain;
If I have eaten the fruits thereof without money,
Or have caused the owners thereof to lose their life;—
Let thistles grow instead of wheat, and cockle instead of barley.

The words of Job are ended.

4

THE SPEECHES OF ELIHU

These abridged readings are taken from the speeches of Elihu, chapters 32–37. They have been so arranged that the substance of Elihu's weak arguments are clear, also his critical, even cruel, attitude toward Job. The reader should be aware throughout Elihu's last words that a storm is arising.

As has been noted in the longer introduction, these speeches are generally accepted as a later insertion into the poem.

So these three men ceased to answer Job, because he was righteous in his own eyes. Then was kindled the wrath of Elihu the Buzite;

against Job was his wrath kindled because he justified himself rather than God. Also against his three friends was his wrath kindled because they had found no answer, and yet had condemned Job.

And Elihu answered, and said:

I am young, and ye are very old;
Wherefore I was afraid and durst not show you my opinion.
I said, Days should speak,
And multitude of years should teach wisdom.
But there is a spirit in man;
And the inspiration of the Almighty giveth them understanding.
Great men are not always wise;
Neither do the aged understand judgment.
Therefore I said, Hearken to me;
I also will show my opinion.
Wherefore, Job, I pray thee, hear my speeches,
And hearken to all my words.

Surely thou hast spoken in mine hearing,
And I have heard the voice of thy words, saying:
I am clean without transgression; I am innocent,
Neither is there iniquity in me.
Behold, in this thou art not just.
I will answer thee that God is greater than man.
He looketh upon men, and if any say, I have sinned,
And perverted that which is right, and it profited me not,
He will deliver his soul from going into the pit,
And his life shall see the light.
Lo, all these things worketh God oftentimes with man,
To bring back his soul from the pit,
To be enlightened with the light of the living.
Mark well, O Job, hearken unto me;
Hold thy peace, and I will speak.

Hear my words, O ye wise men,
And give ear unto me, ye that have knowledge.

For Job hath said, I am righteous,
And God hath taken away my judgment.
What man is like Job who drinketh up scorning like water?
Which goeth in company with the workers of iniquity,
And walketh with wicked men?
Therefore hearken unto me, ye men of understanding:
Far be it from God that he should do wickedness,
And from the Almighty that he should commit iniquity.
For his eyes are upon the ways of men
And he seeth all his goings.
When he giveth quietness, who then can make trouble?
And when he hideth his face, who then can behold him,
Whether it be done against a nation or against a man only?
Surely it is meet to be said unto God:
I have borne chastisement, I will not offend any more.
That which I see not, teach thou me.
If I have done iniquity, I will do no more.
Job hath spoken without knowledge,
And his words were without wisdom.
My desire is that Job may be tried unto the end,
For he addeth rebellion unto his sin,
He clappeth his hands among us,
And multiplieth his words against God.

God thundereth marvellously with his voice;
Great things doeth he, which we cannot comprehend.
For he saith to the snow, Be thou on the earth;
Likewise to the small rain, and to the great rain of his strength.
Out of the south cometh the whirlwind,
And cold out of the north.
Hearken unto this, O Job!
Stand still and consider the wondrous works of God.
Teach us what we shall say unto him,
For we cannot order our speech by reason of darkness.
Shall it be told him that I speak?
If a man speak, surely he shall be swallowed up.

And now men see not the bright light which is in the clouds,
But the wind passeth and cleanseth them.

5

GOD SPEAKS TO JOB OUT OF THE WHIRLWIND

The magnificent passages which follow are rightly held to be the most beautiful of the entire poem. In their dignity of utterance, in their variety and range of imagery, and in their perfection of language, they are unsurpassed by any other poetry, whether ancient or modern. The use of the question which predominates the style adds greatly to the sense of mystery and questioning which pervades the entire poem.

In the pure enjoyment of such poetry as this, the reader should not, however, be unaware of its relation to the poem as a whole. What actually is God revealing to Job through His awful questioning? Why does Job, once he has heard the voice of God and seen the vision which His words create, cry that he is vile, that he abhors himself, that he repents "in dust and ashes." In short, how does this overwhelming vision of God and of His omnipotence quiet and satisfy the bewildered mind of Job?

It is clear that the question of God's justice in His dealings with men, the whole problem of pain and evil in the world, is never answered. To man's finite mind injustice must ever seem to be the law of life, and life itself forever a mystery. God does not explain His hidden ways and purposes to Job; but He does so reveal to him the wonder and the glory of the universe and the worth of life itself that Job no longer needs, or even wants, to question.

Nor should one miss the fact, already suggested, that God commends Job for his questioning, even for his rebellion. Job, and not his three friends, has spoken rightly of God. He is now to deck himself with "majesty and excellency," to bring low all that are proud of heart, and, finally, to understand that his "own right hand," that is, his own honesty of mind, can save his soul.

Then the Lord answered Job out of the whirlwind, and said,
Who is this that darkeneth counsel
By words without knowledge?

Gird up now thy loins like a man;
For I will demand of thee, and answer thou me.

Where wast thou when I laid the foundations of the earth?
Declare, if thou hast understanding.
Who hath laid the measures thereof, if thou knowest?
Or who hath stretched the line upon it?
Whereupon are the foundations thereof fastened?
Or who laid the corner stone thereof,
When the morning stars sang together,
And all the sons of God shouted for joy?
Or who shut up the sea with doors,
When it brake forth, as if it had issued out of the womb?
When I made the cloud the garment thereof,
And thick darkness a swaddlingband for it,
And brake up for it my decreed place,
And set bars and doors,
And said, Hitherto shalt thou come, but no further:
And here shall thy proud waves be stayed?
Hast thou commanded the morning since thy days;
And caused the dayspring to know his place;
That it might take hold of the ends of the earth,
That the wicked might be shaken out of it?
It is turned as clay to the seal;
And they stand as a garment.
And from the wicked their light is withholden,
And the high arm shall be broken.
Hast thou entered into the springs of the sea?
Or hast thou walked in the search of the depth?
Have the gates of death been opened unto thee?
Or hast thou seen the doors of the shadow of death?
Hast thou perceived the breadth of the earth?
Declare if thou knowest it all.
Where is the way where light dwelleth?
And as for darkness, where is the place thereof,
That thou shouldest take it to the bound thereof,

And that thou shouldest know the paths to the house thereof?
Knowest thou it, because thou wast then born?
Or because the number of thy days is great?
Hast thou entered into the treasures of the snow?
Or hast thou seen the treasures of the hail,
Which I have reserved against the time of trouble,
Against the day of battle and war?
By what way is the light parted,
Which scattereth the east wind upon the earth?
Who hath divided a watercourse for the overflowing of waters,
Or a way for the lightning of thunder,
To cause it to rain on the earth, where no man is;
On the wilderness, wherein there is no man;
To satisfy the desolate and waste ground;
And to cause the bud of the tender herb to spring forth?
Hath the rain a father?
Or who hath begotten the drops of dew?
Out of whose womb came the ice?
And the hoary frost of heaven, who hath gendered it?
The waters are hid as with a stone,
And the face of the deep is frozen.
Canst thou bind the sweet influences of Pleiades,
Or loose the bands of Orion?
Canst thou bring forth Mazzaroth in his season?
Or canst thou guide Arcturus with his sons?
Knowest thou the ordinances of heaven?
Canst thou set the dominion thereof in the earth?
Canst thou lift up thy voice to the clouds,
That abundance of waters may cover thee?
Canst thou send lightnings, that they may go,
And say unto thee, Here we are?
Who hath put wisdom in the inward parts?
Or who hath given understanding to the heart?
Who can number the clouds in wisdom?
Or who can stay the bottles of heaven,
When the dust groweth into hardness,

And the clods cleave fast together?
Wilt thou hunt the prey for the lion?
Or fill the appetite of the young lions,
When they couch in their dens,
And abide in the covert to lie in wait?
Who provideth for the raven his food?
When his young ones cry unto God,
They wander for lack of meat.

Knowest thou the time when the wild goats of the rock bring forth?
Or canst thou mark when the hinds do calve?
Canst thou number the months that they fulfil?
Or knowest thou the time when they bring forth?
They bow themselves, they bring forth their young ones,
They cast out their sorrows.
Their young ones are in good liking, they grow up with corn;
They go forth, and return not unto them.
Who hath sent out the wild ass free?
Or who hath loosed the bands of the wild ass?
Whose house I have made the wilderness,
And the barren land his dwellings.
He scorneth the multitude of the city,
Neither regardeth he the crying of the driver.
The range of the mountains is his pasture,
And he searcheth after every green thing.
Will the unicorn be willing to serve thee,
Or abide by thy crib?
Canst thou bind the unicorn with his band in the furrow?
Or will he harrow the valleys after thee?
Wilt thou trust him, because his strength is great?
Or wilt thou leave thy labor to him?
Wilt thou believe him, that he will bring home thy seed,
And gather it into thy barn?
Gavest thou the goodly wings unto the peacocks?
Or wings and feathers unto the ostrich?

Which leaveth her eggs in the earth,
And warmeth them in dust,
And forgetteth that the foot may crush them,
Or that the wild beast may break them.
She is hardened against her young ones, as though they were not hers;
Her labor is in vain without fear,
Because God hath deprived her of wisdom,
Neither hath he imparted to her understanding.
What time she lifteth up herself on high,
She scorneth the horse and his rider.
Hast thou given the horse strength?
Hast thou clothed his neck with thunder?
Canst thou make him afraid as a grasshopper?
The glory of his nostrils is terrible.
He paweth in the valley, and rejoiceth in his strength;
He goeth on to meet the armed men.
He mocketh at fear, and is not affrighted;
Neither turneth he back from the sword.
The quiver rattleth against him,
The glittering spear and the shield.
He swalloweth the ground with fierceness and rage;
Neither believeth he that it is the sound of the trumpet.
He saith among the trumpets, Ha, ha!
And he smelleth the battle afar off,
The thunder of the captains, and the shouting.
Doth the hawk fly by thy wisdom,
And stretch her wings toward the south?
Doth the eagle mount up at thy command,
And make her nest on high?
She dwelleth and abideth on the rock,
Upon the crag of the rock, and the strong place.
From thence she seeketh the prey,
And her eyes behold afar off.
Her young ones also suck up blood;
And where the slain are, there is she.

Moreover the Lord answered Job, and said:

Shall he that contendeth with the Almighty instruct him?
He that reproveth God, let him answer it.

Then Job answered the Lord, and said:

Behold, I am vile. What shall I answer thee?
I will lay mine hand upon my mouth.
Once I have spoken; but I will not answer;
Yea, twice; but I will proceed no further.

Then answered the Lord unto Job out of the whirlwind, and said,
Gird up thy loins now like a man;
I will demand of thee, and declare thou unto me.
Wilt thou also disannul my judgment?
Wilt thou condemn me, that thou mayest be righteous?
Hast thou an arm like God?
Or canst thou thunder with a voice like him?
Deck thyself now with majesty and excellency;
And array thyself with glory and beauty.
Cast abroad the rage of thy wrath;
And behold every one that is proud, and abase him.
Look on every one that is proud, and bring him low;
And tread down the wicked in their place.
Hide them in the dust together;
And bind their faces in secret.
Then will I also confess unto thee
That thine own right hand can save thee.

Behold now behemoth, which I made with thee;
He eateth grass as an ox.
Lo now, his strength is in his loins,
And his force is in the navel of his belly.
He moveth his tail like a cedar;
The sinews of his stones are wrapped together.

His bones are as strong pieces of brass;
His bones are like bars of iron.
He is the chief of the ways of God;
He that made him can make his sword to approach unto him.
Surely the mountains bring him forth food,
Where all the beasts of the field play.
He lieth under the shady trees,
In the covert of the reed, and fens.
The shady trees cover him with their shadow;
The willows of the brook compass him about.
Behold, he drinketh up a river, and hasteth not;
He trusteth that he can draw up Jordan into his mouth.
He taketh it with his eyes;
His nose pierceth through snares.

Canst thou draw out leviathan with an hook?
Or his tongue with a cord which thou lettest down?
Canst thou put an hook into his nose?
Or bore his jaw through with a thorn?
Will he make many supplications unto thee?
Will he speak soft words unto thee?
Will he make a covenant with thee?
Wilt thou take him for a servant forever?
Wilt thou play with him as with a bird?
Or wilt thou bind him for thy maidens?
Shall the companions make a banquet of him?
Shall they part him among the merchants?
Canst thou fill his skin with barbed irons?
Or his head with fish spears?
Lay thine hand upon him,
Remember the battle, do no more.
Behold the hope of him is in vain;
Shall not one be cast down even at the sight of him?
None is so fierce that dare stir him up.
Who then is able to stand before me?
Who hath prevented me, that I should repay him?

Whatsoever is under the whole heaven is mine.
I will not conceal his parts,
Nor his power, nor his comely proportion.
Who can discover the face of his garment?
Or who can come to him with his double bridle?
Who can open the doors of his face?
His teeth are terrible round about,
His scales are his pride,
Shut up together as with a close seal.
One is so near to another,
That no air can come between them.
They are joined one to another,
They stick together, that they cannot be sundered.
By his neesings a light doth shine,
And his eyes are like the eyelids of the morning.
Out of his mouth go burning lamps,
And sparks of fire leap out.
Out of his nostrils goeth smoke,
As out of a seething pot or caldron.
His breath kindleth coals,
And a flame goeth out of his mouth.
In his neck remaineth strength,
And sorrow is turned into joy before him.
The flakes of his flesh are joined together;
They are firm in themselves; they cannot be moved.
His heart is as firm as a stone;
Yea, as hard as a piece of the nether millstone.
When he raiseth up himself, the mighty are afraid;
By reason of breakings they purify themselves.
The sword of him that layeth at him cannot hold:
The spear, the dart, nor the habergeon.
He esteemeth iron as straw,
And brass as rotten wood.
The arrow cannot make him flee;
Slingstones are turned with him into stubble.
Darts are counted as stubble;

He laugheth at the shaking of a spear.
Sharp stones are under him;
He spreadeth sharp pointed things upon the mire.
He maketh the deep to boil like a pot;
He maketh the sea like a pot of ointment.
He maketh a path to shine after him;
One would think the deep to be hoary.
Upon earth there is not his like,
Who is made without fear.
He beholdeth all high things:
He is a king over all the children of pride.

Then Job answered the Lord, and said:

I know that thou canst do everything,
And that no thought can be withholden from thee.
Who is he that hideth counsel without knowledge?
Therefore have I uttered that I understood not;
Things too wonderful for me, which I knew not.
Hear, I beseech thee, and I will speak:
I have heard of thee by the hearing of the ear;
But now mine eye seeth thee.
Wherefore I abhor myself,
And repent in dust and ashes.

-V-

POEMS ON WISDOM

THE poems which follow are among the most beautiful in Hebrew literature. Some are selected from books of the Bible: from Proverbs, Ecclesiastes, and Job; others are from the Apocrypha, a collection of late Hebrew writings in history, narrative, and poetry, not now included in most editions of the Bible except in those used by Roman Catholics.

These poems all belong to the so-called Wisdom Literature of the Bible. But since the word "wisdom" was variously interpreted by those who wrote it, some explanation of its meanings may not come amiss. By far the larger number of writers used the word in a moral or an ethical sense and became the composers, or compilers, of countless proverbs, maxims, or aphorisms which gave men good advice on the most sensible, and even profitable, ways of living. Most of these proverbs are contained in the Old Testament book which bears their name; many others occur in Ecclesiastes and in the Apocryphal book known as Ecclesiasticus.

Other more gifted writers, however, interpreted "wisdom" in a less literal, less realistic sense. To these, wisdom meant religious vision, spiritual richness, that possession of mind and soul which sees beyond the moral law to the mystery of life and which also is aware of the refining effect of that mystery upon human understanding, and, therefore, upon human conduct. To these, wisdom often meant also that mysterious Power "set up from everlasting" and possessed by God "in the beginning of His way," a Power which alone, in its moments of revelation, can transform human life from tragedy to triumph.

These writers were not, like many of the so-called "wise men," teachers and preachers. They were, instead, poets, and among the greatest of poets. It is certain of their poems on Wisdom which I have collected here.

I have brought the poems together in one chapter partly because they deal with the same general subject, whatever their approach to it, partly because certain of them are clearly out of place in the biblical context in which they occur. I have tried also to arrange them in terms of their excellence as poetry; but this arrangement is the result, of course, of a purely personal value-judgment. Whether or not the reader agrees with this judgment, I feel sure that the poems themselves (which close our Old Testament Readings) will be appreciated as noble and beautiful expressions of the Hebrew mind and imagination at its best.

TWO POEMS FROM ECCLESIASTES

I have chosen not to include the book of Ecclesiastes in whole, or even in large part, in these Readings, not surely because of its skepticism, but because much of it is repetitive and also relatively undistinguished as literature. Most of its twelve chapters are in prose, and many of them are given to the repetition of proverbial sayings, most familiar in the book of Proverbs itself. There are, however, in Ecclesiastes some fine poetic passages; and two of these I have given in the form of poetry.

The Preacher, or Koheleth in his Hebrew name, wrote his book around 200 B.C. It really is an essay on the meaning of life, which, Koheleth has discovered, after years spent in searching, has no discernible meaning. God to him is at best but a Cosmic Force, or perhaps even blind Fate or Chance; surely He is no just and merciful creator and ruler of men. Unlike Job, however, this Hebrew thinker does not concern himself in sorrow over the lot of man; nor is he healed by a vision of the wonders of God. His conclusion of the whole matter is that, since the present and the future are obviously governed by chance, one should live one's allotted days with all one's might and draw from them all the good things which they afford.

But that he was not without a sense of the mystery of life or without sympathy for men as they draw near its close, is quite evident from the following poems.[1]

1

The Strange Course of Life

FROM ECCLESIASTES, CHAPTERS 1 AND 9

One generation passeth away, and another generation cometh;
But the earth abideth forever.
The sun also ariseth, and the sun goeth down,
And hasteth to the place where he arose.

[1] A treatment of Ecclesiastes is given in *The Bible and the Common Reader*, Pt. II.

The wind goeth toward the south,
And turneth about unto the north.
It whirleth about continually.
And the wind returneth again according to his circuits.
All the rivers run into the sea;
Yet the sea is not full.
Unto the place from whence the rivers come,
Thither they return again.
The thing that hath been, it is that which shall be;
And that which is done is that which shall be done;
And there is no new thing under the sun.
There is no remembrance of former things;
Neither shall there be any remembrance of things that are to come
With those that shall come after.

I gave my heart to seek and to search out wisdom
Concerning all things that are done under heaven.
I have seen all the works that are done under the sun;
And behold, all is vanity and vexation of spirit.
And I gave my heart to know wisdom,
And to know madness and folly.
I perceived that this also is vexation of spirit.
For in much wisdom is much grief,
And he that increaseth knowledge, increaseth sorrow.

Go thy way, eat thy bread with joy,
And drink thy wine with a merry heart.
Let thy garments be always white;
And let thy head lack no ointment.
Whatsoever thy hand findeth to do, do it with thy might,
For there is no work, nor device, nor knowledge, nor wisdom
In the grave whither thou goest.
I returned, and saw under the sun,
That the race is not to the swift,
Nor the battle to the strong,
Neither yet bread to the wise,

Nor yet riches to men of understanding,
Nor yet favor to men of skill:
But time and chance happeneth to them all.

2

The Sorrows of Old Age

FROM ECCLESIASTES 12

This lovely and touching description of old age is accomplished by means of symbolic images: the keepers of the house are the hands; the darkened windows are the eyes; the grinders are the teeth; the white blossoms of the almond are the hair. The old are afraid of high places, of the traffic on the streets, of handling the lamps and bowls and pitchers.

Rejoice, O young man, in thy youth;
And let thy heart cheer thee in the days of thy youth;
And walk in the ways of thine heart,
And in the sight of thine eyes
While the evil days come not nor the years draw nigh
When thou shalt say, I have no pleasure in them.
While the sun, or the light, or the moon, or the stars
Be not darkened, nor the clouds return after the rain:
In the day when the keepers of the house shall tremble,
And the strong men shall bow themselves,
And the grinders cease because they are few,
And those that look out of the windows be darkened.
And the doors shall be shut in the streets
When the sound of the grinding is low;
And he shall rise up at the voice of the bird;
And all the daughters of music shall be brought low.
Also when they shall be afraid of that which is high,
And fears shall be in the way,
And the almond tree shall flourish,
And the grasshopper shall be a burden,
And desire shall fail:

Because man goeth to his long home
And the mourners go about the streets.
Or ever the silver cord be loosed,
Or the golden bowl be broken,
Or the pitcher be broken at the fountain,
Or the wheel broken at the cistern.

Then shall the dust return to the earth as it was,
And the spirit shall return unto God who gave it.

TWO POEMS FROM PROVERBS

The book of Proverbs is a collection, or better, several collections, of maxims and aphorisms, written and compiled over several centuries and published as a whole some time between 400–200 B.C. Most of the thirty-one chapters which form the book are given entirely to the terse, balanced sayings of those more realistic writers who interpreted wisdom in a moral or ethical sense and who are concerned mainly with good counsel and wise advice. But here and there among their numberless maxims which follow one another with no clear sequence, there are passages, possibly out of place and obviously written by men with a more idealistic conception of life and thought. And at the close of chapter 8 there is a poem filled with such vision, such exalted thought and expression, that most of the rest of the book seems barren by comparison. This poem will close our group of poems on Wisdom because it is, in my opinion, the finest of them all.

The two which are now given here, although, in comparison, of lesser merit than the final poem, hold high place among the best literary passages of our Bible.

1

The Gifts of Wisdom

FROM PROVERBS 3

Happy is the man that findeth wisdom,
And the man that getteth understanding.
For the merchandise of it is better than the merchandise of silver,

And the gain thereof than fine gold.
She is more precious than rubies,
And all the things thou canst desire are not to be compared unto her.
Length of days is in her right hand,
And in her left hand riches and honor.
Her ways are ways of pleasantness,
And all her paths are peace.
She is a tree of life to them that lay hold upon her;
And happy is every one that retaineth her.

2

The Voice of Wisdom

FROM PROVERBS 8 AND 9

Doth not wisdom cry?
And understanding put forth her voice?
She standeth in the top of high places,
By the way, in the places of the paths.
She crieth at the gates, at the entry of the city,
At the coming in at the doors:
Unto you, O men, I call,
And my voice is to the sons of man.
Hear, for I will speak of excellent things;
And the opening of my lips shall be right things.
Receive my instruction, and not silver,
And knowledge rather than choice gold.

Wisdom hath builded her house;
She hath hewn out her seven pillars.
She hath killed her beasts; she hath mingled her wine;
She hath also furnished her table.
She hath sent forth her maidens.
She crieth upon the highest places of the city:
Whoso is simple, let him turn in hither.
Come, eat of my bread,

And drink of the wine which I have mingled.
Forsake the foolish, and live;
And go in the way of understanding.
The fear of the Lord is the beginning of wisdom;
And the knowledge of the Holy is understanding.
For by me thy days shall be multiplied,
And the years of thy life shall be increased.

POEMS FROM THE WISDOM OF SOLOMON

The Wisdom of Solomon in the Apocrypha is a late book written probably not far from the year 100 B.C. Many scholars think that it was originally composed in Greek and later translated into Hebrew.

1

The Souls of the Righteous

FROM CHAPTERS 2 AND 3

For they said within themselves, reasoning not aright:
Short and sorrowful is our life,
And there is no healing when a man cometh to his end.
Because by mere chance were we born,
And hereafter we shall be as though we had never been.
And our name shall be forgotten in time,
And no man shall remember our works.
And our life shall pass away as the traces of a cloud,
And shall be scattered as a mist
When it is chased by the beams of the sun.
For our allotted time is the passing of a shadow.

Come, therefore, and let us enjoy the good things that now are.
And let us use the creation with all our soul.
Let us fill ourselves with costly wine and perfumes,
And let no flower of spring pass us by.
Let us crown ourselves with rosebuds before they be withered.

Thus reasoned they, and they were led astray,
For they knew not the mysteries of God,
Neither hoped they for wages of holiness,
Nor did they judge that there is a prize for blameless souls,
Because God created man for incorruption
And made him an image of his own everlastingness.

But the souls of the righteous are in the hand of God,
And no torment shall touch them.
In the eyes of the foolish they seemed to have died,
And their departure was accounted to be their hurt,
And their journeying away from us to be their ruin.
But they are in peace.
For even if in the sight of men they be punished,
Their hope is full of immortality;
Because God made trial of them,
And found them worthy of himself.
As gold in the furnace he proved them,
And as a whole burnt offering he accepted them.
And in the time of their visitation they shall shine forth,
And as sparks among stubble they shall run to and fro.

2

The Nature of Wisdom

FROM CHAPTERS 6 AND 7

Wisdom is radiant and fadeth not away;
And easily is she beheld of them that love her,
And found of them that seek her.
She forestalleth them that desire to know her,
Making herself first known.
He that riseth up early to seek her shall have no toil,
For he shall find her sitting at his gates.
For to think upon her is perfectness of understanding,
And he that watcheth for her sake shall quickly be free from care.

For her true beginning is desire of discipline;
And the care for discipline is love of her;
And love of her is observance of her laws;
And to give heed to her laws confirmeth incorruption;
And incorruption bringeth near unto God.

But what wisdom is, I will declare,
And I will not hide mysteries from you.
But I will trace her out from the beginning of creation,
And bring the knowledge of her into clear light.

I myself am a mortal man, like to all,
And am sprung from one born of the earth;
And in the womb of a mother was I moulded into flesh
In the time of ten months.
And when I was born, I drew in the common air,
And fell upon the earth, which is of like nature,
And the first voice I uttered was crying, as all others do;
For all men have one entrance into life,
And the like going out.
Wherefore I prayed and understanding was given me;
I called upon God, and the spirit of wisdom came to me.
I preferred her before sceptres and thrones,
And esteemed riches nothing in comparison to her.
I loved her above health and beauty,
And chose to have her instead of light;
For the light that cometh from her never goeth out.
For she is a treasure unto men that never faileth,
Which they that use become the friends of God.

For she is a breath of the power of God,
And a clear effluence of the glory of the Almighty;
Therefore can nothing defiled find entrance into her.
For she is an effulgence from everlasting light,
And an unspotted mirror of the working of God,
And an image of his goodness.

And she hath power to do all things,
And she reneweth all things;
And from generation to generation, passing into holy souls,
She maketh men friends of God and prophets.
She is fairer than the sun,
And above all the constellations of the stars,
And, being compared with light, she is found to be before it.

POEMS FROM ECCLESIASTICUS

The Apocryphal book Ecclesiasticus is a collection of writings by a man called Jesus, the son of Sira. Writing around 180 B.C., he evidently took the book of Proverbs for his model. There are, however, among his countless maxims, several poems on wisdom in her more exalted interpretation; and there is throughout his long book of fifty-one chapters always the evidence of his understanding of human life and of the worth of the individual.

1

The Wisdom of Those Who Work with Their Hands

FROM CHAPTER 38

The wisdom of the scribe cometh by opportunity of leisure.
How shall he become wise that holdeth the plough,
That driveth oxen and is occupied in their labors,
And whose discourse is of the stock of bulls?
He will set his heart upon turning his furrows;
And his wakefulness is to give his heifers their fodder.
So is every artificer and workmaster
That passeth his time by night as by day.
They that cut gravings of signets,
Their diligence is to make great variety;
They will set their heart to preserve likeness in their portraiture,
And will be wakeful to finish their work.
So is the smith, sitting by the anvil,

And considering the unwrought iron.
The vapor of the fire will waste his flesh;
The noise of the hammer will be ever in his ear;
He will set his heart upon perfecting his works,
And he will be wakeful to adorn them perfectly.
So is the potter, sitting at his work,
And turning the wheel about with his feet.
He will fashion the clay with his arm;
He will apply his heart to finish the glazing;
And he will be wakeful to make clean the furnace.

All these put their trust in their hands,
And each becometh wise in his own work.
Without these shall not a city be inhabited.
They shall not be sought for in the council of the people,
And in the assembly they shall not mount on high;
They shall not sit on the seat of the judge,
Neither shall they declare instruction and judgment.
But they will maintain the fabric of the world;
And in the handiwork of their craft is their prayer.

2

Wisdom Speaks in Her Own Praise

FROM CHAPTER 24

Wisdom shall praise herself
And shall glory in the midst of her people.
In the congregation of the Most High shall she open her mouth,
And glory in the presence of his power.

I came forth from the mouth of the Most High,
And covered the earth as a mist.
I dwelt in high places,
And my throne is in the pillar of the cloud.
Alone I compassed the circuit of heaven,

And walked in the depth of the abyss,
In the waves of the sea, and in all the earth.
God created me from the beginning, before the world,
And to the end I shall not fail.
In the Holy Tabernacle I ministered before him,
And so was I established in Zion.
In the beloved city likewise he gave me rest,
And in Jerusalem was my authority.
I was exalted like a cedar in Lebanon,
And as a cypress tree on the mountains of Hermon.
I was exalted like a palm tree on the seashore,
And as rose plants in Jericho,
And as a fair olive tree in the plain.
As the terebinth I stretched out my branches;
And my branches are branches of glory and grace.

Come unto me, ye that are desirous of me,
And be ye filled with my produce.
For my memorial is sweeter than honey,
And mine inheritance than the honeycomb.
They that eat me shall yet be hungry;
And they that drink me shall yet be thirsty.
He that obeyeth me shall not be ashamed;
And they that work in me shall not do amiss.

The Dwelling Place of Wisdom

JOB 28

This magnificent poem is wrongly placed in the Book of Job, at the close of the Argument. It obviously does not belong there. It is given here as one of the noblest examples of Wisdom Literature. Its author and date are unknown.

Surely there is a vein for the silver,
And a place for gold where they fine it.
Iron is taken out of the earth,

And brass is molten out of the stone.
He setteth an end to darkness,
And searcheth out all perfection:
The stones of darkness, and the shadow of death.
The flood breaketh out from the inhabitant;
Even the waters forgotten of the foot;
They are dried up, they are gone away from men.
As for the earth, out of it cometh bread;
And under it is turned up as it were fire.
The stones of it are the place of sapphires;
And it hath dust of gold.
There is a path which no fowl knoweth,
And which the vulture's eye hath not seen;
The lion's whelps have not trodden it,
Nor the fierce lion passed by it.
He putteth forth his hand upon the rocks;
He overturneth the mountains by the roots.
He cutteth out rivers among the rocks;
And his eye seeth every precious thing.
He bindeth the floods from overflowing;
And the thing that is hid bringeth he forth to light.

But where shall wisdom be found?
And where is the place of understanding?
Man knoweth not the price thereof;
Neither is it found in the land of the living.
The depth saith, It is not in me;
And the sea saith, It is not with me.
It cannot be gotten for gold,
Neither shall silver be weighed for the price thereof.
It cannot be valued with the gold of Ophir,
With the precious onyx, or the sapphire.
The gold and the crystal cannot equal it;
And the exchange of it shall not be for jewels of fine gold.
No mention shall be made of coral, or of pearls;
For the price of wisdom is above rubies.

The topaz of Ethiopia shall not equal it,
Neither shall it be valued with pure gold.
Whence then cometh wisdom?
And where is the place of understanding?
Seeing it is hid from the eyes of all living,
And kept close from the fowls of the air.
Destruction and death say,
We have heard the fame thereof with our ears.
God understandeth the way thereof,
And he knoweth the place thereof.
For he looketh to the ends of the earth,
And seeth under the whole heaven,
To make the weight for the winds;
And he weigheth the waters by measure.
When he made a decree for the rain,
And a way for the lightning of the thunder.

The Timelessness of Wisdom

PROVERBS 8:22–31

The Lord possessed me in the beginning of his way,
Before his works of old.
I was set up from everlasting, from the beginning,
Or ever the earth was.
When there were no depths, I was brought forth;
When there were no fountains abounding with water.
Before the mountains were settled,
Before the hills was I brought forth;
While as yet he had not made the earth, nor the fields,
Nor the highest part of the dust of the world.
When he prepared the heavens, I was there;
When he set a compass upon the face of the depth;
When he established the clouds above;
When he strengthened the fountains of the deep;
When he gave to the sea his decree,
That the waters should not pass his commandment;

When he appointed the foundations of the earth;
Then I was by him, as one brought up with him;
And I was daily his delight,
Rejoicing always before him;
Rejoicing in the habitable part of his earth;
And my delights were with the sons of men.

SELECTIONS FROM THE NEW TESTAMENT

EVEN to those who know the Bible but slightly, the New Testament, at least to those of Christian tradition and upbringing, is usually more familiar than is the Old. From the four Gospels they know the Beatitudes, the Lord's Prayer, the Sermon on the Mount, certain of the parables of Jesus, and something, at least, of His life and death; from the Acts of the Apostles and the Pauline Epistles they have some knowledge of the spread of the early Church and of the extraordinary missionary journeys of St. Paul; from the book of Revelation they have gathered an idea, however vague, of a vision of the Next World as a place where there shall be no more sorrow or crying. And yet I think it is safe to say that relatively few readers realize either the many differences between the two great "testaments" which make up our Bible or the close relationship which exists between them.

The New Testament is, of course, very different from the Old. In the first place it is only one-third as long and covers in its literature only a period of at most one hundred years in contrast to the eleven centuries, or more, which are embraced by the literature of the Old Testament. Also, whereas the literature of the Old Testament includes every type and subject, that of the New is confined to one subject only, the life and the teachings of Jesus and of His followers and the results upon men of that life and of those teachings. The Old Testament portrays the history of a people from its beginnings to its tragic conquest by foreign nations; the New Testament has to do only with scattered Christian groups in Palestine and the Mediterranean world and has comparatively little relation to the wider world of its time. The literature of the New Testament, except for a few songs and hymns inherited from the Old, is entirely in prose and was written in the Greek of its day rather than in Hebrew, although its writers, with the possible exception of St. Luke, were all Jewish. The purpose of the New Testament was an overwhelming religious purpose, that of spreading the good tidings of a new faith; whereas the purpose actuating many of the Old Testament writers was both literary and religious. From these distinctions one is not surprised to learn that as a work of literature the New Testament is distinctly inferior to the Old. Its authors, except for St. Paul and St. Luke, were not men of outstanding literary genius, and whatever literary merit the New Testament has (and it has a great deal) arises from the religious fervor which prompted its writing.

And yet with all these differences we must never forget that without the Old Testament there would be no New. St. Augustine was quite right when he said, "The New Testament lies within the Old; the Old Testament is made manifest in the New." The founder of Christianity was Himself of the Jewish race and was brought up under the teachings of the Jewish Law. His teaching by parables was a Jewish inheritance; many of His rules for human conduct had been uttered by the Hebrew prophets before Him. His great work was to reinterpret, humanize, and illumine Jewish teachings; to reveal God to men as He had never been before revealed; to give to an old and tired world new faith and hope, or, in His own words, a more abundant life.

The New Testament, like the Old, is a collection. Its twenty-seven books, together with other manuscripts less valuable, originally comprised the literature of the earliest Christian communities. The first of the twenty-seven in point of time were St. Paul's letters, written between A.D. 50 and 64; the four Gospels and the book of the Acts were written later, between A.D. 70 and 90; the book of Revelation around A.D. 96. The shorter epistles, accredited to various writers, were mostly of a still later date. The New Testament, as we know it today, was not actually compiled until A.D. 367, under the authority of the Church of that time.

To select the best readings from the New Testament and to arrange these with clarity and helpfulness is a difficult task and one upon which I have given much care and thought. In my arrangement I realize acutely that I have departed radically from the methods of other compilers. Most of these, and there are many of them, have, for example, combined the four Gospels on the principle of incorporating into one narrative the best features of all. This method seems to me unfortunate since, in my opinion, the Gospels vary in appeal and in literary quality and since each contains its own peculiar emphasis upon the life of Jesus and upon His teachings. Because to me, as to countless other readers and students of the New Testament, St. Luke's Gospel stands incomparably above the others both in human appeal and in literary charm, I have chosen to take my selections largely from its chapters, although I have occasionally added, or substituted, passages from the other three. I have, moreover, arranged the material so that the purely biographical narratives are kept distinct from those stories characterizing other persons and also from the teachings of Jesus, either by direct exposition or by parables.

As to the readings selected from the Acts, I have grouped these around the individuals with whom they have to do: St. Peter or St. Stephen, St. Philip or St. Paul. From the letters of St. Paul I have chosen what I consider the best passages and have in every case suggested the circumstances under which each was written. Revelation, a most obscure book even in the minds of the early Church Fathers, I have carefully abridged and presented in the clearest way possible, at least to me. The shorter epistles, all of less importance than those accredited to St. Paul by the best scholars, are not included in these readings.

With this nucleus of the New Testament given here, readers interested in the other Gospels and epistles should be able to proceed on their own. Before any reading from these selections is begun, the introduction to the New Testament given under that title in *The Bible and the Common Reader,* Part IV, may prove interesting and helpful.

-I-

READINGS FROM THE GOSPELS

THE LIFE OF JESUS

THE TEACHINGS OF JESUS

CERTAIN PARABLES OF JESUS

THE PEOPLE WHOM JESUS LOVED

FROM ST. JOHN, CHAPTER I

IN THE beginning was the Word, and the Word was with God, and the Word was God. The same was in the beginning with God. All things were made by him; and without him was not any thing made that was made. In him was Life; and the Life was the light of men. And the light shineth in darkness; and the darkness comprehended it not.

That was the true Light which lighteth every man that cometh into the world. He was in the world, and the world was made by him, and the world knew him not. He came unto his own, and his own received him not.

But as many as received him, to them gave he power to become the Sons of God, even to them that believe on his name: Which were born, not of blood, nor of the will of the flesh, nor of the will of man, but of God.

And the Word was made flesh, and dwelt among us, and we beheld his Glory, the glory as of the Only Begotten of the Father, full of Grace and Truth.

THE LIFE OF JESUS

Each of the four men who wrote the Gospels (a word which means *good news*) cherished his own idea about the character of Jesus and the meaning of His life. To St. Mark, Jesus was preeminently the Messiah; to St. Matthew, He was both the Messiah and the Founder of the Christian Church; to St. John, who was more a philosopher and a mystic than the others, He was the Word made flesh, the Incarnate Son of God. To St. Luke, although Jesus was all these, He was above all else a friend to men and women; and He had come to earth to point the way to a more abundant life for all mankind. St. Luke was neither a theologian nor a philosopher, but a biographer and a dramatist, a born storyteller who, more than any of the others, could imbue his narrative with charm and excitement.

We know little about the writers of these Gospels, nor have we time or space here to enter into the numerous controversies concerning them. Of St. Mark and St. Luke we do possess some reliable information since both are mentioned in the letters of St. Paul. Both were evidently his companions on certain of his missionary journeys, Mark perhaps one of his secretaries, Luke, who seems to have been trained in medicine, his "beloved physician."

FROM ST. LUKE

1

There was in the days of Herod, the king of Judea, a certain priest named Zacharias; and his wife was of the daughters of Aaron, and her name was Elisabeth. And they were both righteous before God, walking in all the commandments and ordinances of the Lord blameless. And they had no child, and both were now well stricken in years. And it came to pass, that while he executed the priest's office before God in the order of his course, there appeared unto him an angel of the Lord standing on the right side of the altar of incense. And when Zacharias saw him, he was troubled, and fear fell upon him. But the angel said unto him: Fear not, Zacharias: for thy prayer is heard; and thy wife Elisabeth shall bear thee a son; and thou shalt call his name John. And thou shalt have joy and gladness; and many shall rejoice at his birth. For he shall be great in the sight of the Lord, and shall drink neither wine nor strong drink; and he shall be filled with the Holy Ghost, even from his mother's womb. And many of the children of Israel shall he turn to the Lord their God.

And Zacharias said unto the angel, Whereby shall I know this? For I am an old man, and my wife well stricken in years. And the angel answering said unto him: I am Gabriel that stand in the presence of God; and I am sent to speak unto thee, and to show thee these glad tidings. And, behold, thou shalt be dumb and not able to speak until the day that these things shall be performed because thou believest not my words.

And the people waited for Zacharias and marvelled that he tarried so long in the temple. And when he came out, he could not speak unto them; and they perceived that he had seen a vision in the temple. And as soon as the days of his ministration were accomplished, he departed to his own house.

And after those days his wife Elisabeth conceived and hid herself five months, saying, Thus hath the Lord dealt with me in the days wherein he looked on me, to take away my reproach among men.

2

And in the sixth month the angel Gabriel was sent from God unto a city of Galilee, named Nazareth, to a virgin espoused to a man whose name was Joseph, of the house of David; and the virgin's name was Mary. And the angel came in unto her, and said: Hail, thou that art highly favored! The Lord is with thee. Blessed art thou among women. And when she saw him, she was troubled at his saying, and cast in her mind what manner of salutation this should be.

And the angel said unto her, Fear not, Mary; for thou hast found favor with God. And, behold, thou shalt conceive in thy womb, and bring forth a son, and shalt call his name JESUS. He shall be great, and shall be called the Son of the Highest; and the Lord God shall give unto him the throne of his father David. And he shall reign over the house of Jacob forever; and of his kingdom there shall be no end.

Then said Mary unto the angel, How shall this be, seeing I know not a man?

And the angel answered and said unto her: The Holy Ghost shall come upon thee, and the power of the Highest shall overshadow thee; therefore also that holy thing which shall be born of thee shall be called the Son of God. And, behold, thy cousin Elisabeth, she hath also conceived a son in her old age. For with God nothing shall be impossible.

And Mary said, Behold the handmaid of the Lord. Be it unto me according to thy word. And the angel departed from her. And Mary arose in those days and went into the hill country with haste, into a city of Judah; and she entered into the house of Zacharias and saluted Elisabeth. And it came to pass that, when Elisabeth heard the salutation of Mary, the babe leaped in her womb; and Elisabeth was filled with the Holy Ghost. And she spake out with a loud voice and said, Blessed art thou among women, and blessed is the fruit of thy womb. And whence is this to me that the mother of my Lord should come to me? For, lo, as soon as the voice of thy salutation sounded in mine ears, the babe leaped in my womb for joy.

And Mary said:

My soul doth magnify the Lord,
And my spirit hath rejoiced in God my Savior.
For he hath regarded the low estate of his handmaiden;
For, behold, from henceforth all generations shall call me blessed.
For he that is mighty hath done to me great things;
And holy is his name.
And his mercy is on them that fear him from generation to generation.
He hath showed strength with his arm;
He hath scattered the proud in the imagination of their hearts.
He hath put down the mighty from their seats,
And exalted them of low degree.

He hath filled the hungry with good things;
And the rich he hath sent empty away.
He hath holpen his servant Israel,
In remembrance of his mercy;
As he spake to our fathers,
To Abraham, and to his seed forever.

And Mary abode with her about three months, and returned to her own house.

3

Now Elisabeth's full time came that she should be delivered; and she brought forth a son. And her neighbors and her cousins heard how the Lord had showed great mercy upon her; and they rejoiced with her.

And it came to pass that on the eighth day they came to circumcise the child, and they called him Zacharias after the name of his father. And his mother answered and said, Not so; but he shall be called John. And they said unto her, There is none of thy kindred that is called by this name. And they made signs to his father how he would have him called. And he asked for a writing table and wrote, saying, His name is John. And his mouth was opened immediately, and his tongue loosed, and he was filled with the Holy Ghost, and prophesied, saying:

Blessed be the Lord God of Israel;
For he hath visited and redeemed his people,
And hath raised up an horn of salvation for us
In the house of his servant David;
As he spake by the mouth of his holy prophets, which have been since the world began;
That we should be saved from our enemies, and from the hand of all that hate us;
To perform the mercy promised to our fathers,
And to remember his holy covenant;

The oath which he sware to our father Abraham,
That he would grant unto us, that we, being delivered out of the hand of our enemies,
Might serve him without fear,
In holiness and righteousness before him, all the days of our life.
And thou, child, shalt be called the prophet of the Highest:
For thou shalt go before the face of the Lord to prepare his ways;
To give knowledge of salvation unto his people,
By the remission of their sins,
Through the tender mercy of our God,
Whereby the dayspring from on high hath visited us,
To give light to them that sit in darkness and in the shadow of death,
To guide our feet into the way of peace.

4

And it came to pass in those days that there went out a decree from Caesar Augustus that all the world should be taxed. And all went to be taxed, every one into his own city.

And Joseph also went out from Galilee, out of the city of Nazareth, into Judea, unto the city of David, which is called Bethlehem (because he was of the house and lineage of David); to be taxed with Mary his espoused wife, being great with child. And so it was, that, while they were there, the days were accomplished that she should be delivered. And she brought forth her firstborn son, and wrapped him in swaddling clothes, and laid him in a manger, because there was no room for them in the inn.

And there were in the same country shepherds abiding in the field, keeping watch over their flock by night. And, lo, the angel of the Lord came upon them, and the glory of the Lord shone round about them; and they were sore afraid. And the angel said unto them: Fear not, for behold I bring you good tidings of great joy, which shall be to all people. For unto you is born this day in the city of David a Savior, which is Christ the Lord. And this shall be a sign unto you: Ye shall find the babe wrapped in swaddling clothes, lying in a manger. And suddenly there was with the angel a multitude of the heavenly host praising God, and saying: Glory to God in the highest and on earth peace, good will toward men!

And it came to pass, as the angels were gone away from them into heaven, the shepherds said one to another, Let us now go even unto Bethlehem and see this thing which is come to pass, which the Lord hath made known unto us. And they came with haste and found Mary and Joseph, and the babe lying in a manger.

And when they had seen it, they made known abroad the saying which was told them concerning this child. And all they that heard it wondered at those things which were told them by the shepherds. And the shepherds returned, glorifying and praising God for all the things that they had heard and seen, as it was told unto them.

But Mary kept all these things, and pondered them in her heart.

5

And when eight days were accomplished for the circumcising of the child, his name was called JESUS, which was so named of the angel before he was conceived in the womb. And when the days of her purification according to the law of Moses were accomplished, they brought him to Jerusalem, to present him to the Lord, and to offer a sacrifice according to that which is said in the law of the Lord, A pair of turtledoves, or two young pigeons.

And, behold, there was a man in Jerusalem, whose name was Simeon; and the same man was just and devout, and the Holy Ghost was upon him. And it was revealed unto him by the Holy Ghost, that he should not see death, before he had seen the Lord's Christ. And he came by the Spirit into the temple; and when the parents brought in the child Jesus, to do for him after the custom of the law, then took he him up in his arms, and blessed God, and said:

Lord, now lettest thou thy servant depart in peace,
According to thy word:
For mine eyes have seen thy salvation,
Which thou hast prepared before the face of all people:
A light to lighten the Gentiles,
And the glory of thy people Israel.

And Joseph and his mother marvelled at those things which were spoken of him. And Simeon blessed them, and said unto Mary his mother, Behold, this child is set for the fall and rising again of many in Israel; and for a sign which shall be spoken against, that the thoughts of many hearts may be revealed. (Yea, a sword shall pierce through thy own soul also.)

And there was one Anna, a prophetess; and she was a widow of fourscore and four years, which departed not from the temple, but served God with fastings and prayers night and day. And she coming in that instant gave thanks likewise unto the Lord, and spake of him to all them that looked for redemption in Jerusalem. And when they had performed all things according to the law of the Lord, they returned into Galilee, to their own city Nazareth.

6

And the child grew, and waxed strong in spirit, filled with wisdom; and the grace of God was upon him.

Now his parents went to Jerusalem every year at the feast of the passover. And when he was twelve years old, they went up to Jerusalem after the custom of the feast. And when they had fulfilled the days, as they returned, the child Jesus tarried behind in Jerusalem; and Joseph and his mother knew not of it. But they, supposing him to have been in the company, went a day's journey; and they sought him among their kinsfolk and acquaintance. And when they found him not, they turned back again to Jerusalem, seeking him.

And it came to pass, that after three days they found him in the temple, sitting in the midst of the doctors, both hearing them, and asking them questions. And all that heard him were astonished at his understanding and answers. And when they saw him, they were amazed; and his mother said unto him, Son, why hast thou thus dealt with us? Behold, thy father and I have sought thee sorrowing. And he said unto them, How is it that ye sought me? Wist ye not that I must be about my Father's business? And they understood not the saying which he spake unto them.

And he went down with them, and came to Nazareth, and was

subject unto them; but his mother kept all these sayings in her heart. And Jesus increased in wisdom and stature, and in favor with God and man.

FROM ST. MATTHEW 3

7

In those days came John the Baptist (the son of Zacharias) preaching in the wilderness of Judea, and saying, Repent ye; for the kingdom of heaven is at hand. For this is he that was spoken of by the prophet Esaias, saying, The voice of one crying in the wilderness: Prepare ye the way of the Lord.

And the same John had his raiment of camel's hair and a leathern girdle about his loins; and his meat was locusts and wild honey. Then went out to him Jerusalem and all Judea and all the region round about Jordan; and were baptized of him in Jordan, confessing their sins.

Then cometh Jesus from Galilee to Jordan unto John to be baptized of him. But John forbade him, saying, I have need to be baptized of thee, and comest thou to me? And Jesus answering said unto him, Suffer it to be so now. For thus it becometh us to fulfill all righteousness.

Then he suffered him. And Jesus, when he was baptized, went up straightway out of the water. And, lo, the heavens were opened unto him, and he saw the Spirit of God descending like a dove, and lighting upon him. And, lo, a voice from heaven, saying: This is my beloved Son, in whom I am well pleased.

CONTINUED FROM ST. LUKE

8

And Jesus himself began to be about thirty years of age, being (as was supposed) the son of Joseph. And being full of the Holy Ghost, he returned from Jordan and was led by the Spirit into the wilderness, being forty days tempted of the devil.

And in these days he did eat nothing; and when they were ended, he afterward hungered. And the devil said unto him, If thou be the Son of God, command this stone that it be made bread. And Jesus answered him, saying, It is written, that man shall not live by bread alone, but by every word of God.

And the devil, taking him up into a high mountain, showed unto him all the kingdoms of the world in a moment of time. And the devil said unto him, All this power will I give thee, and the glory of them. If thou therefore wilt worship me, all shall be thine. And Jesus answered and said unto him, Get thee behind me, Satan. For it is written, Thou shalt worship the Lord thy God, and him only shalt thou serve.

And the devil brought him to Jerusalem and set him on a pinnacle of the Temple, and said unto him, If thou be the Son of God, cast thyself down from hence. For it is written, He shall give his angels charge over thee to keep thee. And in their hands they shall bear thee up lest at any time thou dash thy foot against a stone. And Jesus answering said unto him, It is said, Thou shall not tempt the Lord thy God.

And when the devil had ended all the temptation, he departed from him for a season. And Jesus returned in the Spirit into Galilee. And there went out a fame of him through all the region round about. And he taught in their synagogues, being glorified of all.

9

And he came to Nazareth, where he had been brought up; and, as his custom was, he went into the synagogue on the sabbath day, and stood up for to read. And there was delivered unto him the book of the prophet Esaias. And when he had opened the book, he found the place where it was written:

The Spirit of the Lord is upon me,
Because he hath anointed me to preach the gospel to the poor;
He hath sent me to heal the brokenhearted,

To preach deliverance to the captives,
And recovering of sight to the blind,
To set at liberty them that are bruised,
To preach the acceptable year of the Lord.

And he closed the book, and gave it to the minister, and sat down. And the eyes of all them that were in the synagogue were fastened on him. And he began to say unto them, This day is this scripture fulfilled in your ears. And all bare him witness, and wondered at the gracious words which proceeded out of his mouth. And they said, Is not this Joseph's son?

10

Now when the sun was setting, all they that had any sick with divers diseases brought them unto him; and he laid his hands on every one of them and healed them. And when it was day, he departed and went into a desert place; and the people sought him and came unto him and stayed him that he should not depart from them. And he said unto them, I must preach the kingdom of God to other cities also; for therefore am I sent. And he preached in the synagogues of Galilee.

And it came to pass that, as the people pressed upon him to hear the word of God, he stood by the lake of Gennesaret. And he saw two ships standing by the lake; but the fishermen were gone out of them and were washing their nets. And he entered into one of the ships, which was Simon's, and prayed him that he would thrust out a little from the land. And he sat down and taught the people out of the ship.

Now when he had left speaking, he said unto Simon, Launch out into the deep and let down your nets for a draught. And Simon answering said unto him, Master, we have toiled all the night and have taken nothing; nevertheless, at thy word I will let down the net. And when they had this done, they inclosed a great multitude of fishes; and their net brake. And they beckoned unto their partners which were in the other ship that they should come and help them. And they came and filled both the ships so that they began to sink.

When Simon Peter saw it, he fell down at Jesus' knees, saying, Depart from me, for I am a sinful man, O Lord. For he was astonished and all that were with him at the draught of the fishes which they had taken. And so was also James, and John, the sons of Zebedee, which were partners with Simon.

And Jesus said unto Simon, Fear not. From henceforth thou shalt catch men. And when they had brought their ships to land, they forsook all and followed him.

11

And it came to pass in those days that he went out into a mountain to pray and continued all night in prayer to God. And when it was day, he called unto him his disciples; and of them he chose twelve whom also he named apostles: Simon Peter and Andrew his brother, James and John, Philip and Bartholomew, Matthew and Thomas, James the son of Alpheus, and Simon called Zelotes, Judas the brother of James, and Judas Iscariot, which also was the traitor.

And it came to pass afterward that he went throughout every city and village, preaching and showing the glad tidings of the kingdom of God; and the twelve were with him. And he gave them power and authority over all devils and to cure diseases. And he sent them to preach the kingdom of God and to heal the sick. And after these things the Lord appointed other seventy also and sent them two and two before his face into every city and place whither he himself would come.

12

Then he took unto him the twelve and said unto them: Behold, we go up to Jerusalem, and all things that are written by the prophets concerning the Son of man shall be accomplished. For he shall be delivered unto the Gentiles, and shall be mocked and spitefully entreated and spitted on. And they shall scourge him and put him to death; and the third day he shall rise again. And they understood none of these things, neither knew they the things which were spoken.

And it came to pass, when he was come nigh to Bethphage and Bethany, at the mount called the mount of Olives, he sent two of his disciples, saying: Go ye into the village over against you, in the which at your entering ye shall find a colt tied whereon yet never man sat. Loose him and bring him hither. And if any man ask you, Why do ye loose him? thus shall ye say unto him, Because the Lord hath need of him.

And they that were sent went their way and found even as he had said unto them. And as they were loosing the colt, the owners thereof said unto them, Why loose ye the colt? And they said, The Lord hath need of him. And they brought him to Jesus; and they cast their garments upon the colt, and they set Jesus thereon. And as he went, they spread their clothes in the way.

And when he was come nigh, even now at the descent of the mount of Olives, the whole multitude of the disciples began to rejoice and praise God with a loud voice for all the mighty works that they had seen, saying: Blessed be the King that cometh in the name of the Lord! Peace in heaven, and glory in the highest!

And when he was come near, he beheld the city and wept over it, saying: If thou hadst known, even thou, at least in this thy day, the things which belong to thy peace! But now they are hid from thine eyes.

And he went into the temple and began to cast out them that sold therein and them that bought, saying unto them: It is written, My house is the house of prayer; but ye have made it a den of thieves. And in the daytime he was teaching in the temple; and at night he went out and abode in the mount that is called the mount of Olives. And all the people came early in the morning to him in the temple for to hear him.

13

Now the feast of unleavened bread drew nigh which is called the passover. And the chief priests and scribes sought how they might kill him, for they feared the people.

Then entered Satan into Judas surnamed Iscariot. And he went his way and communed with the chief priests and captains how he might betray him unto them. And they were glad and covenanted to give him money. And he promised and sought opportunity to betray him unto them in the absence of the multitude.

Then came the day of unleavened bread when the passover must be killed. And Jesus sent Peter and John, saying, Go and prepare us the passover that we may eat. And they said unto him, Where wilt thou that we prepare? And he said unto them, Behold, when ye are entered into the city, there shall a man meet you, bearing a pitcher of water. Follow him into the house where he entereth in. And ye shall say unto the goodman of the house, The Master saith unto thee, Where is the guest chamber where I shall eat the passover with my disciples? And he shall show you a large upper room, furnished. There make ready. And they went and found as he had said unto them; and they made ready the passover.

And when the hour was come, he sat down and the twelve apostles with him. And he said unto them, With desire I have desired to eat this passover with you before I suffer. And he took bread and gave thanks, and brake it, and gave unto them, saying: *This is my body which is given for you. This do in remembrance of me.* Likewise also the cup after supper, saying: *This cup is the new testament in my blood, which is shed for you.*

And he said, Behold, the hand of him that betrayeth me is with me on the table. And truly the Son of man goeth as it was determined; but woe unto that man by whom he is betrayed! And they began to inquire among themselves which of them it was that should do this thing. And there was also a strife among them, which of them should be accounted the greatest. And he said unto them, He that is greatest among you, let him be as the younger; and he that is chief as he that doth serve.

And the Lord said: Simon, Simon, behold, Satan hath desired to have you that he may sift you as wheat. But I have prayed for thee that thy faith fail not; and when thou art converted, strengthen thy brethren. And Peter said unto him, Lord, I am ready to go with thee, both into prison and to death. And Jesus said: I tell thee,

Peter, the cock shall not crow this day, before that thou shalt thrice deny that thou knowest me.

14

And he came out and went, as he was wont, to the mount of Olives; and his disciples also followed him. And when he was at the place, he said unto them, Pray that ye enter not into temptation. And he was withdrawn from them about a stone's cast, and kneeled down and prayed, saying, Father, if thou be willing, remove this cup from me. Nevertheless, not my will, but thine, be done.

And there appeared an angel unto him from heaven, strengthening him. And being in an agony, he prayed more earnestly; and his sweat was as it were great drops of blood falling to the ground. And when he rose up from prayer and was come to his disciples, he found them sleeping for sorrow, and said unto them, Why sleep ye? Rise and pray, lest ye enter into temptation.

And while he yet spake, behold a multitude; and he that was called Judas went before them and drew near unto Jesus to kiss him. But Jesus said unto him, Judas, betrayest thou the Son of man with a kiss? When they which were about him saw what would follow, they said unto him, Lord, shall we smite with the sword? And one of them smote the servant of the high priest and cut off his right ear. And Jesus said, Suffer ye thus far. And he touched his ear and healed him.

Then Jesus said unto the chief priests and captains of the temple, and the elders, Be ye come out as against a thief with swords and staves? When I was daily with you in the temple, ye stretched forth no hands against me; but this is your hour and the power of darkness.

Then took they him, and led him, and brought him into the high priest's house. And Peter followed afar off. And when they had kindled a fire in the midst of the hall, and were set down together, Peter sat down among them. But a certain maid beheld him as he sat by the fire, and earnestly looked upon him, and said, This man was also with him. And he denied him, saying, Woman, I know him not. And after a little while another saw him, and said, Thou art also of them. And Peter said, Man, I am not. And about the space of one hour after, another confidently affirmed, saying, Of a truth this fellow also was with him; for he is a Galilean. And Peter said, Man, I know not what thou sayest. And immediately, while he yet spake, the cock crew.

And the Lord turned, and looked upon Peter. And Peter remembered the word of the Lord, how he had said unto him, Before the cock crow, thou shalt deny me thrice. And Peter went out, and wept bitterly.

15

And as soon as it was day, the whole multitude of them arose and led him unto Pilate. And they began to accuse him, saying, We found this fellow perverting the nation, and forbidding to give tribute to Caesar, saying that he himself is Christ, a king. And Pilate asked him, saying, Art thou the King of the Jews? And he answered him and said, Thou sayest it. Then said Pilate to the chief priests and to the people, I find no fault in this man. And they were the more fierce, saying, He stirreth up the people, teaching throughout all Jewry, beginning from Galilee to this place.

When Pilate heard of Galilee, he asked whether the man were a Galilean. And as soon as he knew that he belonged unto Herod's jurisdiction, he sent him to Herod, who himself also was at Jerusalem at that time. And when Herod saw Jesus, he was exceeding glad, because he had heard many things of him, and he hoped to have seen some miracle done by him. Then Herod questioned with him in many words; but Jesus answered him nothing. And the chief priests and scribes stood and vehemently accused him. And Herod with his men of war set him at nought, and mocked him, and arrayed him in a gorgeous robe, and sent him again to Pilate. And the same day Pilate and Herod were made friends together, for before they were at enmity between themselves.

And Pilate, when he had called together the chief priests and the rulers and the people, said unto them, Ye have brought this man unto me as one that perverteth the people; and, behold, I have found no fault in this man touching those things whereof ye accuse him. No, nor yet Herod, for I sent you to him; and lo, nothing worthy of death is done unto him. I will therefore chastise him and release him. And they cried out all at once, saying, Away with this man, and release unto us Barabbas! Pilate therefore, willing to release Jesus, spake again to them. But they cried, saying, Crucify him, crucify him! And he said unto them the third time, Why, what evil hath he done? I have found no cause of death in him. And they were instant with loud voices, requiring that he might be crucified. And the voices of them and of the chief priests prevailed.

And Pilate gave sentence that it should be as they required. And he released unto them Barabbas, who for sedition and murder was cast into prison; but he delivered Jesus to their will.

16

And as they led him away, they laid hold upon one Simon, a Cyrenian, coming out of the country, and on him they laid the cross, that he might bear it after Jesus. And there followed him a great company of people, and of women, which also bewailed and lamented him. But Jesus, turning unto them, said, Daughters of Jerusalem, weep not for me, but weep for yourselves, and for your children. For, behold, the days are coming, in the which they shall say, Blessed are the barren, and the wombs that never bare, and the paps which never gave suck. Then shall they begin to say to the mountains, Fall on us; and to the hills, Cover us. For if they do these things in a green tree, what shall be done in the dry?

And there were also two other, malefactors, led with him to be put to death. And when they were come to the place, which is called Calvary, there they crucified him, and the malefactors, one on the right hand, and the other on the left. Then said Jesus, Father, forgive them; for they know not what they do. And they parted his raiment, and cast lots. And the people stood beholding. And the rulers also with them derided him, saying, He saved others; let him save himself, if he be Christ, the chosen of God. And the soldiers also mocked him, coming to him, and offering him vinegar, and saying, If thou be the king of the Jews, save thyself. And a superscription also was written over him in letters of Greek, and Latin, and Hebrew, THIS IS THE KING OF THE JEWS.

And one of the malefactors which were hanged railed on him, saying, If thou be Christ, save thyself and us. But the other answering rebuked him, saying, Dost not thou fear God, seeing thou art in the same condemnation? And we indeed justly, for we receive the due reward of our deeds; but this man hath done nothing amiss. And he said unto Jesus, Lord, remember me when thou comest intc thy kingdom. And Jesus said unto him, Verily I say unto thee, Today shalt thou be with me in paradise.

And it was about the sixth hour, and there was a darkness over all the earth until the ninth hour. And the sun was darkened, and the veil of the temple was rent in the midst. And when Jesus had cried with a loud voice, he said, Father, into thy hands I commend my spirit; and having said thus, he gave up the ghost. Now when the centurion saw what was done, he glorified God, saying, Certainly this was a righteous man. And all the people that came together to that sight, beholding the things which were done, smote their breasts, and returned. And all his acquaintance, and the women that followed him from Galilee, stood afar off, beholding these things.

And, behold, there was a man named Joseph, a counsellor; and he was a good man, and a just; he was of Arimathaea, a city of the Jews, who also himself waited for the kingdom of God. This man went unto Pilate, and begged the body of Jesus. And he took it down, and wrapped it in linen, and laid it in a sepulchre that was hewn in stone, wherein never man before was laid. And that day was the preparation, and the sabbath drew on. And the women also, which came with him from Galilee, followed after, and beheld the sepulchre, and how his body was laid. And they returned, and prepared spices and ointments; and rested the sabbath day according to the commandment.

17

Now upon the first day of the week, very early in the morning, they came unto the sepulchre, bringing the spices which they had prepared. And they found the stone rolled away from the sepulchre. And they entered in, and found not the body of the Lord Jesus.

And it came to pass, as they were much perplexed thereabout, behold, two men stood by them in shining garments. And as they were afraid and bowed down their faces to the earth, they said unto them: Why seek ye the living among the dead? He is not here, but is risen. Remember how he spake unto you when he was yet in Galilee, saying, The Son of man must be delivered into the hands of sinful men, and be crucified, and the third day rise again.

And they remembered his words and returned from the sepulchre, and told all these things unto the eleven and to all the rest. It was Mary Magdalene, and Joanna, and Mary the mother of James, and other women that were with them which told these things unto the apostles. And their words seemed to them as idle tales, and they believed them not. Then arose Peter and ran unto the sepulchre. And stooping down, he beheld the linen clothes laid by themselves, and departed, wondering in himself at that which was come to pass.

And, behold, two of them went that same day to a village called Emmaus, which was from Jerusalem about threescore furlongs. And they talked together of all these things which had happened. And it came to pass, that, while they communed together and reasoned, Jesus himself drew near, and went with them. But their eyes were holden that they should not know him.

And he said unto them, What manner of communications are these that ye have one to another, as ye walk, and are sad? And the one of them, whose name was Cleopas, answering said unto him, Art thou only a stranger in Jerusalem, and hast not known the things which are come to pass there in these days? And he said unto them, What things? And they said unto him, Concerning Jesus of Nazareth, which was a prophet mighty in deed and word before God and all the people; and how the chief priests and our rulers delivered him to be condemned to death, and have crucified him.

But we trusted that it had been he which should have redeemed Israel; and beside all this, today is the third day since these things were done. Yea, and certain women also of our company made us astonished, which were early at the sepulchre; and when they found not his body, they came, saying, that they had also seen a vision of angels, which said that he was alive. And certain of them which were with us went to the sepulchre, and found it even so as the women had said; but him they saw not.

Then he said unto them, O fools, and slow of heart to believe all that the prophets have spoken! Ought not Christ to have suffered these things, and to enter into his glory? And beginning at Moses and all the prophets, he expounded unto them in all the scriptures the things concerning himself.

And they drew nigh unto the village, whither they went; and he made as though he would have gone further. But they constrained him, saying, Abide with us; for it is toward evening, and the day is far spent. And he went in to tarry with them. And it came to pass, as he sat at meat with them, he took bread, and blessed it, and brake, and gave to them. And their eyes were opened, and they knew him; and he vanished out of their sight. And they said one to another, Did not our heart burn within us, while he talked with us by the way, and while he opened to us the scriptures?

And they rose up the same hour and returned to Jerusalem, and found the eleven gathered together, and them that were with them, saying, The Lord is risen indeed, and hath appeared to Simon. And they told what things were done in the way and how he was known to them in breaking of bread.

And as they thus spake, Jesus himself stood in the midst of them and saith unto them, Peace be unto you. But they were terrified and affrighted, and supposed that they had seen a spirit. And he said unto them, Why are ye so troubled? And why do thoughts arise in your hearts? Behold my hands and my feet, that it is I myself. And while they yet believed not for joy, and wondered, he said unto them, Have ye here any meat? And they gave him a piece of a broiled fish and of an honeycomb. And he took it and did eat before them.

And he said unto them: These are the words which I spake unto you while I was yet with you, that all things must be fulfilled, which were written in the law, and in the prophets, and in the psalms, concerning me. Then opened he their understanding, that they might understand the scriptures, and said unto them that repentance and remission of sins should be preached in his name among all nations, beginning at Jerusalem.

And he led them out as far as to Bethany, and he lifted up his hands and blessed them. And it came to pass, while he blessed them, he was parted from them and carried up into heaven. And they worshipped him, and returned to Jerusalem with great joy; and were continually in the temple, praising and blessing God.

THE TEACHINGS OF JESUS

Jesus used two forms of teaching: the sermon and the parable. The best known of His sermons is, of course, the Sermon on the Mount. This in a shorter version is recorded by St. Luke; but because it is both more complete and more familiar as recorded by St. Matthew, that version, only slightly abridged, is given in these Readings. The Sermon on the Mount, seemingly the first preached by Jesus (and perhaps given in parts rather than as a whole), is held by all to be a noble, and by many even a complete, summary of His teachings, both ethical and religious.

The sermon which follows it in these pages was apparently the last given by Him. Perhaps more a farewell message than a sermon, since it was spoken to His disciples the night before His death, it differs from the Sermon on the Mount in being wholly spiritual, even mystical, in character. Given in St. John's Gospel, it echoes in simpler words, and yet puzzling even to its listeners, the exalted thoughts of those first verses of St. John, placed as a foreword to these Readings from the Gospels.

The parable, so often employed by Jesus as a more intimate form of teaching, was an inheritance from the Old Testament, where it frequently occurs. It was, in fact, a method of teaching long used by Jewish priests and rabbis and as such was familiar to Jesus, who used it with incomparable power and skill. The word parable in the Greek means *to throw across*, a meaning which in itself suggests the indirect yet persuasive force of these simple narratives.

Most of the parables given here are from St. Luke because, to me at least, he has written them with greater charm than St. Mark or St. Matthew (there are no parables in St. John's Gospel) and because the two best known, The Prodigal Son and The Good Samaritan, occur only in his work.

The Sermon on the Mount

FROM ST. MATTHEW 5, 6, 7

And seeing the multitudes, he went up into a mountain; and when he was set, his disciples came unto him; and he opened his mouth, and taught them, saying:

Blessed are the poor in spirit:
For theirs is the kingdom of heaven.
Blessed are they that mourn:
For they shall be comforted.
Blessed are the meek:
For they shall inherit the earth.
Blessed are they which do hunger and thirst after righteousness:
For they shall be filled.
Blessed are the merciful:
For they shall obtain mercy.
Blessed are the pure in heart:
For they shall see God.
Blessed are the peacemakers:
For they shall be called the children of God.
Blessed are they which are persecuted for righteousness' sake:
For theirs is the kingdom of heaven.
Blessed are ye, when men shall revile you, and persecute you,
And shall say all manner of evil against you falsely, for my sake.
Rejoice, and be exceeding glad: for great is your reward in heaven:
For so persecuted they the prophets which were before you.

Ye are the salt of the earth; but if the salt have lost his savor, wherewith shall it be salted? It is thenceforth good for nothing, but to be cast out, and to be trodden under foot of men.

Ye are the light of the world. A city that is set on an hill cannot be hid. Neither do men light a candle, and put it under a bushel, but on a candlestick; and it giveth light unto all that are in the house. Let your light so shine before men, that they may see your good works, and glorify your Father which is in heaven.

Think not that I am come to destroy the law, or the prophets. I am not come to destroy, but to fulfil. For verily I say unto you, Till heaven and earth pass, one jot or one tittle shall in no wise pass from the law, till all be fulfilled. Whosoever therefore shall break one of these least commandments, and shall teach men so, he shall be called the least in the kingdom of heaven; but whosoever shall do and teach them, the same shall be called great in the kingdom of heaven. For I say unto you, That except your righteousness shall exceed the righteousness of the scribes and Pharisees, ye shall in no case enter into the kingdom of heaven.

Ye have heard that it was said by them of old time, Thou shalt not kill; and whosoever shall kill shall be in danger of judgment. But I say unto you, That whosoever is angry with his brother without a cause shall be in danger of the judgment; and whosoever shall say to his brother, Raca,[1] shall be in danger of the council; but whosoever shall say, Thou fool, shall be in danger of hell fire. Therefore if thou bring thy gift to the altar, and there rememberest that thy brother hath aught against thee, leave there thy gift before the altar, and go thy way. First be reconciled to thy brother, and then come and offer thy gift.

Ye have heard that it was said by them of old time, Thou shalt not commit adultery. But I say unto you, That whosoever looketh on a woman to lust after her, hath committed adultery with her already in his heart. And if thy right eye offend thee, pluck it out, and cast it from thee; for it is profitable for thee that one of thy members should perish, and not that thy whole body should be cast into hell. And if thy right hand offend thee, cut it off, and cast it from thee; for it is profitable for thee that one of thy members should perish, and not that thy whole body should be cast into hell.

Ye have heard that it hath been said, An eye for an eye, and a

[1] A term of deep reproach.

tooth for a tooth. But I say unto you, That ye resist not evil; but whosoever shall smite thee on thy right cheek, turn to him the other also. And if any man will sue thee at the law, and take away thy coat, let him have thy cloak also. And whosoever shall compel thee to go a mile, go with him twain. Give to him that asketh thee, and from him that would borrow of thee turn not thou away.

Ye have heard that it hath been said, Thou shalt love thy neighbor and hate thine enemy. But I say unto you, Love your enemies, bless them that curse you, do good to them that hate you, and pray for them which despitefully use you and persecute you; that ye may be the children of your Father which is in heaven. For he maketh his sun to rise on the evil and on the good, and sendeth rain on the just and on the unjust. For if ye love them which love you, what reward have ye? Do not even the publicans the same? And if ye salute your brethren only, what do ye more than others? Do not even the publicans so? Be ye therefore perfect, even as your Father which is in heaven is perfect.

Take heed that ye do not your alms before men, to be seen of them; otherwise ye have no reward of your Father which is in heaven. Therefore when thou doest thine alms, do not sound a trumpet before thee, as the hypocrites do in the synagogues and in the streets, that they may have glory of men. Verily I say unto you, They have their reward. But when thou doest alms, let not thy left hand know what thy right hand doeth, that thine alms may be in secret; and thy Father which seeth in secret himself shall reward thee openly.

And when thou prayest, thou shalt not be as the hypocrites are; for they love to pray standing in the synagogues and in the corners of the streets, that they may be seen of men. Verily I say unto you, They have their reward. But thou, when thou prayest, enter into thy closet, and when thou hast shut thy door, pray to thy Father which is in secret; and thy Father which seeth in secret shall reward thee openly. But when ye pray, use not vain repetitions, as the heathen do; for they think that they shall be heard for their much speaking. Be not ye therefore like unto them; for your Father knoweth what things ye have need of, before ye ask him.

After this manner therefore pray ye:

Our Father which art in heaven,
Hallowed be thy name.
Thy kingdom come.
Thy will be done
In earth, as it is in heaven.
Give us this day our daily bread.
And forgive us our debts,
As we forgive our debtors.
And lead us not into temptation,
But deliver us from evil:
For thine is the kingdom,
And the power,
And the glory,
Forever. Amen.

For if ye forgive men their trespasses, your heavenly Father will also forgive you; but if ye forgive not men their trespasses, neither will your Father forgive your trespasses.

Moreover, when ye fast, be not, as the hypocrites, of a sad countenance; for they disfigure their faces, that they may appear unto men to fast. Verily I say unto you, They have their reward. But thou, when thou fastest, anoint thine head, and wash thy face; that thou appear not unto men to fast, but unto thy Father which is in secret; and thy Father, which seeth in secret, shall reward thee openly.

Lay not up for yourselves treasures upon earth, where moth and rust doth corrupt, and where thieves break through and steal; but lay up for yourselves treasures in heaven where neither moth nor rust doth corrupt, and where thieves do not break through nor steal; for where your treasure is, there will your heart be also. The light of the body is the eye. If therefore thine eye be single, thy whole body shall be full of light. But if thine eye be evil, thy whole body shall be full of darkness. If therefore the light that is in thee be darkness, how great is that darkness! No man can serve two masters; for either he will hate the one, and love the other; or else he will hold to the one, and despise the other. Ye cannot serve God and mammon. Therefore I say unto you, Take no thought for your life, what ye shall eat, or what ye shall drink; nor yet for your body, what ye shall put on. Is not the life more than meat, and the body than raiment? Behold the fowls of the air: For they sow not, neither do they reap, nor gather into barns; yet your heavenly Father feedeth them. Are ye not much better than they? Which of you by taking thought can add one cubit unto his stature? And why take ye thought for raiment? Consider the lilies of the field, how they grow; they toil not, neither do they spin; and yet I say unto you, that even Solomon in all his glory was not arrayed like one of these. Wherefore, if God so clothe the grass of the field, which today is, and tomorrow is cast into the oven, shall he not much more clothe you, O ye of little faith? Therefore take no thought, saying, What shall we eat? or, What shall we drink? or, Wherewithal shall we be clothed? (for after all these things do the Gentiles seek.) For your heavenly Father knoweth that ye have need of all these things. But seek ye first the kingdom of God, and his righteousness; and all these things shall be added unto you. Take therefore no thought for the morrow; for the morrow shall take thought for the things of itself. Sufficient unto the day is the evil thereof.

Judge not, that ye be not judged. For with what judgment ye judge, ye shall be judged; and with what measure ye mete, it shall be measured to you again. And why beholdest thou the mote that is in thy brother's eye, but considerest not the beam that is in thine own eye? Or how wilt thou say to thy brother, Let me pull out the mote out of thine eye; and, behold, a beam is in thine own eye? Thou hypocrite, first cast out the beam out of thine own eye; and then shalt thou see clearly to cast out the mote out of thy brother's eye.

Give not that which is holy unto the dogs, neither cast ye your pearls before swine, lest they trample them under their feet, and turn again and rend you.

Ask, and it shall be given you; seek, and ye shall find; knock, and it shall be opened unto you. For every one that asketh receiveth; and he that seeketh findeth; and to him that knocketh it shall be opened.

Or what man is there of you, whom if his son ask bread, will he give him a stone? Or if he ask a fish, will he give him a serpent?

If ye then, being evil, know how to give good gifts unto your children, how much more shall your Father which is in heaven give good things to them that ask him? Therefore all things whatsoever ye would that men should do to you, do ye even so to them. For this is the law and the prophets.

Enter ye in at the strait gate; for wide is the gate, and broad is the way, that leadeth to destruction, and many there be which go in thereat. Because strait is the gate, and narrow is the way, which leadeth unto life, and few there be that find it.

Beware of false prophets, which come to you in sheep's clothing, but inwardly they are ravening wolves. Ye shall know them by their fruits. Do men gather grapes of thorns, or figs of thistles? Even so every good tree bringeth forth good fruit; but a corrupt tree bringeth forth evil fruit. A good tree cannot bring forth evil fruit, neither can a corrupt tree bring forth good fruit. Every tree that bringeth not forth good fruit is hewn down, and cast into the fire. Wherefore by their fruits ye shall know them.

Not every one that saith unto me, Lord, Lord, shall enter into the kingdom of heaven; but he that doeth the will of my Father which is in heaven. Many will say to me in that day, Lord, Lord, have we not prophesied in thy name? And in thy name have cast out devils? And in thy name done many wonderful works? And then will I profess unto them, I never knew you. Depart from me, ye that work iniquity.

Therefore whosoever heareth these sayings of mine, and doeth them, I will liken him unto a wise man, which built his house upon a rock. And the rain descended, and the floods came, and the winds blew, and beat upon that house; and it fell not; for it was founded upon a rock. And every one that heareth these sayings of mine, and doeth them not, shall be likened unto a foolish man, which built his house upon the sand. And the rain descended, and the floods came, and the winds blew, and beat upon that house; and it fell; and great was the fall of it.

ST. JOHN 14

Let not your heart be troubled. Ye believe in God, believe also in me. In my Father's house are many mansions; if it were not so, I would have told you. I go to prepare a place for you. And if I go and prepare a place for you, I will come again, and receive you unto myself, that where I am, there ye may be also. And whither I go ye know, and the way ye know. Thomas saith unto him, Lord, we know not whither thou goest; and how can we know the way? Jesus saith unto him, I am the way, the truth, and the life. No man cometh unto the Father, but by me. If ye had known me, ye should have known my Father also; and from henceforth ye know him, and have seen him. Philip saith unto him, Lord, show us the Father, and it sufficeth us. Jesus saith unto him, Have I been so long time with you, and yet hast thou not known me, Philip? He that hath seen me hath seen the Father; and how sayest thou then, Show us the Father? Believest thou not that I am in the Father, and the Father in me? The words that I speak unto you I speak not of myself; but the Father, that dwelleth in me, he doeth the works. Believe me that I am in the Father, and the Father in me; or else believe me for the very works' sake. Verily, verily, I say unto you. He that believeth on me, the works that I do shall he do also; and greater works than these shall he do, because I go unto my Father. And whatsoever ye shall ask in my name, that will I do, that the Father may be glorified in the Son. If ye shall ask any thing in my name, I will do it.

If ye love me, keep my commandments. And I will pray the Father, and he shall give you another Comforter, that he may abide with you forever; even the Spirit of truth, whom the world cannot receive, because it seeth him not, neither knoweth him; but ye know him; for he dwelleth with you, and shall be in you. I will not leave you comfortless; I will come to you. Yet a little while, and the world seeth me no more; but ye see me; because I live, ye shall live also. At that day ye shall know that I am in my Father, and ye in me, and I in you. He that hath my commandments and keepeth them, he it is that loveth me; and he that loveth me shall be loved of my Father, and I will love him, and will manifest myself to him. Judas saith unto him (not Iscariot), Lord, how is it that thou wilt manifest thyself unto us, and not unto the world? Jesus answered and said unto him, If a man love me, he will keep my words; and my Father will love him, and we will come unto him, and make our abode with him. He that loveth me not keepeth not my sayings; and the word which ye hear is not mine, but the Father's which sent me. These things have I spoken unto you, being yet present with you. But the Comforter, which is the Holy Ghost, whom the Father will send in my name, he shall teach you all things and bring all things to your remembrance, whatsoever I have said unto you.

Peace I leave with you, my peace I give unto you. Not as the world giveth, give I unto you. Let not your heart be troubled, neither let it be afraid.

CERTAIN PARABLES OF JESUS

The Pharisee and the Publican

FROM ST. LUKE 18

And he spake this parable unto certain which trusted in themselves that they were righteous, and despised others.

Two men went up into the temple to pray: the one a Pharisee, and the other a publican. The Pharisee stood and prayed thus with himself: God, I thank thee, that I am not as other men are, extortioners, unjust, adulterers, or even as this publican. I fast twice in the week; I give tithes of all that I possess. And the publican, standing afar off, would not lift up so much as his eyes unto heaven, but smote upon his breast, saying, God be merciful to me a sinner. I tell you, this man went down to his house justified rather than the other; for every one that exalteth himself shall be abased; and he that humbleth himself shall be exalted.

The Rich Man and the Beggar

FROM ST. LUKE 16

There was a certain rich man, which was clothed in purple and fine linen, and fared sumptuously every day. And there was a certain beggar named Lazarus, which was laid at his gate, full of sores, and desiring to be fed with the crumbs which fell from the rich man's table; moreover the dogs came and licked his sores. And it came to pass, that the beggar died, and was carried by the angels into Abraham's bosom. The rich man also died, and was buried; and in hell he lifted up his eyes, being in torments, and seeth Abraham afar off, and Lazarus in his bosom. And he cried and said, Father Abraham, have mercy on me, and send Lazarus, that he may dip the tip of his finger in water, and cool my tongue; for I am tormented in this flame. But Abraham said, Son, remember that thou in thy lifetime receivedst thy good things, and likewise Lazarus evil things; but now he is comforted, and thou art tormented. And beside all this, between us and you there is a great gulf fixed, so that they which would pass from hence to you cannot; neither can they pass to us, that would come from thence.

Then he said, I pray thee therefore, father, that thou wouldest send him to my father's house, for I have five brethren, that he may testify unto them, lest they also come into this place of torment. Abraham saith unto him, They have Moses and the prophets; let them hear them. And he said, Nay, father Abraham; but if one went unto them from the dead, they will repent. And he said unto him, If they hear not Moses and the prophets, neither will they be persuaded, though one rose from the dead.

The Lost Sheep and the Lost Coin

FROM ST. LUKE 15

Then drew near unto him all the publicans and sinners for to hear him. And the Pharisees and scribes murmured, saying, This man receiveth sinners, and eateth with them.

And he spake this parable unto them, saying: What man of you, having a hundred sheep, if he lose one of them, doth not leave the ninety and nine in the wilderness, and go after that which is lost, until he find it? And when he hath found it, he layeth it on his shoulders, rejoicing. And when he cometh home, he calleth together his friends and neighbors, saying unto them, Rejoice with me; for I have found my sheep which was lost. I say unto you, that likewise joy shall be in heaven over one sinner that repenteth, more than over ninety and nine just persons, which need no repentance.

Either what woman having ten pieces of silver, if she lose one piece, doth not light a candle, and sweep the house, and seek diligently till she find it? And when she hath found it, she calleth her friends and her neighbors together, saying, Rejoice with me; for I have found the piece which I had lost. Likewise, I say unto you, there is joy in the presence of the angels of God over one sinner that repenteth.

The Foolish Rich Man

FROM ST. LUKE 12

And one of the company said unto him, Master, speak to my brother, that he divide the inheritance with me. And he said unto him, Man, who made me a judge or a divider over you? And he said unto them, Take heed, and beware of covetousness; for a man's life consisteth not in the abundance of the things which he possesseth.

And he spake a parable unto them, saying: The ground of a certain rich man brought forth plentifully. And he thought within himself, saying, What shall I do, because I have no room where to bestow my fruits? And he said, This will I do: I will pull down my barns, and build greater; and there will I bestow all my fruits and my goods. And I will say to my soul, Soul, thou hast much goods laid up for many years. Take thine ease, eat, drink, and be merry. But God said unto him, Thou fool, this night thy soul shall be required of thee. Then whose shall those things be, which thou hast provided?

So is he that layeth up treasure for himself, and is not rich toward God.

The Guests at the Supper

FROM ST. LUKE 14

And it came to pass that he went into the house of one of the chief Pharisees to eat bread on the sabbath day. And he put forth a parable to those which were bidden when he marked how they chose out the chief rooms, saying unto them: When thou art bidden of any man to a wedding, sit not down in the highest room, lest a more honorable man than thou be bidden of him, and he that bade thee and him come and say to thee, Give this man place; and thou begin with shame to take the lowest room. But when thou art bidden, go and sit down in the lowest room, that when he that bade thee cometh, he may say unto thee, Friend, go up higher. For whosoever exalteth himself shall be abased; and he that humbleth himself shall be exalted.

Then said he also to him that bade him, When thou makest a dinner or a supper, call not thy friends, nor thy brethren, neither thy kinsmen, nor thy rich neighbors, lest they also bid thee again, and a recompense be made thee. But when thou makest a feast, call the poor, the maimed, the lame, the blind. And thou shalt be blessed, for they cannot recompense thee; but thou shalt be recompensed at the resurrection of the just.

And when one of them that sat at meat with him heard these things, he said unto him, Blessed is he that shall eat bread in the kingdom of God. Then said he unto him: A certain man made a great supper, and bade many, and sent his servant at supper time to say to them that were bidden, Come; for all things are now ready. And they all with one consent began to make excuse. The first said unto him, I have bought a piece of ground, and I must needs go and see it; I pray thee have me excused. And another said, I have bought five yoke of oxen, and I go to prove them; I pray thee have me excused. And another said, I have married a wife, and therefore I cannot come.

So that servant came, and showed his lord these things. Then the master of the house being angry said to his servant, Go out quickly into the streets and lanes of the city, and bring in hither the poor, and the maimed, and the halt, and the blind. And the servant said, Lord, it is done as thou hast commanded, and yet there is room. And the Lord said unto the servant, Go out into the highways and hedges, and compel them to come in, that my house may be filled. For I say unto you, That none of those men which were bidden shall taste of my supper.

The Talents

FROM ST. MATTHEW 25

For the kingdom of heaven is as a man travelling into a far country, who called his own servants, and delivered unto them his goods. And unto one he gave five talents, to another two, and to another one; to every man according to his several ability; and straightway took his journey. Then he that had received the five talents went and traded with the same, and made them other five talents. And likewise he that had received two, he also gained other two. But he that had received one went and digged in the earth, and hid his lord's money.

After a long time the lord of those servants cometh, and reckoneth with them. And so he that had received five talents came and brought other five talents, saying, Lord, thou deliveredst unto me five talents; behold, I have gained beside them five talents more. His lord said unto him, Well done, thou good and faithful servant! Thou hast been faithful over a few things; I will make thee ruler over many things. Enter thou into the joy of thy lord. He also that had received two talents came and said, Lord, thou deliveredst unto me two talents; behold, I have gained two other talents beside them. His lord said unto him, Well done, good and faithful servant! Thou hast been faithful over a few things; I will make thee ruler over many things. Enter thou into the joy of thy lord. Then he which had received the one talent came and said, Lord, I knew thee that thou art an hard man, reaping where thou hast not sown, and gathering where thou hast not strawed; and I was afraid, and went and hid thy talent in the earth. Lo, there thou hast that is thine. His lord answered and said unto him, Thou wicked and slothful servant, thou knewest that I reap where I sowed not, and gather where I have not strawed. Thou oughtest therefore to have put my money to the exchangers, and then at my coming I should have received mine own with usury. Take therefore the talent from him, and give it unto him which hath ten talents. For unto every one that hath shall be given, and he shall have abundance; but from him that hath not shall be taken away even that which he hath.

The Wise and the Foolish Virgins

FROM ST. MATTHEW 25

Then shall the kingdom of heaven be likened unto ten virgins, which took their lamps, and went forth to meet the bridegroom. And five of them were wise, and five were foolish. They that were foolish took their lamps, and took no oil with them; but the wise took oil in their vessels with their lamps. While the bridegroom tarried, they all slumbered and slept. And at midnight there was a cry made, Behold, the bridegroom cometh! Go ye out to meet him. Then all those virgins arose, and trimmed their lamps. And the foolish said unto the wise, Give us of your oil; for our lamps are gone out. But the wise answered, saying, Not so; lest there be not enough for us and you; but go ye rather to them that sell, and buy for yourselves.

And while they went to buy, the bridegroom came; and they that were ready went in with him to the marriage; and the door was shut. Afterward came also the other virgins, saying, Lord, Lord, open to us. But he answered and said, Verily I say unto you, I know you not.

Watch therefore, for ye know neither the day nor the hour wherein the Son of man cometh.

The Prodigal Son

FROM ST. LUKE 15

And he said, A certain man had two sons; and the younger of them said to his father, Father, give me the portion of goods that falleth to me. And he divided unto them his living. And not many days after, the younger son gathered all together, and took his journey into a far country, and there wasted his substance with riotous living. And when he had spent all, there arose a mighty famine in that land; and he began to be in want. And he went and joined himself to a citizen of that country; and he sent him into his fields to feed swine. And he would fain have filled his belly with the husks that the swine did eat; and no man gave unto him. And when he came to himself, he said, How many hired servants of my father's have bread enough and to spare, and I perish with hunger! I will arise and go to my father, and will say unto him, Father, I have sinned against heaven, and before thee, and am no more worthy to be called thy son. Make me as one of thy hired servants.

And he arose, and came to his father. But when he was yet a great way off, his father saw him, and had compassion, and ran, and fell on his neck, and kissed him. And the son said unto him, Father, I have sinned against heaven, and in thy sight, and am no more worthy to be called thy son. But the father said to his servants, Bring forth the best robe, and put it on him; and put a ring on his hand, and shoes on his feet; and bring hither the fatted calf, and kill it; and let us eat, and be merry. For this my son was dead, and is alive again; he was lost, and is found. And they began to be merry.

Now his elder son was in the field; and as he came and drew nigh to the house, he heard music and dancing. And he called one of the servants, and asked what these things meant. And he said unto him, Thy brother is come; and thy father hath killed the fatted calf, because he hath received him safe and sound. And he was angry, and would not go in; therefore came his father out, and intreated him. And he answering said to his father, Lo, these many years do I serve thee, neither transgressed I at any time thy commandment; and yet thou never gavest *me* a kid, that I might make merry with my friends. But as soon as this thy son was come, which hath devoured thy living with harlots, thou hast killed for him the fatted calf. And he said unto him, Son, thou art ever with me, and all that I have is thine. It was meet that we should make merry and be glad. For this thy brother was dead, and is alive again; and was lost, and is found.

The Good Samaritan

FROM ST. LUKE 10

And, behold, a certain lawyer stood up, and tempted him, saying, Master, what shall I do to inherit eternal life? He said unto him, What is written in the law? How readest thou? And he answering said, Thou shalt love the Lord thy God with all thy heart, and with all thy soul, and with all thy strength, and with all thy mind; and thy neighbor as thyself. And he said unto him, Thou hast answered right. This do, and thou shalt live. But he, willing to justify himself, said unto Jesus, And who is my neighbor?

And Jesus answering said, A certain man went down from Jerusalem to Jericho, and fell among thieves, which stripped him of his raiment, and wounded him, and departed, leaving him half dead. And by chance there came down a certain priest that way; and when he saw him, he passed by on the other side. And likewise a Levite, when he was at the place, came and looked on him, and passed by on the other side. But a certain Samaritan, as he journeyed, came where he was; and when he saw him, he had compassion on him, and went to him, and bound up his wounds, pouring in oil and wine, and set him on his own beast, and brought him to an inn, and took care of him. And on the morrow, when he departed, he took out two pence, and gave them to the host, and said unto him, Take care of him; and whatsoever thou spendest more, when I come again, I will repay thee. Which now of these three, thinkest thou, was neighbor unto him that fell among the thieves? And he said, He that showed mercy on him. Then said Jesus unto him, Go and do thou likewise.

THE PEOPLE WHOM JESUS LOVED

Throughout all the Gospels there are many stories which portray the concern of Jesus over all sorts and conditions of men. Living in the Roman world of His day with its slavery, its rigorous class distinctions, and its tyranny, He revealed no quality more characteristic of Himself than His interest in the individual, His sense of the value and the dignity of human life, His overflowing compassion for those in sorrow or in need.

Although all four writers stress this care and concern, none does it with such vividness or such drama as does St. Luke, whose pages are filled with people of every description and in all manner of situations; and although frequently the other writers tell the same story, that story under his pen assumes a brighter reality. This superior genius is best shown in his incomparable account of the woman with the alabaster box of ointment, an incident which is told also by St. Mark (chapter 14) and by St. Matthew (chapter 26). Since, to me, this story is not only the most beautiful single narrative of the New Testament, but contains as well within itself the complete meaning and message, inspiration and vision, of the life and teachings of Jesus, I have chosen it as the conclusion to these Readings from the Gospels.

The Children

FROM ST. MARK 10

And they brought young children to him, that he should touch them; and his disciples rebuked those that brought them. But when Jesus saw it, he was much displeased, and said unto them, Suffer the little children to come unto me, and forbid them not; for of such is the kingdom of God. Verily I say unto you, Whosoever shall not receive the kingdom of God as a little child, he shall not enter therein. And he took them up in his arms, put his hands upon them, and blessed them.

FROM ST. MATTHEW 18

At the same time came the disciples unto Jesus, saying, Who is the greatest in the kingdom of heaven? And Jesus called a little child unto him, and set him in the midst of them and said:

Verily, I say unto you, Except ye be converted, and become as little children, ye shall not enter into the kingdom of heaven. Whosoever therefore shall humble himself as this little child, the same is greatest in the kingdom of heaven. And whoso shall receive one such little child in my name, receiveth me. But whoso shall offend one of these little ones which believe in me, it were better for him that a millstone were hanged about his neck, and that he were drowned in the depth of the sea. Take heed that ye despise not one of these little ones; for I say unto you, That in heaven their angels do always behold the face of my Father which is in heaven.

The Hungry People

FROM ST. MARK 6 AND ST. JOHN 6

And the apostles gathered themselves together unto Jesus, and told him all things, both what they had done, and what they had taught. And he said unto them, Come ye yourselves apart into a desert place, and rest a while; for there were many coming and going, and they had no leisure so much as to eat. And they departed into a desert place by ship privately. And the people saw them departing, and many knew him, and ran afoot thither out of all cities, and outwent them, and came together unto him. And Jesus, when he came out, saw much people, and was moved with compassion toward them, because they were as sheep not having a shepherd; and he began to teach them many things.

And when the day was now far spent, his disciples came unto him, and said, This is a desert place, and now the time is far passed. Send them away, that they may go into the country round about, and into the villages, and buy themselves bread; for they have nothing to eat. He answered and said unto them, Give ye them to eat. And they say unto him, Shall we go and buy two hundred pennyworth of bread, and give them to eat? He saith unto them, How many loaves have ye? Go and see.

One of his disciples, Andrew, Simon Peter's brother, saith unto him, There is a lad here, which hath five barley loaves, and two small fishes; but what are they among so many?

And Jesus said, Make the men sit down. Now there was much grass in the place, so the men sat down, in number about five thousand. And Jesus took the loaves; and when he had given thanks, he distributed to the disciples, and the disciples to them that were set down; and likewise of the fishes as much as they would. When they were filled, he said unto his disciples, Gather up the fragments that remain, that nothing be lost. Therefore they gathered them together, and filled twelve baskets with the fragments of the five barley loaves, which remained over and above unto them that had eaten.

The Woman Taken in Adultery

FROM ST. JOHN 8

And the scribes and Pharisees brought unto him a woman taken in adultery; and when they had set her in the midst, they say unto him, Master, this woman was taken in adultery, in the very act. Now Moses in the law commanded us, that such should be stoned; but what sayest thou? This they said, tempting him, that they might have to accuse him. But Jesus stooped down, and with his finger wrote on the ground, as though he heard them not. So when they continued asking him, he lifted up himself, and said unto them, He that is without sin among you, let him first cast a stone at her. And again he stooped down, and wrote on the ground. And they which heard it, being convicted by their own conscience, went out one by one, beginning at the eldest, even unto the last; and Jesus was left alone, and the woman standing in the midst. When Jesus had lifted up himself, and saw none but the woman, he said unto her, Woman, where are those thine accusers? Hath no man condemned thee? She said, No man, Lord. And Jesus said unto her, Neither do I condemn thee. Go, and sin no more.

The Blind Beggar

FROM ST. LUKE 18

And it came to pass, that as he was come nigh unto Jericho, a certain blind man sat by the wayside begging. And hearing the multitude pass by, he asked what it meant. And they told him, that Jesus of Nazareth passeth by. And he cried, saying, Jesus, thou Son of David, have mercy on me! And they which went before rebuked him, that he should hold his peace; but he cried so much the more, Thou Son of David, have mercy on me. And Jesus stood, and commanded him to be brought unto him; and when he was come near, he asked him, Saying, What wilt thou that I shall do unto thee? And he said, Lord, that I may receive my sight. And Jesus said unto him, Receive thy sight. Thy faith hath saved thee. And immediately he received his sight, and followed him, glorifying God; and all the people, when they saw it, gave praise unto God.

The Ten Lepers

FROM ST. LUKE 17

And it came to pass, as he went to Jerusalem, that he passed through the midst of Samaria and Galilee. And as he entered into a certain village, there met him ten men that were lepers, which stood afar off. And they lifted up their voices and said, Jesus, Master, have mercy on us. And when he saw them, he said unto them, Go show yourselves unto the priests. And it came to pass, that, as they went they were cleansed. And one of them, when he saw that he was healed, turned back, and with a loud voice glorified God, and fell down on his face at his feet, giving him thanks; and he was a Samaritan. And Jesus answering said, Were there not ten cleansed? But where are the nine? There are not found that returned to give glory to God, save this stranger. And he said unto him, Arise, go thy way. Thy faith hath made thee whole.

The Syrophenician Woman

FROM ST. MARK 7

And from thence he arose, and went into the borders of Tyre and Sidon, and entered into a house, and would have no man know it; but he could not be hid. For a certain woman, whose young daughter had an unclean spirit, heard of him, and came and fell at his feet. The woman was a Greek, a Syrophenician by nation; and she besought him that he would cast forth the devil out of her daughter. But he answered her not a word. And his disciples came and besought him, saying, Send her away; for she crieth after us. But he answered and said, I am not sent but unto the lost sheep of the house of Israel. Then came she and worshipped him saying, Lord, help me. But Jesus said unto her, Let the children first be filled; for it is not meet to take the children's bread, and to cast it unto the dogs. And she answered and said unto him, Yes, Lord; yet the dogs under the table eat of the children's crumbs. And he said unto her, For this saying go thy way; the devil is gone out of thy daughter. And when she was come to her house, she found the devil gone out, and her daughter laid upon the bed.

The Roman Centurion and His Servant

FROM ST. LUKE 7

Now when he had ended all his sayings in the audience of the people, he entered into Capernaum. And a certain centurion's servant, who was dear unto him, was sick, and ready to die. And when he heard of Jesus, he sent unto him the elders of the Jews, beseeching him that he would come and heal his servant. And when they came to Jesus, they besought him instantly, saying, That he was worthy for whom he should do this, for he loveth our nation, and he hath built us a synagogue.

Then Jesus went with them. And when he was now not far from the house, the centurion sent friends to him, saying unto him, Lord, trouble not thyself; for I am not worthy that thou shouldest enter under my roof. Wherefore neither thought I myself worthy to come unto thee; but say in a word, and my servant shall be healed. For I also am a man set under authority, having under me soldiers; and I say unto one, Go, and he goeth; and to another, Come, and he cometh; and to my servant, Do this, and he doeth it.

When Jesus heard these things, he marvelled at him, and turned him about, and said unto the people that followed him, I say unto you, I have not found so great faith, no, not in Israel. And they that were sent, returning to the house, found the servant whole that had been sick.

Zaccheus

FROM ST. LUKE 19

And Jesus entered and passed through Jericho. And, behold, there was a man named Zaccheus, which was the chief among the publicans, and he was rich. And he sought to see Jesus who he was; and could not for the press, because he was little of stature. And he ran before, and climbed up into a sycamore tree to see him; for he was to pass that way. And when Jesus came to the place, he looked up, and saw him, and said unto him, Zaccheus, make haste, and come down; for today I must abide at thy house. And he made haste, and came down, and received him joyfully. And when they saw it, they all murmured, saying, that he was gone to be guest with a man that is a sinner. And Zaccheus stood, and said unto the Lord, Behold, Lord, the half of my goods I give to the poor; and if I have taken any thing from any man by false accusation, I restore him fourfold. And Jesus said unto him, This day is salvation come to this house. For the Son of man is come to seek and to save that which was lost.

The Woman of Samaria

FROM ST. JOHN 4

Jesus left Judea, and departed again into Galilee. And he must needs go through Samaria. Then cometh he to a city of Samaria, which is called Sychar, near to the parcel of ground that Jacob gave to his son Joseph. Now Jacob's well was there. Jesus therefore, being wearied with his journey, sat thus on the well; and it was about the sixth hour.

There cometh a woman of Samaria to draw water. Jesus saith unto her, Give me to drink. (For his disciples were gone away unto the city to buy meat.) Then saith the woman of Samaria unto him, How is it that thou, being a Jew, askest drink of me, which am a woman of Samaria? For the Jews have no dealings with the Samaritans. Jesus answered and said unto her, If thou knewest the gift of God, and who it is that saith to thee, Give me to drink, thou wouldest have asked of him, and he would have given thee living water.

The woman saith unto him, Sir, thou hast nothing to draw with, and the well is deep; from whence then hast thou that living water? Art thou greater than our father Jacob, which gave us the well, and drank thereof himself, and his children, and his cattle? Jesus answered and said unto her, Whosoever drinketh of this water shall thirst again; but whosoever drinketh of the water that I shall give him shall never thirst; but the water that I shall give him shall be in him a well of water springing up into everlasting life. The woman saith unto him, Sir, give me this water, that I thirst not, neither come hither to draw. Jesus saith unto her, Go, call thy husband, and come hither. The woman answered and said, I have no husband. Jesus said unto her, Thou hast well said, I have no husband; for thou hast had five husbands; and he whom thou now hast is not thy husband; in that saidst thou truly. The woman saith unto him, Sir, I perceive that thou art a prophet. Our fathers worshipped in this mountain; and ye say, that in Jerusalem is the place where men ought to worship. Jesus saith unto her, Woman, believe me, the hour cometh, when ye shall neither in this mountain, nor yet at Jerusalem, worship the Father. Ye worship, ye know not what;

we know what we worship; for salvation is of the Jews. But the hour cometh, and now is when the true worshippers shall worship the Father in spirit and in truth; for the Father seeketh such to worship him. God is a spirit; and they that worship him must worship him in spirit and in truth. The woman saith unto him, I know that Messias cometh, which is called Christ. When he is come, he will tell us all things. Jesus saith unto her, I that speak unto thee am he.

And upon this came his disciples and marvelled that he talked with the woman; yet no man said, What seekest thou? or, Why talkest thou with her? The woman then left her waterpot and went her way into the city, and saith to the men, Come, see a man which told me all things that ever I did. Is not this the Christ?

Then they went out of the city and came unto him.

The Rich Young Man

FROM ST. MATTHEW 19

And, behold, one came and said unto him, Good Master, what good thing shall I do, that I may have eternal life? And he said unto him, Why callest thou me good? There is none good but one, that is, God. But if thou wilt enter into life, keep the commandments. He saith unto him, Which? Jesus said, Thou shalt do no murder, Thou shalt not commit adultery, Thou shalt not steal, Thou shalt not bear false witness, Honor thy father and thy mother; and, Thou shalt love thy neighbor as thyself. The young man saith unto him, All these things have I kept from my youth up. What lack I yet? Jesus said unto him, If thou wilt be perfect, go and sell that thou hast, and give to the poor, and thou shalt have treasure in heaven; and come and follow me. But when the young man heard that saying, he went away sorrowful; for he had great possessions.

Martha and Mary

FROM ST. LUKE 10

Now it came to pass, as they went, that he entered into a certain village; and a certain woman named Martha received him into her house. And she had a sister called Mary, which also sat at Jesus' feet, and heard his word. But Martha was cumbered about much serving, and came to him, and said, Lord, dost thou not care that my sister hath left me to serve alone? Bid her therefore that she help me.

And Jesus answered and said unto her, Martha, Martha, thou art careful and troubled about many things. But one thing is needful; and Mary hath chosen that good part, which shall not be taken away from her.

The Woman with the Alabaster Box

FROM ST. LUKE 7

And one of the Pharisees desired him that he would eat with him. And he went into the Pharisee's house, and sat down to meat. And, behold, a woman in the city, which was a sinner, when she knew that Jesus sat at meat in the Pharisee's house, brought an alabaster box of ointment. And she stood at his feet behind him weeping, and began to wash his feet with tears, and did wipe them with the hairs of her head, and kissed his feet, and anointed them with the ointment.

Now when the Pharisee which had bidden him saw it, he spake within himself, saying, This man, if he were a prophet, would have known who and what manner of woman this is that toucheth him; for she is a sinner.

And Jesus answering said unto him, Simon, I have somewhat to say unto thee. And he saith, Master, say on. There was a certain creditor which had two debtors: the one owed five hundred pence, and the other fifty. And when they had nothing to pay, he frankly forgave them both. Tell me therefore, which of them will love him most? Simon answered and said, I suppose that he to whom he forgave most. And he said unto him, Thou hast rightly judged.

And he turned to the woman, and said unto Simon: Seest thou this woman? I entered into thine house. Thou gavest me no water for my feet; but she hath washed my feet with tears, and wiped them with the hairs of her head. Thou gavest me no kiss; but this woman, since the time I came in, hath not ceased to kiss my feet. My head with oil thou didst not anoint; but this woman hath anointed my feet with ointment. Wherefore I say unto thee, Her sins, which are many, are forgiven; for she loved much. But to whom little is forgiven, the same loveth little. And he said unto her, Thy sins are forgiven.

And they that sat at meat with him began to say within themselves, Who is this that forgiveth sins also? And he said to the woman, Thy faith hath saved thee. Go in peace.

-II-

THE ACTS OF THE APOSTLES

THE Acts of the Apostles is in reality a continuation of St. Luke's Gospel and probably was originally published with that biography of Jesus as one book. Just when it was detached from the Gospel or given its present title, we do not know. Since it is our one surviving account of the earliest Christian age and of the spread of Christian communities and churches throughout the Mediterranean world, it has great historical value. Part of the book, from chapter 16:10 to its close, was obviously based on a diary or journal kept by its author as he travelled with St. Paul during certain of the years between A.D. 50 and 64, around which latter date St. Paul died in Rome.

The book of the Acts is a difficult one to read as a unit because it contains within a relatively small space so much seemingly diverse material: brilliant single episodes; long sententious speeches (a literary convention of the time and perhaps not actual speeches, but rather ones reconstructed by St. Luke); missionary journeys, often difficult to disentangle. Perhaps the best way to become acquainted with the book is to read it entire from one's Bible in order to see it, first, as a whole, even though that sight may be a confused one. Suggestions for such reading are given in *The Bible and the Common Reader,* Part IV.

The charm of the book, however, consists not in its historical background, important as that may be, but rather in those dramatic episodes and incidents which center about its various characters. These, in my opinion, give to the book its peculiar and distinctive value as literature. From its second chapter, which relates those amazing happenings in the "upper room" in Jerusalem, St. Luke misses no opportunity to imbue his stories with drama, excitement, and wonder. Indeed, this sense of wonder which surrounds and penetrates them all becomes the atmosphere of his book.

Since I feel so deeply that the episodes in themselves form the most memorable portions of the Acts, I have chosen for these Readings the best of them and have arranged them around the persons with whom they have to do.

THE DAY OF PENTECOST

FROM ACTS 2

And when the day of Pentecost was fully come, they were all with one accord in one place. And suddenly there came a sound from heaven as of a rushing mighty wind, and it filled all the house where they were sitting. And there appeared unto them cloven tongues like as of fire, and it sat upon each of them. And they were all filled with the Holy Ghost, and began to speak with other tongues, as the Spirit gave them utterance. And there were dwelling in Jerusalem Jews, devout men, out of every nation under heaven. Now when this was noised abroad, the multitude came together, and were confounded, because that every man heard them speak in his own language.

And they were all amazed and marvelled, saying one to another, Behold, are not all these which speak Galileans? And how hear we every man in our own tongue, wherein we were born? Parthians, and Medes, and Elamites, and the dwellers in Mesopotamia, and in Judea, and Cappadocia, in Pontus, and Asia, Phrygia, and Pamphylia, in Egypt, and in the parts of Libya about Cyrene, and strangers of Rome, Jews and proselytes, Cretes and Arabians—we do hear them speak in our tongues the wonderful works of God!

STORIES ABOUT ST. PETER

Peter and the Lame Beggar

FROM ACTS 3

Now Peter and John went up together into the temple at the hour of prayer, being the ninth hour. And a certain man, lame from his mother's womb, was carried, whom they laid daily at the gate of the temple which is called Beautiful, to ask alms of them that entered into the temple; who, seeing Peter and John about to go into the temple, asked an alms. And Peter, fastening his eyes upon him with John, said, Look on us. And he gave heed unto them, expecting to receive something of them.

Then Peter said, Silver and gold have I none; but such as I have give I thee: In the name of Jesus Christ of Nazareth rise up and walk. And he took him by the right hand, and lifted him up; and immediately his feet and ankle bones received strength. And he, leaping up, stood, and walked, and entered with them into the temple, walking, and leaping, and praising God. And all the people saw him walking and praising God. And they knew that it was he which sat for alms at the Beautiful gate of the temple; and they were filled with wonder and amazement at that which had happened unto him. And as the lame man which was healed held Peter and John, all the people ran together unto them in the porch that is called Solomon's, greatly wondering.

Ananias and Sapphira

FROM ACTS 5

But a certain man named Ananias, with Sapphira his wife, sold a possession, and kept back part of the price, his wife also being privy to it, and brought a certain part, and laid it at the apostles' feet. But Peter said, Ananias, why hath Satan filled thine heart to lie to the Holy Ghost, and to keep back part of the price of the land? While it remained, was it not thine own? And after it was sold, was it not in thine own power? Why hast thou conceived this thing in thine heart? Thou hast not lied unto men, but unto God.

And Ananias hearing these words fell down, and gave up the ghost; and great fear came on all them that heard these things. And the young men arose, wound him up, and carried him out, and buried him.

And it was about the space of three hours after, when his wife, not knowing what was done, came in. And Peter answered unto her, Tell me whether ye sold the land for so much? And she said, Yea, for so much. Then Peter said unto her, How is it that ye have agreed together to tempt the Spirit of the Lord? Behold, the feet of them which have buried thy husband are at the door, and shall carry thee out.

Then fell she down straightway at his feet, and yielded up the ghost; and the young men came in, and found her dead, and, carrying her forth, buried her by her husband. And great fear came upon all the church, and upon as many as heard these things.

The Story of Dorcas

FROM ACTS 9

Now there was at Joppa a certain disciple named Tabitha, which by interpretation is called Dorcas. This woman was full of good works and almsdeeds which she did. And it came to pass in those days that she was sick and died, whom, when they had washed, they laid in an upper chamber. And forasmuch as Lydda was nigh to Joppa, and the disciples had heard that Peter was there, they sent unto him two men desiring him that he would not delay to come to them.

Then Peter arose and went with them. When he was come, they brought him into the upper chamber; and all the widows stood by him weeping, and showing the coats and garments which Dorcas made while she was with them. But Peter put them all forth, and kneeled down, and prayed; and turning him to the body said, Tabitha, arise. And she opened her eyes; and when she saw Peter, she sat up. And he gave her his hand, and lifted her up; and when he had called the saints and widows, he presented her alive. And it was known throughout all Joppa; and many believed in the Lord. And it came to pass, that he tarried many days in Joppa with one Simon a tanner.

Cornelius the Centurion

FROM ACTS 10

There was a certain man in Caesarea called Cornelius, a centurion of the band called the Italian band, a devout man, and one that feared God with all his house, which gave much alms to the people, and prayed to God always. He saw in a vision evidently, about the ninth hour of the day, an angel of God coming in to him, and saying unto him, Cornelius. And when he looked on him, he was afraid, and said, What is it, Lord? And he said unto him, Thy prayers and thine alms are come up for a memorial before God. And now send men to Joppa, and call for one Simon, whose surname is Peter. He lodgeth with one Simon a tanner, whose house is by the sea side; he shall tell thee what thou oughtest to do. And when the angel which spake unto Cornelius was departed, he called two of his household servants, and a devout soldier of them that waited on him continually; and when he had declared all these things unto them, he sent them to Joppa.

On the morrow, as they went on their journey, and drew nigh unto the city, Peter went up upon the housetop to pray about the sixth hour. And he became very hungry, and would have eaten; but while they made ready, he fell into a trance. And he saw heaven opened, and a certain vessel descending unto him, as it had been a great sheet knit at the four corners, and let down to the earth, wherein were all manner of four-footed beasts of the earth, and wild beasts, and creeping things, and fowls of the air. And there came a voice to him, Rise, Peter, kill, and eat. But Peter said, Not so, Lord; for I have never eaten any thing that is common or unclean. And the voice spake unto him again the second time, What God hath cleansed, that call not thou common. This was done thrice; and the vessel was received up again into heaven.

Now while Peter doubted in himself what this vision he had seen should mean, behold, the men which were sent from Cornelius had made inquiry for Simon's house, and stood before the gate, and called, and asked whether Simon, which was surnamed Peter, were lodged there. While Peter thought on the vision, the Spirit said unto him, Behold, three men seek thee. Arise therefore, and get thee down, and go with them, doubting nothing; for I have sent them.

Then Peter went down to the men which were sent unto him from Cornelius; and said, Behold, I am he whom ye seek. What is the cause wherefore ye are come? And they said, Cornelius the centurion, a just man, and one that feareth God, and of good report among all the nation of the Jews, was warned from God by a holy angel to send for thee into his house, and to hear words of thee. Then called he them in, and lodged them. And on the morrow Peter went away with them; and certain brethren from Joppa accompanied him. And the morrow after they entered into Caesarea. And Cornelius waited for them, and had called together his kinsmen and near friends.

And as Peter was coming in, Cornelius met him, and fell down at his feet, and worshipped him. But Peter took him up, saying, Stand up; I myself also am a man. And as he talked with him, he went in, and found many that were come together. And he said unto them, Ye know how that it is an unlawful thing for a man that is a Jew to keep company, or come unto one of another nation; but God hath showed me that I should not call any man common or unclean. Of a truth I perceive that God is no respecter of persons. But in every nation he that feareth him, and worketh righteousness, is accepted with him. . . .

While Peter yet spake these words, the Holy Ghost fell on all them which heard the word. And they of the circumcision which believed were astonished, as many as came with Peter, because that on the Gentiles also was poured out the gift of the Holy Ghost. For they heard them speak with tongues, and magnify God. Then answered Peter, Can any man forbid water, that these should not be baptized, which have received the Holy Ghost as well as we? And he commanded them to be baptized in the name of the Lord.

Peter's Escape from Prison

FROM ACTS 12

Now, about that time Herod the king stretched forth his hands to vex certain of the church. And he killed James the brother of John with the sword. And because he saw it pleased the Jews, he proceeded further to take Peter also. And when he had apprehended him, he put him in prison, and delivered him to four quaternions of soldiers to keep him, intending after Easter to bring him forth to the people. Peter therefore was kept in prison; but prayer was made without ceasing of the church unto God for him.

And when Herod would have brought him forth, the same night Peter was sleeping between two soldiers, bound with two chains; and the keepers before the door kept the prison. And, behold, the angel of the Lord came upon him, and a light shined in the prison; and he smote Peter on the side, and raised him up, saying, Arise up quickly. And his chains fell off from his hands. And the angel said unto him, Gird thyself, and bind on thy sandals. And so he did. And he saith unto him, Cast thy garment about thee, and follow me. And he went out and followed him; and wist not that it was true which was done by the angel, but thought he saw a vision. When they were past the first and the second ward, they came unto the iron gate that leadeth unto the city, which opened to them of his own accord; and they went out, and passed on through one street; and forthwith the angel departed from him.

And when Peter was come to himself, he said, Now I know of a surety, that the Lord hath sent his angel, and hath delivered me out of the hand of Herod, and from all the expectation of the people of the Jews. And when he had considered the thing, he came to the house of Mary the mother of John, whose surname was Mark, where many were gathered together praying. And as Peter knocked at the door of the gate, a damsel came to hearken, named Rhoda. And when she knew Peter's voice, she opened not the gate for gladness, but ran in, and told how Peter stood before the gate. And they said unto her, Thou art mad. But she constantly affirmed that it was even so. Then said they, It is his angel. But Peter continued knocking; and when they had opened the door, and saw him, they were astonished. But he, beckoning unto them with the hand to hold their peace, declared unto them how the Lord had brought him out of the prison. And he said, Go, show these things unto James, and to the brethren. And he departed, and went into another place.

Now as soon as it was day, there was no small stir among the soldiers, what was become of Peter. And when Herod had sought for him, and found him not, he examined the keepers, and commanded that they should be put to death. And Peter went down from Judea to Caesarea, and there abode.

ST. STEPHEN: HIS MARTYRDOM

FROM ACTS 6, 7, 8

And Stephen, full of faith and power, did great wonders and miracles among the people. Then there arose certain of the synagogue, which is called the synagogue of the Libertines, and Cyrenians, and Alexandrians, and of them of Cilicia and of Asia, disputing with Stephen. And they were not able to resist the wisdom and the spirit by which he spake. Then they suborned men, which said, We have heard him speak blasphemous words against Moses, and against God. And they stirred up the people, and the elders, and the scribes, and came upon him, and caught him, and brought him to the council, and set up false witnesses, which said, This man ceaseth not to speak blasphemous words against this holy place, and the law; for we have heard him say that this Jesus of Nazareth shall destroy this place, and shall change the customs which Moses delivered us. And all that sat in the council, looking steadfastly on him, saw his face as it had been the face of an angel.

Then said the high priest, Are these things so? And Stephen said: Men, brethren, and fathers, hearken! The God of glory appeared unto our father Abraham when he was in Mesopotamia, before he dwelt in Charran. . . . Ye stiffnecked and uncircumcised in heart and ears, ye do always resist the Holy Ghost; as your fathers did, so do ye. Which of the prophets have not your fathers persecuted? And they have slain them which showed before of the coming of the Just One, of whom ye have been now the betrayers and murderers, who have received the law by the disposition of angels, and have not kept it.

When they heard these things, they were cut to the heart, and they gnashed on him with their teeth. But he, being full of the Holy Ghost, looked up steadfastly into heaven, and saw the glory of God, and Jesus standing on the right hand of God. And he said, Behold, I see the heavens opened, and the Son of man standing on the right hand of God.

Then they cried out with a loud voice, and stopped their ears, and ran upon him with one accord, and cast him out of the city, and stoned him. And the witnesses laid down their clothes at a young man's feet, whose name was Saul. And they stoned Stephen, calling upon God, and saying, Lord Jesus, receive my spirit. And he kneeled down, and cried with a loud voice, Lord, lay not this sin to their charge. And when he had said this, he fell asleep.

And Saul was consenting unto his death. And at that time there was a great persecution against the church which was at Jerusalem; and they were all scattered abroad throughout the regions of Judea and Samaria, except the apostles. And devout men carried Stephen to his burial, and made great lamentation over him.

As for Saul, he made havoc of the church, entering into every house, and, haling men and women, committed them to prison. Therefore they that were scattered abroad went everywhere preaching the word.

ST. PHILIP AND THE ETHIOPIAN

FROM ACTS 8

Then Philip went down to the city of Samaria and preached Christ unto them. And the people with one accord gave heed unto those things which Philip spake, hearing and seeing the miracles which he did. And there was great joy in that city.

And the angel of the Lord spake unto Philip, saying, Arise, and go toward the south unto the way that goeth down from Jerusalem unto Gaza, which is desert. And he arose and went. And, behold, a man of Ethiopia, an eunuch of great authority under Candace queen of the Ethiopians, who had the charge of all her treasure, and had come to Jerusalem for to worship, was returning, and, sitting in his chariot, read Esaias the prophet.

Then the Spirit said unto Philip, Go near, and join thyself to this chariot. And Philip ran thither to him, and heard him read the prophet Esaias, and said, Understandest thou what thou readest? And he said, How can I, except some man should guide me? And he desired Philip that he would come up and sit with him.

The place of the scripture which he read was this:

He was led as a sheep to the slaughter;
And like a lamb dumb before his shearer,
So opened he not his mouth.
In his humiliation his judgment was taken away;
And who shall declare his generation?
For his life is taken from the earth.

And the eunuch answered Philip, and said, I pray thee, of whom speaketh the prophet this? Of himself, or of some other man?

Then Philip opened his mouth, and began at the same scripture, and preached unto him Jesus. And as they went on their way, they came unto a certain water; and the eunuch said, See, here is water. What doth hinder me to be baptized? And Philip said, If thou believest with all thine heart, thou mayest. And he answered and said, I believe that Jesus Christ is the Son of God.

And he commanded the chariot to stand still; and they went down both into the water, both Philip and the eunuch; and he baptized him. And when they were come up out of the water, the Spirit of the Lord caught away Philip, that the eunuch saw him no more; and he went on his way rejoicing.

STORIES ABOUT ST. PAUL

The stories about St. Paul, except for the thrilling account of his conversion on the road to Damascus, are less appealing than are the preceding stories about the other apostles. Although he was unquestionably the greatest of them all in terms of human personality and influence, he seems, in St. Luke's accounts of him, more remote than lovable, of heroic stature surely, yet neither warm nor companionable. Much of this impression is clearly the result of St. Luke's manner of writing in the last half of the Acts. Apparently, when he came to record events for his travel notes or journals, his power as a recreator of personality was either deliberately set aside or dimmed by the multiplicity of the events themselves. The drama latent in many of these latter stories is often lost in the long speeches made by St. Paul in his own defense before various state officials.

The stories given here have to do with his missionary journeys to Asia Minor, Macedonia, and Greece, with his appearance as a prisoner before King Agrippa at Caesarea, and finally with his stormy voyage toward Rome.

Saul on the Damascus Road

FROM ACTS 9

And Saul, yet breathing out threatenings and slaughter against the disciples of the Lord, went unto the high priest, and desired of him letters to Damascus to the synagogues, that if he found any of this way, whether they were men or women, he might bring them bound into Jerusalem.

And as he journeyed, he came near Damascus; and suddenly there shined round about him a light from heaven. And he fell to the earth, and heard a voice saying unto him, Saul, Saul, why persecutest thou me? And he said, Who art thou, Lord? And the Lord said, I am Jesus whom thou persecutest. It is hard for thee to kick against the pricks. And he, trembling and astonished, said, Lord, what wilt thou have me to do? And the Lord said unto him, Arise, and go into the city, and it shall be told thee what thou must do. And the men which journeyed with him stood speechless, hearing a voice, but seeing no man. And Saul arose from the earth; and when his eyes were opened, he saw no man; but they led him by the hand, and brought him into Damascus. And he was three days without sight, and neither did eat or drink.

And there was a certain disciple named Ananias; and to him said the Lord in a vision, Ananias. And he said, Behold, I am here, Lord. And the Lord said unto him, Arise and go into the street which is called Straight, and inquire in the house of Judas for one called Saul, of Tarsus; for, behold, he prayeth. And he hath seen in a vision a man named Ananias coming in and putting his hand on him that he might receive his sight.

Then Ananias answered, Lord, I have heard by many of this man, how much evil he hath done to thy saints at Jerusalem. And here he hath authority from the chief priests to bind all that call on thy name. But the Lord said unto him, Go thy way. For he is a chosen vessel unto me to bear my name before the Gentiles and kings and the children of Israel. For I will show him how great things he must suffer for my name's sake.

And Ananias went his way and entered into the house; and putting his hands on him said, Brother Saul, the Lord, even Jesus, that appeared unto thee in the way as thou camest, hath sent me that thou mightest receive thy sight and be filled with the Holy Ghost. And immediately there fell from his eyes as it had been scales; and he received sight forthwith, and arose and was baptized. And when he had received meat, he was strengthened.

Then was Saul certain days with the disciples which were at Damascus. And straightway he preached Christ in the synagogues, that he is the Son of God. But all that heard him were amazed and said: Is not this he that destroyed them which called on this name in Jerusalem?

Paul in Prison in Macedonia

FROM ACTS 16

And a vision appeared to Paul in the night: There stood a man of Macedonia, and prayed him, saying, Come over into Macedonia, and help us. And after he had seen the vision, immediately we endeavored to go into Macedonia, assuredly gathering that the Lord had called us for to preach the gospel unto them. Therefore loosing from Troas, we came with a straight course to Samothracia, and the next day to Neapolis; and from thence to Philippi, which is the chief city of that part of Macedonia, and a colony; and we were in that city abiding certain days. And on the sabbath we went out of the city by a river side, where prayer was wont to be made; and we sat down, and spake unto the women which resorted thither.

And a certain woman named Lydia, a seller of purple, of the

city of Thyatira, which worshipped God, heard us, whose heart the Lord opened, that she attended unto the things which were spoken of Paul. And when she was baptized, and her household, she besought us, saying, If ye have judged me to be faithful to the Lord, come into my house, and abide there. And she constrained us.

And it came to pass, as we went to prayer, a certain damsel possessed with a spirit of divination met us, which brought her masters much gain by soothsaying. The same followed Paul and us, and cried, saying, These men are the servants of the most high God, which show unto us the way of salvation. And this did she many days. But Paul, being grieved, turned and said to the spirit, I command thee in the name of Jesus Christ to come out of her. And he came out the same hour.

And when her masters saw that the hope of their gains was gone, they caught Paul and Silas, and drew them into the market place unto the rulers, and brought them to the magistrates, saying, These men, being Jews, do exceedingly trouble our city, and teach customs, which are not lawful for us to receive, neither to observe, being Romans. And the multitude rose up together against them; and the magistrates rent off their clothes, and commanded to beat them. And when they had laid many stripes upon them, they cast them into prison, charging the jailor to keep them safely, who, having received such a charge, thrust them into the inner prison, and made their feet fast in the stocks.

And at midnight Paul and Silas prayed, and sang praises unto God; and the prisoners heard them. And suddenly there was a great earthquake, so that the foundations of the prison were shaken; and immediately all the doors were opened, and every one's bands were loosed. And the keeper of the prison awaking out of his sleep, and seeing the prison doors open, he drew out his sword, and would have killed himself, supposing that the prisoners had been fled. But Paul cried with a loud voice, saying, Do thyself no harm; for we are all here. Then he called for a light, and sprang in, and came trembling, and fell down before Paul and Silas, and brought them out, and said, Sirs, what must I do to be saved? And they said, Believe on the Lord Jesus Christ, and thou shalt be saved and thy house.

And they spake unto him the word of the Lord, and to all that were in his house. And he took them the same hour of the night, and washed their stripes; and was baptized, he and all his, straightway. And when he had brought them into his house, he set meat before them and rejoiced, believing in God with all his house.

And when it was day, the magistrates sent the sergeants, saying, Let those men go. And the keeper of the prison told this saying to Paul, The magistrates have sent to let you go. Now therefore depart, and go in peace. But Paul said unto them, They have beaten us openly uncondemned, being Romans, and have cast us into prison; and now do they thrust us out privily? Nay verily; but let them come themselves and fetch us out. And the sergeants told these words unto the magistrates; and they feared, when they heard that they were Romans. And they came and besought them, and brought them out, and desired them to depart out of the city. And they went out of the prison, and entered into the house of Lydia; and when they had seen the brethren, they comforted them, and departed.

Paul at Athens

FROM ACTS 17

Now while Paul waited at Athens, his spirit was stirred in him when he saw the city wholly given to idolatry. Therefore disputed he in the synagogue with the Jews, and with the devout persons, and in the market daily with them that met with him. Then certain philosophers of the Epicureans, and of the Stoics, encountered him. And some said, What will this babbler say? Other some, He seemeth to be a setter forth of strange gods. And they took him, and brought him unto Areopagus, saying, May we know what this new doctrine whereof thou speakest is? For thou bringest certain strange things to our ears. We would know therefore what these things mean. (For all the Athenians and strangers which were there spent their time in nothing else, but either to tell, or to hear some new thing.)

Then Paul stood in the midst of Mars' hill, and said: Ye men of Athens, I perceive that in all things ye are too superstitious. For as I passed by, and beheld your devotions, I found an altar with this inscription, TO THE UNKNOWN GOD. Whom therefore ye ignorantly worship, him declare I unto you. God that made the world and all things therein, seeing that he is Lord of heaven and earth, dwelleth not in temples made with hands, neither is worshipped with men's hands, as though he needed any thing, seeing he giveth to all life, and breath, and all things; and hath made of one blood all nations of men for to dwell on all the face of the earth, and hath determined the times before appointed, and the bounds of their habitation, that they should seek the Lord, if haply they might feel after him, and find him, though he be not far from every one of us. For in him we live, and move, and have our being; as certain also of your own poets have said, For we are also his offspring. Forasmuch then as we are the offspring of God, we ought not to think that the Godhead is like unto gold, or silver, or stone, graven by art and man's device. And the times of this ignorance God winked at; but now commandeth all men everywhere to repent, because he hath appointed a day, in the which he will judge the world in righteousness by that man whom he hath ordained; whereof he hath given assurance unto all men, in that he hath raised him from the dead.

And when they heard of the resurrection of the dead, some mocked; and others said, We will hear thee again of this matter. So Paul departed from among them. Howbeit certain men clave unto him, and believed.

A Town Clerk of Ephesus

FROM ACTS 19

And the same time there arose no small stir about that way. For a certain man named Demetrius, a silversmith, which made silver shrines for Diana, brought no small gain unto the craftsmen, whom he called together with the workmen of like occupation, and said, Sirs, ye know that by this craft we have our wealth. Moreover ye see and hear that not alone at Ephesus, but almost throughout all Asia, this Paul hath persuaded and turned away much people, saying that they be no gods which are made with hands. So that not only this our craft is in danger to be set at nought; but also that the temple of the great goddess Diana should be despised, and her magnificence should be destroyed, whom all Asia and the world worshippeth. And when they heard these sayings, they were full of wrath, and cried out, saying, Great is Diana of the Ephesians! And the whole city was filled with confusion; and having caught Gaius and Aristarchus, men of Macedonia, Paul's companions in travel, they rushed with one accord into the theatre.

And when Paul would have entered in unto the people, the disciples suffered him not. And certain of the chief of Asia, which were his friends, sent unto him, desiring him that he would not adventure himself into the theatre. Some therefore cried one thing, and some another; for the assembly was confused; and the more part knew not wherefore they were come together. And they drew Alexander out of the multitude, the Jews putting him forward. And Alexander beckoned with the hand, and would have made his defense unto the people. But when they knew that he was a Jew, all with one voice about the space of two hours cried out, Great is Diana of the Ephesians!

And when the town clerk had appeased the people, he said, Ye men of Ephesus, what man is there that knoweth not how that the city of the Ephesians is a worshipper of the great goddess Diana, and of the image which fell down from Jupiter? Seeing then that these things cannot be spoken against, ye ought to be quiet, and to do nothing rashly. For ye have brought hither these men, which are neither robbers of churches, nor yet blasphemers of your goddess. Wherefore if Demetrius, and the craftsmen which are with him, have a matter against any man, the law is open, and there are deputies. Let them implead one another. But if ye enquire anything concerning other matters, it shall be determined in a lawful assembly. For we are in danger to be called in question for this day's uproar, there being no cause whereby we may give an account of this concourse. And when he had thus spoken, he dismissed the assembly.

Paul Before King Agrippa

FROM ACTS 25, 26

And after certain days king Agrippa and Bernice came unto Caesarea to salute Festus. And when they had been there many days, Festus declared Paul's cause unto the king, saying:

There is a certain man left in bonds by Felix, about whom, when I was at Jerusalem, the chief priests and the elders of the Jews informed me, desiring to have judgment against him. To whom I answered, It is not the manner of the Romans to deliver any man to die, before that he which is accused have the accusers face to face, and have license to answer for himself concerning the crime laid against him. Therefore, when they were come hither, without any delay on the morrow I sat on the judgment seat, and commanded the man to be brought forth. Against whom when the accusers stood up, they brought none accusation of such things as I supposed, but had certain questions against him of their own superstition, and of one Jesus, which was dead, whom Paul affirmed to be alive. And because I doubted of such manner of questions, I asked him whether he would go to Jerusalem, and there be judged of these matters. But when Paul had appealed to be reserved unto the hearing of Augustus, I commanded him to be kept till I might send him to Caesar.

Then Agrippa said unto Festus, I would also hear the man myself. Tomorrow, said he, thou shalt hear him. And on the morrow, when Agrippa was come, and Bernice, with great pomp, and was entered into the place of hearing with the chief captains, and principal men of the city, at Festus' commandment Paul was brought forth. And Festus said, King Agrippa, and all men which are here present with us, ye see this man, about whom all the multitude of the Jews have dealt with me, both at Jerusalem, and also here, crying that he ought not to live any longer. But when I found that he had committed nothing worthy of death, and that he himself hath appealed to Augustus, I have determined to send him. Of whom I have no certain thing to write unto my lord. Wherefore I have brought him forth before you, and specially before thee, O king Agrippa, that, after examination had, I might have somewhat to write. For it seemeth to me unreasonable to send a prisoner, and not withal to signify the crimes laid against him.

Then Agrippa said unto Paul, Thou art permitted to speak for thyself. Then Paul stretched forth the hand, and answered for himself: I think myself happy, king Agrippa, because I shall answer for myself this day before thee touching all the things whereof I am accused of the Jews; especially because I know thee to be expert in all customs and questions which are among the Jews. Wherefore I beseech thee to hear me patiently. My manner of life from my youth, which was at the first among mine own nation at Jerusalem, know all the Jews, which knew me from the beginning, if they would testify, that after the most straitest sect of our religion I lived a Pharisee. And now I stand and am judged for the hope of the promise made of God unto our fathers. For which hope's sake, king Agrippa, I am accused of the Jews.

Why should it be thought a thing incredible with you that God should raise the dead? I verily thought with myself, that I ought to do many things contrary to the name of Jesus of Nazareth, which thing I also did in Jerusalem; and many of the saints did I shut up in prison, having received authority from the chief priests; and when they were put to death, I gave my voice against them. And I punished them oft in every synagogue, and compelled them to blaspheme; and being exceedingly mad against them, I persecuted them even unto strange cities.

[Here Paul tells of his conversion on the road to Damascus.]

Whereupon, O king Agrippa, I was not disobedient unto the heavenly vision. But I showed first unto them of Damascus, and at Jerusalem, and throughout all the coasts of Judea, and then to the Gentiles, that they should repent and turn to God, and do works meet for repentance. For these causes the Jews caught me in the temple, and went about to kill me. Having therefore obtained help of God, I continue unto this day, witnessing both to small and great, saying none other things than those which the prophets and Moses did say should come: That Christ should suffer, and that he should be the first that should rise from the dead and should show light unto the people and to the Gentiles.

And as he thus spake for himself, Festus said with a loud voice, Paul, thou art beside thyself! Much learning doth make thee mad. But he said, I am not mad, most noble Festus; but I speak forth the words of truth and soberness. For the king knoweth of these things before whom also I speak freely. King Agrippa, believest thou the prophets? I know that thou believest.

Then Agrippa said unto Paul, Almost thou persuadest me to be a Christian! And Paul said, I would to God that not only thou, but also all that hear me this day were both almost and altogether such as I am, except these bonds. And when he had thus spoken, the king rose up and the governor and Bernice, and they that sat with them. And when they were gone inside, they talked between themselves, saying, This man doeth nothing worthy of death or of bonds.

The Voyage to Italy

FROM ACTS 27, 28

And when it was determined that we should sail into Italy, they delivered Paul and certain other prisoners unto one named Julius, a centurion of Augustus' band. And entering into a ship of Adramyttium, we launched, meaning to sail by the coasts of Asia, one Aristarchus, a Macedonian of Thessalonica, being with us. And the next day we touched at Sidon. And Julius courteously entreated Paul, and gave him liberty to go unto his friends to refresh himself. And when we had launched from thence, we sailed under Cyprus, because the winds were contrary. And when we had sailed over the sea of Cilicia and Pamphylia, we came to Myra, a city of Lycia. And there the centurion found a ship of Alexandria sailing into Italy; and he put us therein. And when we had sailed slowly many days, and scarce were come over against Cnidus, the wind not suffering us, we sailed under Crete, over against Salmone; and, hardly passing it, came unto a place which is called The Fair Havens; nigh thereunto was the city of Lasea.

Now when much time was spent, and when sailing was now dangerous, Paul admonished them, and said unto them, Sirs, I perceive that this voyage will be with hurt and much damage, not only of the lading and ship, but also of our lives. Nevertheless the centurion believed the master and the owner of the ship more than those things which were spoken by Paul. And because the haven was not commodious to winter in, the more part advised to depart thence also, if by any means they might attain to Phenice, and there to winter, which is an haven of Crete, and lieth toward the southwest and northwest. And when the south wind blew softly, supposing that they had obtained their purpose, loosing thence, they sailed close by Crete.

But not long after there arose against it a tempestuous wind, called Euroclydon. And when the ship was caught, and could not bear up into the wind, we let her drive. And running under a certain island which is called Clauda, we had much work to come by the boat, which when they had taken up, they used helps, undergirding the ship; and, fearing lest they should fall into the quicksands, struck sail, and so were driven. And we being exceedingly tossed with a tempest, the next day they lightened the ship; and the third day we cast out with our own hands the tackling of the ship. And when neither sun nor stars in many days appeared, and no small tempest lay on us, all hope that we should be saved was then taken away.

But after long abstinence, Paul stood forth in the midst of them, and said, Sirs, ye should have hearkened unto me, and not have loosed from Crete, and to have gained this harm and loss. And now I exhort you to be of good cheer; for there shall be no loss of man's life among you, but of the ship. For there stood by me this night the angel of God, whose I am, and whom I serve, Saying, Fear not, Paul; thou must be brought before Caesar; and, lo, God hath given thee all them that sail with thee. Wherefore, sirs, be of good cheer; for I believe God, that it shall be even as it was told me. Howbeit we must be cast upon a certain island.

But when the fourteenth night was come, as we were driven up and down in Adria, about midnight the shipmen deemed that they drew near to some country; and sounded, and found it twenty fathoms; and when they had gone a little further, they sounded again, and found it fifteen fathoms. Then fearing lest we should have fallen upon rocks, they cast four anchors out of the stern, and wished for the day. And as the shipmen were about to flee out of the ship, when they had let down the boat into the sea, under color as though they would have cast anchors out of the foreship, Paul said to the centurion and to the soldiers, Except these abide in the ship, ye cannot be saved. Then the soldiers cut off the ropes of the boat, and let her fall off.

And while the day was coming on, Paul besought them all to take meat, saying, This day is the fourteenth day that ye have tarried and continued fasting, having taken nothing. Wherefore I pray you to take some meat; for this is for your health; for there shall not a hair fall from the head of any of you. And when he had thus spoken, he took bread, and gave thanks to God in presence of them all; and when he had broken it, he began to eat. Then were they all of good cheer, and they also took some meat. And we were in all in the ship two hundred threescore and sixteen souls. And when they had eaten enough, they lightened the ship, and cast out the wheat into the sea.

And when it was day, they knew not the land; but they discovered a certain creek with a shore, into the which they were minded, if it were possible, to thrust in the ship. And when they had taken up the anchors, they committed themselves unto the sea, and loosed the rudder bands, and hoisted up the mainsail to the wind, and made toward shore. And falling into a place where two seas met, they ran the ship aground; and the forepart stuck fast, and remained unmovable, but the hinder part was broken with the violence of the waves. And the soldiers' counsel was to kill the prisoners, lest any of them should swim out, and escape. But the centurion, willing to save Paul, kept them from their purpose; and he commanded that they which could swim should cast themselves first into the sea, and get to land, and the rest, some on boards, and some on broken pieces of the ship. And so it came to pass, that they escaped all safe to land.

And when they were escaped, then they knew that the island was called Melita.[1] And the barbarous people showed us no little kindness; for they kindled a fire and received us every one because of the present rain and because of the cold. And when Paul had gathered a bundle of sticks and laid them on the fire, there came a viper out of the heat and fastened on his hand. And when the barbarians saw the venomous beast hang on his hand, they said among themselves, No doubt this man is a murderer, whom, though he hath escaped the sea, yet vengeance suffereth not to live.

And Paul shook off the beast into the fire and felt no harm. Howbeit they looked when he should have swollen or fallen down dead suddenly; but after they had looked a great while and saw no harm come to him, they changed their minds and said that he was a god.

In the same quarters were possessions of the chief man of the island whose name was Publius, who received us and lodged us three days courteously. And it came to pass that the father of Publius lay sick of a fever, to whom Paul entered in and prayed and laid his hands on him and healed him. So when this was done, others also which had diseases in the island came and were healed. These also honored us with many honors; and when we departed, they laded us with such things as were necessary.

And after three months we departed in a ship of Alexandria, which had wintered in the isle. And landing at Syracuse, we tarried there three days. And from thence we came to Rhegium; and we came the next day to Puteoli, where we found brethren and were desired to tarry with them seven days. And so we went toward Rome.

And from thence when the brethren heard of us, they came to meet us as far as Appi Forum and the Three Taverns, whom, when Paul saw, he thanked God and took courage. And when we came to Rome, the centurion delivered the prisoners to the captain of the guard. But Paul was suffered to dwell by himself with a soldier that kept him.

[1] The island was Malta.

-III-

THE LETTERS OF ST. PAUL

If, as I have earlier suggested, the stories about St. Paul in the Acts of the Apostles fail to reveal him as vividly as we might wish, he himself in his letters gloriously repairs any such sense of disappointment. For his letters are his unconscious portrait of himself as the most brilliant single figure of the first century of the Christian era and as one of the most remarkable personalities of any age. Within their impassioned sentences, their lofty flights of rhetoric, their swift changes of mood, their commands, adjurations, pleadings, and reproaches, is all of St. Paul: his logical and agile mind; his powers of argument; his sometimes amusing prejudices; his prodigious vitality both physical and spiritual; his volatile nature, now dejected, now uplifted; his common sense and care for minutest detail; his bitter scorn of apathy and of idleness; his boastful pride in his sufferings; his courtesy, gratitude, and even tenderness; and, above all else, his astounding and almost incredible faith.

Although the exact date of each of the ten Epistles, now accredited to him by the best scholars, is impossible to ascertain, St. Paul surely wrote his letters between the years 51 and 64 A.D. They were, as all know, written to the struggling new churches in Asia Minor, Greece, and Rome, most of which his own missionary zeal had founded. Although parts of them are models of literary composition, they were apparently not composed with any thought of publication. Instead they were written and sent as messages of concern, advice, and comfort to groups of people whom he looked upon not only as his charges but as his children. And as each of the communities to which he wrote was peculiar to itself, so each letter deals with the matters and problems of particular interest to that community.[1]

The letters which remain to us (for there were doubtless others now lost) are, of course, of inestimable value as the earliest existing documents of the Christian religion and as the nucleus of the New Testament. Yet to readers not interested primarily in fine points of doctrine

[1] *The Bible and the Common Reader*, Pt. IV, gives a relatively full account of each church and community and of its religious and social problems. It gives also a sketch of the life and personality of St. Paul.

or in theological argument, their appeal, I feel sure, lies rather in their revelation of a gifted and unique human being and in their distinction both as great pieces of literature and as equally great affirmations of "those things that cannot be shaken." This assurance has, therefore, determined the number and the nature of the passages which I have chosen to include here.

I have thought best also to abandon any chronological arrangement, but instead to place the selections in the order of their merit as literature, regardless of the date of composition. And in every case I have given in brief introductory notes the circumstances under which the letter was written and the conditions which dictated its contents.

A LETTER TO THE CHURCH AT EPHESUS

St. Paul wrote his letter to the church at Ephesus, where he had lived and worked for three years, some time after A.D. 60 and while he was a prisoner in Rome. The letter is, more than any other, a kind of religious meditation, mystical in nature, in which its writer seems to be quietly gathering together in his mind those indestructible, deathless truths by which he has lived since his conversion. It has been suggested that perhaps a presentiment of his own death in the near future is responsible for the material and the atmosphere of his letter.

FROM EPHESIANS 4, 5, 6, 3

I, therefore, the prisoner of the Lord, beseech you that ye walk worthy of the vocation wherewith ye are called, with all lowliness and meekness, with long-suffering, forbearing one another in love; endeavoring to keep the unity of the Spirit in the bond of peace. There is one body, and one Spirit, even as ye are called in one hope of your calling; one Lord, one faith, one baptism; one God and Father of all, who is above all, and through all, and in you all. But unto every one of us is given grace according to the measure of the gift of Christ.

And he gave some, apostles; and some, prophets; and some, evangelists; and some, pastors and teachers, for the perfecting of the saints, for the work of the ministry, for the edifying of the body of Christ. Till we all come in the unity of the faith, and of the knowledge of the Son of God, unto a perfect man, unto the measure of the stature of the fulness of Christ. That we henceforth be no more children, tossed to and fro, and carried about with every wind of doctrine, by the sleight of men, and cunning craftiness, whereby they lie in wait to deceive; but speaking the truth in love, may grow up into him in all things, which is the head, even Christ.

Wherefore putting away lying, speak every man truth with his neighbor; for we are members one of another. Be ye angry, and sin not. Let not the sun go down upon your wrath, neither give place to the devil. Let all bitterness, and wrath, and anger, and clamor, and evil speaking, be put away from you, with all malice; and be ye kind one to another, tender-hearted, forgiving one another, even as God for Christ's sake hath forgiven you.

Be ye therefore followers of God, as dear children; and walk in love, as Christ also hath loved us, and hath given himself for us an offering and a sacrifice to God for a sweet-smelling savor. Let no man deceive you with vain words, for because of these things cometh the wrath of God upon the children of disobedience. Be not ye therefore partakers with them. For ye were sometime darkness, but now are ye light in the Lord. Walk as children of light, redeeming the time, because the days are evil. Wherefore be ye not unwise, but understanding what the will of the Lord is.

Finally, my brethren, be strong in the Lord, and in the power of his might. Put on the whole armor of God, that ye may be able to stand against the wiles of the devil. For we wrestle not against flesh and blood, but against principalities, against powers, against the rulers of the darkness of this world, against spiritual wickedness in high places.

Wherefore take unto you the whole armor of God, that ye may be able to withstand in the evil day, and having done all, to stand. Stand therefore, having your loins girt about with truth, and having on the breastplate of righteousness; and your feet shod with the preparation of the gospel of peace; above all, taking the shield of faith, wherewith ye shall be able to quench all the fiery darts of the wicked.

And take the helmet of salvation, and the sword of the Spirit, which is the word of God, praying always with all prayer and supplication in the Spirit, and watching thereunto with all perseverance and supplication for all saints. And for me, that utterance may be given unto me, that I may open my mouth boldly, to make known the mystery of the gospel, for which I am an ambassador in bonds; that therein I may speak boldly, as I ought to speak.

For this cause I bow my knees unto the Father of our Lord Jesus Christ, of whom the whole family in heaven and earth is named, that he would grant you, according to the riches of his glory, to be strengthened with might by his Spirit in the inner man; that Christ may dwell in your hearts by faith; that ye, being rooted and grounded in love, may be able to comprehend with all saints what is the breadth, and length, and depth, and height; and to know the love of Christ, which passeth knowledge, that ye might be filled with all the fulness of God.

Now unto him that is able to do exceeding abundantly, above all that we ask or think, according to the power that worketh in us, unto him be glory in the church by Christ Jesus throughout all ages, world without end.

A LETTER TO THE CHURCH AT PHILIPPI

St. Paul's letter to his "beloved" at Philippi is the most personal and informal of all his Epistles, and, therefore, perhaps the most appealing. The church there was the first founded by him on the continent of Europe, and it was quite evidently the one closest to his heart. Always proud of working at his trade of tent-making to support himself even during his missionary journeys and reluctant to accept gifts of money, he is, as his letter proves, grateful and even happy to receive such a gift from his children at Philippi, and equally grateful for their sending of Epaphroditus to help him at Rome. For, according to most scholars, his letter was written during his last months there and shortly before his death.

Paul and Timothy, the servants of Jesus Christ, to all the saints in Christ Jesus which are at Philippi, with the bishops and deacons: Grace be unto you, and peace from God our Father and from the Lord Jesus Christ. I thank my God upon every remembrance of you, always in every prayer of mine for you all making request with joy, for your fellowship in the gospel from the first day until now; being confident of this very thing, that he which hath begun a good work in you will perform it until the day of Jesus Christ. For God is my record, how greatly I long after you all.

But I would ye should understand, brethren, that the things which happened unto me have fallen out rather unto the furtherance of the gospel, so that my bonds in Christ are manifest in all the palace, and in all other places; and many of the brethren in the Lord, waxing confident by my bonds, are much more bold to speak the word without fear.

For I know that this shall turn to my salvation through your prayer, and the supply of the Spirit of Jesus Christ, according to my earnest expectation and my hope, that in nothing I shall be ashamed, but that with all boldness, as always, so now also Christ shall be magnified in my body, whether it be by life, or by death. For to me to live is Christ, and to die is gain. But if I live in the flesh, this is the fruit of my labor; yet what I shall choose, I wot not. For I am in a strait betwixt two, having a desire to depart, and to be with Christ, which is far better; nevertheless to abide in the flesh is more needful for you. And having this confidence, I know that I shall abide and continue with you all for your furtherance and joy of faith.

Only let your conversation be as it becometh the gospel of Christ: that whether I come and see you, or else be absent, I may hear of your affairs, that ye stand fast in one spirit, with one mind striving together for the faith of the gospel, and in nothing terrified by your adversaries. For unto you it is given in the behalf of Christ, not only to believe on him, but also to suffer for his sake, having the same conflict which ye saw in me, and now hear to be in me.

If there be therefore any consolation in Christ, if any comfort of love, if any fellowship of the Spirit, fulfil ye my joy, that ye be likeminded, having the same love, being of one accord, of one mind. Let nothing be done through strife or vainglory; but in lowliness of mind let each esteem other better than themselves.

Let this mind be in you, which was also in Christ Jesus, who, being in the form of God, thought it not robbery to be equal with God; but made himself of no reputation, and took upon him the form of a servant, and was made in the likeness of men. And being found in fashion as a man, he humbled himself, and became obedient unto death, even the death of the cross. Wherefore God also hath highly exalted him, and given him a name which is above every name: That at the name of Jesus every knee should bow, of things in heaven, and things in earth, and things under the earth; and that every tongue should confess that Jesus Christ is Lord, to the glory of God the Father.

Wherefore, my beloved, as ye have always obeyed, not as in my presence only, but now much more in my absence, work out your own salvation with fear and trembling. For it is God which worketh in you both to will and to do of his good pleasure. Do all things without murmurings and disputings, that ye may be blameless and harmless, the sons of God, without rebuke, in the midst of a crooked and perverse nation, among whom ye shine as lights in the world, holding forth the word of life, that I may rejoice in the day of Christ, that I have not run in vain, neither labored in vain. Yea, and if I be offered upon the sacrifice and service of your faith, I joy, and rejoice with you all. For the same cause also do ye joy, and rejoice with me.

But I trust in the Lord Jesus to send Timothy shortly unto you, that I also may be of good comfort when I know your state. For I have no man likeminded, who will naturally care for your state. For all seek their own, not the things which are Jesus Christ's. But ye know the proof of him, that, as a son with the father, he hath served with me in the gospel. Him therefore I hope to send presently, so soon as I shall see how it will go with me. But I trust in the Lord that I also myself shall come shortly.

Yet I supposed it necessary to send to you Epaphroditus, my brother and companion in labor, and fellow soldier, your messenger, and he that ministered to my wants. For he longed after you all, and was full of heaviness, because that ye had heard that he had been sick. For indeed he was sick nigh unto death; but God had mercy on him; and not on him only, but on me also, lest I should have sorrow upon sorrow. I sent him therefore the more carefully, that, when ye see him again, ye may rejoice, and that I may be the less sorrowful. Receive him therefore in the Lord with all gladness.

Finally, my brethren, rejoice in the Lord. To write the same things to you, to me indeed is not grievous, but for you it is safe. For we are the circumcision, which worship God in the spirit, and rejoice in Christ Jesus and have no confidence in the flesh. If any other man thinketh that he hath whereof he might trust in the flesh, I more: Circumcised the eighth day, of the stock of Israel, of the tribe of Benjamin, a Hebrew of the Hebrews; as touching the law, a Pharisee; concerning zeal, persecuting the church; touching the righteousness which is in the law, blameless. But what things were gain to me, those I counted loss for Christ.

Yea doubtless, and I count all things but loss for the excellency of the knowledge of Christ Jesus my Lord; for whom I have suffered the loss of all things, and do count them but dung that I may win Christ; that I may know him, and the power of his resurrection, and the fellowship of his sufferings, if by any means I might attain unto the resurrection of the dead. Brethren, I count not myself to have apprehended; but this one thing I do: Forgetting those things which are behind, and reaching forth unto those things which are before, I press toward the mark for the prize of the high calling of God in Christ Jesus.

Brethren, be followers together of me, and mark them which walk so as ye have us for an ensample. For our conversation is in heaven, from whence also we look for the Savior, the Lord Jesus Christ. Who shall change our vile body, that it may be fashioned like unto his glorious body, according to the working whereby he is able even to subdue all things unto himself. Therefore, my brethren dearly beloved and longed for, my joy and crown, so stand fast in the Lord, my dearly beloved.

Rejoice in the Lord always; and again I say, Rejoice. Let your moderation be known unto all men. The Lord is at hand. Be careful for nothing; but in everything by prayer and supplication with thanksgiving let your requests be made known unto God. And the peace of God, which passeth all understanding, shall keep your hearts and minds through Christ Jesus.

Finally, brethren, whatsoever things are true, whatsoever things are honest, whatsoever things are just, whatsoever things are pure, whatsoever things are lovely, whatsoever things are of good report; if there be any virtue, and if there be any praise, think on these things. Those things, which ye have both learned, and received, and heard, and seen in me, do; and the God of peace shall be with you.

But I rejoiced in the Lord greatly, that now at the last your care of me hath flourished again; wherein ye were also careful, but ye lacked opportunity. Not that I speak in respect of want; for I have learned, in whatsoever state I am, therewith to be content. I know both how to be abased, and I know how to abound. Everywhere and in all things I am instructed both to be full and to be hungry, both to abound and to suffer need. I can do all things through Christ which strengtheneth me. Notwithstanding, ye have well done, that ye did communicate with my affliction.

Now ye Philippians know also, that in the beginning of the gospel, when I departed from Macedonia, no church communicated with me as concerning giving and receiving, but ye only. For even in Thessalonica ye sent once and again unto my necessity. Not because I desire a gift; but I desire fruit that may abound to your account. But I have all, and abound; I am full, having received of Epaphroditus the things which were sent from you, an odor of a sweet smell, a sacrifice acceptable, well pleasing to God. But my God shall supply all your need according to his riches in glory by Christ Jesus.

Salute every saint in Christ Jesus. The brethren which are with me greet you. All the saints salute you, chiefly they that are of Caesar's household. The grace of our Lord Jesus Christ be with you all. Amen.

A PERSONAL LETTER TO A FRIEND

Much more interesting than the obscure Epistle to the Colossians, not given here even in part, is the following personal letter to an old friend of St. Paul's, Philemon, who lived in Colossae, in Phrygia, and who apparently gave his house as the meeting place of the church. One of Philemon's slaves, Onesimus, after robbing his master, had fled to Rome, probably remembering St. Paul and relying on an old friendship for protection. Converted by the apostle in Rome, he had been persuaded to return to his master; and St. Paul's letter to Philemon is written as a request for forgiveness and mercy. The letter is a charming one, delicately written and with an undertone of humor and even of playfulness. We can be sure that Philemon did receive his runaway slave, now his brother in Christ; and we can enjoy, at least in our imaginations, the tradition that this same slave became the bishop named Onesimus, who was prominent in Ephesus early in the next century.

Paul, a prisoner of Jesus Christ, and Timothy our brother, unto Philemon, our dearly beloved, and fellow laborer, and to the church in thy house: Grace to you, and peace, from God our Father and the Lord Jesus Christ.

I thank my God, making mention of thee always in my prayers, hearing of thy love and faith, which thou hast toward the Lord Jesus, and toward all saints, that the communication of thy faith may become effectual by the acknowledging of every good thing which is in you in Christ Jesus. For we have great joy and consolation in thy love, because the bowels of the saints are refreshed by thee, brother.

Wherefore, though I might be much bold in Christ to enjoin thee that which is convenient, yet for love's sake I rather beseech thee, being such a one as Paul the aged, and now also a prisoner of Jesus Christ, I beseech thee for my son Onesimus, whom I have begotten in my bonds, which in time past was to thee unprofitable, but now profitable to thee and to me, whom I have sent again. Thou therefore receive him, that is, mine own bowels, whom I would have retained with me, that in thy stead he might have ministered unto me in the bonds of the gospel. But without thy mind would I do nothing; that thy benefit should not be as it were of necessity, but willingly.

For perhaps he therefore departed for a season, that thou shouldest receive him forever, not now as a servant, but above a servant, a brother beloved, specially to me; but how much more unto thee, both in the flesh, and in the Lord? If thou count me therefore a partner, receive him as myself. If he hath wronged thee, or oweth thee aught, put that on mine account. I, Paul, have written it with mine own hand, I will repay it. Albeit I do not say to thee how thou owest unto me even thine own self besides!

Yea, brother, let me have joy of thee in the Lord. Having confidence in thy obedience, I wrote unto thee, knowing that thou wilt also do more than I say. But withal prepare me also a lodging, for I trust that through your prayers I shall be given unto you. There salute thee Epaphras, my fellow prisoner in Christ Jesus, Marcus, Aristarchus, Demas, Lucas, my fellow laborers. The grace of our Lord Jesus Christ be with your spirit. Amen.

A LETTER TO THE CHURCH AT ROME

St. Paul's letter to the Romans, of which the passages which follow are but a small part, was written about A.D. 56, when he was planning his journey to the Imperial City. It differs from his other letters in being far less personal in tone and far more finished in expression.

The reasons for these differences are, I think, easily explained. St. Paul, although his reputation was widespread, was not personally known to the Christian community at Rome, since the church there, unlike the others to which he wrote his letters, had not been founded by him; and because he felt less personal connection with the Roman Christians, the tone of his letter would naturally be less intimate. Its literary quality, which one must think conscious, had its source doubtless both in his sense of the power and position of Rome as the capital city of a great empire and in his hope and desire to make the best impression possible on people with whom he was not acquainted. His aim, therefore, in writing with care and even with caution was clearly to acquaint this church with his own position on matters of faith and dogma in order to ensure for himself the welcome and the support which he longed for.

The somewhat elaborate arguments of much of his letter lend to it the rather formal character of a theological dissertation; yet it is a genuine letter, which, especially in the portions given here, reveals the underlying emotions responsible in large part for its eloquence.

FROM ROMANS 12, 13, 14, 8

I beseech you therefore, brethren, by the mercies of God, that ye present your bodies a living sacrifice, holy, acceptable unto God, which is your reasonable service. And be not conformed to this world; but be ye transformed by the renewing of your mind, that ye may prove what is that good, and acceptable, and perfect will of God. For I say, through the grace given unto me, to every man that is among you, not to think of himself more highly than he ought to think; but to think soberly, according as God hath dealt to every man the measure of faith. For as we have many members in one body, and all members have not the same office; so we, being many, are one body in Christ, and every one members one of another.

Having then gifts differing according to the grace that is given to us, whether prophecy, let us prophesy according to the proportion of faith; or ministry, let us wait on our ministering; or he that teacheth, on teaching; or he that exhorteth, on exhortation. He that giveth, let him do it with simplicity; he that ruleth, with diligence; he that showeth mercy, with cheerfulness. Let love be without dissimulation. Abhor that which is evil; cleave to that which is good. Be kindly affectioned one to another with brotherly love, in honor preferring one another; not slothful in business; fervent in spirit; serving the Lord; rejoicing in hope; patient in tribulation; continuing instant in prayer; distributing to the necessity of saints; given to hospitality. Bless them which persecute you; bless, and curse not. Rejoice with them that do rejoice, and weep with them that weep.

Be of the same mind one toward another. Mind not high things, but condescend to men of low estate. Be not wise in your own conceits. Recompense to no man evil for evil. Provide things honest in the sight of all men. If it be possible, as much as lieth in you, live peaceably with all men. Dearly beloved, avenge not yourselves, but rather give place unto wrath; for it is written, Vengeance is mine; I will repay, saith the Lord. Therefore if thine enemy hunger, feed him; if he thirst, give him drink; for in so doing thou shalt heap coals of fire on his head. Be not overcome of evil, but overcome evil with good.

Owe no man anything, but to love one another; for he that loveth another hath fulfilled the law. For this, Thou shalt not commit adultery, Thou shalt not kill, Thou shalt not steal, Thou shalt not bear false witness, Thou shalt not covet; and if there be any other commandment, it is briefly comprehended in this saying, namely, Thou shalt love thy neighbor as thyself. Love worketh no ill to his neighbor; therefore love is the fulfilling of the law. And that, knowing the time, that now it is high time to awake out of sleep; for now is our salvation nearer than when we believed. The night is far spent, the day is at hand! Let us therefore cast off the works of darkness, and let us put on the armor of light.

Him that is weak in the faith receive ye, but not to doubtful disputations. For one believeth that he may eat all things; another, who is weak, eateth herbs. Let not him that eateth despise him that eateth not; and let not him which eateth not judge him that eateth; for God hath received him. One man esteemeth one day above another; another esteemeth every day alike. Let every man be fully persuaded in his own mind.

For none of us liveth to himself, and no man dieth to himself. For whether we live, we live unto the Lord; and whether we die, we die unto the Lord. Whether we live therefore, or die, we are the Lord's. For to this end Christ both died, and rose, and revived, that he might be Lord both of the dead and living. But why dost thou judge thy brother? Or why dost thou set at nought thy brother? For we shall all stand before the judgment seat of Christ. I know, and am persuaded by the Lord Jesus, that there is nothing unclean of itself; but to him that esteemeth anything to be unclean, to him it *is* unclean. For the kingdom of God is not meat and drink; but righteousness, and peace, and joy in the Holy Ghost. Let us therefore follow after the things which make for peace, and things wherewith one may edify another. It is good neither to eat flesh, nor to drink wine, nor anything whereby thy brother stumbleth, or is offended, or is made weak.

There is therefore now no condemnation to them which are in Christ Jesus, who walk not after the flesh, but after the Spirit. For the law of the Spirit of life in Christ Jesus hath made me free from the law of sin and death. For what the law could not do, in that it was weak through the flesh, God sending his own Son in the likeness of sinful flesh. For they that are after the flesh do mind the things of the flesh; but they that are after the Spirit, the things of the Spirit. For to be carnally minded is death; but to be spiritually minded is life and peace. And if Christ be in you, the body is dead because of sin; but the Spirit is life because of righteousness. But if the Spirit of him that raised up Jesus from the dead dwell in you, he that raised up Christ from the dead shall also quicken your mortal bodies by his Spirit that dwelleth in you. For if ye live after the flesh, ye shall die; but if ye through the Spirit do mortify the deeds of the body, ye shall live.

For as many as are led by the Spirit of God, they are the sons of God. For ye have not received the spirit of bondage again to fear; but ye have received the Spirit of adoption, whereby we cry, Abba, Father. The Spirit itself beareth witness with our spirit, that we are the children of God. And if children, then heirs; heirs of God, and joint-heirs with Christ, if so be that we suffer with him, that we may be also glorified together.

For I reckon that the sufferings of this present time are not worthy to be compared with the glory which shall be revealed in us. For we know that the whole creation groaneth and travaileth in pain together until now. And not only they, but ourselves also, which have the firstfruits of the Spirit, even we ourselves groan within ourselves, waiting for the adoption, to wit, the redemption of our body. For we are saved by hope; but hope that is seen is not hope; for what a man seeth, why doth he yet hope for? But if we hope for that we see not, then do we with patience wait for it. Likewise the Spirit also helpeth our infirmities; for we know not what we should pray for as we ought; but the Spirit itself maketh intercession for us with groanings which cannot be uttered. And we know that all things work together for good to them that love God.

What shall we then say to these things? If God be for us, who can be against us? He that spared not his own Son, but delivered him up for us all, how shall he not with him also freely give us all things? Who shall lay anything to the charge of God's elect? It is God that justifieth. Who is he that condemneth? It is Christ that died, yea rather, that is risen again, who is even at the right hand of God, who also maketh intercession for us. Who shall separate us from the love of Christ? Shall tribulation, or distress, or persecution, or famine, or nakedness, or peril, or sword? As it is written, For thy sake we are killed all the day long; we are accounted as sheep for the slaughter. Nay, in all these things we are more than conquerors, through him that loved us. For I am persuaded that neither death, nor life, nor angels, nor principalities, nor powers, nor things present, nor things to come, nor height, nor depth, nor any other creature, shall be able to separate us from the love of God, which is in Christ Jesus our Lord.

A LETTER TO THE HEBREWS

In the King James Version, the last of the fourteen Epistles of Paul the Apostle is that written to the Hebrews. Like those to Timothy and to Titus, the letter to the Hebrews was actually not written by St. Paul, but instead by some unknown and gifted author during the last years of the first century after Christ. Yet because it contains certain chapters of great literary and spiritual value, which no reader of the New Testament should miss, I have selected here the best and most familiar of its passages for inclusion in these Readings. And because it has for centuries appeared under St. Paul's name, we will set aside the fact that he did not write it, in the sure and certain knowledge that no one could admire and echo more eagerly than he its passionate affirmation of that Faith to which he gave his life.

Now faith is the substance of things hoped for, the evidence of things not seen. For by it the elders obtained a good report. Through faith we understand that the worlds were framed by the word of God, so that things which are seen were not made of things which do appear.

By faith Abel offered unto God a more excellent sacrifice than Cain, by which he obtained witness that he was righteous, God testifying of his gifts; and by it he, being dead, yet speaketh. But without faith it is impossible to please him; for he that cometh to God must believe that he is, and that he is a rewarder of them that diligently seek him.

By faith Noah, being warned of God of things not seen as yet, moved with fear, prepared an ark to the saving of his house, by the which he condemned the world, and became heir of the righteousness which is by faith.

By faith Abraham, when he was called to go out into a place which he should after receive for an inheritance, obeyed; and he went out, not knowing whither he went. By faith he sojourned in the land of promise, as in a strange country, dwelling in tabernacles with Isaac and Jacob, the heirs with him of the same promise. For he looked for a city which hath foundations, whose builder and maker is God.

These all died in faith, not having received the promises, but having seen them afar off, and were persuaded of them, and embraced them, and confessed that they were strangers and pilgrims on the earth. For they that say such things declare plainly that they seek a country. And truly, if they had been mindful of that country from whence they came out, they might have had opportunity to have returned. But now they desire a better country, that is, a heavenly; wherefore God is not ashamed to be called their God, for he hath prepared for them a city.

By faith Abraham, when he was tried, offered up Isaac; and he that had received the promises offered up his only begotten son. By faith Isaac blessed Jacob and Esau concerning things to come. By faith Jacob, when he was a dying, blessed both the sons of Joseph; and worshipped, leaning upon the top of his staff. By faith Joseph, when he died, made mention of the departing of the children of Israel, and gave commandment concerning his bones.

By faith Moses, when he was born, was hid three months of his parents, because they saw he was a proper child, and they were not afraid of the king's commandment. By faith Moses, when he was come to years, refused to be called the son of Pharaoh's daughter, choosing rather to suffer affliction with the people of God, than to enjoy the pleasures of sin for a season, esteeming the reproach of Christ greater riches than the treasures in Egypt. By faith he forsook Egypt, not fearing the wrath of the king; for he endured, as seeing him who is invisible. By faith they passed through the Red sea as by dry land, which the Egyptians assaying to do were drowned. By faith the walls of Jericho fell down, after they were compassed about seven days.

And what shall I more say? For the time would fail me to tell of Gideon, and of Barak, and of Samson, and of Jephthah; of David also, and Samuel, and of the prophets, who through faith subdued kingdoms, wrought righteousness, obtained promises, stopped the mouths of lions, quenched the violence of fire, escaped the edge of the sword, out of weakness were made strong, waxed valiant in fight, turned to flight the armies of the aliens. Women received their dead raised to life again; and others were tortured, not accepting deliverance, that they might obtain a better resurrection. And others had trial of cruel mockings and scourgings, yea, moreover of bonds and imprisonment. They were stoned, they were sawn asunder, were tempted, were slain with the sword; they wandered about in sheepskins and goatskins, being destitute, afflicted, tormented; they wandered in deserts, and in mountains, and in dens and caves of the earth.

Wherefore, seeing we also are compassed about with so great a cloud of witnesses, let us lay aside every weight, and the sin which doth so easily beset us, and let us run with patience the race that is set before us, looking unto Jesus, the author and finisher of our faith, who for the joy that was set before him endured the cross, despising the shame, and is set down at the right hand of the throne of God. . . . For whom the Lord loveth, he chasteneth.

Now no chastening for the present seemeth to be joyous, but grievous; nevertheless, afterward it yieldeth the peaceable fruit of righteousness unto them that are exercised thereby. Wherefore lift up the hands which hang down and the feeble knees; and make straight paths for your feet lest that which is lame be turned out of the way. Follow peace with all men, and holiness without which no man shall see God.

For ye are not come unto the mount that might be touched and that burned with fire, nor unto blackness and darkness and tempest. But ye are come unto mount Sion and unto the city of the Living God, the heavenly Jerusalem, and to an innumerable company of angels; to the general assembly and church of the firstborn, which are written in heaven, and to God the Judge of all, and to the spirits of just men made perfect; and to Jesus the mediator of the New Covenant.

See that ye refuse not him that speaketh. For if they escaped not who refused him that spake on earth, much more shall not we escape if we turn away from him that speaketh from heaven. But now he hath promised, saying: Yet once more I shake not the earth only, but also heaven. And this word, *Yet once more,* signifieth the removing of those things that are shaken, that those things which cannot be shaken may remain.

TWO LETTERS TO THE CHURCH AT CORINTH

Few scholars or critics would question the statement that St. Paul's letters to the church at Corinth contain the noblest of his writing and the most exalted of his thoughts. Here most surely the chief of the apostles places himself among the greatest of literary artists by that magical power which he possessed of translating the inner rhythm of his spirit into the perfection of words.

Perhaps not a little of the exercise of that power arose from St. Paul's concern over his Corinthian children. Just as none of his churches afforded him so much joy as did that at Philippi, no other provided him with so much anxiety as did that at Corinth. For although he must have rejoiced over the vitality of the lively Corinthians, he had frequent seasons of "fear and much trembling" over the behavior resulting from that very liveliness.

Corinth, situated on the isthmus connecting the two halves of Greece and a center, therefore, of trade and commerce, was not only a famous seat of Greek culture and learning, but also a city which bore, to St. Paul at least, the rather sinister reputation of one given over to pleasure and sensuous excitement. To him the Corinthian Christians were, indeed, "babes in Christ"; and their equal delight in philosophic speculation and in the manifold joys of this world called forth in his letters to them careful and patient explanation of their new obligations as Christians and stern warnings against the many temptations of their gay city.

The passages selected from the letters to Corinth should be read with the nature of the recipients clearly in mind. For example, the familiar and beautiful description of charity is understood far more rightly when one realizes that the Corinthians were, indeed, like children in their eager acceptance of pleasure, that they loved to speak "with tongues," and that they found often irksome the rigorous duties and "seemly behavior" of their new life as Christians. It is to *them* and not to his other churches that St. Paul feels called upon to boast of his own sufferings, *they* who need to be told of the "terrestrial and the celestial," "the earthy and the heavenly."

His letters to them were written around A.D. 54, some years before many of the others; and yet here, as in none of the others, we possess the unsurpassed literary treasures of the New Testament.

FROM II CORINTHIANS 6 AND 11

We then, as workers together with him, beseech you also that ye receive not the grace of God in vain. (For he saith, I have heard thee in a time accepted, and in the day of salvation have I succoured thee. Behold, now is the accepted time; behold, now is the day of salvation.) Giving no offence in anything, that the ministry be not blamed; but in all things approving ourselves as the ministers of

God, in much patience, in afflictions, in necessities, in distresses, in stripes, in imprisonments, in tumults, in labors, in watchings, in fastings; by pureness, by knowledge, by longsuffering, by kindness, by the Holy Ghost, by love unfeigned, by the power of truth, by the power of God, by the armor of righteousness on the right hand and on the left, by honor and dishonor, by evil report and good report; as deceivers, and yet true; as unknown, and yet well known; as dying, and, behold, we live; as chastened, and not killed; as sorrowful, yet alway rejoicing; as poor, yet making many rich; as having nothing, and yet possessing all things.

I speak as concerning reproach, as though we had been weak. Howbeit, whereinsoever any is bold (I speak foolishly), I am bold also. Are they Hebrews? So am I. Are they Israelites? So am I. Are they the seed of Abraham? So am I. Are they ministers of Christ? (I speak as a fool) I am more; in labors more abundant, in stripes above measure, in prisons more frequent, in deaths oft. Of the Jews five times received I forty stripes save one. Thrice was I beaten with rods, once I was stoned, thrice I suffered shipwreck, a night and a day I have been in the deep. In journeyings often, in perils of waters, in perils of robbers, in perils by mine own countrymen, in perils by the heathen, in perils in the city, in perils in the wilderness, in perils in the sea, in perils among false brethren. In weariness and painfulness, in watchings often, in hunger and thirst, in fastings often, in cold and nakedness. Beside those things that are without, that which cometh upon me daily, the care of all the churches.

Who is weak, and I am not weak? Who is offended, and I burn not? If I must needs glory, I will glory of the things which concern mine infirmities. The God and Father of our Lord Jesus Christ, which is blessed for evermore, knoweth that I lie not.

FROM I CORINTHIANS 13 AND 15

Though I speak with the tongues of men and of angels, and have not charity, I am become as sounding brass, or a tinkling cymbal. And though I have the gift of prophecy, and understand all mysteries, and all knowledge; and though I have all faith, so that I could remove mountains, and have not charity, I am nothing. And though I bestow all my goods to feed the poor, and though I give my body to be burned, and have not charity, it profiteth me nothing.

Charity suffereth long, and is kind; charity envieth not; charity vaunteth not itself, is not puffed up, doth not behave itself unseemly, seeketh not her own, is not easily provoked, thinketh no evil; rejoiceth not in iniquity, but rejoiceth in the truth; beareth all things, believeth all things, hopeth all things, endureth all things. Charity never faileth; but whether there be prophecies, they shall fail; whether there be tongues, they shall cease; whether there be knowledge, it shall vanish away. For we know in part, and we prophesy in part. But when that which is perfect is come, then that which is in part shall be done away.

When I was a child, I spake as a child, I understood as a child, I thought as a child; but when I became a man, I put away childish things. For now we see through a glass, darkly; but then face to face. Now I know in part; but then shall I know even as also I am known.

And now abideth faith, hope, charity, these three; but the greatest of these is charity.

But some man will say, How are the dead raised up? and with what body do they come? Thou fool, that which thou sowest is not quickened, except it die; and that which thou sowest, thou sowest not that body that shall be, but bare grain, it may chance of wheat, or of some other grain; but God giveth it a body as it hath pleased him, and to every seed his own body. All flesh is not the same flesh; but there is one kind of flesh of men, another flesh of beasts, another of fishes, and another of birds. There are also celestial bodies, and bodies terrestrial; but the glory of the celestial is one, and the glory of the terrestrial is another. There is one glory of the sun, and another glory of the moon, and another glory of the stars; for one star differeth from another star in glory.

So also is the resurrection of the dead. It is sown in corruption; it is raised in incorruption. It is sown in dishonor; it is raised in glory. It is sown in weakness; it is raised in power. It is sown a natural body; it is raised a spiritual body. There is a natural body, and there is a spiritual body. And so it is written. The first man Adam was made a living soul; the last Adam was made a quickening spirit. Howbeit that was not first which is spiritual, but that which is natural; and afterward that which is spiritual. The first man is of the earth, earthy; the second man is the Lord from heaven. As is the earthy, such are they also that are earthy; and as is the heavenly, such are they also that are heavenly. And as we have borne the image of the earthy, we shall also bear the image of the heavenly.

Now this I say, brethren, that flesh and blood cannot inherit the kingdom of God; neither doth corruption inherit incorruption. Behold, I show you a mystery: We shall not all sleep, but we shall all be changed, in a moment, in the twinkling of an eye, at the last trump. For the trumpet shall sound, and the dead shall be raised incorruptible, and we shall be changed. For this corruptible must put on incorruption, and this mortal must put on immortality. So when this corruptible shall have put on incorruption, and this mortal shall have put on immortality, then shall be brought to pass the saying that is written, Death is swallowed up in victory. O death, where is thy sting? O grave, where is thy victory? The sting of death is sin; and the strength of sin is the law. But thanks be to God, which giveth us the victory through our Lord Jesus Christ.

-IV-

THE BOOK OF REVELATION

THE book of Revelation, or, as it is entitled in the King James Version, The Revelation of St. John the Divine, is a highly imaginative work which belongs to a type of literature called *apocalyptic,* or *vision* literature, from the Greek word meaning *to reveal.* This form of writing was not uncommon between 200 B.C. and A.D. 100, and is well exemplified in the Old Testament Book of Daniel, a late book written at some time between 168–165 B.C., and springing from much the same background as does Revelation.[1]

Revelation has usually been considered the most mysterious of biblical writings largely because the background from which it sprung is unfamiliar to the average reader and because its wealth of strange and even fantastic images, its cryptic numbers, and its ever shifting scenes result in confusion. Its obscurity is, however, lessened once one understands, first, the conditions of its time, and, second, the underlying form in which it is presented, even although that form is, it is true, often difficult to discern.

It was written around A.D. 96 by a Jewish Christian who had lived for some time in Palestine before he had moved to Ephesus in Asia Minor. Although his name was John, he should probably not be identified with the author of the Gospel According to St. John. Just who he was, in fact, remains a mystery even to the best scholars; but from his introduction to his series of visions we may safely gather that he had been sentenced as a Christian martyr to the island of Patmos in the Aegean Sea. There were stone quarries on Patmos; and he may well have been condemned to labor in them to further the mighty building projects of ambitious Roman emperors.

His book, like that of the author of Daniel, arose out of a time of bitter, even of horrible persecution. Just as in the time of Daniel a cer-

[1] A description of the Book of Daniel is given in *The Bible and the Common Reader,* Pt. II. Although no selections are given from Daniel in these Readings (since it is difficult to see the book as a purely Old Testament work), it may well be read as a preface to the study of Revelation, a much later work to which it bears a close relation.

tain Syrian king, Antiochus IV, attempted with ruthless cruelty to stamp out the Jewish religion in Palestine, so at the time of Revelation the Emperor Domitian, who saw himself as a god and demanded homage and even worship from all his subjects, allowed and encouraged widespread persecution and martyrdom of thousands, both Jews and Christians, who refused to bow before his image. This persecution was at its worst in Asia Minor, which region with its various Christian communities was the chief center of the new religion. The author of Revelation, for this reason, addresses his vision of a glorious eventual future to the seven churches of Asia, to each of which he promises, through God, final deliverance if each will stand firm in the Faith and "overcome" the sorrows and tribulations of this desperate time.

The scene of Revelation is laid in Heaven before the throne of God, where a succession of dramatic and symbolic actions follow one another in sometimes bewildering swiftness. Some of these are descriptive of the heavenly rewards awaiting those souls who have suffered on this earth for their faith; others are prophetic of dire calamities which shall beset the world before its end; still others foretell the certain doom of Rome (Babylon, the Mother of Harlots) and of her Empire. The book will be more clearly understood if we look upon it as a heavenly drama constructed in three great acts, even although those acts are often hard to follow because of the obscurity of certain of their scenes and because of the countless and sometimes indefinable images and symbols in which the entire book abounds.

I have, therefore, attempted, with the help of careful and, I think, necessary deletion of the more meaningless portions, to present the book as such a drama with prologue, setting, acts, and epilogue, for only in this way, it seems to me, can it be at all understood and appreciated. It must not, of course, be interpreted literally, but must rather be read with the imagination in full play. For it is a poetic and symbolic book, remarkable for its description of a bitter crisis in the early history of Christianity, for its extraordinary literary qualities, and for its exultant promise of the final victory of the spiritual powers of men. It is, to be sure, a tract for its times; yet no such prosaic title should be allowed to dim its great poetic and spiritual beauty.

THE INTRODUCTION TO THE BOOK

FROM REVELATION 1–3

I John, who also am your brother and companion in tribulation, and in the kingdom and patience of Jesus Christ, was in the isle that is called Patmos, for the word of God, and for the testimony of Jesus Christ. I was in the Spirit on the Lord's day, and heard behind me a great voice, as of a trumpet, saying: I am Alpha and Omega, the first and the last. What thou seest, write in a book, and send it unto the seven churches which are in Asia.

And I turned to see the voice that spake with me. And being turned, I saw seven golden candlesticks, and in the midst of the seven candlesticks one like unto the Son of man, clothed with a garment down to the foot, and girt about the paps with a golden girdle. His head and his hairs were white like wool, as white as snow; and his eyes were as a flame of fire; and his feet like unto fine brass, as if they burned in a furnace; and his voice as the sound of many waters. And he had in his right hand seven stars; and out of his mouth went a sharp two-edged sword; and his countenance was as the sun shineth in his strength.

And when I saw him, I fell at his feet as dead. And he laid his right hand upon me, saying unto me, Fear not. I am the first and the last. I am he that liveth, and was dead; and, behold, I am alive for evermore, and have the keys of hell and of death. Write the things which thou hast seen, the things which are, and the things which shall be hereafter. The mystery of the seven stars which thou sawest in my right hand, and the seven golden candlesticks: the seven stars are the angels of the seven churches; and the seven candlesticks which thou sawest are the seven churches. . . .

To him that overcometh will I grant to sit with me in my throne, even as I also overcame and am set down with my Father in his throne. He that hath an ear, let him hear what the Spirit saith unto the churches.

THE SETTING OF THE DRAMA IN HEAVEN

FROM REVELATION 4

After this I looked, and, behold, a door was opened in heaven; and the first voice which I heard was as it were of a trumpet talking with me, which said, Come up hither, and I will show thee things which must be hereafter. And immediately I was in the Spirit; and, behold, a throne was set in heaven, and one sat on the throne. And he that sat was to look upon like a jasper and a sardine stone; and there was a rainbow round about the throne, in sight like unto an emerald. And round about the throne were four and twenty seats; and upon the seats I saw four and twenty elders sitting, clothed in white raiment; and they had on their heads crowns of gold. And out of the throne proceeded lightnings and thunderings and voices; and there were seven lamps of fire burning before the throne, which are the seven Spirits of God.

And before the throne there was a sea of glass like unto crystal; and in the midst of the throne, and round about the throne, were four beasts full of eyes before and behind. And the first beast was like a lion, and the second beast like a calf, and the third beast had a face as a man, and the fourth beast was like a flying eagle. And the four beasts had each of them six wings about him; and they were full of eyes within. And they rest not day and night, saying, Holy, holy, holy, Lord God Almighty, which was, and is, and is to come.

THE PROLOGUE

FROM REVELATION 5

And I saw in the right hand of him that sat on the throne a book written within and on the back side, sealed with seven seals. And I saw a strong angel proclaiming with a loud voice, Who is worthy to open the book, and to loose the seals thereof? And no man in heaven, nor in earth, neither under the earth, was able to open the book, neither to look thereon. And I wept much, because no man was found worthy to open and to read the book, neither to look thereon. And one of the elders saith unto me, Weep not. Behold, the Lion of the tribe of Judah, the Root of David, hath prevailed to open the book, and to loose the seven seals thereof.

And I beheld, and, lo, in the midst of the throne and of the four beasts, and in the midst of the elders, stood a Lamb as it had been slain, having seven horns and seven eyes, which are the seven Spirits of God sent forth into all the earth. And he came and took the book out of the right hand of him that sat upon the throne. And when he had taken the book, the four beasts and four and twenty elders fell down before the Lamb, having every one of them harps, and golden vials full of odors, which are the prayers of saints. And they sung a new song, saying, Thou art worthy to take the book, and to open the seals thereof; for thou wast slain, and hast redeemed us to God by thy blood out of every kindred, and tongue, and people, and nation. And I beheld, and I heard the voice of many angels round about the throne; and the number of them was ten thousand times ten thousand and thousands of thousands, saying with a loud voice: Worthy is the Lamb that was slain to receive power, and riches, and wisdom, and strength, and honor, and glory, and blessing!

ACT I: THE OPENING OF THE SEVEN SEALS

FROM REVELATION 6, 7, 8

And I saw when the Lamb opened one of the seals, and I heard, as it were the noise of thunder, one of the four beasts saying, Come and see. And I saw, and behold a white horse. And he that sat on him had a bow; and a crown was given unto him; and he went forth conquering, and to conquer. And when he had opened the second seal, I heard the second beast say, Come and see. And there went out another horse that was red. And power was given to him that sat thereon to take peace from the earth, and that they should kill one another; and there was given unto him a great sword. And when he had opened the third seal, I heard the third beast say, Come and see. And I beheld, and lo a black horse. And he that sat on him had a pair of balances in his hand. And I heard a voice in the midst of the four beasts say, A measure of wheat for a penny; and three measures of barley for a penny; and see thou hurt not the oil and the wine. And when he had opened the fourth seal, I heard the voice of the fourth beast say, Come and see. And I looked, and behold a pale horse. And his name that sat on him was Death, and Hell followed with him. And power was given unto them over the fourth part of the earth, to kill with sword, and with hunger, and with death, and with the beasts of the earth.[2]

And when he had opened the fifth seal, I saw under the altar the souls of them that were slain for the word of God, and for the testimony which they held. And they cried with a loud voice, saying, How long, O Lord, holy and true, dost thou not judge and avenge our blood on them that dwell on the earth? And white robes were given unto every one of them; and it was said unto them that they should rest yet for a little season, until their fellow servants also and their brethren, that should be killed as they were, should be fulfilled.

And I beheld when he had opened the sixth seal, and, lo, there was a great earthquake; and the sun became black as sackcloth of hair, and the moon became as blood. And the stars of heaven fell unto the earth, even as a fig tree casteth her untimely figs, when she is shaken of a mighty wind. And the heaven departed as a scroll when it is rolled together; and every mountain and island were moved out of their places. And the kings of the earth, and the great men, and the rich men, and the chief captains, and the mighty men, and every bondman, and every free man, hid themselves in the dens and in the rocks of the mountains, and said to the mountains and rocks, Fall on us, and hide us from the face of him that sitteth on the throne, and from the wrath of the Lamb. For the great day of his wrath is come; and who shall be able to stand?

And after these things I saw four angels standing on the four corners of the earth, holding the four winds of the earth, that the wind should not blow on the earth, nor on the sea, nor on any tree. And I saw another angel ascending from the east, having the seal

[2] The famous four horses symbolize tragic events to come upon the earth: the white horse symbolizes the invasion of barbarians; the red, revolution and civil strife; the black, famine; and the pale horse, death.

of the living God; and he cried with a loud voice to the four angels, to whom it was given to hurt the earth and the sea, saying, Hurt not the earth, neither the sea, nor the trees, till we have sealed the servants of our God in their foreheads. And I heard the number of them which were sealed; and there were sealed a hundred and forty and four thousand of all the tribes of the children of Israel.

After this I beheld, and, lo, a great multitude, which no man could number, of all nations, and kindreds, and people, and tongues, stood before the throne, and before the Lamb, clothed with white robes, and palms in their hands, and cried with a loud voice, saying: Salvation to our God which sitteth upon the throne, and unto the Lamb!

And one of the elders answered, saying unto me, What are these which are arrayed in white robes? And whence came they? And I said unto him, Sir, thou knowest. And he said to me, These are they which came out of great tribulation, and have washed their robes, and made them white in the blood of the Lamb.

Therefore are they before the throne of God,
And serve him day and night in his temple.
And he that sitteth on the throne shall dwell among them.
They shall hunger no more, neither thirst any more;
Neither shall the sun light on them, nor any heat.
For the Lamb which is in the midst of the throne shall feed them,
And shall lead them unto living fountains of waters.
And God shall wipe away all tears from their eyes.

And when he had opened the seventh seal, there was silence in heaven about the space of half an hour.

ACT II: THE SOUNDING OF THE SEVEN TRUMPETS[3]

FROM REVELATION 8, 9, 10, 11

And I saw the seven angels which stood before God; and to them were given seven trumpets. And the seven angels which had the seven trumpets prepared themselves to sound.

The first angel sounded, and there followed hail and fire min-

[3] This Act, the most obscure portion of Revelation, has been carefully abridged in order to make it as clear as possible.

gled with blood, and they were cast upon the earth; and the third part of trees was burnt up, and all green grass was burnt up. And the second angel sounded, and as it were a great mountain burning with fire was cast into the sea; and the third part of the sea became blood. And the third angel sounded, and there fell a great star from heaven, burning as it were a lamp, and it fell upon the rivers and the fountains of waters. And many men died of the waters, because they were made bitter. And the fourth angel sounded, and the third part of the sun was smitten, and the third part of the moon, and the third part of the stars. And I beheld and heard an angel flying through the midst of heaven, saying with a loud voice: Woe, woe, woe to the inhabiters of the earth by reason of the other voices of the trumpets of the three angels, which are yet to sound.

And the fifth angel sounded, and I saw a star fall from heaven unto the earth; and to him was given the key of the bottomless pit. And he opened the bottomless pit; and there arose a smoke out of the pit, as the smoke of a great furnace; and the sun and the air were darkened by reason of the smoke of the pit. And there came out of the smoke locusts upon the earth; and unto them was given power, as the scorpions of the earth have power. And it was commanded them that they should not hurt the grass of the earth, neither any green thing, neither any tree; but only those men which have not the seal of God in their foreheads. And to them it was given that they should not kill them, but that they should be tormented; and their torment was as the torment of a scorpion when he striketh a man. And in those days shall men seek death and shall not find it. And the shapes of the locusts were like unto horses prepared unto battle.

And the sixth angel sounded, and I heard a voice from the four horns of the golden altar which is before God, saying to the sixth angel which had the trumpet, Loose four angels. And the four angels were loosed, and the number of their army of horsemen were two hundred thousand thousand; and the heads of the horses were as the heads of lions, and out of their mouths issued fire and smoke and brimstone.

By these was the third part of men killed. And the rest of the men which were not killed by these plagues repented not of the works of their hands, that they should not worship idols of gold, and silver, and brass, and stone, and of wood. Neither repented they of their murders, nor of their sorceries, nor of their fornication, nor of their thefts.

And I saw another mighty angel come down from heaven, clothed with a cloud; and a rainbow was upon his head, and his face was as it were the sun. And he cried with a loud voice and sware by him that liveth forever and ever, who created heaven and the things that therein are, and the earth, and the sea, that there should be time no longer. But that, when the seventh angel shall begin to sound, the mystery of God should be finished.

And the seventh angel sounded, and there were great voices in heaven, saying, The kingdoms of this world are become the kingdom of our Lord and of his Christ; and he shall reign forever and ever. And the temple of God was opened in heaven, and there was seen in his temple the ark of his testament. And there were lightnings, and voices, and thunderings, and an earthquake, and great hail.

INTERLUDES

A War in Heaven

FROM REVELATION 12

And there was war in heaven: Michael and his angels fought against the dragon; and the dragon fought and his angels, and prevailed not; neither was their place found any more in heaven. And the great dragon was cast out, that old serpent, called the Devil, and Satan, which deceiveth the whole world. He was cast out into the earth, and his angels were cast out with him. And I heard a loud voice saying in heaven, Now is come salvation, and strength, and the kingdom of our God, and the power of his Christ; for the accuser of our brethren is cast down, which accused them before our God day and night. And they overcame him by the blood of the Lamb, and by the word of their testimony; and they loved not their lives unto the death.

Therefore rejoice, ye heavens, and ye that dwell in them. Woe to the inhabiters of the earth and of the sea! For the devil is come down unto you, having great wrath because he knoweth that he hath but a short time.

A Beast: The Roman Emperor

FROM REVELATION 13

And I stood upon the sand of the sea, and saw a beast rise up out of the sea, having seven heads and ten horns, and upon his horns ten crowns, and upon his heads the name of blasphemy. And they worshipped the dragon which gave power unto the beast; and they worshipped the beast, saying, Who is like unto the beast? Who is able to make war with him? And there was given unto him a mouth speaking great things and blasphemies. And it was given unto him to make war with the saints, and to overcome them; and power was given him over all kindreds, and tongues, and nations. And all that dwell upon the earth shall worship him, whose names are not written in the book of life of the Lamb slain from the foundation of the world.

ACT III: THE OPENING OF THE SEVEN VIALS

FROM REVELATION 15, 16, 17, 18

And I saw another sign in heaven, great and marvellous, seven angels having the seven last plagues; for in them is filled up the wrath of God. And the seven angels came out of the temple clothed in pure and white linen and having their breasts girded with golden girdles. And one of the four beasts gave unto the seven angels seven golden vials full of the wrath of God, who liveth forever and ever.

And I heard a great voice out of the temple saying to the seven angels: Go your ways and pour out the vials of the wrath of God upon the earth. And the first went and poured out his vial upon the earth. And there fell a noisome and grievous sore upon the men which had the mark of the beast and upon them which worshipped his image. And the second angel poured out his vial upon the sea; and it became as the blood of a dead man; and every living soul died in the sea. And the third angel poured out his vial upon the rivers and fountains of water; and they became blood. And I heard the angel of the waters say, Thou art righteous, O Lord, which art, and wast, and shalt be, because thou hast judged thus. For they have shed the blood of saints and prophets, and thou hast given them blood to drink.

And the fourth angel poured out his vial upon the sun; and power was given unto him to scorch men with fire. And men were scorched with great heat and blasphemed the name of God. And the fifth angel poured out his vial upon the seat of the beast; and his kingdom was full of darkness; and they gnawed their tongues for pain. And the sixth angel poured out his vial upon the great river Euphrates; and the water thereof was dried up that the way of the kings of the east might be prepared.

And the seventh angel poured out his vial into the air; and there came a great voice out of the temple of heaven from the throne, saying, It is done. And there were voices, and thunders, and lightnings; and there was a great earthquake such as was not since men were upon the earth. And the great city was divided into three parts, and the cities of the nations fell. And great Babylon came in remembrance before God to give unto her the cup of the wine of the fierceness of his wrath.

And there came one of the seven angels which had the seven vials, and talked with me, saying unto me, Come hither. I will show unto thee the judgment of the great whore that sitteth upon many waters. So he carried me away in the spirit into the wilderness; and I saw a woman sit upon a scarlet-colored beast, full of names of blasphemy, having seven heads and ten horns. And the woman was arrayed in purple and scarlet color, and decked with gold and precious stones and pearls, having a golden cup in her hand full of abominations and filthiness. And upon her forehead was a name written, MYSTERY, BABYLON THE GREAT, THE MOTHER OF HARLOTS AND ABOMINATIONS OF THE EARTH. And I saw the woman drunken with the blood of the saints, and with the blood of the martyrs of Jesus; and when I saw her, I wondered with great admiration.

And the angel said unto me, Wherefore didst thou marvel? I will tell thee the mystery of the woman, and of the beast that carrieth her, which hath the seven heads and ten horns. The seven heads are seven mountains, on which the woman sitteth. And he saith unto me, The waters which thou sawest, where the whore sitteth, are peoples, and multitudes, and nations and tongues. And the ten horns which thou sawest upon the beast, these shall hate the whore, and shall make her desolate and naked, and shall eat her flesh, and burn her with fire. And the woman which thou sawest is that great city, which reigneth over the kings of the earth.

And after these things I saw another angel come down from heaven, having great power; and the earth was lightened with his glory. And he cried mightily with a strong voice, saying:

Babylon the great is fallen, is fallen,
And is become the habitation of devils,
And the hold of every foul spirit,
And a cage of every unclean and hateful bird.
For all nations have drunk of the wine of the wrath of her fornication,
And the kings of the earth have committed fornication with her,
And the merchants of the earth are waxed rich through the abundance of her delicacies.

And I heard another voice from heaven, saying:

Come out of her, my people, that ye be not partakers of her sins,
And that ye receive not of her plagues.
For her sins have reached unto heaven,
And God hath remembered her iniquities.
Therefore shall her plagues come in one day, death, and mourning, and famine;
And she shall be utterly burned with fire;
For strong is the Lord God, who judgeth her.

And the merchants of the earth shall weep and mourn over her; for no man buyeth their merchandise any more: The merchandise of gold, and silver, and precious stones, and of pearls, and fine linen, and purple, and silk, and scarlet; and all manner vessels of ivory, and all manner vessels of most precious wood, and of brass, and iron, and marble; and cinnamon, and odors, and ointments, and frankincense, and wine, and oil, and fine flour, and wheat; and beasts, and sheep, and horses, and chariots, and slaves, and souls of men. The merchants of these things, which were made rich by her, shall stand afar off for the fear of her torment, weeping and wailing. For in one hour so great riches is come to nought.

And every shipmaster, and all the company in ships, and sailors, and as many as trade by sea, stood afar off, and cried when they saw the smoke of her burning, saying, What city is like unto this great city! And they cast dust on their heads, and cried, weeping and wailing, saying, Alas, alas, that great city, wherein were made rich all that had ships in the sea by reason of her costliness! For in one hour is she made desolate.

THE EPILOGUE: A SERIES OF VISIONS

FROM REVELATION 19, 20, 21, 22

And after these things I heard a great voice of much people in heaven, saying, Alleluia! Salvation and glory, and honor, and power unto the Lord our God! And again they said, Alleluia! And the four and twenty elders and the four beasts fell down and worshipped God that sat on the throne, saying, Amen! Alleluia! And I heard as it were the voice of a great multitude and as the voice of many waters and as the voice of mighty thunderings, saying Alleluia! For the Lord God omnipotent reigneth!

And I saw a great white throne, and him that sat on it, from whose face the earth and the heaven fled away. And I saw the dead, small and great, stand before God; and the books were opened; and another book was opened, which is the book of life. And the dead were judged out of those things which were written in the books, according to their works. And the sea gave up the dead which were in it; and death and hell delivered up the dead which were in them; and they were judged every man according to their works. And whosoever was not found written in the book of life was cast into the lake of fire. And I saw a new heaven and a new earth; for the first heaven and the first earth were passed away, and there was no more sea.

And I, John, saw the holy city, New Jerusalem, coming down from God out of heaven, prepared as a bride adorned for her husband. And I heard a great voice out of heaven saying:

Behold, the tabernacle of God is with men,
And he will dwell with them,
And they shall be his people,
And God himself shall be with them, and be their God.
And God shall wipe away all tears from their eyes;
And there shall be no more death, neither sorrow nor crying,
Neither shall there be any more pain;
For the former things are passed away.

And he that sat upon the throne said, Behold, I make all things new. And he said unto me, Write: for these words are true and faithful. And he said unto me, It is done. I am Alpha and Omega, the beginning and the end. I will give unto him that is athirst of the fountain of the water of life freely. He that overcometh shall inherit all things; and I will be his God, and he shall be my son.

And there came unto me one of the seven angels which had the seven vials full of the seven last plagues, and talked with me, saying, Come hither. I will show thee the bride, the Lamb's wife. And he carried me away in the spirit to a great and high mountain, and showed me that great city, the holy Jerusalem, descending out of heaven from God, having the glory of God. And her light was like unto a stone most precious, even like a jasper stone, clear as crystal. And she had a wall great and high, and had twelve gates, and at the gates twelve angels, and names written thereon, which are the names of the twelve tribes of the children of Israel. And the wall of the city had twelve foundations, and in them the names of the twelve apostles of the Lamb.

And the building of the wall of it was of jasper; and the city was pure gold, like unto clear glass. And the foundations of the wall of the city were garnished with all manner of precious stones. The first foundation was jasper; the second, sapphire; the third, a chalcedony; the fourth, an emerald; the fifth, sardonyx; the sixth, sardius; the seventh, chrysolite; the eighth, beryl; the ninth, a topaz; the tenth, a chrysoprasus; the eleventh, a jacinth; the twelfth, an amethyst. And the twelve gates were twelve pearls. Every several gate was of one pearl; and the street of the city was pure gold, as it were transparent glass.

And I saw no temple therein; for the Lord God Almighty and the Lamb are the temple of it. And the city had no need of the sun, neither of the moon, to shine in it; for the glory of God did lighten it, and the Lamb is the light thereof. And the nations of them which are saved shall walk in the light of it; and the kings of the earth do bring their glory and honor into it. And the gates of it shall not be shut at all by day; for there shall be no night there. And they shall bring the glory and honor of the nations into it. And there shall in no wise enter into it any thing that defileth, neither whatsoever worketh abomination, or maketh a lie; but they which are written in the Lamb's book of life.

And he showed me a pure river of water of life, clear as crystal, proceeding out of the throne of God and of the Lamb. In the midst of the street of it, and on either side of the river, was there the tree of life, which bare twelve manner of fruits, and yielded her fruit every month; and the leaves of the tree were for the healing of the nations.

And there shall be no more curse;
But the throne of God and of the Lamb shall be in it;
And his servants shall serve him.
And they shall see his face,
And his name shall be in their foreheads.
And there shall be no night there;
And they need no candle, neither light of the sun;
For the Lord God giveth them light,
And they shall reign forever and ever.